Usability Testing
and Research

THE ALLYN AND BACON SERIES IN TECHNICAL COMMUNICATION

Series Editor: Sam Dragga, Texas Tech University

Thomas T. Barker
*Writing Software Documentation:
A Task-Oriented Approach*

Carol M. Barnum
Usability Testing and Research

Deborah S. Bosley
*Global Contexts: Case Studies in International
Technical Communication*

Paul Dombrowski
Ethics in Technical Communication

David Farkas and Jean Farkas
Principles of Web Design

Laura J. Gurak
Oral Presentations for Technical Communication

Sandra W. Harner and Tom G. Zimmerman
Technical Marketing Communication

Richard Johnson-Sheehan
Writing Proposals: Rhetoric for Managing Change

Dan Jones
Technical Writing Style

Charles Kostelnick and David D. Roberts
*Designing Visual Language: Strategies for
Professional Communicators*

Carolyn Rude
Technical Editing, Third Edition

Gerald J. Savage and Dale L. Sullivan
*Writing a Professional Life: Stories of
Technical Communicators On and Off the Job*

Usability Testing and Research

Carol M. Barnum

Southern Polytechnic State University

Longman

New York   San Francisco   Boston
London   Toronto   Sydney   Tokyo   Singapore   Madrid
Mexico City   Munich   Paris   Cape Town   Hong Kong   Montreal

To Jack

Senior Vice President/Publisher: Joseph Opiela
Vice President/Publisher: Eben W. Ludlow
Marketing Manager: Christopher Bennem
Supplements Editor: Donna Campion
Production Manager: Mark Naccarelli
Project Coordination, Text Design, and Electronic Page Makeup: Nesbitt Graphics, Inc.
Cover Design Manager: Nancy Danahy
Cover Designer: Caryl Silvers
Senior Manufacturing Buyer: Dennis J. Para
Printer and Binder: Hamilton Printing Company
Cover Printer: Coral Graphic Services

Library of Congress Cataloging-in-Publication Data

Barnum, Carol M.
    Usability testing and research/Carol M. Barnum.
        p. cm.
    Includes bibliographical references and index.
    ISBN 0-205-31519-4
    1. User interfaces (Computer systems)—Testing. 2. Human-computer interaction.   I. Title.

QA76.9.U83 B362 2002
004'.01'9—dc21   2001029542

Please visit our website at http://www.ablongman.com

ISBN 0-205-31519-4

2 3 4 5 6 7 8 9 10—HT—10 09 08 07 06 05

CONTENTS

CHAPTER

7   Conducting the Usability Test   230

CHAPTER

8   Analyzing and Reporting Results   268

CHAPTER

9 Web Usability

APPENDIX

Making It Work as a Team

FOREWORD
by the Series Editor

The Allyn and Bacon Series in Technical Communication is designed to meet the continuing education needs of professional technical communicators, both those who desire to upgrade or update their own communication abilities as well as those who train or supervise writers, editors, and artists within their organization. This series also serves the growing number of students enrolled in undergraduate and graduate programs in technical communication. Such programs offer a wide variety of courses beyond the introductory technical writing course—advanced courses for which fully satisfactory and appropriately focused textbooks have often been impossible to locate.

The chief characteristic of the books in this series is their consistent effort to integrate theory and practice. The books offer both research-based and experienced-based instruction, describing not only what to do and how to do it but explaining why. The instructors who teach advanced courses and the students who enroll in these courses are looking for more than rigid rules and ad hoc guidelines. They want books that demonstrate theoretical sophistication and a solid foundation in the research of the field as well as pragmatic advice and perceptive applications. Instructors and students will also find these books filled with activities and assignments adaptable to the classroom and to the self-guided learning processes of professional technical communicators.

To operate effectively in the field of technical communication, today's technical communicators require extensive training in the creation, analysis, and design of information for both domestic and international audiences, for both paper and electronic environments. The books in the Allyn and Bacon Series address those subjects that are most frequently taught at the undergraduate and graduate levels as a direct response to both the educational needs of students and the practical demands of business and industry. Additional books will be developed for the series in order to satisfy or anticipate changes in writing technologies, academic curricula, and the profession of technical communication.

Sam Dragga
Texas Tech University

PREFACE

Communication equals remembering what it's like not to know.
—RICHARD SAUL WURMAN

From the moment you know enough to talk about a product—any product, whether it's hardware, software, games, or Web pages—you know too much to be able to tell if the product would be usable for a human being who doesn't know what you know. As Jakob Nielsen, one of the major proponents of usability in product design, puts it, "Your best guess is not good enough" (10). Bad guesses or misguided hunches are the reason usability came into the world: first as an effort to stem the rising tide of complaints about designs that didn't work for users, then as a discipline that encompasses many areas, including computer science, cognitive science, engineering, psychology, and technical communication. The aim of the discipline is to set aside the developers' knowledge about products and put in its place knowledge about users. Thus, the watchword for the discipline, which goes by many names, is *user-centered design*, a term that encompasses human factors, ergonomics, information architecture, instructional design, software engineering, and usability. Although representatives from these various disciplines may claim responsibility for one area or another of the development of the product, all must embrace the philosophy of user-centered design and work together to create products that work for real users performing real tasks to attain real goals. This book is about the part that usability testing plays in the user-centered design process.

How Did We Get Here?

The history of usability and its place in user-centered design is a short, but rapidly expanding one. Although work in human factors (or ergonomics, as it is more commonly called in Europe) got its start during World War II as a result of specialists' study of human interaction with new tools and technology operating on land, at sea, and in space, the focus of attention initially was on improving the efficiency of existing systems and human interaction with them. The Human Factors and Ergonomics Society was formed in 1957 with the International Ergonomics Association formed shortly afterward in 1959. Human–computer interaction interest didn't come until later in the 1970s, following the introduction of mainframe computers into commercial use in the 1960s. In 1960 there were 2000 computers in the United States. By 1970 there were 125,000 and by 1985 there were close to 500,000, following the introduction of the Apple II in 1978, the IBM PC in 1981, and the Apple Macintosh in 1984 (Landauer 14; Schriver 42). The Internet had its start in the 1960s but the World Wide Web didn't come into use until the early 1990s.

As the 1980s saw the rapid expansion of computer use in offices and homes, interest in computer–human interaction emerged, tying together the fields of computer science, graphic design, psychology, and technical communication. Two breakthrough works, appearing one year apart, introduced the concept of a design methodology that focused on the user, rather than the technology: Gould and Lewis (1985) described the principles that came to be recognized as the basis for user-centered design, and Norman and Draper edited a collection of essays called *User Centered System Design* (1986). At the same time, new organizations were forming that addressed the issues associated with usability. In addition to the Human Factors and Ergonomics Society (HFES), four other organizations with overlapping interests in this area were established:

- SIGCHI: the Association for Computing Machinery (ACM) Special Interest Group on Computer–Human Interaction (formed in 1982)
- SIGDOC: the Association for Computing Machinery (ACM) Special Interest Group on Documentation (formed in 1983)
- UPA: the Usability Professionals' Association (formed in 1991)
- Usability SIG of STC: the Society for Technical Communication's Special Interest Group on Usability (formed in 1992)

Where Do You Fit into This Field?

Your interest in this subject could come from your interest in any of the many overlapping disciplines that have a hand in making usable products. You could be in the field of computer science, cognitive science or psychology, human factors engineering, or any of the other engineering disciplines. You could be a technical communicator, information developer, or information architect. You could be a Web developer or graphic designer. Or you could be a content specialist in science, medicine, health care, environmental issues, or a myriad of other areas where information and products touch people's lives.

If you're a student pursuing a degree in any of these fields, this book will help you understand the process of usability testing, give you the principles and the tools to practice usability testing, and, hopefully, give you the inspiration and motivation to advocate usability in the companies and organizations you will join after graduation.

If you're a professional in any of the disciplines described earlier, you may already be doing usability testing. For you, this book provides a systematic approach to expand what you already do, as you work to incorporate usability testing into a user-centered design process. If you are a member of a usability team or a cross-functional team, your team may want to read the book as a source for new ideas, supported by current research in usability testing methodologies. If you haven't already participated in a usability test but you want to learn how to do it, this book will provide the groundwork to help you get started.

How Is the Book Organized to Assist You?

The chapter organization is as follows:

1. What Is Usability and What Is Usability Testing?
2. Other Methods for Getting Feedback about Product Usability
3. User and Task Analysis
4. Iterative Testing for User-Centered Design
5. Planning for Usability Testing
6. Preparing for Usability Testing
7. Conducting the Usability Test
8. Analyzing and Reporting Results
9. Web Usability

Appendix: Making It Work as a Team

Depending on your interest in the subject and your current knowledge and experience, you may want to read the book chapter by chapter, or you may want to skip around. Some advice about how to take either approach follows.

If You're a Student or New to the Field

If you're a student or new to the field of usability testing, you will most likely want to begin at the beginning of the book and progress through each chapter. The first chapter provides you with an introduction to usability, usability testing, and user-centered design, and to some basic terminology to understand how usability testing can be done with or without a lab or in the user's home or business. It also provides you with information that documents the ways in which usability testing can be cost-justified by showing the savings from usability testing as well as the costs of not testing.

Following this foundation, which provides a working vocabulary for the chapters that follow, Chapter 2 presents other methods used to get feedback from users. Although some call these other methods *usability testing*, most see them as part of a usability engineering lifecycle contributing to a user-centered design process, with usability testing being one part of the process. As user-centered design is a multistage process, this chapter provides information about some of the other methods used.

Chapter 3 provides information at the heart of the process of building user-centered design products: understanding the user and the user's tasks. You will learn methods for performing this vital investigation into user and task analysis. Armed with this information about who your users are and what their goals are with the product, you can begin developing and testing products that are user-centered. Chapter 4 demonstrates how testing should not be viewed as a once-and-done activity, but should be seen, instead, as an iterative process, repeated throughout the development of the product. Techniques for incorporating iterative testing into the design process are presented, and you will learn what can be discovered at each phase in the design and which approaches work best in different phases.

While the first half of the book establishes the basis for user-centered design activities, the second half focuses on the planning, preparation, and activities of a usability test. Chapters 5, 6, and 7 focus on these testing plans and actions. Examples from both student projects and client projects support the guidelines provided. Using these, you should be able to put together your own test plan and organize the tasks for testing so that the testing days go smoothly and produce results that can be turned into actions for product improvement. Chapter 8 provides guidance on ways to report the results to your organization, including oral, written, and videotaped reports. The last chapter looks at the hot topic in usability today: Web usability. Although discussions of usability issues affecting the Web are included throughout the book, this chapter turns the spotlight on the research findings and special issues regarding Web testing and Web usability.

If you're going to be doing usability testing as a member of a team, you will want to read the Appendix, probably before the team meets for the first time, as it can give you some important guidelines on how to be an effective team member and have a productive and satisfying team experience.

If You're Already Familiar with Usability Testing

If you're already familiar with usability testing or perhaps have done some of the steps in a user-centered design process, you may want to skip the first chapter. If your main interest is putting together a plan for conducting a test, you may want to go directly to Chapters 5, 6, and 7. If you're going to be doing usability testing as a member of a cross-functional team, you should read the Appendix, and you may want to encourage your team members to also read this information. If, however, your main interest is Web testing, you will probably want to begin with the last chapter and then move back into the chapters on planning, preparing, and conducting a usability test, followed by the chapter on reporting the results, as these chapters contain examples about Web usability testing projects.

What Are the Special Features of This Book?

The special features of this book are these:

- A broad approach to usability testing that places the subject within a user-centered design process
- Relevant, up-to-date research to support the underlying assumptions and guidelines with an overall view of applying the relevant research to the development of a useful process
- A focus on iterative design and testing, including paper prototyping and "discount" usability testing that emphasizes frequent, inexpensive testing as the core of a user-centered design process
- Student and professional examples of all phases of planning, preparing, conducting, and reporting results

- Special attention given to issues and examples of interest to technical communicators, including examples from paper and online documentation, tutorials and help, and computer-based training
- An extended case with examples of a Web-based product
- Sidebars throughout the book with examples, stories, and anecdotes (both serious and humorous), illustrating usability issues
- Checklists, photographs, and line drawings to illustrate the methods and approaches for testing in different situations
- A separate chapter on Web usability and Web-testing issues for those with a particular interest in this topic
- End-of-chapter summaries with links to the information of the next chapter in "Coming Up" sections
- End-of-chapter references to sources cited in each chapter, which can be used for additional reading and reference
- End-of-chapter discussion questions and exercises, which can be used in the classroom, training room, or team meetings

Additional Resources

Depending on your needs and interests, you may find either or both of the following additional resources helpful to you.

Companion Web Site

A companion Web site, located at www.ablongman.com/barnum will supply you with additional information as well as new information. Whether you are a student, working professional, or instructor, you should check the Web site for supplementary information, including downloadable forms and templates, additional usability test reports, additional photographs of laboratory set-ups, tutorials for videotape editing, a top-10 list of usability resources, and links to useful Web sites and relevant professional organizations.

Because the field of usability testing is continually evolving, the companion Web site will also include the most recent and relevant new resources, as well as provide highlights of new findings. By checking the Web site regularly, you can keep up with the latest developments in this rapidly growing field.

Instructor's Manual

To support new instructors in the field of usability testing, as well as provide some ideas for seasoned instructors, an instructor's manual is available. It includes sample syllabi for a semester-length and quarter-length course. It also includes suggested approaches for structuring assignments related to the development of a test plan and conducting a usability test, plus additional ideas for teaching assignments, as well as strategies for teaching the course via the Internet. Suggested responses and general guidelines for using some of the end-of-chapter exercises are also provided.

Acknowledgments

There are many people who have helped me grow and learn in the field of usability and others who have helped shape this book. I want to thank them and acknowledge my debt to them here.

To My Colleagues and Mentors in Usability

- To *Ginny Redish,* whose book (written with Joe Dumas) *A Practical Guide to Usability Testing* has served as my usability bible for all these years, and to Ginny herself for all her guidance and support through our shared interests, personally and professionally.
- To *Jeff Rubin,* whose *Handbook of Usability Testing* expanded my knowledge in usability testing, and to Jeff himself for our shared conversations over the years about usability and publishing.
- To *Loren Burke* of The Usability Center, who helped me get started teaching usability testing by team-teaching my first course with me and offering the use of his lab to our students.
- To *Dave Rinehart* of The Usability Group, who has visited my usability testing class frequently to talk about the management side of usability testing and to share wonderful stories from usability testing sessions.
- To *Reed Johnson* of Usability Systems, who worked closely with me not only to build our lab at Southern Polytechnic, but also to patiently answer all my questions about how to keep it up and running through the inevitable glitches that any state-of-the-art technology presents.

To Allyn and Bacon/Longman and the Series Editor

- To *Eben Ludlow,* Vice President of Longman, who has been part of my publishing life (even if sometimes tangentially) for many years, and who toasted the occasion of my signing the book contract, which gave the project a special sense of merit.
- To *Sam Dragga,* Series Editor, with whom the idea for this project started as a conversation as we floated along a river together at a conference, and for his patience in supporting the project from the concept stage to the end.
- To *Maria McColligan,* Project Manager, Nesbitt Graphics, Inc., for guiding me so patiently through the production process.

To the Reviewers of This Book

- To *Clay Spinuzzi*/University of Texas at Austin, *Mark Zachry*/Utah State University, and *Judith Ramey*/University of Washington, for their thoughtful, careful, and extremely helpful review of the manuscript. Their support and suggestions have guided my revision of the manuscript for final submission.

To My Students in Usability Testing

To my graduate students in Usability Testing at Southern Polytechnic, who learned along with me what worked and what didn't in the early years of teaching the course, and whose efforts and enthusiasm about usability testing inspired me to write the book. As well, I am grateful for the excellent examples of their work included in this book, which are a testament to how much they learned and how much they taught me.

Carol M. Barnum
Southern Polytechnic State University

References

Dumas, Joseph S., and Janice C. Redish. *A Practical Guide to Usability Testing.* Norwood, NJ: Ablex, 1993.

Gould, John D., and Clayton Lewis. "Designing for Usability: Key Principles and What Designers Think." *Communications of the ACM* 20.3 (Mar 1985): 300–311.

Landauer, Thomas K. *The Trouble with Computers: Usefulness, Usability, and Productivity.* Cambridge, MA: MIT Press, 1995.

Nielsen, Jakob. *Usability Engineering.* Boston: Academic Press, 1993.

Norman, Donald A., and Stephen W. Draper, eds. *User Centered System Design: New Perspectives on Human-Computer Interaction.* Hillsdale, NJ: Erlbaum, 1986.

Rubin, Jeffrey. *Handbook of Usability Testing: How to Plan, Design, and Conduct Effective Tests.* New York: Wiley, 1994.

Schriver, Karen A. *Dynamics of Document Design: Creating Texts for Readers.* New York: Wiley, 1997.

Wurman, Richard Saul. *Information Anxiety: Follow the Yellow Brick Road.* New York: Doubleday, 1989. 130.

What Is Usability and What Is Usability Testing?

 "Personal computers are just too **hard** to use, and it isn't your fault." Walt Mossberg began with these words in his first "Personal Technology" column in *The Wall Street Journal*. Although Mossberg made this statement in 1991, many would agree that little has changed today. Among them is Marc Andreessen, chief technology officer of America Online, who opened PC Expo '99 with the observation that "the computer industry is failing its customers by not making its products simpler and easier to use" (see Martinez). Perhaps he was aware of a worldwide poll of network managers, which revealed that 83% had found "abusive or violent behavior of users" against their computers ("Road Rage"). A survey, seeking to document such incidents of computer rage, found that:

- 14% of respondents said that computer problems interrupted their work day at least once per day.
- 17% reported that it takes more than an hour per day to fix the problems.
- 21% reported missed work deadlines because of computer problems.
- 46% were frustrated by error messages they couldn't understand (see Barbash).

And computers are not the only source of rage. Comedian Steve Martin, writing in *The New Yorker*, presents the following scenario:

> The burning gates of Hell were opened and the designer of CD packaging entered to the Devil's fanfare. "We've been wanting him down here for a long time," The One of Pure Evil said to his infernal minions, "but we decided to wait, because he was doing such good work above, wrapping the CDs with cellophane and that sticky tape strip. Ask him to dinner and be sure to invite the computer-manual people too." (53)

What makes computer and electronic products—the hardware and software and accompanying documentation—so difficult for the average user to use? Some claim that the problem lies with the engineers and computer analysts who are out

1

of touch with the intended users but who spearhead the design effort. Andreessen agrees, stating that computer designers and programmers have "followed their own inclinations rather than the needs of consumers." With their love of the technology and inquisitiveness about the limits of the tool, they have driven the effort to add feature upon feature to new products. Egged on, perhaps, by marketing specialists who claim that the products will be more competitive with more features, and backed up by salespeople who report that their customers are demanding more features, it's not surprising that the products that you and I want to use are frequently just too hard to use. Who doesn't know someone who can't program a VCR, but instead uses an after-market product like VCR Plus to simplify the process? How many of us can just walk up and use an unfamiliar microwave oven, or cellular phone, or programmable coffeemaker? And how many of us have struggled to learn how to use a new computer or software tool? Who doesn't understand the success of the "dummies" books, which have rushed in to fill the gap left by unclear documentation that doesn't clarify, but only further confuses users?

Why didn't product designers and manufacturers ask us, the users of these products, what we wanted? Why didn't they let us try out the product in development to see if it matched our goals and expectations, as well as our own process for performing the task at hand? Why didn't they bring us into the design and development of the product early enough in the development cycle so that our issues and problems concerning the product could be used to make the product work for us? In fact, why didn't they ask us how we performed tasks and what we wanted in products instead of designing what they thought we wanted or presumed we needed? In the next section, we address these questions and provide some answers, set against the background of the changing marketplace and the changing population of users of high-tech products.

This book is about the place that usability testing, as well as other related research methods, holds within the process of developing products that work for users. We can all understand the problem of products that don't work for us in the way we want. But it's interesting to see how usability has become an increasingly important issue in product development as the user population, the audience for technical products, has changed. So, we begin with a look at the changing demographics of users. Then, we define the terms that will establish the basis of the discussion—usability, usability testing, and user-centered design—and provide an example that shows where usability testing fits into a user-centered design process. With this foundation, we discuss the different models of testing with and without a lab, as well as in the field. Because you may find yourself in a situation where you will want some support to justify your request to begin usability testing in your company, we conclude with some compelling arguments regarding the benefits of testing as well as the risks of not testing.

The Times Have Changed

Out of market necessity, resulting from changes in the user population and the increased competitiveness of the marketplace, has come a need for usable products with the resulting need for usability testing as a key element in what has come to be called *user-centered design*. John Carroll, one of the early proponents of this much-needed change, provides some background for the change that began in the 1980s:

> In the midst of a revolution in technology to support human activity, people were being terrorized by word processors. The user population for computers was increasing and diversifying rapidly; programmers and engineers were being replaced by secretaries and professionals as the typical users. But companies did not understand the needs of these new users, and they were not prepared technically to support them. (2)

Alan Cooper, a usability specialist who did pioneering work at Apple, characterizes this transformation in the user population as "the democratization of consumer power" (34). He describes the transition from complex mechanical devices, requiring highly trained, highly skilled expert users, to the advent of "silicon brains" in tools and systems that placed them in the hands of "untrained amateurs." Typical examples include self-pump gas stations replacing trained service station attendants and ATMs replacing bank tellers. The problem, however, is that "the engineering process doesn't discern between the creation of a complex system that will be operated by a trained, paid professional and one that is to be operated by an indifferent amateur" (34).

As early as the 1970s, Gould and Lewis, researchers in human factors, were advocating design principles for usability that fell on the deaf ears of the developers, for reasons based on the following commonly-held belief systems (303–306):

- Users are similar to designers—because designers have limited contact with users, they don't understand how different users can be from designers.
- Users don't know what they need—because many users have not considered how systems might improve what they do or because designers may unwittingly intimidate users, causing them to be unresponsive.
- The job does not require or permit interaction with users—because designers are kept far removed from users and receive information about them through others in the organization.
- Reason will prevail—systems based on logical design and reason will naturally be logical and reasonable to users.
- Design guidelines should be sufficient—because rules of design will lead to effective designs.
- Good design means getting it right the first time—in keeping with the concept of designing for "zero defects."
- The power of technology will triumph—because users need what the technology provides, despite the difficulty of learning or use.

Even when it is understood that products must be designed to be useful, usable, and desirable, design is complicated by the following realities:

- Products that are usable and desirable may not be useful.
- Products that are useful and usable may not be desirable.

In the past, a product was deemed successful if it met at least two of these three criteria. This is no longer true. Now the largest segment of the market demands that products match all three criteria: usefulness, usability, and desirability

(Sanders). However, developers may still be focusing too much on the first users of their products.

In *Crossing the Chasm*, Geoffrey Moore calls these first users the "innovators." As Table 1.1 shows, there are five groups of users for high-tech products, each with the following distinct *psychographic* (a combination of psychology and demographics) profile (12–14).

Although there are cracks between each group, a chasm exists between the Early Adopters and the Early Majority, and many companies fall into this chasm for failing to realize that they must be thinking of the "crossing" and planning for it when they begin product design. As Moore explains, "The early majority want to buy a *productivity improvement* for existing operations. They are looking to minimize the discontinuity with the old ways. They want evolution, not revolution. They want technology to enhance, not overthrow, established ways of doing business" (21). Out of this chaos and confusion, this crossing the chasm from the emerging technology embraced by a few technowizards to the expansion of the technology to the general population, comes the concept of usability and usability testing. As Moore states, "*It is almost always the end user and his or her application that give the market its defining characteristics*" (105; italics in original).

User Interface Engineering, a usability consulting firm, applies its own terminology to the product development lifecycle, dividing it into four stages related to a product's usability ("Market Maturity"):

1. Raw iron
2. Checklist battles
3. Productivity wars
4. Transparency

In the *raw iron* stage, usability is not a concern or a consideration, as creating something new and getting it to market are the major drivers in product development. If the product survives its entry into the market, it must make the perilous transition to the *checklist battles* stage, in which features predominate. Usability is not an issue at this stage; rather, it is seen as a barrier to the addition of features required to outpace the competition.

The next stage, called the *productivity wars,* is where usability becomes a major consideration, and that usually means a major redesign of the product to consider issues of ease of learning and ease of use, which haven't been addressed before. As an example of a product moving from the second to the third stage, a reviewer of Microsoft's Excel spreadsheet characterized it as "powerful and intimidating," but then praised the improved Excel 98 version, because the programmers "wisely switched strategy" to make the product easier to use rather than adding more features (Haddad).

The final transition is to the *transparency stage,* in which the product is now invisible, and all competing products are similar in design (think of modems, disk drives, and memory as examples of products in this stage). Customers don't know and don't care what makes the product effective because the effectiveness is built into the product. In this stage, the marketing advantage becomes lowest cost and best performance. Few products reach this final stage, and many do not make it to the third stage in which they are designed for usability.

TABLE 1.1	Five Groups of High-Tech Users
Group	**Psychographic Profile**
Innovators ("techies")	Pursue new technology aggressively because technology is a central interest in their life, regardless of what function the technology performs. They represent a very small but valuable portion of the adoption life cycle.
Early Adopters (visionaries)	Like innovators, they buy into new product concepts early, but unlike innovators, they are not technologists. Instead, they find it easy to imagine the usefulness of the product.
Early Majority (pragmatists)	Although they can relate to the perceived benefits of the technology, they are driven by the practicality of the product in improving productivity in some way. They are willing to wait and see what the early adopters find out. They represent one-third of the total buying population.
Late Majority (conservatives)	They share many of the characteristics of the early majority, but with one major difference: they are not comfortable with the technology. They wait to see if a standard gets established and if there's lots of support for the product. This group also comprises one-third of the total buying population.
Laggards (skeptics)	These are the technophobic members of the population who buy only after the technology is transparent or buried within the product.

Source: Adapted from Geoffrey A. Moore, *Crossing the Chasm: Marketing and Selling Technology Products to Mainstream Customers.* New York: Harper Business, 1991, pp.12–14.

Perhaps this product development process is being speeded up today, moving more quickly to the stage where usability becomes an issue. Some attribute this change to the increasing use of the World Wide Web by customers performing "e-commerce" transactions, which in traditional "brick and mortar" businesses are done by trained sales personnel. Again, we are reminded of Cooper's model of transition from experts to amateurs. If the Web site is a barrier to the successful completion of the sale, business will be lost. Thus, for the customer who is a discretionary shopper, usability is typically the critical factor in a buying decision. If it's not easy, customers will jump ship for another site, a belief confirmed by a study that shows that "27% of all Web transactions are abandoned at the payment screen" (Binstock). It used to be customary to blame the user for failing to be able to perform the process; however, this argument no longer prevails. Now, the need to satisfy the demands of the user is taking an increasingly important place in design decisions and product development. In the next section, we explore the meaning of usability and the role that usability testing plays in achieving the creation of products that are easier to use.

 ## What Is Usability?

To get at the meaning of *usability*, it might seem odd, but nonetheless useful, to begin with an explanation of what usability is not. Usability is *not:*

- Quality assurance
- Zero defects
- Utility of design features
- Intrinsic in products

These terms reflect issues related to the product itself, not to the interaction of a person with the product. The presence of these qualities may validate a product from the standpoint of utility, while saying little about its usability.

Although some contend that efforts to come up with a clear and concise definition of usability "can be aptly compared to attempts to nail a blob of Jell-O to the wall" (Gray and Salzman 242), the following definitions of usability show a marked similarity:

- "The extent to which a product can be used by specified users to achieve specified goals in a specified context of use with effectiveness, efficiency, and satisfaction" (ISO 9241–11 International Organization for Standardization)
- "The measure of the quality of the user experience when interacting with something—whether a Web site, a traditional software application, or any other device the user can operate in some way or another" (Nielsen, "What Is 'Usability'"?)
- "Usability means that the *people who use the product* can do so *quickly and easily* to accomplish *their own tasks*" (Dumas and Redish, 4; italics in original)

Encompassing all these ideas in an expanded definition of usability, Jakob Nielsen, a usability specialist, identifies the following components, or attributes, of usability (*Usability Engineering* 26):

- *Learnability.* The system should be easy to learn so that the user can rapidly start doing some work.
- *Efficiency.* The system should be efficient to use, so that once it is learned, the user can achieve a high level of productivity.
- *Memorability.* The system should be easy to remember, so that the casual user is able to return to the system after a time and not have to learn it all over again.
- *Errors.* The system should have a low error rate, so that users make few errors and can easily recover from them.
- *Satisfaction.* The system should be pleasant to use, so that users are subjectively satisfied when using it; they like it.

In all these definitions of usability, the focus is on the user, not on the product. A product's usability is determined by the user's *perception* of the quality of the product, based on the user's ease of use, ease of learning and relearning, the product's intuitiveness for the user, and the user's appreciation of the usefulness of a product. Usefulness is defined in terms of the user's *need* for the product in the context of the user's *goals*. In every case, usability must be understood as matching the needs of a particular user for a particular use. If the product doesn't add value to the way in which the user currently performs tasks, then the user will have no use for the product. For instance, if the user perceives that the envelope template in word processing software is too complicated to set up and use, then the user is more likely to use a typewriter for this function or hand write the envelope or purchase an add-on label maker to create an address label for the envelope.

Beyond usefulness, however, is the critical criterion of *satisfaction*, which no amount of validation testing or quality assurance testing will reveal. That measure can only come from the user. Is the user satisfied with the legibility of the font and the display of the information on the page or screen? Is the spacing between the lines appropriate for the user, given his or her visual capacity? Is the choice of color pleasing to the user? Is the design of the screen attractive to the user? These are but a few of the subjective issues that can be determined only by the user. User-centered design, the method of product development that will result in products containing these attributes, is the subject of the next section of this chapter.

What Is User-Centered Design?

With the shift in product design away from a validation of features and capabilities to a focus on the user's perceptions of usefulness and feeling of satisfaction has come a change in terminology from *product usability* to *user-centered design*. Finally, the trumpet call put forth by Gould and Lewis, starting in the 1970s, has been heard, and their three critical principles of design have become the watchword for user-centered design, as it is practiced today (300):

1. *Early focus on users and tasks* that involves understanding the users, the tasks that users perform, and the environment in which users perform these tasks.
2. *Empirical measurement* of product usage that involves users providing information about ease of learning, ease of use, and related usability issues.
3. *Iterative design* that fixes the problems found by users in usability testing as part of the product development lifecycle.

These three principles inform the process of user-centered design because they require that product developers and technical communicators, those who prepare the product for users, gather information about users and tasks before they begin the product development process, then evaluate the product with users as the product is under development, and repeat this process to learn whether changes made improve the product as it moves through development. As Figure 1.1 shows, the user-centered design process can be divided into three phases: analysis, development, and post-release. At each phase, information by and about users is central to learning what to design, how to design it, and how to improve the next release in a cycle of continuous product improvement. Other evaluation techniques, such as heuristic evaluation and cognitive walkthroughs, involve "experts" inspecting the product for usability issues. These other aspects of data gathering are discussed in Chapter 2. Paper prototyping and the iterative design process are discussed in Chapter 4. But the heart of the process, as well as the bulk

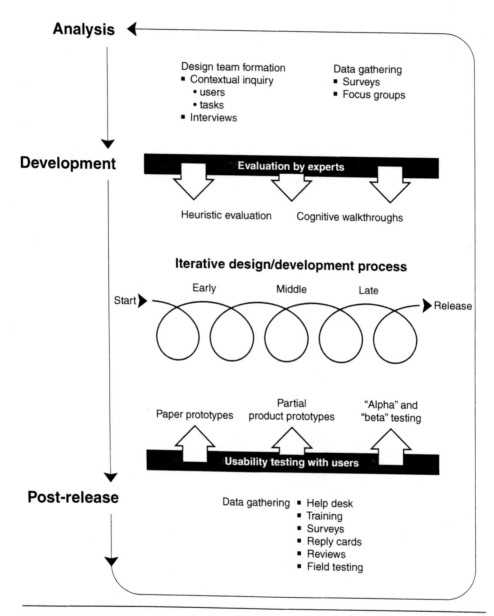

Figure 1.1   User-centered design process
(Used with permission from Bev Arends.)

of the chapters in this book, is dependent on usability testing as the best method to feed direct information about users' perceptions of satisfaction and problems back to the development team. In the next section, we address the way in which this user-centered design process is supported through usability testing.

What Is Usability Testing?

User-centered design focuses on users, tasks, and environments. So, how do developers learn about these factors? The process that incorporates user-centered design into product development is sometimes called *usability engineering,* which relates it in concept and importance to software engineering as a critical part of product development. The process of learning from users about a product's usability by observing them using the product, one aspect of usability engineering, is called *usability testing.* A further distinction is to view most usability engineering methods—other than usability testing—as "analytical" and to view usability testing as "empirical," meaning that the information comes from the experiences of the user (Gray and Salzman).

Usability testing generally has the following characteristics (Dumas and Redish 22):

1. The primary goal is to improve the usability of a product. For each test, there must be specific goals and concerns that you articulate when planning the test.
2. The participants represent real users.
3. The participants do real tasks.
4. The team observes and records what participants do and say.
5. The team analyzes the data, diagnoses the problems, and recommends changes to fix these problems.

Although these characteristics describe a standard approach to usability testing, it is important to recognize that the term usability testing can mean different things to different people, depending on their training and experience. As Jeff Rubin, a usability consultant, observes, "I have noticed that the term *usability testing* is often used rather indiscriminately to refer to *any* technique used to evaluate a product or system" (25; italics in original). However, Rubin uses the term usability testing to mean the "process that employs participants who are representative of the target population to evaluate the degree to which a product meets specific usability criteria. This inclusion of representative users eliminates labeling as usability testing such techniques as expert evaluations, walk-throughs, and the like that do not require representative users as part of the process" (25).

Like Rubin, and Dumas and Redish, we will use the term usability testing to mean the process that involves live feedback from actual users performing real tasks. Even while using such a definition of usability testing, it is important to clarify what usability testing is not. Just as usability is not quality assurance or zero defects, usability testing is also *not* any of the following:

- *Function testing.* Verifies that users are able to perform certain tasks.
- *Reliability testing.* Verifies that the product performs as designed.
- *Validation testing.* Verifies that the product performs without errors or "bugs."

Although, of course, these tests must be performed to assure the accuracy and validity of a product, none of these types of tests affirms a match with users' wants, needs, and desires. For instance, function testing verifies that the system performs as designed and that it contains the features deemed most useful. Usability testing, in contrast, determines whether the users can find and use the features in the amount of time and effort they are *willing* to expend searching.

Traditional Approach to Usability Testing

Usability testing, as it was commonly practiced well into the 1980s, was expensive, time-consuming, and scientific in approach. Labs, where such tests were conducted, were managed by usability experts who typically had education and training as cognitive scientists, experimental psychologists, or human factors engineers. Because tests were viewed as research experiments, they typically required 30 to 50 test "subjects." Jakob Nielsen, in his capacity as a human factors engineer, was prominent among those who published research findings using such statistical samples, believed to be required for validity. Thus, when Nielsen presented a paper at the 1989 Human-Computer Interaction (HCI) conference entitled "Usability Engineering at a Discount" (later entitled "Guerrilla HCI: Using Discount Usability Engineering to Penetrate the Intimidation Barrier," in Bias and Mayhew), it caused a paradigm shift in the practice of usability testing. For, what Nielsen learned from his own research contradicted "the perception that anybody touching usability will come down with a bad case of budget overruns" (245). It is no wonder that such a perception existed, however, when the *Communications of the ACM* (monthly publication of the Association for Computing Machinery) reported in 1988 that "'the costs required to add human factors elements to the development of software' was $128,330" (Mantei and Teorey, reported in Nielsen, "Guerrilla HCI" 246). Add to the dollar expense the time involved in performing tests on 30 to 50 test subjects plus the time required to analyze the results, and it is easy to see why development schedules rarely afforded such time, even when budgets allowed the expense. When testing wasn't a part of product development, design issues were resolved without the benefit of user reaction.

Nielsen approached the problem of trying to get results with lower cost from the following perspective:

> If *no* information is available, you might as well choose by tossing a coin, and you will have a 50% probability of choosing the best interface. If a small amount of user testing has been done, you may find that interface A is better than interface B at the 20% level of significance. Even though 20% is considered "not significant," your tests have actually improved your chance of choosing the best interface from 50/50 to 4-to-1, meaning that you would be foolish not to take the data into account when choosing. ("Guerrilla HCI" 248)

Thus, Nielsen concluded that something was better than nothing, and he set out to learn how few users would be required to get valid results. For another view, decidedly tongue-in-cheek, of why products are not made to be usable, see the sidebar entitled "Excuses, Excuses, Excuses" (Horton 29).

Excuses, Excuses, Excuses
William Horton

Excuses by managers

Many managers, especially midlevel technical managers who "cut their teeth on glass teletypes and machine code," seem to regard usability as a bureaucratic waste.

Economy—Sure it's awkward, but we can explain it in documentation . . . in training . . . with phone support.

Urgency—We don't have time for usability testing. We barely have time to finish the product.

Continuity—It may be bad but our customers are used to it by now.

Marketing—We designed exactly what our customers said they wanted.

Pride—Our customers are so intelligent, educated, and motivated, they can handle it.

Force—They'll use it because it's their job to use it.

Excuses by product managers

On some projects the engineers, programmers, and technical gurus seem to view usability as an unnecessary frill, a fad of interest only to technowimps.

Inertia—If it ain't broke, don't fix it.

Absolutism—We can't make it totally obvious, so let's not even try.

Puritanism—It's a computer. It's supposed to be hard.

Denial—It's NOT a bug. That's the way we designed it.

Elitism—If our customers can't figure it out, we should get new customers.

Legality—We followed the user-interface standards manual.

Excuses by technical communicators

Yes, even writers, editors, trainers, and customer-support engineers sometimes resist efforts to make products more useful.

Protectionism—Obviousness would eliminate my job or what I like about it.

Bureaucracy—It's not my job.

Ignorance—I don't have a Ph.D. in ergonomics.

Impotence—They won't let me.

Defense—Everything users need to know is in the manual. It's not our fault they won't read it.

Exasperation—We don't have time to simplify the product. We're too busy documenting it.

Source: William Horton. "Let's Do Away with Manuals . . . Before They Do Away with Us." *Technical Communication* (First Quarter, 1993), p. 29. Reprinted with permission from *Technical Communication,* the journal of the Society for Technical Communication, Arlington, VA, U.S.A.

Discount Usability Testing

Nielsen, along with fellow researcher Tom Landauer, determined that "the maximum benefit-cost ratio is achieved when using between three and five subjects" (reported in Nielsen, "Guerrilla HCI" 251). It was also determined that the test did not need to be recorded in a lab, because note takers could capture the essential findings by hand. This combination of a very small number of test subjects and a room with human recorders rather than video recorders gave birth to the concept of *discount usability testing,* an approach that wasn't originally considered "best" but still "good enough" to produce usable results.

The year following Nielsen's report on his research, Robert Virzi reported identical results from his own research at the Human Factors Society Annual Meeting in 1990. Virzi concluded, as had Nielsen, that "(1) with between 4 and 5 subjects, 80% of the usability problems are detected and (2) that additional subjects are less and less likely to reveal new information" (291). The same number of subjects was confirmed by James Lewis and reported in 1994.

The implications for usability testing were immediate and dramatic:

1. Usability testing could be incorporated into the development of the product at little cost.
2. Usability testing could be incorporated into the development of the product without adversely affecting the development time.
3. Usability testing could be done early and often, using the process called iterative testing, so that the results of testing could be incorporated cheaply while the product was still under development.
4. Usability testing did not require the expense of a lab to be effective.
5. Incorporating this discount usability testing approach into the normal development cycle of products provided a practical way for companies to move to a user-centered design process.

Thus, 1990 ushered in a new way of thinking about usability testing, which allowed for Gould and Lewis' long-advocated, but little-used early focus on the user, iterative testing, and incorporation of improvements while the product is under development. Although it was originally conceived as "good enough," discount usability testing is now viewed as an acceptable model for testing, so long as it is understood to be a "diagnostic test" rather than "a research experiment" (Dumas). In the next section, we look at the different testing models commonly used.

Testing Models

Usability testing can be done with a lab, without a lab, or in the "field," meaning the place where users actually perform their tasks with the product. Field testing, which typically takes place after a product has been released, is a *summative* evaluation, meaning that it is conducted at the end of the development process, whereas testing that takes place during the development process, with or without a lab, is a *formative* evaluation, meaning that the data gathered can be applied to the continuing development of the product that is still forming. In a survey about usability testing methods conducted by the Usability Professionals' Association in 1991–92 (Rosenbaum), the most common method of testing occurred in a lab (32 out of 33 respondents); however, usability testing without a lab was not a choice. A discussion of testing methods follows in the next sections, beginning with lab testing.

Testing with a Lab

Lab testing brings users into a controlled environment, in which they are asked to do specific tasks within specified timeframes. The lab shown in Figure 1.2 is typical of those in use today. This lab shows two rooms, divided by a one-way mirror in

Figure 1.2   Typical two-room usability lab
(Used with permission from Southern Polytechnic State University and the subjects photographed.)

the wall between the two rooms. One room provides a place for the user, or evaluator, to perform the tasks required of the test. This room is typically called the *evaluation room* or *evaluator room*. The glass wall dividing this room from the other room looks like a mirror that the user cannot see through. The other room, where the test administrator or team observes the evaluator and records the activities on videotape for later review, is typically called the *observation room* or *control room*. The team can look through this glass wall to observe the evaluator at work. A schematic of this concept, adapted for an existing space, is shown in Figure 1.3.

Some labs also have a third room, called the *executive viewing room*, that allows executives and others with an interest in the test to observe without interfering with the work being done by the test administrator or team. This room is sometimes separated by a clear glass opening in the wall that allows the visitors to see through the observation room into the evaluation room. Figure 1.4 shows the schematic drawing of such a three-room setup.

In other cases, this room is physically separated from the usability lab, and the visitors observe and hear the activities going on in the evaluation room by watching a TV monitor. Other labs have a reception area, which provides a place to meet and greet the evaluators.

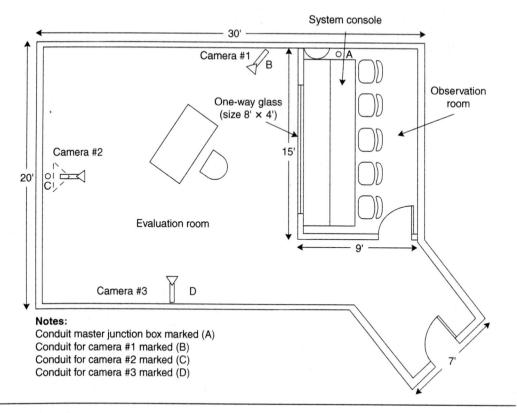

Figure 1.3   Schematic of two-room usability lab

The key features of a typical usability lab are:

■ *One-way mirror* that allows the test administrator or test team to look through the glass to observe the user performing the tasks, while the user cannot see back through the mirror to observe the administrator or team.

■ *Adjustable lighting* so that the test administrator or team can see well enough to perform work during the test, without being seen by the user through the one-way mirror; the light can then be turned up after each test for setup for the next user.

■ *Camera or cameras* that can be set and adjusted (with pan/tilt/zoom) to record the actions of the user (typically using a mouse, keyboard, or documentation), the body language of the user (facial expressions, posture, movement), and the computer screen (to observe what the user is seeing on the screen).

■ *Monitor or bank of monitors* that shows the test administrator or team what is being captured by each of the cameras; one monitor shows what is being recorded onto videotape for later review.

■ *Videotape recorder* that captures the activities of the evaluator on videotape and then allows for later review; two videotape recorders allow for tape editing for a highlights tape.

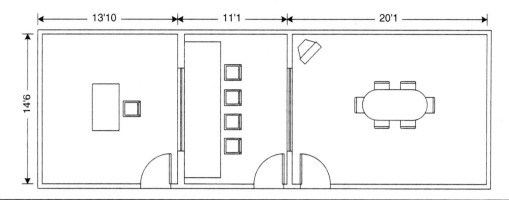

Figure 1.4   Schematic of three-room usability lab
(Used with permission from Usability Systems, Inc.)

- *Composite mixing board* that allows the test administrator or team to capture on videotape one or more camera activities at once (e.g., the user and the computer screen) through split-screen or picture-in-picture options.
- *Scan converter* that provides "direct feed" from the computer screen to the monitors inside the observation room and also to the video recording equipment. This is not found in all labs, as a video camera can be focused onto the computer screen, although this creates scan lines across the video image. The direct feed provides an undistorted view of the screen captured on video and observed by the team or administrator.
- *Logging computer* with software that allows the test administrator or team to record observations, using either the capabilities of a standard word-processing package or a specialized logging software tool for capturing observations in an event log. It is especially helpful to have a time stamp feature to coordinate events described in the log with the corresponding incidents recorded on videotape. A macro can be created for this purpose in most word-processing software products.
- *Multidirectional, wireless microphone* that transmits everything the user says, as well as any sounds coming from the computer.
- *Headsets* (optional) that allow the team to speak to each other and to the logger to share observations at a low voice level (as lack of soundproofing can create distractions for the user) and to hear everything that the evaluator is saying. Without headsets, the evaluation room needs the microphone wired through the wall into the observation room so that the user's voice can be heard.
- *Telephone or intercom* that allows the user to call for help if he or she gets stuck or to call the administrator when the user feels the task is completed.

A 1994 survey of 13 usability labs reported the following (Nielsen, "Usability Laboratories"):

- The defining characteristics of a usability lab are video cameras (used in all labs) and a one-way mirror (used in 92% of labs).

- Usability labs are a fairly recent phenomenon, with the median year of the first usability lab being 1989.
- Only slightly less than half of the labs in the survey used scan converters at the time of the survey, but with prices dropping, it is anticipated that many more are doing so now.

For a list of guidelines for designing a usability lab, see the sidebar entitled "Guidelines for Designing a Usability Lab," also located on the Society for Technical Communication (STC) Web site. In addition, the STC Web site (<http://www.stcsig

---

Guidelines for Designing a Usability Lab
Chauncey Wilson

1. Sound proofing is an important design consideration. Make sure that all "holes" between rooms are properly sound-proofed (including the ceiling).
2. Make sure that you have adjustable lighting in the observation room so you can dim the lights when a participant is in the testing room.
3. You might want to include a second piece of glass angled to prevent a "drum effect" and to insure that noises don't propogate easily through the mirror.
4. Make sure that you can easily run new cables between the two rooms.
5. Purchase scan converters at the highest resolution that your users will be working on.
6. If your company is international, consider buying one recorder that can record in both PAL and NTSC. That way you can record a tape and send it overseas without the need to send it out.
7. Make sure that your lab is accessible by wheelchair.
8. Consider locating your lab near a waiting area or lounge so participants have a place to wait in comfort.
9. Consider a white noise generator for the participant side of the lab if you have a really quiet room. I worked in a lab once that was so quiet you could easily hear the mo-

tors on the cameras. A $50 white noise generator or small air cleaner (I've used both) can be used for a little (not a lot of) background noise.
10. I visited a lab once where the team had originally placed a camera directly over the user's head so they could see the keyboard and paper documentation. There were strong complaints that the overhead camera was a bit voyeuristic and intrusive. The camera was mounted behind the user at an angle and the complaints ceased.
11. Consider curtains or blinds for the mirror. Participants expect a mirror, but it might be distracting when you are using the room for other activities. Also, a few pieces of reasonable artwork (not corporate advertising posters!!) make the room a little less intimidating.
12. Provide enough outlets in the observation room for observers who may want to plug in their laptops to take notes.
13. Have some nice signs on the doors to the lab that indicate a test is in progress. Make the sign assertive so people aren't tempted to walk in during a test.
14. You might consider running a video feed to a conference room nearby if you expect to have large groups of observers and your lab is small.

Source: Chauncey Wilson, Guidelines for Designing a Usability Lab <http://www.stcsig.org/usability/topics/index.html>.

.org/usability/>) contains information under the topic "usability labs" about lab vendors and companies that rent their labs.

Although a permanent lab offers the advantage of being set up and ready to go on short notice, some companies use portable labs that can be set up in a conference room or taken to the "field" for usability testing. A portable lab can be stored when not in use and rolled in and set up quickly when needed for tests. A portable lab can also be packed into a few suitcases and taken on a plane or placed in the trunk of a car for transportation to a remote location. The lab equipment can be separated from the user with a portable screen or put in another room with remote camera hook-up into the evaluator room. A portable lab can be as simple as a computer, a monitor, and a video camera, or it can be as sophisticated as the one shown in Figure 1.5, which packs into two suitcases and contains the following:

- Two digital color cameras
- Remote control from the console to avoid user interruption
- Three LCD color monitors to preview video input sources
- One 10-in. LCD color monitor for composite view of images
- 1024 × 768 scan converter to capture the computer image
- Two audio systems: a desk microphone to record user comments and a wireless microphone to communicate with the user

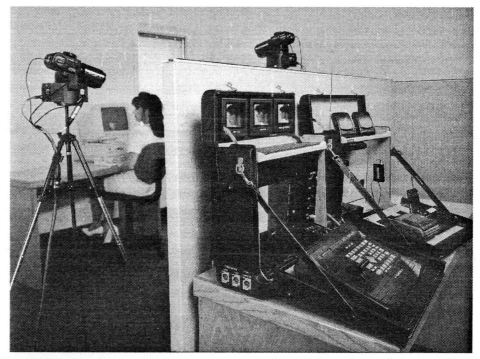

Figure 1.5 Portable usability lab
(Used with permission from Usability Systems, Inc.)

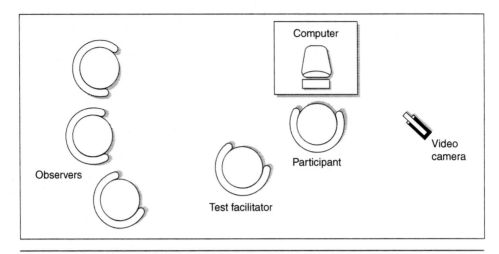

Figure 1.6   Usability testing setup without a lab
(Used with permission from Bev Arends.)

Although a usability lab provides certain advantages, it is not a requirement for companies interested in doing usability testing. The next section looks at the requirements of testing without a lab.

Testing Without a Lab

To conduct usability testing without a lab, all that is required is a room large enough to house the equipment needed for the user, plus space for the test administrator and observers (or team) to sit to the side of the user, as shown in Figure 1.6. It is best to position the observers so that they are still within the peripheral vision of the user, but not directly in his or her line of sight (Rubin 50–51). In this way, the user is aware of the activities going on in the background, without being distracted by them. One observer typically uses a stopwatch to record the time on tasks, noting the information on a form that records the tasks, the times, and the observer's comments. Other observers record actions observed with comments for later discussion. Figure 1.7 is an example of a simple form. A video camera can be set up to record the user performing the tasks, or an audiotape recorder can be used for recording comments from the user. Debriefing meetings can be held to productively involve all observers and increase team interest in product improvement.

At its simplest level, usability testing without a lab requires nothing more than a stopwatch, pencils, some note cards and some sticky notes. Lotus Development began usability testing with just such a "low-tech usability starter kit" (Butler). The contents of the starter kit for each observer were as follows:

- Index cards
- Observer pen
- Observer instructions:

- Write down anything you want to record.
- Put one idea per card.
- Leave your cards on the desk when you go.

After the observers had completed their work, a debriefing meeting (with food as an incentive) was scheduled to gather the results. The facilitator of the meeting was instructed to:

- Attach one piece of tape to each card created by observers.
- Post all the cards in one place on a wall.

When the participants (former observers) arrived at the meeting, they received instructions to:

- Move the cards as needed to:
  - Establish categories.
  - Label categories using sticky notes.
- Decide on a ranking scheme, perhaps with each team member voting on a 1-to-10 scale.
- Determine final rankings by consensus.
- Create a final report in a table of results.

Although much useful information can be learned from usability testing with or without a lab, another equally rich source of information about usability comes from field testing. In the next section, we look at approaches to field testing.

Start time: _____

Actions	Comments	Types of assists	Types of errors

Stop time: _____

Figure 1.7 Data log sheet

Field Testing

In our use of the term, *field testing* means going into the "field" to evaluate products used in the office, an industrial setting, or a home. It is not to be confused with *field studies*, which also send observers into the field, but whose purpose is to gather information about users and tasks *before* a product is developed. Field studies are discussed in Chapter 3. Here, we discuss field testing, which evaluates a product after it has been released from production. As a usability testing method, it provides several advantages, as well as several disadvantages, over lab testing.

Here are some of the advantages of field testing:

1. You go to the user, rather than asking the user to come to you.
2. You get to observe the actual environment in which the user works or lives, rather than attempting to simulate it artificially; thus, you gain an understanding of the availability of work space, access to manuals, type of computer used, lighting conditions, and other aspects of use.
3. You get to see how the user works with the product in the user's real work setting, complete with interruptions, disruptions, and distractions (typically not present in lab testing).
4. You get to study the artifacts in the user's environment, such as sticky notes on the user's monitor, personal job aids, and other techniques created by the user to remember certain tasks or functions.
5. You learn whether the user has access to documentation and where it is located (and used).

Here are some of the disadvantages of field testing:

1. You cannot control the environment, so it becomes difficult to perform timed tasks.
2. You cannot remove yourself from the environment, as lab testing allows you to do.
3. You may not be able to hold the user's undivided attention, as the distractions of the workplace might interfere.
4. You typically cannot test as many users, as companies may be unwilling to allow frequent disruptions (not to mention the additional time and expense required for the product developers to be out of the office).
5. Because field testing is usually a summative evaluation, complex problems uncovered during the testing generally cannot be changed on the product tested.

Field testing can be done in one of two ways:

- *Structured observations.* With this type of test, the user is asked to perform the kinds of tasks that might also be done in a lab. This technique is excellent for learning about how the user will use the product in his or her actual environment, as the influence of environment is often a critical factor in the usability of a product. It is also used very late in product development to determine whether the product fits into the environment for which it has been developed. However, when done late in the product development cycle, the results of such testing are typically not incorporated until the next release of the product. In another type of field testing, called *beta testing,* users are asked to test the product in their own setting and report the results through a questionnaire. Typically, though, this type of testing does not involve observations by the developer or test team. Also, typically, it is used more for validation testing rather than for usability testing.

- *Longitudinal field studies.* Although field tests are typically a snapshot of one or more visits to the field to see how users interact with a particular product at a particular time, a longitudinal field test studies users interacting with products over time as they progress from novice to intermediate to expert. By scheduling return visits to see the same users progressing in their use of a product, developers can learn what happens to users interacting with their product as the users' proficiency improves. Whereas lab testing most commonly determines what a novice user wants from a particular product in development, longitudinal field studies reveal the changing requirements of the same user as he or she moves through stages of proficiency with the product. Of course, longitudinal field studies take time and money; for this reason, they are not commonly performed because of the demand for rapid development of products.

However, when a new type of product is introduced to the market, it is critical to the success of the product to learn from users how it works in their own environment. When WebTV was introduced, the usability team understood that lab testing alone would not provide enough information about the use of the product to address all aspects of usability, so they arranged for field testing and longitudinal field studies in customers' homes. During in-home visits, the field researchers asked users to perform tasks using the printer adapter. These tasks were based on the same scenarios and questionnaires developed in lab testing. At the conclusion of the initial home visit, the researchers gave the participants a tape recorder with a list of questions about the printer taped on the recorder. Participants were encouraged to record comments in response to the questions as they used the printer over a 3-week period. When the researchers returned to pick up the tape recorders, they asked additional questions of the participants. The findings were so useful that the results were presented to a broad group within the company organization (Gomoll et al.).

In this example, the company believed in the value of such testing and was willing to pay the expense involved. However, such an enlightened view may not exist within your company. Whether the cost is minimal or significant, you may find yourself working for a company that doesn't conduct usability testing because the cost seems too high, no matter what it is. In this situation, you may have to make a case for usability testing. In the next section, we provide some strategies for making that case.

Cost-Justifying Usability

Costs of Testing

A fully developed, state-of-the-art usability lab costs $75,000 to $150,000, depending on the specific needs of the company for testing products. A state-of-the-art portable lab system ranges in price from $30,000 to $50,000. Certainly, as discussed earlier, a lab can be built for much less expense, and usability testing can be conducted without a lab.

Even without the expense of a lab or costly usability equipment, usability testing is not without some expense. The simplest tests can take many person-hours of development and analysis. For example, one research study showed that it takes 39 hours to conduct a usability test of a Web site the first time (Molich and Gram; reported in Nielsen, "Cost"). This time included planning the test, recruiting participants, testing five users, analyzing the data, and reporting the results. The cost for the test developers' time does not include the cost of paying participants, feeding and housing them, as needed, or paying a company, such as a temporary employment agency, to recruit the participants. Nor does it include the cost of the equipment for testing or the use of a lab. Nielsen reports that once the learning curve of testing is accomplished, testing can be done in less time: tests can be written in 2 hours, recruiting done by outsourcing (at a cost of less than $1,000 for five users), reporting can be handled in a 1-hour meeting with no more than an executive summary of findings that takes 2 or 3 hours to write for a total of 2 days' effort ("Cost"). However, even with low cost outlays, some managers are reluctant to provide the time or money for usability testing. Typically, these are managers who don't see the value of testing because they haven't observed users doing usability testing on their products. In such situations, an argument may need to be made that weighs the costs of testing against those of not testing. In the next section, we examine the typical hidden costs of *not testing*.

Costs of Not Testing

A common lesson learned the hard way in the software development industry is that it costs 100 times more to make a change in the next release of a product than to make it at the beginning of the project development cycle (Nielsen, "Mud-Throwing").

The costs of not testing are frequently calculated as the costs of the following:

- *Support calls.* How much do help calls increase whenever a new product is released?
- *Training.* How much is required to support the user community?
- *Competitive advantage.* How does the user community assess your product against the competition? Can you afford to wait until the product is released to find out?
- *Image and reputation.* Does the product measure up to its billing as easy to use, designed for users, and so forth? Does it enhance the existing product

line and increase the company's credibility? Do the reviews help sell the product or kill it?

■ *Efficient use of the customer's time.* How much money is lost by companies when their employees cannot use products efficiently and effectively?

An examination of the cost of even one second of added time to a product can make a big difference to an employer's bottom line, as demonstrated by Table 1.2.

TABLE 1.2	A Small Inefficiency Can Lead to Heavy Costs	
User's salary	Suppose your product is used by an accountant earning $50,000.00 per year.	$50,000.00
Salary multiplier	The employer also pays for insurance, office space, and other benefits. These typically add 50% to 100% to the salary.	× 1.5
Annual cost	The result is the annual cost of the employee's time.	$75,000.00
Work days per year	This salary represents work performed over a year. Let's assume a typical American 5-day work week with 2 weeks' vacation.	÷ 250
Cost per day	This gives the employee cost per day.	$300
Hours per day	Let's use a standard workday.	÷ 8
Cost per hour	This tells what 1 hour of work costs.	$37.50
Seconds per hour	Divide this by 60 seconds per minute times 60 minutes an hour.	÷ 3,600
Cost per second	This tells the cost of 1 second of the user's time.	$0.0142

This amount—about a penny and a half—may seem miniscule to you, but it is critical to corporate managers. Complex, awkward procedures can waste considerable time. For instance:

User's time cost	What we calculated for the cost of 1 second of the user's time.	$0.0142
Time wasted by awkward procedure	How much time does the user waste because a procedure is hard to remember (must look up or read instructions) or is performed with unnecessary steps? Let's assume a value of 10 seconds.	× 10
Cost per use	The result shows how much is wasted each time one user performs the procedure.	$0.142
Frequency of use	How often does the user perform such procedures during the period of the calculation? Let's assume 10 times a day on 250 workdays per year.	× 2,500
Cost per user	This gives the total cost for each user.	$260.42
Number of users	Multiply this by the number of users of the product, say, 1,000.	× 1,000
Total cost	This tells the total cost to all users of the awkward features.	$260,420

Source: William Horton. "Let's Do Away with Manuals . . . Before They Do Away with Us." *Technical Communication* (First Quarter, 1993), p. 30. (Reprinted with permission from *Technical Communication,* the journal of the Society for Technical Communication, Arlington, VA, U.S.A.)

It shows how quickly the costs can mount when a product has not been designed and tested to demonstrate maximum efficiency and ease of use.

Taking a "life-cycle" perspective on costs is critical, according to Ginny Redish, a usability specialist, who reports one engineer's estimate that "70% of software life-cycle costs occur in the maintenance phase" (27). Another research study finds that 80% of the maintenance costs are due to an inability to anticipate user requirements (Karat 48). Still another reports that the 90 person-hours required to usability test a software product with 152 users showed a 56% "correct" response rate on the original design. The revised design produced 75% "correct" responses. The author, usability specialist James Prekeges, reasons that this is a highly-leveraged investment, using the following argument:

> If the 90 hours is averaged out over the 152 users, the cost was 35 minutes per user. Will they save an average of 35 minutes each over the life of the product due to being 76% effective, rather than 56% effective? The answer is a resounding YES. They will probably see a payback within the first day of using it, and over the long term the benefit is staggering.

Recognizing the increasing interest in a product's usability as part of a buying decision, *PC/Computing* instituted its own usability testing process for software and hardware products, assigning usability scores derived from comparison testing. An early test reported in March 1994 presented a face-off between two software products: WordPerfect 6.0 vs. Microsoft Word 6.0 (both for Windows). The result of the face-off was a "usability-approved" score of 88 for WordPerfect and 82 for Word, based on a number of factors that testers were asked to consider. Although the results are, indeed, interesting in light of the subsequent history and market share of these two products since the test was conducted, the point is not to discuss which product was marketed more effectively, but which was *rated and reviewed* as the better product. When it comes to marketing, Geoffrey Moore points out that "in fact, feature for feature, the less successful product is often arguably superior" (4).

Because so many reviews include usability issues as part of product assessment, usability can become a strong selling point in persuading management that it is better to find and fix problems before a reviewer finds and reports problems with your product. Case in point: a usability consultant was hired to conduct usability testing on a new product already released in a limited way to beta testers (early users of the product who provide feedback before formal release). Based on the large number of problems found in the beta tests, the company decided to delay release of the product until they addressed the major usability issues. Thus, they were quite surprised and somewhat perplexed to see the results of two vastly different product reviews reported in separate publications: one extremely favorable and the other extremely unfavorable. Curious as to the reason for the disparity of views, they followed up with both reviewers and learned that the favorable review had been based on the product released after the improvements were made, whereas the unfavorable review had been based on the beta version before the improvements were made.

In 1993, approximately 155 reviews in microcomputer trade journals focused on user-friendliness and usability of software products. Surely, much more space is devoted to these topics in today's trade publications. When the issue of the costs involved in usability testing arises, responses to use with your organization must show the costs accrued from not testing, as well as the savings to be derived from usability testing. In the next section, we look at the benefits of testing, which can be part of the argument made for cost savings.

Benefits of Testing

The benefits of testing can be calculated by looking at the costs of not testing and assuming the benefits to be derived when testing is added to product development. In a 1991 study documented by Wixon and Jones (reported in Karat 49), usability engineering resulted in a revenue increase of 80% over the first release of the product, which had not been usability-engineered. What's more, the second release produced revenues that were 60% over projections, with customers citing the usability of the product in their buying decisions. As we've said, the benefits of testing include reduced training time, reduced support calls, reduced maintenance, better marketability, increased satisfaction, and the like. They also include increased productivity for the development team as they incorporate learning about usability from previous product tests into new product development. This, in turn, can improve the development cycle, as less trial and error is involved and a more accurate definition of user requirements can be compiled.

But let's take a closer look at how some of these benefits are calculated. A 1997 study makes the case for incorporating usability into product development by looking at business PCs to analyze whether the cost improves productivity. At an average cost of $3,000 each, or about $1,000 a year over the average life span of a typical computer, the actual cost of computers must include the related costs to use them, which include:

- Technicians to keep the computers and networks going $1,170
- Links to a network and required basic software $1,730
- Technical support $3,510
- Lost time for employees (waiting for programs to run or help to arrive, or playing games packaged with software) $5,590

This makes the total annual cost of the computer not $1,000, but $13,000. Added to that cost is the difficulty of using many systems, which requires employees to use up to 10% of their work time helping coworkers with computer problems, making the total annual cost of a PC $23,500 (Gibbs 87–88).

Typically, high productivity losses are attributed to poor interface design. But productivity gains can result from even very small changes, as Ben Shneiderman, in an address to the Usability Professionals' Association, presented in these two examples:

1. If you change the size or position of buttons on a computer screen, you slow down users by 5 to 10%.
2. If you change the word on a single button (for instance, from "search" to "query"), you slow down users 10 to 20%.

Need more ammunition? Here are more studies to make the case. Recognizing the importance of productivity and a need for productivity improvement, the New York Stock Exchange brought in a design firm to upgrade the four main computers used on the trading floor. The improvements made on the basis of usability testing as part of a user-centered design process resulted in the workload capacity doubling and the error rate falling by a factor of 10 (Gibbs 88). When American Express redesigned its computer interface for bank authorizations, training times dropped from 12 hours to 2 hours and task time from 17 minutes to 4 minutes (Gibbs 89). For still more examples of companies' documented savings from usability testing, see *Cost-Justifying Usability* (Bias and Mayhew), which establishes a framework for making the business case for usability testing as part of the product development process.

Perhaps the benefits are obvious. However, as Table 1.3 shows, when we look at the results of a survey to determine which work processes were most frequently used to ensure the quality of information products, we see that usability testing came in fourth out of five methods used every time (Ramey 43):

TABLE 1.3	Work Processes Used Every Time to Ensure Quality		
Method	**Percentage Who Use Every Time**
Inspection for technical quality	73.2
Inspection for communication quality (editing)	60.6
Peer reviews	47.7
Usability testing	9.1
Field studies, contextual inquiry, etc.	6.6

Source: Judith Ramey, "What Technical Communicators Think About Measuring Value Added: Report on a Questionnaire." *Technical Communication* 42.1 (1995), p. 30. (Reprinted with permission from *Technical Communication*, the journal of the Society for Technical Communication, Arlington, VA, U.S.A.)

Most likely, these results have improved, even dramatically, given that the survey was conducted in 1994 and the focus was on information products only. Although the study did point out that 59.1% of the respondents do usability testing occasionally, it also found that 40.9% of respondents never do usability testing. Thus, even with the likelihood of improved numbers today, there is still a need for cost-justifying usability testing to increase the outcome of usability testing being done every time on every product.

It is interesting to note that Bias and Mayhew conclude their book on cost-justifying methods by stating that "ten years ago, it was unusual for usability to be on equal footing with 'product function' and 'schedule' in the business decision equation. Ten years from now, this book will be unnecessary, except perhaps to help new usability professionals with their level of usability-justification efforts" ("Summary" 322). If you find that your manager or organization no longer needs to be "sold" on the benefits of usability testing, that's progress. If, however, you meet resistance, you will need to employ the arguments presented here to justify the cost and prove the value of testing.

Summary

In this chapter, we have presented:

- A definition of usability, explaining what it *is not* as well as what it *is*
- An explanation of the user-centered design process, which encompasses the early and repetitive focus on users as key to the development of usable products
- A definition of usability testing, explaining what it *is not* as well as what it *is*
- An explanation of the traditional approach to usability testing
- The breakthrough that resulted from an understanding of the validity of discount usability testing
- Current approaches to usability testing, with and without a lab, as well as in the field
- Descriptions of different types of lab setups
- Descriptions of options for testing without a lab
- A presentation, with examples, of the costs of not conducting usability tests
- A presentation (with examples) of the methods of cost-justifying usability testing by selling the benefits of testing vs. the costs

Coming Up

In the next chapter, we look at other methods of conducting research and getting information from usability experts and from users as part of a usability engineering process.

Questions/Topics for Discussion

1. How is usability testing different from quality assurance? Make one list of all the words you think would be on a list for usability testing and another list of all the words on a list for quality assurance. In what ways are the lists different? Are there any similarities or overlaps in the two lists?
2. Think of a product you have bought that was difficult to learn to use. What made it difficult? Who do you think the intended user of the product is? If you are the intended user, what would you recommend to the designers to make the product more usable for you?
3. Using Moore's categories of users for high-tech products, how would you categorize yourself? Describe your attitude toward technology and learning new tools as a member of one of the five categories of users. What are the most important usability issues for you as a member of a particular group of users?
4. What do we mean when we speak of *discount* usability testing? What are the requirements of a discount usability test? How has this approach made

usability testing much more practical as part of a user-centered design process?

5. If you were asked to cost-justify usability testing, that is, to make a case for the return on investment of the expense of a usability test, what points would you present? Be prepared to address both the benefits of testing as well as the costs and problems that occur when testing is not done.

Exercises

1. Bring in the instructions for a product you have found difficult to use. Be prepared to lead a discussion, either in a small group or for the class, about the usability issues you faced in trying to follow the instructions.
2. From these usability issues or problems with the instructions, create a list of solutions to make this set of instructions usable. If you're working in a small group, the group should select a set of instructions for this exercise.
3. From this list of solutions, create a list of usability guidelines for any set of instructions.
4. Using the World Wide Web, search for job openings with the word "usability" either in the title or in the job description. Bring your list to class and discuss how many similarities and how many differences there are in jobs addressing usability. You may want to narrow your search by also using the words "technical communication" to see how many matches you get with "usability."
5. Using the World Wide Web, locate a Web site or listserv that addresses usability issues. In addition to identifying the URL (Web address) or listserv address, describe the objective of the Web site or listserv. Also evaluate its usefulness to you and the members of the class. Describe the features or topics that make it useful.

References

Barbash, Fred. "Terminal Tantrums." *Washington Post* 7 June 1999: Business 20–21.

Bias, Randolph G., and Deborah J. Mayhew, eds. *Cost-Justifying Usability*. Boston: Academic Press, 1994.

———. "Summary: A Place at the Table." *Cost-Justifying Usability*. Eds. Randolph G. Bias and Deborah J. Mayhew. Boston: Academic Press, 1994. 319–25.

Binstock, Andrew. "New Mantra: Usability." *Information Week Online* 6 Sept. 1999 <http://www.informationweek.com/751/51adusa.htm>.

Butler, Mary Beth. "Usability Testing Starter Kit." Paper presented at STC 41st Annual Conference, Minneapolis, MN, 15–18 May, 1994.

Carroll, John M. "Reconstructing Minimalism." *Minimalism Beyond the Nurnberg Funnel*. Ed. John M. Carroll. Cambridge, MA: MIT Press, 1988. 1–17.

Cooper, Alan. *The Inmates Are Running the Asylum.* Indianapolis, IN: SAMS, 1999.

Dumas, Joe. "Usability Testing Methods: When Does a Usability Test Become a Research Experiment?" *Common Ground* 9.2 (May 1999): 1+.

Dumas, Joseph S., and Janice C. Redish. *A Practical Guide to Usability Testing.* Norwood, NJ: Ablex, 1993.

Gibbs, W. Wayt. "Taking Computers to Task." *Scientific American* (July 1997): 82–89.

Gomoll, Kate, et al. "Stories from the Living Room: In-Home Visits with WebTV Users." *Proceedings of Usability Professionals' Association 1998 Conference.* Washington, DC, 25–26 June, 1998. 229–33.

Gould, John D., and Clayton Lewis. "Designing for Usability: Key Principles and What Designers Think." *Communications of the ACM* 28.3 (Mar. 1985): 300–311.

Gray, Wayne D., and Marilyn C. Salzman. "Damaged Merchandise? A Review of Experiments That Compare Usability Evaluation Methods." *Human–Computer Interaction* 13 (1998): 203–61.

Haddad, Charles. "Excel Makes Better Use of Mac's Innovations." *Atlanta Journal-Constitution* 28 June 1998: C2.

Horton, William. "Let's Do Away with Manuals . . . Before They Do Away with Us." *Technical Communication* (First Quarter 1993): 26–34.

International Organization for Standardization <http://www.iso.ch/>.

Karat, Clare-Marie. "Business Case Approach to Usability Cost Justification." *Cost-Justifying Usability.* Eds. Randolph G. Bias and Deborah J. Mayhew. Boston: Academic Press, 1994: 45–70.

Lewis, James R. "Sample Sizes for Usability Studies: Additional Considerations." *Human Factors* 36.2 (1994): 368–78.

"Market Maturity." *Eye for Design* Jan.–Feb. 1997 User Interface Engineering <http://world.std.com/~uieweb/market.htm>.

Martin, Steve. "Designer of Audio CD Packaging Enters Hell." *The New Yorker,* 19 April 1999: 53.

Martinez, Michael. "Simplify, Simplify: AOL Chief Opens PC Expo with Customers-First Call." ABCNews.com, 22 June 1999 <http://www.abcnews.go.com/sections/tech/DailyNews/pcexpo990622.html>.

Moore, Geoffrey A. *Crossing the Chasm: Marketing and Selling Technology Products to Mainstream Customers.* New York: Harper Business, 1991.

Mossberg, Walter S. "Personal Technology." *The Wall Street Journal* 17 Oct. 1991: B1.

Nielsen, Jakob. "Cost of User Testing a Website." *Alertbox,* 3 May 1998 <http://www.useit.com/alertbox/980503.html>.

———. "Guerrilla HCI: Using Discount Usability Engineering to Penetrate the Intimidation Barrier." *Cost-Justifying Usability.* Eds. Randolph G. Bias and Deborah J. Mayhew. Boston: Academic Press, 1994. 242–72.

———. "The Mud-Throwing Theory of Usability." *Alertbox,* 2 Apr. 2000 <http://www.useit.com/alertbox/20000402.html>.

———. *Usability Engineering.* Boston: Academic Press, 1993.

———. "Usability Laboratories: A 1994 Survey" <http://www.useit.com/papers/uselabs.html>.

————. "What Is 'Usability'?" 29 Sept. 1998 <http://www.zdnet.com>.

Prekeges, James G. "Usability Testing for Non-Testers." Paper presented at STC 40th Annual Conference, Dallas, TX, 6–9 June 1993.

Ramey, Judith. "What Technical Communicators Think About Measuring Value Added: Report on a Questionnaire." *Technical Communication* 42.1 (1995): 40–51.

Redish, Janice (Ginny). "Adding Value as a Professional Communicator." *Technical Communication* 42.1 (1995): 26–39.

"Road Rage on the Information Superhighway." *CNN Interactive* 12 Mar 1999. <http://www.cnn.com/TECH/computing/9903/12/network.rage/>.

Rosenbaum, Stephanie, ed. "Results of Member Survey: Usability Professionals' Association." *Proceedings of Usability Professionals' Association Conference.* Seattle, WA, 21 July 1993. 1–27.

Rubin, Jeffrey. *Handbook of Usability Testing.* New York: Wiley, 1994.

Sanders, Elizabeth B.-N. "Converging Perspectives in Product Development Research." *Interface '93 Proceedings.* HFES, Raleigh, NC, 5–8, May 1993. 236–41.

Shneiderman, Ben. "The Golden Age of Usability." Keynote address presented at the Usability Professionals' Association Conference 1998, Washington, DC, 25 June 1998.

Virzi, Robert A. "Streamlining the Design Process: Running Fewer Subjects." *Proceedings of the Human Factors Society 34th Annual Meeting,* Orlando, FL, 8–12 Oct. 1990. 291–94.

Wilson, Chauncey. "Guidelines for Designing a Usability Lab" <http://www.stcsig.org/usability/topics/index.html>.

Other Methods for Getting Feedback About Product Usability

 In Chapter 1, we outlined the user-centered design process and showed the place of usability testing, as well as other methods of research, within it. In this chapter, we explore these other methods for getting feedback about a product's usability. These include methods for getting feedback from experts and methods for getting feedback from users. Any of these methods, used in combination with usability testing, provides a more complete picture of the usability of the product than one single method can.

Usability engineering is frequently viewed as the umbrella term that describes the set of activities underlying the process of creating user-centered product designs. They include usability testing, of course, but also a variety of other methods for obtaining information about the usability of products. This chapter discusses these other methods by dividing the process into two approaches:

1. Methods using feedback from experts
2. Methods using feedback from users

For a list of usability methods that specifically address documentation, see the sidebar entitled "Documentation Usability Techniques" (Wilson).

Feedback from Experts

Usability inspection is the term that applies to those activities involving experts "inspecting" or "examining" usability-related aspects of a product (Nielsen and Mack). Typically, usability inspection focuses on the user interface. We use the term *interface* to mean all the elements of a product with which the user comes in contact. These include the hardware, software, online help, and documentation,

(continued on page 35)

31

Documentation Usability Techniques

Chauncey E. Wilson

Method	Focus	Notes
Read and locate test	General sense of ease of navigation and organization of information.	Need a fairly large sample and must spend time on representative questions.
Laboratory testing	Use to verify unique features of all types of online help. If performance isn't an issue, participants are generally asked to "think aloud."	Finding participants is the biggest issue. Can be used for performance testing (how fast, how many errors).
Summary test	Use to see if users grasp key concepts (e.g., security).	Users read a section of documentation and reflect on what they think it means. Scoring may not be easy.
Usability edit	Detailed edit of instructions. User is asked to read through text and mark up anything that is hard to understand, wordy, inconsistent, etc.	Useful for procedural help to see if language is clear, anything is missing, terminology is consistent.
User interface inspections	Formal inspection of document with focus on usability, readability, and consistency issues. A common user interface design technique.	Catches many details. Should have writers from different groups involved in the inspection to improve consistency. Requires some minimal training. Should not be the only method used.
Diaries of documentation usage	Users keep a diary of their experience with the documentation (and product).	Requires dedicated users.
Audio diaries	Use audio computers found on most computers to create an audio diary.	Need a microphone. Users can e-mail their audio file to you. Easy to turn on and off. Can be used for surveys and diaries.
Pop-up Web surveys	A window pops up once for each user asking if the user will fill out a short survey. If the person says, "yes," the survey appears. A user only gets one instance of this.	See <www.surveysite.com> for an example.
Logging of online help usage	Wire up some customers so that their use of help is logged. Have them send back logs once a week.	Security issues. Must develop or purchase logging software that will log all forms of help usage and point to the topic of interest.

Method	Focus	Notes
Mark-up of documentation	Ask users to mark up the hard copy with comments and send it to you.	Requires some dedication and some mark-up training.
Critical incident questionnaire	Ask users about critical incidents involving any form of documentation.	Critical incident questionnaires allow the gathering of critical issue and frequency data. Critical incidents can be successes or failures.
Telephone survey of documentation usage	Get general feedback about documentation issues.	Hard for users to remember things if cold-called. Best technique is to contact users, get them to commit to a study of a particular length, send them questions of interest, and ask that they jot down notes before the phone interview.
Tape recorder with big button	Detailed, real-time feedback. User hits button to record a comment; hits button again to stop recording.	Requires OK from users and may involve security issues. Collection of tapes can be a problem. Analysis is detailed, but time-consuming.
Documentation survey (mail questionnaire)	A good questionnaire requires design and testing; focus on key questions.	Some incentive is needed here for dedicated customers.
Beta questionnaire	Information on product and documentation; requires careful design.	Many customers don't use the documentation much during beta so this method often disappoints the beta team.
Summaries of product reviews	What is said about your documentation or your competitor's documentation in product reviews?	Magazines, journals, and Web sites have reviews of product documentation. Some reviews rate documentation on specific usability criteria.
Email surveys	Put out a survey through an e-mail list. Problem here is that the sample may be somewhat biased.	Get names of potential recipients from support, marketing, or user group lists.
Web survey	Put out a survey on the Web or send the survey to selected users. Problem here is that the sample may be somewhat biased	Get names of potential recipients from support.
Training classes	Sit in on training classes. Work with the instructor to provide some training on the documentation.	Ask trainees to note problems with documentation and let you know about them during exercises or at breaks.

(continued)

Method	Focus	Notes
Information race	Give users a set of questions and tell them that they are racing each other to find the answer in the documentation.	More for expert users who have strong egos.
Support debriefings	Meet with support once a month or so and review any recurrent usability or documentation problems.	Good information on places where the user interface or documentation could be better.
Screen movies	Ask users to do screen movies of their work or documentation usage. You can use screen-recording tools like Lotus ScreenCam. Users can start recording when they are using documentation or want to show how they use a product. They can stop recording until the next documentation "incident."	Takes lots of disk space. Most screen-recording software can handle voice so users can think aloud and give you a screen movie.
Remote usability testing	Use software like NetMeeting or PCAnywhere to view the screen of a user at a distant site. You can hear the user over a regular phone line while observing what the user is doing on the screen.	Takes some practice. Useful internally, but more difficult working with clients because of firewalls and security issues.
Competitive testing	Check out features of other products to see how usable they are.	Often done informally, but results hard to interpret.
Paper-and-pencil testing of individual elements of publications	Early feedback on document structure, language, and graphics.	Create samples of proposed publications and have users walk through scenarios. Check out things like terminology, heading levels, task sequences, use of illustrations and examples, and index entries.
User group feedback	Meet with user groups during conferences, shows, etc. Prepare a list of questions to ask.	General feedback, but good way to make contact for more detailed information.
Online focus groups	Participants are selected according to a user profile. Participants are given passwords to prototype products and can use them before the focus group.	Cheaper than regular focus groups and people can use products to get more detailed data than face-to-face focus groups.
Coordination with product management when customers visit	Work with product management/marketing to get some time with customers who are visiting your site.	Prepare a list of questions to have ready.

Method	Focus	Notes
Field visits	Field visits can be used to gather a lot of information, including documentation use.	Must focus on the whole product. Trips to get info on "just documentation" are not all that successful.

Source: Chauncey E. Wilson, "Documentation Usability Techniques." <http://www.stcsig.org/usability/resources>.

as well as any other elements that shape the user's experience with the product. In a formal usability inspection (also called a *design review*), the designers, acting as the inspectors, follow a prescribed format for reviewing a product and detecting "defects." The objective of such a design review is to locate inconsistencies, especially those that do not comply with a set of development standards.

A less formal type of inspection or design review is *storyboarding*. Storyboards are outlines, prototypes, or design elements, typically with explanations of graphics and text contained on each board. When posted on the walls of a meeting room, the storyboards provide a way for the development team—which might include the product manager, developers, technical experts, user representative, editor, technical communicator, graphics/production staff, and others connected with the product—to "walk the walls" and visualize the product from the storyboard displays. Used in the early stage of product development, issues of design, flow, and content can be resolved quickly and changes made easily.

Although formal inspections and informal storyboard techniques are used often, the most common types of usability inspection are:

- *Heuristic evaluations,* in which usability experts judge the usability of a product against a specific set of heuristics, or principles.
- *Cognitive walkthroughs,* in which experts trained in cognitive processes evaluate the effectiveness of a product design according to its ability to match the problem-solving process users would employ.

These have gained widespread acceptance because they:

- Are inexpensive
- Do not require special equipment or a usability lab
- Can be integrated easily into the product development lifecycle
- Produce "instant gratification" since problems and recommendations are generated without delay (Nielsen and Mack xvi)

In the next sections, we examine these two methods, beginning with the heuristic evaluation.

Heuristic Evaluation

Heuristic evaluation is the most popular of the usability inspection methods. Nielsen describes heuristic evaluation as one of two "discount" usability methods, the other being usability testing with a small number of participants (as described in Chapter 1). Heuristic evaluation is a discount method because it is cheap and effective. Whereas one evaluator discovers only 35% of usability problems, using a small set of evaluators, typically three to five, produces a high degree of overlap in their findings (Nielsen; Nielsen and Mack).

In a heuristic evaluation, each evaluator works alone to inspect the product against a set of rules or principles. In some cases, the evaluators are given a typical-use scenario, listing the steps a user would take to perform typical tasks. Each evaluator then goes through the interface at least twice: once to become familiar with it and a second time to inspect the elements against the list of recognized rules. Because the evaluators are not necessarily using the product to perform real tasks, this method can be used for interfaces that exist only on paper, allowing the inspection to take place early in the product development cycle.

The results of each evaluator's individual inspection can be collected and documented in a report, recorded by an observer, or collated in a meeting of all inspectors to share their results. The report produces a list of usability problems with explanations of the principle violated by each one. Although it is not a requirement to produce a list of recommendations, these are frequently obvious. For example, if the evaluator determines that the system does not provide feedback to the user at a critical point, the recommendation to provide feedback is readily apparent. A debriefing session with the developers following the heuristic evaluation allows for quick solutions to be generated for the less obvious problems.

The Heuristics

Much of the work of developing heuristics for analysis of user interfaces derives from research conducted by John Carroll and his fellow cognitive scientists at IBM's Watson Research Center. Applying a minimalist approach, by which they used an action- and task-oriented approach to developing documentation, they tested documentation that included only enough information to get users started right away on their tasks (Carroll, *Nurnberg Funnel* and *Minimalism Beyond*). Table 2.1 presents the four major design principles and the corresponding heuristics for designing minimalist instruction (van der Meij and Carroll 21). For more information about research on users and tasks, see Chapter 3.

Regardless of whether the interface being inspected is documentation (print or online), the software user interface, or the World Wide Web, the underlying principle of heuristic evaluation is that the rules are logical and intuitive for any expert who understands what a good product should and should not do. By establishing a set of heuristics, these underlying principles become standardized so that several evaluators can focus on the same categories for the purpose of cataloging the results. Although a set of heuristics can contain several hundred items, a popular model developed by Nielsen (in Nielsen and Mack 30) contains the ten principles outlined in Table 2.2 on page 38.

Clearly, this set of heuristics pertains to interface design issues primarily, which was its original intent. Although this list of rules has been widely adopted, there are other lists, such as the one developed by Gerhardt-Powals (192–93) and shown in Table 2.3 on page 39. Despite some similarities, this set of heuristics appears to more specifically address the domain of cognitive scientists. For a set of heuristics to apply when looking at Web sites, see Chapter 9.

TABLE 2.1	Four Major Design Principles and Their Heuristics for Designing Minimalist Instruction	
Principle 1: Choose an action-oriented approach.	**Heuristic 1.1**	Provide an immediate opportunity to act.
	Heuristic 1.2	Encourage and support exploration and innovation.
	Heuristic 1.3	Respect the integrity of the user's activity.
Principle 2: Anchor the tool in the task domain.	**Heuristic 2.1**	Select or design instructional activities that are real tasks.
	Heuristic 2.2	The components of the instruction should reflect the task structure.
Principle 3: Support error recognition and recovery.	**Heuristic 3.1**	Prevent mistakes whenever possible.
	Heuristic 3.2	Provide error information when actions are error-prone or when correction is difficult.
	Heuristic 3.3	Provide error information that supports detection, diagnosis, and recovery.
	Heuristic 3.4	Provide on-the-spot error information.
Principle 4: Support reading to do, study, and locate.	**Heuristic 4.1**	Be brief; don't spell out everything.
	Heuristic 4.2	Provide closure for chapters.

Source: Hans van der Meij and John M. Carroll. "Principles and Heuristics for Designing Minimalist Instruction." *Minimalism Beyond the Nurnberg Funnel* Ed. John M. Carroll, Cambridge, MA: MIT Press, 1998, p. 21. (Used with permission. © 1998 Massachusetts Institute of Technology.)

Companies typically adapt an existing set of heuristics to their own uses. In Appendix 2.2 at the end of this chapter, a detailed example developed at Xerox is presented. It provides a review checklist that expands upon Nielsen's model.

The Heuristics Applied to Documentation

A further adaptation of Nielsen's heuristics by Daugherty shows the ways in which they can be used for an inspection of documentation. (See Table 2.4 on page 40.) A sample checklist for one part of such a heuristic evaluation of a manual might look like the one shown in Table 2.5 on page 41, also compiled by Daugherty.

Another way to conduct a heuristic evaluation of documentation is to perform a *usability edit*. Although an edit frequently means the same thing as a heuristic evaluation, it may be different in that the "rules" may not be explicitly defined. Rather, the evaluators may be provided with some questions to answer as they analyze the effectiveness of the documentation. A different approach to this question technique is to ask negative questions (what did we do wrong?) or make negative statements to determine whether the documentation measures up. The negative statements illustrated in Table 2.6 on page 42 (Hart 54), can focus reviewers' comments on specific aspects of the text, illustration, and page layout.

Other Uses for Heuristic Evaluation

In addition to inspecting documentation or the interface for software or hardware, a usability inspection can also be applied to other products. For example, an inspection was made of the journal *Technical Communication,* following its redesign. The report of that inspection is provided at the end of this chapter in Appendix 2.3. It shows how the evaluators adapted Nielsen's set of 10 heuristics, creating a list of 17 items for the inspection.

TABLE 2.2	Nielsen's Ten Usability Heuristics
1. Visibility of system status	The system should always keep users informed about what is going on, through appropriate feedback within reasonable time.
2. Match between system and the real world	The system should speak the user's language, with words, phrases, and concepts familiar to the user, rather than system-oriented terms. Follow real-world conventions, making information appear in a natural and logical order.
3. User control and freedom	Users often choose system functions by mistake and will need a clearly marked "emergency exit" to leave the unwanted state without having to go through an extended dialogue. Support undo and redo.
4. Consistency and standards	Users should not have to wonder whether different words, situations, or actions mean the same thing. Follow platform conventions.
5. Error prevention	Even better than good error messages is a careful design which prevents a problem from occurring in the first place.
6. Recognition rather than recall	Make objects, actions, and options visible. The user should not have to remember information from one part of the dialogue to another. Instructions for use of the system should be visible or easily retrievable whenever appropriate.
7. Flexibility and efficiency of use	Accelerators—unseen by the novice user—may often speed up the interaction for the expert user to such an extent that the system can cater to both inexperienced and experienced users. Allow users to tailor frequent actions.
8. Aesthetic and minimalist design	Dialogues should not contain information that is irrelevant or rarely needed. Every extra unit of information in a dialogue competes with the relevant units of information and diminishes their relative visibility.
9. Help users recognize, diagnose, and recover from errors	Error messages should be expressed in plain language (no codes), precisely indicate the problem, and constructively suggest a solution.
10. Help and documentation	Even though it is better if the system can be used without documentation, it may be necessary to provide help and documentation. Any such information should be easy to search, focused on the user's task, list concrete steps to be carried out, and not be too large.

Source: Jakob Nielsen, "Heuristic Evaluation." *Usability Inspection Methods.* Eds. Jakob Nielsen and Robert L. Mack. New York: Wiley, 1994, p. 30. © 1994 John Wiley & Sons, Inc. (Reprinted by permission of John Wiley & Sons, Inc.)

In the next section, we discuss another type of expert inspection: the cognitive walkthrough.

Cognitive Walkthroughs

A *cognitive walkthrough* is a usability inspection method designed to evaluate "ease of learning, particularly by exploration" (Wharton et al. 105). This focus derives from the principle of minimalism, as explored by John Carroll and others, which identifies

TABLE 2.3	Gerhardt-Powals's Ten Cognitive Design Principles
1. Automate unwanted workload	Eliminate mental calculations, estimations, comparisons, and any unnecessary thinking to free cognitive resources for high-level tasks.
2. Reduce uncertainty	Display data in a manner that is clear and obvious.
3. Fuse data	Bring together lower-level data into a higher-level summation to reduce cognitive load.
4. Present new information with meaningful aids to interpretation	Use a familiar framework, making it easier to absorb; use everyday terms, metaphors, etc.
5. Use names that are conceptually related to function	Names and labels should be context-dependent to improve recall and recognition.
6. Group data in consistently meaningful ways	Within a screen, group data logically; across screens, group data consistently to reduce search time.
7. Limit data-driven tasks	Reduce the time spent assimilating raw data by using appropriate colors and graphics.
8. Include in the displays only that information needed by the operator at a given time	Exclude extraneous information that is not relevant to common tasks so that users can focus on critical data.
9. Provide multiple coding of data	Provide data in multiple formats or levels of detail to satisfy different user preferences.
10. Practice judicious redundancy	To resolve the possible conflict between principles 6 and 8, it is sometimes necessary to include more information than is needed.

Source: Adapted from Jill Gerhardt-Powals. "Cognitive Engineering Principles for Enhancing Human-Computer Performance." *International Journal of Human-Computer Interaction* 8.2 (1996), pp. 192–193.

users' preferences for learning by exploration. In a cognitive walkthrough, the reviewers evaluate the interface in the context of tasks that users would perform. Table 2.7 on page 43 shows an overview of the process (Wharton et al. 106).

Before the walkthrough begins, the participants must agree on the user profile and the representative tasks to be analyzed. They must also receive information from the developer about the perceived order of steps that users should take to complete tasks. This process is called "crafting the credible story." The stories are the descriptions of users' anticipated actions based on agreed upon assumptions about the users' background knowledge and goals. The team decides what users may know from experience and what users will be able to determine from system responses to choices of action by the users. In step 3, the walkthrough itself, the group considers the actions that a user would take following one path to solve a problem. The process often uses a systematic question-and-answer approach, such as:

- Will users know which key to select here?
- Will users understand what the system tells them at this point?
- Will users be able to determine which pulldown menu contains the action they are looking for?

TABLE 2.4	Nielsen's Heuristics Adapted for Documentation Usability
User/audience awareness	From Nielsen's "match between system and real world." Speak the user's language, use familiar terminology, be aware of international audiences.
Appropriate information	From Nielsen's "aesthetic and minimalist design." Eliminate unnecessary information. Provide all relevant information.
Memory load	Minimize user's memory load. Chunk information; use cross-references to refresh user's memories.
Consistency	Ensure consistency in document design and word choice.
Appropriate organization	Present information in task-oriented approach, putting most important information first.
Feedback	Indicate results and outcomes of actions following an instruction. Reinforce correct actions.
Troubleshooting information	From Nielsen's "error recovery, recognition, and diagnosis." Provide solutions to potential problems in plain language.
Flexibility and efficiency of use	Use "accelerators" such as quick reference cards to allow expert users to get up to speed quickly.
Retrieval aids	Provide access to information through an index, table of contents, cross-references, headings.
Design	Make the layout inviting to the user. Consider other issues affecting usability such as size, medium, durability, and portability.

Source: Adapted from M. Shannon Daugherty. "The Usability Evaluation: A 'Discount' Approach to Usability Testing." *Intercom* Dec. 1997, pp. 16–20. (Used with permission from *Intercom,* the magazine of the Society for Technical Communication, Arlington, VA, U.S.A.)

This approach simulates the problem-solving process that users are expected to take in completing the tasks they would want to perform. The evaluators in the walkthrough use this information to tell a story about what the intended user is most likely to do to solve the "problem" of completing the task.

Although cognitive walkthroughs focus on one aspect of usability—ease of learning—they naturally uncover issues related to ease of use and the functionality of the application. The method finds inconsistencies in the designers' plan and the users' use of the product. These could be related to poor word choice (a word or term that doesn't match the user's vocabulary), inconsistent word choice, or lack of feedback when an action is performed.

The key advantage to this inspection method is that it can identify problems with the design very early in development, before the design is ready to be tested by the actual users. The key disadvantage is that the process is effective only when the evaluators are trained in cognitive psychology or the process of the cognitive walkthrough. Untrained evaluators produce poor results, as research shows when comparing findings by software engineers not trained in the discipline vs. cognitive psychologists with background and training in the discipline (Wharton et al.).

However, a recent development, which will require further study, is the creation of software that simulates the behavior of typical users and provides cognitive feedback to the developers. As reported at CHI (Computer-Human Interac-

TABLE 2.5	**Sample Checklist for Heuristic Evaluation of Documentation**

Retrieval Aids

Feature	Requirements	Status/Notes
Table of contents	Layout is clear and well designed	
	Structure is parallel	
	Three levels are shown	
	Wording is task-oriented	
Headings	Levels are clearly distinguished	
	Headings stand out from text	
	Wording is task-oriented	
	Section content is well summarized	
Headers and footers	Users can easily find their place in the text	
	Wording is task-oriented	
	Users can locate a section or page number easily	
Index	Index includes:	
	Appropriate number of entries	
	Acronyms and abbreviations used in text	
	Topics and terms used in text	
	Descriptive entries	
	Synonyms for topics and terms used	
	Appropriate cross-referenced entries	

Source: M. Shannon Daugherty. "The Usability Evaluation: A 'Discount' Approach to Usability Testing." *Intercom* Dec. 1997, p. 19. (Used with permission from *Intercom*, the magazine of the Society for Technical Communication, Arlington, VA, U.S.A.)

tion) '97, one such program has "a programmable production-rule cognitive processor" that is built on "constraints synthesized from human performance literature." The program then "generates a specific sequence of perceptual, cognitive, and motor activities required to perform each specific instance of the task" (Hornof and Kieras 107). Designers merely specify the cognitive strategy they want to use. According to the *User Interface Design Update Newsletter*, which reported these findings, "Eventually, this will allow designers to conduct initial, and very effective usability tests, without requiring real users to perform the tasks" (Bailey). If that becomes the case, you will no longer need this book. In the meantime, however, there are a number of studies that compare the advantages and disadvantages of conducting heuristic evaluations, cognitive walkthroughs, and lab testing. We discuss these in the next section.

Comparison of Methods

The research (reported in Nielsen and Mack) shows that in general:

- Heuristic evaluation is a better predictor than cognitive walkthroughs of end-user problems (those found in lab testing).
- No inspection method predicts end-user problems as well as actual user testing.

TABLE 2.6	Focused Statements for Review of Documentation

Statements About Text

Language and jargon	Identify unfamiliar words, or words that are used incorrectly.
Sentence and paragraph structure	Identify sentences/paragraphs that are unnecessarily complex.
Comprehension	Provide examples of test that is misunderstood on first reading.
Organization	Identify where there are too many/too few headings or an overly complex organizational structure.
Access	Identify any information you couldn't find easily in the table of contents, index, or other aids.

Statements About Illustrations

Quality	Identify any illustrations that were hard to understand because of the poor quality of reproduction (blurry, labeling too small, etc.).
Comprehension	Identify any illustrations that are too complex.
Correctness	Identify any illustration that is misleading or incorrect, or that contradicts the text.
Completeness	Identify any concepts that would be enhanced by an illustration.

Statements About Page Layout

Positioning	Indicate where it was hard to find a table or figure referred to in the text or where the position of an item was confusing or interfered with your ability to read or scan text or seemed irrelevant.
Structure	Indicate any layout techniques that interfered with reading comprehension (quotations, sidebars).
Readability	Indicate where text is too small or tightly spaced or where the visual style made text hard to read.

Source: Adapted from Geoff Hart. "Accentuate the Negative: Obtaining Effective Reviews Through Focused Questions." *Technical Communication* 44.1 (1997), pp. 52–57. (Used with permission from *Technical Communication,* the journal of the Society for Technical Communication, Arlington, VA, U.S.A.)

- Inspection methods are generally better at finding problems than at determining the appropriate improvement (although some improvements are obvious).
- User testing and inspection methods do not have a high degree of overlapping findings.

Table 2.8 on page 44 shows a comparison of three methods of testing, based on the types of findings each uncovers (Desurvire 185). Although the experts, using heuristic evaluation and cognitive walkthroughs, predicted an equal percentage of errors that were likely to cause problems for users, a higher correlation of users' severe problems was found in the heuristic evaluation than in the cognitive walkthrough. However, it is particularly interesting to note that the experts using heuristic evaluation found 80% of the minor annoyances that users might experi-

TABLE 2.7	Overview of the Cognitive Walkthrough Process
1. Define inputs to the walk-through	Identification of the users.
	Sample tasks for evaluation.
	Action sequences for completing the tasks.
	Description or implementation of the interface.
2. Convene the analysts	
3. Walk through the action sequences for each task	Tell a credible story, considering . . .
	Will the user try to achieve the right effect?
	Will the user notice that the correct action is available?
	Will the user associate the correct action with the effect that the user is trying to achieve?
	If the correct action is performed, will the user see that progress is being made toward a solution of the task?
4. Record critical information	User knowledge requirements.
	Assumptions about the user population.
	Notes about side issues and design changes.
	The credible success story.
5. Revise the interface to fix the problems	

Source: Cathleen Wharton, et al. "The Cognitive Walkthrough Method: A Practitioner's Guide." *Usability Inspection Methods.* Eds. Jakob Nielsen and Robert L. Mack. New York: Wiley, 1994, p. 106. © 1994 John Wiley & Sons, Inc. (Reprinted by permission of John Wiley & Sons, Inc.)

ence, but only 29% of the problems that were likely to cause task failure (the most severe problems).

Another study found that nonexperts (those without experience in usability and interface design) uncovered many interface "errors" that did not, in fact, turn out to occur with actual users. These "false positives" provided results that couldn't be validated. If changes were made on the basis of such inspections alone, good things about a product might have been changed and bad things left unchanged, particularly serious problems that might have been overlooked.

The conclusion from these studies is that these "alternative methods still fall short of the empirical experiments," using actual users (Desurvire 195). Based on these findings, it is best not to rely on any one method for determining the usability of a product, but to use a variety of methods. In the next section, we examine other methods of obtaining feedback from users.

Feedback from Users

Feedback from users can come from a variety of sources. These include focus groups, surveys and interviews, and other user feedback channels. We discuss these methods of getting feedback from users in the following sections of this chapter, beginning with focus groups, which is a technique typically used before product development begins.

TABLE 2.8	Comparison of Testing Methods' Effectiveness			
		Problem Severity Code		
Method	**Evaluators**	**Minor Annoyance/ Confusion**	**Problem Caused Error**	**Problem Caused Task Failure**
Lab	Observed with users	5	3	17
Heuristic evaluation	Experts	80%	67%	29%
	Software developers	40%	0%	12%
	Nonexperts	20%	0%	6%
Cognitive walkthrough	Experts	40%	67%	18%
	Software developers	0%	0%	12%
	Nonexperts	20%	0%	6%

Source: Heather W. Desurvire. "Faster Cheaper!! Are Usability Inspection Methods as Effective as Empirical Testing?" *Usability Inspection Methods.* Eds. Jakob Nielsen and Robert L. Mack. New York: Wiley, 1994, p. 185. © 1994 John Wiley & Sons, Inc. (Reprinted by permission of John Wiley & Sons, Inc.)

Focus Groups

Focus groups have a long history of use in social science settings, beginning in World War II, where they were used to investigate the effectiveness of military training materials. After the war, they became a frequent tool for conducting market research for new product development. Focus groups provide qualitative data about people's needs, wants, and desires. As a method of gathering qualitative data, they fall in between open-ended interviews and contextual inquiry (a subject we treat in Chapter 3). Because focus groups are most useful for exploring and discovering information, they are typically used before product development begins. For product development purposes, focus groups can get at some of the issues users have about the current products they use or their desires about a product they would like to see developed. Companies can learn from focus groups what consumers think of the company and its products and what they're willing to pay for new products. Thus, focus groups can support user and task analysis efforts (discussed in Chapter 3). They can also be useful in gathering information about competitors' products—to learn what users like and don't like— as an aid in designing a new product that will be marketed against the competitors' products.

In addition to providing information about preferences, focus groups can also provide the baseline for establishing usability *metrics,* or measures, to be used later in usability testing. For instance, in discussions with focus group participants, developers can learn how much time users are willing to spend working on tasks and which tasks are most important to them. In addition to revealing how much time users are willing to spend on certain tasks, focus groups can identify how much time users typically spend on tasks and how much time they would like to spend (which may, in fact, be different from how much time they are willing to spend). From this information, usability metrics, such as the following, can be established for a usability test (Hammer 246):

- Users will be able to install and configure the product within 10 minutes.
- Brand-new users will be able to add an account to the database within 15 minutes of starting the software.
- After completing the tutorial, users will be able to successfully perform a complex task with the software in less than 10 minutes.
- Users will rate the usability of the QuickStart tutorial as a 4 or 5 on a 5-point scale, where 5 indicates it is extremely easy to use.

Traditional Focus Groups

A traditional focus group brings 6 to 12 people together for 2 hours with a facilitator. The people are selected from the user community. The discussion can be held in a conference room or meeting room and can be audiotaped. If held in a usability lab or market research firm with a one-way mirror, it can be observed and videotaped.

The role of the moderator, or facilitator, in a focus group is critical to the success of the effort. Although focus groups may appear to be freewheeling sessions to the participants, in reality, the facilitator has a specific agenda that matches the goals of the developers about what they want to learn from the participants. The facilitator must not only keep the group on track, without appearing to steer them, but must also make sure that all members have a chance to contribute, and that one or two members do not dominate and move the group in a particular direction. To ensure the validity of the findings, several focus group sessions should be conducted so that the data can be compared from each group. A report on the results of all the focus group sessions captures the key findings.

A typical agenda for a focus group might be as follows:

1. *Waiting room exercise.* A screening survey for participants before entering the focus group room.
2. *Introductions.* The facilitator introduces himself or herself to the group and the participants, in turn, introduce themselves.
3. *Background discussion.* The appearance of an open-ended discussion of the product or concept, but one that is actually highly structured and planned by the facilitator.
4. *Key questions.* Carefully crafted by the facilitator to be open-ended and to avoid leading the participants in a particular direction.
5. *Product or concept demonstration.* "Live" or on video.
6. *Summary of findings.* To collate and confirm findings from participants.

An alternative strategy is to use brainstorming, but in a more structured format. In one brainstorming approach, each person in the focus group is given a stack of index cards and asked to write down one idea per card. Then the facilitator goes around the room, asking each participant to share one new idea from the stack. All these ideas are captured on an easel until no new ideas are generated.

This technique allows for equal participation of the members in a focus group (Miller).

A modification of the focus group is the *customer research group*, in which 12 to 15 users are invited to come in at the same time. Instead of having a single facilitator conduct the focus group, there is a facilitator for each customer, so that multiple discussions take place simultaneously. Customers are asked to perform several exercises, such as a card-sorting exercise, and explain to their personal facilitator why they ordered the cards in the way they did. The design team members then share all the data they have gathered (Beck).

Electronic Focus Groups

Focus groups can also take place when the participants are not actually in the same room, through the use of specialized software to connect participants via computer or through teleconferencing equipment. Software captures electronic discussions and makes it simpler for the moderator to analyze the data afterward. Because the interaction takes place online, there tends to be less discussion, but this can be viewed as positive in that it restricts the likelihood that one person will dominate the discussion, a frequently cited problem in face-to-face focus groups.

The Web or Internet can also be used to approximate a focus group, by posting questions on a Web site or with a newsgroup or listserv. The disadvantage is that the questions are "public" rather than private, and the respondents in such online discussions are much more likely to be "power users," who may not represent the typical user of the product. There also may be a built-in bias from the respondents, arising from the nature of the group where the posting is placed. However, this method provides a very inexpensive way to gather feedback about user preferences.

Although focus groups can be used to get reactions from users about early concepts or prototypes for a product or to validate information gathered from other sources, focus groups cannot confirm what users would actually do with or want from products, only what they say they would do or want. As well, focus groups cannot confirm any aspects of the usability of a product. Thus, focus groups, as with all the other methods discussed in this chapter, should not be used as the sole source of information-gathering about user preferences.

Surveys and Interviews

Surveys

Another way of getting feedback from users is from surveys. These can be distributed through the mail, conducted via telephone, or made available on the company's Web site. Questions can be open-ended or limited. As with focus groups, surveys can be used to obtain information about user preferences, although they typically don't provide the depth of responses available in a focus group. However, surveys can be distributed widely to a large number of people at a low cost, making it possible to receive a large number of responses, certainly much larger than can typically be afforded by focus groups.

Designing surveys requires some expertise or training to create questions that are unambiguous and unbiased and that prompt users to respond in a consistent way. The consistency of response is frequently verified by framing the same type of question in two different places or by asking for a certain kind of information in two different ways. Another challenge in using surveys is that they must be long enough to be useful to the developers, but short enough to encourage participation from potential respondents. They should be pilot-tested with users who represent the potential audience before being distributed so that problems can be addressed and corrected before administering them.

Survey questions can be created with yes/no responses, but these are likely to force respondents into one specific choice or the other, negating the possibility of seeing how strongly the respondent is committed to one choice or the other. More commonly, surveys use a scale: typically 4 or 5 points. Some survey developers prefer a 4-point scale, as this requires the respondent to make a choice because the neutral central point is eliminated. Others prefer a 5-point scale, as this allows respondents to choose the neutral central point.

The most common 5-point scale is the Likert scale, which asks respondents to rate the degree to which they agree or disagree with a statement. Typically, such a scale might have the following values:

1 = strongly disagree
2 = partly disagree
3 = neither agree nor disagree
4 = partly agree
5 = strongly agree

For example, a statement using this model might be:

The installation process was easy.

Modifications to the Likert model allow for responses that reflect values other than those of agreement or disagreement. For instance, a question might be framed as follows:

How easy or difficult was the installation process?

Responses could include the following:

1 = very easy
2 = somewhat easy
3 = neither easy nor difficult
4 = somewhat difficult
5 = very difficult

For examples of various Likert scales, see Chapter 6, which presents questionnaires created as part of preparing for a usability test.

Scales of more or less than five items are also used. For instance, a statement might ask users to rate the ease of installation of the software on a scale of 1 to 7, with 1 being very difficult and 7 very easy. Some researchers find that the number of items on the scale is not as significant as the fact that there should be an odd number, thus providing a neutral point, which a 4-point scale would not provide. However, *the error of central tendency,* which is the tendency to avoid the extremes for the middle, comes into play with the larger scale (Anastasi and Urbina, reported in Dumas). For instance, participants using a 7-point scale are less likely to choose either 1 or 7, avoiding the extremes of the scale on both ends.

Open-ended questions, which ask participants to respond in their own words, are useful, but much more time-consuming for respondents to complete and for analysts to interpret and compare. If a survey contains too many open-ended questions with lots of blank lines, respondents are more likely to discard it. However, a limited number of places for additional responses will glean some interesting results, especially at the end of a section of closed-type questions. Demographic information, if requested, should be placed at the end of the survey, not at the beginning, because some respondents find this information threatening or an invasion of privacy.

How many is enough for validating the return? Unlike the magic number of 4% used as a success marker by advertising and marketing people, a 4% response rate to a survey would be considered invalid. In fact, a smaller random sampling of the target audience with a higher percentage rate, at 65% or higher, yields far more reliable data than a larger distribution with a smaller than 65% return. Therefore, it is often necessary to invest in follow-up mechanisms like a postcard or letter reminder to encourage more responses. Some companies include incentives, such as small gifts or gift certificates, for completion of the survey.

In addition to the mail or telephone survey, another type of survey that provides feedback from users is the response card that comes with some technical documentation and software products. Although the actual percentage of returned cards is typically low and those who return them do not necessarily represent a valid sampling of the customer base, the information can be added to other sources of information about user satisfaction. This information, however, is about products already in the marketplace, whereas the mail or telephone survey can gather information about potential customers and their preferences for products yet to be developed.

Because of the convenience and affordability, companies with Web sites are now using their sites to collect information about their users. Not only does the site tell how many people are visiting, but it can also document where they look and what links they make. Some companies are adding surveys to their Web site to learn more from their visitors. These survey responses are even less representative of the user community than response cards, because they come only from those who visit the company's Web site, but such information can still provide useful data about this part of the user population. And, of course, if the entire user population is Web-based, such as an online stock-trading site, then the responses will bear a strong correlation to the user community.

Some companies are establishing participant recruiting databases, using Web-based forms that gather demographic information and request permission to contact participants for future surveys. This approach allows the company to select from the database those they want to sample in a survey. One company uses this approach to compile information on customer satisfaction, requirements-gathering, task analysis, terminology, icon recognition, design review, and so forth. The company can send out a survey from its participant database and receive results in 3 days (Vredenburg, McInerney, and Isensee).

Interviews

When open-ended responses are the goal of information-gathering, an interview works better than a survey. Interview questions would need to be standardized in advance of the interviews so that the same person or a group of interviewers is asking the same questions in the same sequence to all those interviewed. The interviews can be arranged in advance, using lists provided by market research firms, customer files, or the company's Web site, or the interviews can be random. As random interviews tend to fall in the annoying category of telemarketing, the more effective approach for many companies is to identify a target audience and arrange the interviews at a convenient time for the participants. The information can be recorded for later transcription, or each interviewer can work from a template designed to quickly capture the most likely responses, with room for additional notes. The main advantage of interviewing over survey responses is that participants are generally more willing to go into greater detail about their attitudes and opinions than they would if required to put their views in writing in a survey. The main disadvantages are that it costs more to conduct personal interviews, it takes more time for both the interviewer and interviewee (typically resulting in a small sample of participants), and the interviewer can inject bias by voice tone and inflection.

Although surveys and interviews provide valuable information from customers or potential customers, others sources within companies can also be used for customer feedback. We discuss these alternate ways of gathering data from users in the next section.

Internal Sources of Customer Feedback

Companies that provide technical support and training have ready-made internal sources of feedback about customer problems. Interviewing staff in these departments can provide valuable data to improve the usability of products in future releases or to create new products that better address customer needs. Analyzing data gathered by each of these groups can provide insight as well.

Technical Support

Technical support (the help desk) can provide insight into problems users experience with a product after it has gone to market. These problems could be about the design of the product or the documentation. In some cases, the answer to a problem is explained in the documentation but the user cannot find it. By researching the types of calls that come in to technical support, developers can get a good understanding of what causes problems for customers so as to improve the next release of the product. Some developers pose "the question of the week" to technical support, asking them to query their customers at the end of a technical support call. At no cost to the company and no real inconvenience to the customer, this information helps developers get quick feedback about issues as they arise.

A frequent measure of the improvements resulting from usability testing is to evaluate a drop in calls to the help desk with the new release of a product, as compared to the calls logged with an earlier release that hadn't been usability-tested. In some cases, usability testing can be cost-justified by this one measure of cost savings.

Training

Trainers are an excellent source of information about the usability of products. Information can be collected systematically through a questionnaire that trainers give to customers during training, or it can be collected from the trainers themselves through focus groups with the trainers or personal interviews. Interviews with trainers can reveal what parts of the training are most difficult for them to deliver, and why. If trainers use a questionnaire in their training classes, usability issues can be included. Or trainers can ask users to suggest usability improvements.

Of course, it's an eye-opening experience to sit in a training class to see first-hand what problems users experience with the product. Improving the usability of the product can also provide a cost-savings in reducing the training time required to learn how to use it.

Summary

In this chapter, we have presented other methods for getting feedback about product usability, as part of a user-centered design process. One method uses experts to perform inspections of two types:

- *Heuristic evaluation*, which applies a set of rules or principles to an inspection of the user interface.
- *Cognitive walkthrough*, which evaluates the learnability of a product by posing questions about the ways in which users would perform tasks.

We presented the advantages and disadvantages of this method using experts and compared the results of these inspections with those from usability testing.

We also examined methods for obtaining feedback from users, other than the method of usability testing. These methods include:

- *Focus groups*, which bring together 6 to 12 people with a trained moderator to explore issues about users' needs, wants, and desires relating to products in the market or under consideration.
- *Surveys*, which can mailed, administered by phone, or made available on a company's Web site, to get information about products in the marketplace as well as determine potential interest in products under consideration.

■ *Interviews*, which gather opinions and attitudes from users in response to open-ended questions.

■ *Internal sources of customer feedback*, which provide a rich resource about problems that users report to the help desk or experience when using new products in training sessions. Developers can use this information to improve the next release or the next product.

All these methods of obtaining feedback about products and users can be valuable resources in creating user-centered products. A comparison of methods, such as those discussed in this chapter, allows key findings to be replicated and confirmed. However, as Nielsen and many others advocate, "User testing with real users is the most fundamental usability method and is in some sense irreplaceable, since it provides direct information about how people use computers and what their exact problems are with the concrete interface being tested" (Nielsen 165).

Coming Up

Although some of the methods described in this chapter provide information about users that can help developers understand users' wants, in the next chapter, we look at methodologies to analyze users and the tasks they perform in their own environments to not only hear from them what they want, but also to see how they work and study what they do. Because this information is a valuable part of a user-centered design process, it is best gathered even before product development begins so that the product developed will match users' wishes, hopes, and needs.

Questions/Topics for Discussion

1. How is usability engineering different from usability testing? What processes does usability engineering entail?
2. Expert reviews are sometimes called *usability inspections.* How is the word "inspection" used in this context to describe expert reviews?
3. One type of inspection is called a heuristic evaluation. Why is it considered one of the discount usability methods described by Jakob Nielsen? Describe the steps in a heuristic review and the number of people who should be involved in performing this type of evaluation.
4. Another type of expert review is the cognitive walkthrough. Describe its features and the differences between this type of expert review and a heuristic evaluation.
5. Which of the two expert review processes—heuristic review or cognitive walkthrough—provides better information about end-user problems? Why would developers want to use one or the other method, and what would be the advantage of using both methods? How do both methods compare to usability testing?

6. When should focus groups be used? What kinds of information do focus groups produce and how can this information be applied to product development? How can the information from focus groups be used in planning the goals of a usability test?

7. List some of the other methods of obtaining feedback from users. Describe the advantages and disadvantages of each of these methods. How does information from each of these methods help in the development of usable products?

Exercises

1. Using a set of instructions that have usability problems, apply one of the sets of heuristics in this chapter to conduct a heuristic evaluation of the instructions. Be prepared to provide examples of rules violations, as seen in the instructions.

2. Create a survey to get information about the users of the instructions, using one of the sample scales (Likert or other 5-point scales) provided in this chapter.

3. Test these instructions on another class member or with other members of your group. Clarify any questions that may cause confusion or misunderstanding.

4. Conduct a cognitive walkthrough of the instructions by creating a typical task scenario. Exchange your walkthrough procedures with another member of the class (or group) and observe the process. What usability issues did the walkthrough produce? Were any missed that you think might cause problems for the end user? If so, discuss these with your partner or group.

5. Conduct a heuristic evaluation of the three-fold brochure (Chapter Appendix 2.1), which was produced by the Information Technology department of a university to inform faculty and staff about how to use email on the computer network and how to access administrative databases. *Note:* The terms "Kiwi" and "Eudora" refer to two types of email systems on the network. When you have completed your evaluation, think about the issues affecting the intended users. Make a list of these, grouped by categories. Assign labels for each category. Be prepared to discuss your categories with the class.

For Your Project

1. Conduct a heuristic evaluation of the product you will be using for a usability test. If you are working in a team, each member should conduct the evaluation separately. Then the team should meet to compare results and create a list of problems you will want to address in planning for the test.

2. Conduct a heuristic evaluation of a competing product. Compare the results of this evaluation with those of your evaluation of the product you

will test. If the competing product has better results, you may want to use this information to establish usability performance objectives.
3. Informally review several competing products to study the ways in which they present information or arrange tasks. Make a list of the aspects of the competing products you like and compare these to the product you will be testing.

References

Bailey, Bob. *User Interface Design Update Newsletter*, Nov. 1998 Human Factors International <http://www.humanfactors.com/Newsletters>.

Beck, Doug. "Customer Research Groups" <http://www.stcsig.org/usability/topics/index.html>.

Carroll, John M., ed. *Minimalism Beyond the Nurnberg Funnel*. Cambridge, MA: MIT Press, 1998.

———. *The Nurnberg Funnel: Designing Minimalist Instruction for Practical Computer Skill*. Cambridge, MA: MIT Press, 1990.

Daugherty, M. Shannon. "The Usability Evaluation: A 'Discount' Approach to Usability Testing." *Intercom* (Dec. 1997): 16–20.

Desurvire, Heather W. "Faster, Cheaper!! Are Usability Inspection Methods as Effective as Empirical Testing?" *Usability Inspection Methods* Eds. Jakob Nielsen and Robert L. Mack. New York: Wiley, 1994. 173–202.

Dumas, Joe. "Usability Testing Methods: Subjective Measures. Part 1—Creating Effective Questions and Answers." *Common Ground* 8.3 (July 1998): 5–10.

Gerhardt-Powals, Jill. "Cognitive Engineering Principles for Enhancing Human-Computer Performance." *International Journal of Human-Computer Interaction* 8.2 (1996): 189–211.

Hammer, Molly. "Involving Customers in Developing Usability Metrics." Proceedings of the STC 45th Annual Conference, Anaheim, CA, 17–20 May 1998. 246–47.

Hart, Geoff. "Accentuate the Negative: Obtaining Effective Reviews Through Focused Questions." *Technical Communication* 44.1 (1997): 52–57.

Hornof, Anthony J., and David E. Kieras. "Cognitive Modeling Reveals Menu Search is Both Random and Systematic." *Proceedings of CHI '97* Atlanta, GA, 22–27 Mar. 1997. 107–14.

Miller, Dick. "Brainstorming Techniques in Focus Groups" <http://www.stcsig.org/usability/topics/index.html>.

Nielsen, Jakob. *Usability Engineering*. Boston: Academic Press, 1993.

Nielsen, Jakob, and Robert L. Mack, eds. *Usability Inspection Methods*. New York: Wiley, 1994.

van der Meij, Hans, and John M. Carroll. "Principles and Heuristics for Designing Minimalist Instruction." *Minimalism Beyond the Nurnberg Funnel*. Ed. John M. Carroll. Cambridge, MA: MIT Press, 1998. 19–53.

Vredenburg, Karel, Paul McInerney, and Scott Isensee. "Getting Rapid and Representative User Input Using the Web." *Usability Professionals' Association Conference*. 25–26 June 1998. 289–90.

Wharton, Cathleen, et al. "The Cognitive Walkthrough Method: A Practitioner's Guide." *Usability Inspection Methods*. Eds. Jakob Nielsen and Robert L. Mack. New York: Wiley, 1994. 105–140.

Wilson, Chauncey E. "Documentation Usability Techniques" <http://www.stcsig.org/usability/resources>.

Information Technology

CTNet
Reference Card
1.0

See inner flap for instructions.

Special Notes for Kiwi and Eudora

If you use Kiwi or Eudora for e-mail, you'll have to do the following after you change your administrative password. If you change your administrative password but don't do the following, you won't be able to retrieve your mail!

In Kiwi, Choose Special | Configuration. In the "Password" block, enter your current administrative password. Then click OK to keep that password.

In Eudora, choose Special | Forget Password. This will make Eudora erase your password. The next time you check your mail, Eudora will prompt you for your new password.

How to Use This Card

This card is designed to help you fix the most common problems encountered on CTNet. Those problems include:

- Frozen terminals
- Password problems
- "Host Timeout" messages in Kiwi
- "No response" messages in Eudora
- Garbage characters on your screen

To use this card, you should:

1 Follow the steps in **Sanity Check** section to be sure you have a problem.

2 Follow the steps in the **General Troubleshooting** section to fix your problem.

3 Refer to this card when changing your password.

If you can't fix the problem using this card, or if you repeatedly encounter the same error, contact Information Technology at x123 for help.

Three-fold brochure (side 1)

Sanity Checks

You should perform the following Sanity Checks to make sure you have a problem before you try to fix anything.

1 Check your network cable at the network outlet and on your machine to make sure you are plugged in to the network.

2 If you have an A/B switch on your computer, make sure it is set to "Network".

3 Make sure you aren't trying to run your mail software and your terminal software at the same time. If you do, you'll have problems. The two most common errors are shown below.

• If you try to run Eudora and Connect at the same time, you'll see the following whenever Eudora tries to check your mail:

"Don't blame me, blame the CTB. The connection is not open."

• If you try to run Kiwi and Kermit at the same time, you'll get unpredictable results.

If you're not sure you have a problem, continue with the steps listed on the next column.

General Troubleshooting

After you perform the Sanity Checks, start here to fix your network problem.

1 Start the software that gets you into the campus network. That's usually Kermit or Connect.

2 Press **CTRL+Q**.

3 Press **ENTER** a few times.

You may see a lot of garbage pass by on the screen; that's OK, as long as you see the network menu at the end. If you still don't see the network menu, find your machine in the following table, press the corresponding keystrokes, and then press **ENTER**.

Machine	Press the following
PC	ALT+B
Mac	Option+Dash or Apple+B
Terminal	ALT+Break or Break

If you still have problems, call Information Technology x123 for help!

Changing Your Password

Starting in February, administrative passwords will be expired periodically for security reasons. You'll know this has happened when you get the message:

"Your password has expired. Please choose a new one."

during logon. You'll be prompted for your old password (to confirm you're really you!) and then for your new password. You won't see your new password as you type it in order to keep it secret. Finally, the system will ask you for your new password one more time to make sure you typed it correctly.

Keep in mind the following when you choose a new password:

• Your password must have a minimum of **4 letters and 2 numbers**. Don't include a space, "@" or "#" in your password!

• Your password should be easy for you to remember but difficult for others to guess.

• Never, *never* write down your password!

Kiwi and Eudora users should see the back of this card for more instructions on updating your password.

Xerox Heuristic Evaluation Checklist

1. Visibility of System Status

The system should always keep user informed about what is going on, through appropriate feedback within reasonable time.

#	Review Checklist	Yes	No	N/A	Comments
1.1	Does every display begin with a title or header that describes screen contents?	☐	☐	☐	
1.2	Is there a consistent icon design scheme and stylistic treatment across the system?	☐	☐	☐	
1.3	Is a single, selected icon clearly visible when surrounded by unselected icons?	☐	☐	☐	
1.4	Do menu instructions, prompts, and error messages appear in the same place(s) on each menu?	☐	☐	☐	
1.5	In multipage data entry screens, is each page labeled to show its relation to others?	☐	☐	☐	
1.6	If overtype and insert mode are both available, is there a visible indication of which one the user is in?	☐	☐	☐	
1.7	If pop-up windows are used to display error messages, do they allow the user to see the field in error?	☐	☐	☐	
1.8	Is there some form of system feedback for every operator action?	☐	☐	☐	
1.9	After the user completes an action (or group of actions), does the feedback indicate that the next group of actions can be started?	☐	☐	☐	
1.10	Is there visual feedback in menus or dialog boxes about which choices are selectable?	☐	☐	☐	
1.11	Is there visual feedback in menus or dialog boxes about which choice the cursor is on now?	☐	☐	☐	
1.12	If multiple options can be selected in a menu or dialog box, is there visual feedback about which options are already selected?	☐	☐	☐	
1.13	Is there visual feedback when objects are selected or moved?	☐	☐	☐	
1.14	Is the current status of an icon clearly indicated?	☐	☐	☐	
1.15	Is there feedback when function keys are pressed?	☐	☐	☐	

#	Review Checklist	Yes	No	N/A	Comments
1.16	If there are observable delays (greater than 15 seconds) in the system's response time, is the user kept informed of the system's progress?	☐	☐	☐	
1.17	Are response times appropriate to the task?	☐	☐	☐	
1.18	Typing, cursor motion, mouse selection: 50–150 milliseconds	☐	☐	☐	
1.19	Simple, frequent tasks: less than 1 second	☐	☐	☐	
1.20	Common tasks: 2–4 seconds	☐	☐	☐	
1.21	Complex tasks: 8–12 seconds	☐	☐	☐	
1.22	Are response times appropriate to the user's cognitive processing?	☐	☐	☐	
1.23	Continuity of thinking is required and information must be remembered throughout several responses: less than 2 seconds.	☐	☐	☐	
1.24	High levels of concentration aren't necessary and remembering information is not required: 2–15 seconds.	☐	☐	☐	
1.25	Is the menu-naming terminology consistent with the user's task domain?	☐	☐	☐	
1.26	Does the system provide *visibility:* that is, by looking, can the user tell the state of the system and the alternatives for action?	☐	☐	☐	
1.27	Do GUI menus make obvious which item has been selected?	☐	☐	☐	
1.28	Do GUI menus make obvious whether deselection is possible?	☐	☐	☐	
1.29	If users must navigate between multiple screens, does the system use context labels, menu maps, and place markers as navigational aids?	☐	☐	☐	

2. Match Between System and the Real World

The system should speak the user's language, with words, phrases and concepts familiar to the user, rather than system-oriented terms. Follow real-world conventions, making information appear in a natural and logical order.

#	Review Checklist	Yes	No	N/A	Comments
2.1	Are icons concrete and familiar?	☐	☐	☐	
2.2	Are menu choices ordered in the most logical way, given the user, the item names, and the task variables?	☐	☐	☐	

#	Review Checklist	Yes	No	N/A	Comments
2.3	If there is a natural sequence to menu choices, has it been used?	☐	☐	☐	
2.4	Do related and interdependent fields appear on the same screen?	☐	☐	☐	
2.5	If shape is used as a visual cue, does it match cultural conventions?	☐	☐	☐	
2.6	Do the selected colors correspond to common expectations about color codes?	☐	☐	☐	
2.7	When prompts imply a necessary action, are the words in the message consistent with that action?	☐	☐	☐	
2.8	Do keystroke references in prompts match actual key names?	☐	☐	☐	
2.9	On data entry screens, are tasks described in terminology familiar to users?	☐	☐	☐	
2.10	Are field-level prompts provided for data entry screens?	☐	☐	☐	
2.11	For question and answer interfaces, are questions stated in clear, simple language?	☐	☐	☐	
2.12	Do menu choices fit logically into categories that have readily understood meanings?	☐	☐	☐	
2.13	Are menu titles parallel grammatically?	☐	☐	☐	
2.14	Does the command language employ user jargon and avoid computer jargon?	☐	☐	☐	
2.15	Are command names specific rather than general?	☐	☐	☐	
2.16	Does the command language allow both full names and abbreviations?	☐	☐	☐	
2.17	Are input data codes meaningful?	☐	☐	☐	
2.18	Have uncommon letter sequences been avoided whenever possible?	☐	☐	☐	
2.19	Does the system automatically enter leading or trailing spaces to align decimal points?	☐	☐	☐	
2.20	Does the system automatically enter a dollar sign and decimal for monetary entries?	☐	☐	☐	
2.21	Does the system automatically enter commas in numeric values greater than 9999?	☐	☐	☐	
2.22	Do GUI menus offer activation: that is, make obvious how to say *"now do it"*?	☐	☐	☐	

#	Review Checklist	Yes	No	N/A	Comments
2.23	Has the system been designed so that keys with similar names do not perform opposite (and potentially dangerous) actions?	☐	☐	☐	
2.24	Are function keys labeled clearly and distinctively, even if this means breaking consistency rules?	☐	☐	☐	

3. User Control and Freedom

Users should be free to select and sequence tasks (when appropriate), rather than having the system do this for them. Users often choose system functions by mistake and will need a clearly marked "emergency exit" to leave the unwanted state without having to go through an extended dialogue. Users should make their own decisions (with clear information) regarding the costs of exiting current work. The system should support undo and redo.

#	Review Checklist	Yes	No	N/A	Comments
3.1	If setting up windows is a low-frequency task, is it particularly easy to remember?	☐	☐	☐	
3.2	In systems that use overlapping windows, is it easy for users to rearrange windows on the screen?	☐	☐	☐	
3.3	In systems that use overlapping windows, is it easy for users to switch between windows?	☐	☐	☐	
3.4	When a user's task is complete, does the system wait for a signal from the user before processing?	☐	☐	☐	
3.5	Can users type-ahead in a system with many nested menus?	☐	☐	☐	
3.6	Are users prompted to confirm commands that have drastic, destructive consequences?	☐	☐	☐	
3.7	Is there an "undo" function at the level of a single action, a data entry, and a complete group of actions?	☐	☐	☐	
3.8	Can users cancel out of operations in progress?	☐	☐	☐	
3.9	Are character edits allowed in commands?	☐	☐	☐	
3.10	Can users reduce data entry time by copying and modifying existing data?	☐	☐	☐	
3.11	Are character edits allowed in data entry fields?	☐	☐	☐	
3.12	If menu lists are long (more than seven items), can users select an item either by moving the cursor or by typing a mnemonic code?	☐	☐	☐	

#	Review Checklist	Yes	No	N/A	Comments
3.13	If the system uses a pointing device, do users have the option of either clicking on menu items or using a keyboard shortcut?	☐	☐	☐	
3.14	Are menus broad (many items on a menu) rather than deep (many menu levels)?	☐	☐	☐	
3.15	If the system has multiple menu levels, is there a mechanism that allows users to go back to previous menus?	☐	☐	☐	
3.16	If users can go back to a previous menu, can they change their earlier menu choice?	☐	☐	☐	
3.17	Can users move forward and backward between fields or dialog box options?	☐	☐	☐	
3.18	If the system has multipage data entry screens, can users move backward and forward among all the pages in the set?	☐	☐	☐	
3.19	If the system uses a question and answer interface, can users go back to previous questions or skip forward to later questions?	☐	☐	☐	
3.20	Do function keys that can cause serious consequences have an undo feature?	☐	☐	☐	
3.21	Can users easily reverse their actions?	☐	☐	☐	
3.22	If the system allows users to reverse their actions, is there a retracing mechanism to allow for multiple undos?	☐	☐	☐	
3.23	Can users set their own system, session, file, and screen defaults?	☐	☐	☐	

4. Consistency and Standards

Users should not have to wonder whether different words, situations, or actions mean the same thing. Follow platform conventions.

#	Review Checklist	Yes	No	N/A	Comments
4.1	Have industry or company formatting standards been followed consistently in all screens within a system?	☐	☐	☐	
4.2	Has a heavy use of all uppercase letters on a screen been avoided?	☐	☐	☐	
4.3	Do abbreviations not include punctuation?	☐	☐	☐	
4.4	Are integers right-justified and real numbers decimal-aligned?	☐	☐	☐	
4.5	Are icons labeled?	☐	☐	☐	

#	Review Checklist	Yes	No	N/A	Comments
4.6	Are there no more than twelve to twenty icon types?	☐	☐	☐	
4.7	Are there salient visual cues to identify the active window?	☐	☐	☐	
4.8	Does each window have a title?	☐	☐	☐	
4.9	Are vertical and horizontal scrolling possible in each window?	☐	☐	☐	
4.10	Does the menu structure match the task structure?	☐	☐	☐	
4.11	Have industry or company standards been established for menu design, and are they applied consistently on all menu screens in the system?	☐	☐	☐	
4.12	Are menu choice lists presented vertically?	☐	☐	☐	
4.13	If "exit" is a menu choice, does it always appear at the bottom of the list?	☐	☐	☐	
4.14	Are menu titles either centered or left-justified?	☐	☐	☐	
4.15	Are menu items left-justified, with the item number or mnemonic preceding the name?	☐	☐	☐	
4.16	Do embedded field-level prompts appear to the right of the field label?	☐	☐	☐	
4.17	Do on-line instructions appear in a consistent location across screens?	☐	☐	☐	
4.18	Are field labels and fields distinguished typographically?	☐	☐	☐	
4.19	Are field labels consistent from one data entry screen to another?	☐	☐	☐	
4.20	Are fields and labels left-justified for alpha lists and right-justified for numeric lists?	☐	☐	☐	
4.21	Do field labels appear to the left of single fields and above list fields?	☐	☐	☐	
4.22	Are attention-getting techniques used with care?	☐	☐	☐	
4.23	Intensity: two levels only	☐	☐	☐	
4.24	Size: up to four sizes	☐	☐	☐	
4.25	Font: up to three	☐	☐	☐	
4.26	Blink: two to four hertz	☐	☐	☐	
4.27	Color: up to four (additional colors for occasional use only)	☐	☐	☐	
4.28	Sound: soft tones for regular positive feedback, harsh for rare critical conditions	☐	☐	☐	
4.29	Are attention-getting techniques used only for exceptional conditions or for time-dependent information?	☐	☐	☐	

#	Review Checklist	Yes	No	N/A	Comments
4.30	Are there no more than four to seven colors, and are they far apart along the visible spectrum?	☐	☐	☐	
4.31	Is a legend provided if color codes are numerous or not obvious in meaning?	☐	☐	☐	
4.32	Have pairings of high-chroma, spectrally extreme colors been avoided?	☐	☐	☐	
4.33	Are saturated blues avoided for text or other small, thin-line symbols?	☐	☐	☐	
4.34	Is the most important information placed at the beginning of the prompt?	☐	☐	☐	
4.35	Are user actions named consistently across all prompts in the system?	☐	☐	☐	
4.36	Are system objects named consistently across all prompts in the system?	☐	☐	☐	
4.37	Do field-level prompts provide more information than a restatement of the field name?	☐	☐	☐	
4.38	For question and answer interfaces, are the valid inputs for a question listed?	☐	☐	☐	
4.39	Are menu choice names consistent, both within each menu and across the system, in grammatical style and terminology?	☐	☐	☐	
4.40	Does the structure of menu choice names match their corresponding menu titles?	☐	☐	☐	
4.41	Are commands used the same way, and do they mean the same thing, in all parts of the system?	☐	☐	☐	
4.42	Does the command language have a consistent, natural, and mnemonic syntax?	☐	☐	☐	
4.43	Do abbreviations follow a simple primary rule and, if necessary, a simple secondary rule for abbreviations that otherwise would be duplicates?	☐	☐	☐	
4.44	Is the secondary rule used only when necessary?	☐	☐	☐	
4.45	Are abbreviated words all the same length?	☐	☐	☐	
4.46	Is the structure of a data entry value consistent from screen to screen?	☐	☐	☐	
4.47	Is the method for moving the cursor to the next or previous field consistent throughout the system?	☐	☐	☐	
4.48	If the system has multipage data entry screens, do all pages have the same title?	☐	☐	☐	
4.49	If the system has multipage data entry screens, does each page have a sequential page number?	☐	☐	☐	
4.50	Does the system follow industry or company standards for function key assignments?	☐	☐	☐	

#	Review Checklist	Yes	No	N/A	Comments
4.51	Are high-value, high-chroma colors used to attract attention?	☐	☐	☐	

5. Help Users Recognize, Diagnose, and Recover from Errors

Error messages should be expressed in plain language (NO CODES).

#	Review Checklist	Yes	No	N/A	Comments
5.1	Is sound used to signal an error?	☐	☐	☐	
5.2	Are prompts stated constructively, without overt or implied criticism of the user?	☐	☐	☐	
5.3	Do prompts imply that the user is in control?	☐	☐	☐	
5.4	Are prompts brief and unambiguous?	☐	☐	☐	
5.5	Are error messages worded so that the system, not the user, takes the blame?	☐	☐	☐	
5.6	If humorous error messages are used, are they appropriate and inoffensive to the user population?	☐	☐	☐	
5.7	Are error messages grammatically correct?	☐	☐	☐	
5.8	Do error messages avoid the use of exclamation points?	☐	☐	☐	
5.9	Do error messages avoid the use of violent or hostile words?	☐	☐	☐	
5.10	Do error messages avoid an anthropomorphic tone?	☐	☐	☐	
5.11	Do all error messages in the system use consistent grammatical style, form, terminology, and abbreviations?	☐	☐	☐	
5.12	Do messages place users in control of the system?	☐	☐	☐	
5.13	Does the command language use normal action-object syntax?	☐	☐	☐	
5.14	Does the command language avoid arbitrary, non-English use of punctuation, except for symbols that users already know?	☐	☐	☐	
5.15	If an error is detected in a data entry field, does the system place the cursor in that field or highlight the error?	☐	☐	☐	
5.16	Do error messages inform the user of the error's severity?	☐	☐	☐	
5.17	Do error messages suggest the cause of the problem?	☐	☐	☐	

#	Review Checklist	Yes	No	N/A	Comments
5.18	Do error messages provide appropriate semantic information?	☐	☐	☐	
5.19	Do error messages provide appropriate syntactic information?	☐	☐	☐	
5.20	Do error messages indicate what action the user needs to take to correct the error?	☐	☐	☐	
5.21	If the system supports both novice and expert users, are multiple levels of error-message detail available?	☐	☐	☐	

6. Error Prevention

Even better than good error messages is a careful design which prevents a problem from occurring in the first place.

#	Review Checklist	Yes	No	N/A	Comments
6.1	If the database includes groups of data, can users enter more than one group on a single screen?	☐	☐	☐	
6.2	Have dots or underscores been used to indicate field length?	☐	☐	☐	
6.3	Is the menu choice name on a higher-level menu used as the menu title of the lower-level menu?	☐	☐	☐	
6.4	Are menu choices logical, distinctive, and mutually exclusive?	☐	☐	☐	
6.5	Are data inputs case-blind whenever possible?	☐	☐	☐	
6.6	If the system displays multiple windows, is navigation between windows simple and visible?	☐	☐	☐	
6.7	Are the function keys that can cause the most serious consequences in hard-to-reach positions?	☐	☐	☐	
6.8	Are the function keys that can cause the most serious consequences located far away from low-consequence and high-use keys?	☐	☐	☐	
6.9	Has the use of qualifier keys been minimized?	☐	☐	☐	
6.10	If the system uses qualifier keys, are they used consistently throughout the system?	☐	☐	☐	
6.11	Does the system prevent users from making errors whenever possible?	☐	☐	☐	
6.12	Does the system warn users if they are about to make a potentially serious error?	☐	☐	☐	
6.13	Does the system intelligently interpret variations in user commands?	☐	☐	☐	

#	Review Checklist	Yes	No	N/A	Comments
6.14	Do data entry screens and dialog boxes indicate the number of character spaces available in a field?	☐	☐	☐	
6.15	Do fields in data entry screens and dialog boxes contain default values when appropriate?	☐	☐	☐	

7. Recognition Rather Than Recall

Make objects, actions, and options visible. The user should not have to remember information from one part of the dialogue to another. Instructions for use of the system should be visible or easily retrievable whenever appropriate.

#	Review Checklist	Yes	No	N/A	Comments
7.1	For question and answer interfaces, are visual cues and white space used to distinguish questions, prompts, instructions, and user input?	☐	☐	☐	
7.2	Does the data display start in the upper-left corner of the screen?	☐	☐	☐	
7.3	Are multiword field labels placed horizontally (not stacked vertically)?	☐	☐	☐	
7.4	Are all data a user needs on display at each step in a transaction sequence?	☐	☐	☐	
7.5	Are prompts, cues, and messages placed where the eye is likely to be looking on the screen?	☐	☐	☐	
7.6	Have prompts been formatted using white space, justification, and visual cues for easy scanning?	☐	☐	☐	
7.7	Do text areas have "breathing space" around them?	☐	☐	☐	
7.8	Is there an obvious visual distinction made between "choose one" menu and "choose many" menus?	☐	☐	☐	
7.9	Have spatial relationships between soft function keys (on-screen cues) and keyboard function keys been preserved?	☐	☐	☐	
7.10	Does the system gray out or delete labels of currently inactive soft function keys?	☐	☐	☐	
7.11	Is white space used to create symmetry and lead the eye in the appropriate direction?	☐	☐	☐	
7.12	Have items been grouped into logical zones, and have headings been used to distinguish between zones?	☐	☐	☐	
7.13	Are zones no more than twelve to fourteen characters wide and six to seven lines high?	☐	☐	☐	

#	Review Checklist	Yes	No	N/A	Comments
7.14	Have zones been separated by spaces, lines, color, letters, bold titles, rules lines, or shaded areas?	☐	☐	☐	
7.15	Are field labels close to fields, but separated by at least one space?	☐	☐	☐	
7.16	Are long columnar fields broken up into groups of five, separated by a blank line?	☐	☐	☐	
7.17	Are optional data entry fields clearly marked?	☐	☐	☐	
7.18	Are symbols used to break long input strings into "chunks"?	☐	☐	☐	
7.19	Is reverse video or color highlighting used to get the user's attention?	☐	☐	☐	
7.20	Is reverse video used to indicate that an item has been selected?	☐	☐	☐	
7.21	Are size, boldface, underlining, color, shading, or typography used to show relative quantity or importance of different screen items?	☐	☐	☐	
7.22	Are borders used to identify meaningful groups?	☐	☐	☐	
7.23	Has the same color been used to group related elements?	☐	☐	☐	
7.24	Is color coding consistent throughout the system?	☐	☐	☐	
7.25	Is color used in conjunction with some other redundant cue?	☐	☐	☐	
7.26	Is there good color and brightness contrast between image and background colors?	☐	☐	☐	
7.27	Have light, bright, saturated colors been used to emphasize data and have darker, duller, and desaturated colors been used to de-emphasize data?	☐	☐	☐	
7.28	Is the first word of each menu choice the most important?	☐	☐	☐	
7.29	Does the system provide *mapping:* that is, are the relationships between controls and actions apparent to the user?	☐	☐	☐	
7.30	Are input data codes distinctive?	☐	☐	☐	
7.31	Have frequently confused data pairs been eliminated whenever possible?	☐	☐	☐	
7.32	Have large strings of numbers or letters been broken into chunks?	☐	☐	☐	
7.33	Are inactive menu items grayed out or omitted?	☐	☐	☐	
7.34	Are there menu selection defaults?	☐	☐	☐	

#	Review Checklist	Yes	No	N/A	Comments
7.35	If the system has many menu levels or complex menu levels, do users have access to an on-line spatial menu map?	☐	☐	☐	
7.36	Do GUI menus offer affordance: that is, make obvious where selection is possible?	☐	☐	☐	
7.37	Are there salient visual cues to identify the active window?	☐	☐	☐	
7.38	Are function keys arranged in logical groups?	☐	☐	☐	
7.39	Do data entry screens and dialog boxes indicate when fields are optional?	☐	☐	☐	
7.40	On data entry screens and dialog boxes, are dependent fields displayed only when necessary?	☐	☐	☐	

8. Flexibility and Minimalist Design

Accelerators—unseen by the novice user—may often speed up the interaction for the expert user such that the system can cater to both inexperienced and experienced users. Allow users to tailor frequent actions. Provide alternative means of access and operation for users who differ from the "average" user (e.g., physical or cognitive ability, culture, language, etc.).

#	Review Checklist	Yes	No	N/A	Comments
8.1	If the system supports both novice and expert users, are multiple levels of error message detail available?	☐	☐	☐	
8.2	Does the system allow novices to use a keyword grammar and experts to use a positional grammar?	☐	☐	☐	
8.3	Can users define their own synonyms for commands?	☐	☐	☐	
8.4	Does the system allow novice users to enter the simplest, most common form of each command, and allow expert users to add parameters?	☐	☐	☐	
8.5	Do expert users have the option of entering multiple commands in a single string?	☐	☐	☐	
8.6	Does the system provide function keys for high-frequency commands?	☐	☐	☐	
8.7	For data entry screens with many fields or in which source documents may be incomplete, can users save a partially filled screen?	☐	☐	☐	
8.8	Does the system automatically enter leading zeros?	☐	☐	☐	
8.9	If menu lists are short (seven items or fewer), can users select an item by moving the cursor?	☐	☐	☐	

#	Review Checklist	Yes	No	N/A	Comments
8.10	If the system uses a type-ahead strategy, do the menu items have mnemonic codes?	☐	☐	☐	
8.11	If the system uses a pointing device, do users have the option of either clicking on fields or using a keyboard shortcut?	☐	☐	☐	
8.12	Does the system offer "find next" and "find previous" shortcuts for database searches?	☐	☐	☐	
8.13	On data entry screens, do users have the option of either clicking directly on a field or using a keyboard shortcut?	☐	☐	☐	
8.14	On menus, do users have the option of either clicking directly on a menu item or using a keyboard shortcut?	☐	☐	☐	
8.15	In dialog boxes, do users have the option of either clicking directly on a dialog box option or using a keyboard shortcut?	☐	☐	☐	
8.16	Can expert users bypass nested dialog boxes with either type-ahead, user-defined macros, or keyboard shortcuts?	☐	☐	☐	

9. Aesthetic and Minimalist Design

Dialogues should not contain information which is irrelevant or rarely needed. Every extra unit of information in a dialogue competes with the relevant units of information and diminishes their relative visibility.

#	Review Checklist	Yes	No	N/A	Comments
9.1	Is only (and all) information essential to decision making displayed on the screen?	☐	☐	☐	
9.2	Are all icons in a set visually and conceptually distinct?	☐	☐	☐	
9.3	Have large objects, bold lines, and simple areas been used to distinguish icons?	☐	☐	☐	
9.4	Does each icon stand out from its background?	☐	☐	☐	
9.5	If the system uses a standard GUI interface where menu sequence has already been specified, do menus adhere to the specification whenever possible?	☐	☐	☐	
9.6	Are meaningful groups of items separated by white space?	☐	☐	☐	
9.7	Does each data entry screen have a short, simple, clear, distinctive title?	☐	☐	☐	
9.8	Are field labels brief, familiar, and descriptive?	☐	☐	☐	

#	Review Checklist	Yes	No	N/A	Comments
9.9	Are prompts expressed in the affirmative, and do they use the active voice?	☐	☐	☐	
9.10	Is each lower-level menu choice associated with only one higher-level menu?	☐	☐	☐	
9.11	Are menu titles brief, yet long enough to communicate?	☐	☐	☐	
9.12	Are there pop-up or pull-down menus within data entry fields that have many, but well-defined, entry options?	☐	☐	☐	

10. Help and Documentation

Even though it is better if the system can be used without documentation, it may be necessary to provide help and documentation. Any such information should be easy to search, focused on the user's task, list concrete steps to be carried out, and not be too large.

#	Review Checklist	Yes	No	N/A	Comments
10.1	If users are working from hard copy, are the parts of the hard copy that go on-line marked?	☐	☐	☐	
10.2	Are on-line instructions visually distinct?	☐	☐	☐	
10.3	Do the instructions follow the sequence of user actions?	☐	☐	☐	
10.4	If menu choices are ambiguous, does the system provide additional explanatory information when an item is selected?	☐	☐	☐	
10.5	Are data entry screens and dialog boxes supported by navigation and completion instructions?	☐	☐	☐	
10.6	If menu items are ambiguous, does the system provide additional explanatory information when an item is selected?	☐	☐	☐	
10.7	Are there memory aids for commands, either through on-line quick reference or prompting?	☐	☐	☐	
10.8	Is the help function visible; for example, a key labeled HELP or a special menu?	☐	☐	☐	
10.9	Is the help system interface (navigation, presentation, and conversation) consistent with the navigation, presentation, and conversation interfaces of the application it supports?	☐	☐	☐	
10.10	Navigation: Is information easy to find?	☐	☐	☐	
10.11	Presentation: Is the visual layout well designed?	☐	☐	☐	
10.12	Conversation: Is the information accurate, complete, and understandable?	☐	☐	☐	

#	Review Checklist	Yes	No	N/A	Comments
10.13	Is the information relevant?	☐	☐	☐	
10.14	Goal-oriented (What can I do with this program?)	☐	☐	☐	
10.15	Descriptive (What is this thing for?)	☐	☐	☐	
10.16	Procedural (How do I do this task?)	☐	☐	☐	
10.17	Interpretive (Why did that happen?)	☐	☐	☐	
10.18	Navigational (Where am I?)	☐	☐	☐	
10.19	Is there context-sensitive help?	☐	☐	☐	
10.20	Can the user change the level of detail available?	☐	☐	☐	
10.21	Can users easily switch between help and their work?	☐	☐	☐	
10.22	Is it easy to access and return from the help system?	☐	☐	☐	
10.23	Can users resume work where they left off after accessing help?	☐	☐	☐	

11. Skills

The system should support, extend, supplement, or enhance the user's skills, background knowledge, and expertise—not replace them.

#	Review Checklist	Yes	No	N/A	Comments
11.1	Can users choose between iconic and text display of information?	☐	☐	☐	
11.2	Are window operations easy to learn and use?	☐	☐	☐	
11.3	If users are experts, usage is frequent, or the system has a slow response time, are there fewer screens (more information per screen)?	☐	☐	☐	
11.4	If users are novices, usage is infrequent, or the system has a fast response time, are there more screens (less information per screen)?	☐	☐	☐	
11.5	Does the system automatically color-code items, with little or no user effort?	☐	☐	☐	
11.6	If the system supports both novice and expert users, are multiple levels of detail available?	☐	☐	☐	
11.7	Are users the initiators of actions rather than the responders?	☐	☐	☐	
11.8	Does the system perform data translations for users?	☐	☐	☐	
11.9	Do field values avoid mixing alpha and numeric characters whenever possible?	☐	☐	☐	

#	Review Checklist	Yes	No	N/A	Comments
11.10	If the system has deep (multilevel) menus, do users have the option of typing ahead?	☐	☐	☐	
11.11	When the user enters a screen or dialog box, is the cursor already positioned in the field users are most likely to need?	☐	☐	☐	
11.12	Can users move forward and backward within a field?	☐	☐	☐	
11.13	Is the method for moving the cursor to the next or previous field both simple and visible?	☐	☐	☐	
11.14	Has auto-tabbing been avoided except when fields have fixed lengths or users are experienced?	☐	☐	☐	
11.15	Do the selected input device(s) match user capabilities?	☐	☐	☐	
11.16	Are cursor keys arranged in either an inverted T (best for experts) or a cross configuration (best for novices)?	☐	☐	☐	
11.17	Are important keys (for example, <u>ENTER</u>, <u>TAB</u>) larger than other keys?	☐	☐	☐	
11.18	Are there enough function keys to support functionality, but not so many that scanning and finding are difficult?	☐	☐	☐	
11.19	Are function keys reserved for generic, high-frequency, important functions?	☐	☐	☐	
11.20	Are function key assignments consistent across screens, subsystems, and related products?	☐	☐	☐	
11.21	Does the system correctly anticipate and prompt for the user's probable next activity?	☐	☐	☐	

12. Pleasurable and Respectful Interaction with the User

The user's interactions with the system should enhance the quality of her or his work-life. The user should be treated with respect. The design should be aesthetically pleasing—with artistic as well as functional value.

#	Review Checklist	Yes	No	N/A	Comments
12.1	Is each individual icon a harmonious member of a family of icons?	☐	☐	☐	
12.2	Has excessive detail in icon design been avoided?	☐	☐	☐	
12.3	Has color been used with discretion?	☐	☐	☐	

#	Review Checklist	Yes	No	N/A	Comments
12.4	Has the amount of required window housekeeping been kept to a minimum?	☐	☐	☐	
12.5	If users are working from hard copy, does the screen layout match the paper form?	☐	☐	☐	
12.6	Has color been used specifically to draw attention, communicate organization, indicate status changes, and establish relationships?	☐	☐	☐	
12.7	Can users turn off automatic color coding if necessary?	☐	☐	☐	
12.8	Are typing requirements minimal for question and answer interfaces?	☐	☐	☐	
12.9	Do the selected input device(s) match environmental constraints?	☐	☐	☐	
12.10	If the system uses multiple input devices, has hand and eye movement between input devices been minimized?	☐	☐	☐	
12.11	If the system supports graphical tasks, has an alternative pointing device been provided?	☐	☐	☐	
12.12	Is the numeric keypad located to the right of the alpha key area?	☐	☐	☐	
12.13	Are the most frequently used function keys in the most accessible positions?	☐	☐	☐	
12.14	Does the system complete unambiguous partial input on a data entry field?	☐	☐	☐	

13. Privacy

The system should help the user to protect personal or private information—belonging to the user or to his/her clients.

#	Review Checklist	Yes	No	N/A	Comments
13.1	Are protected areas completely inaccessible?	☐	☐	☐	
13.2	Can protected or confidential areas be accessed with certain passwords?	☐	☐	☐	
13.3	Is this feature effective and successful?	☐	☐	☐	

Source: "Xerox Heuristic Evaluation—A System Checklist" <http://www.stcsig.org/usability/resources>.

Usability Inspection of *Technical Communication*

Team 1C: Final Report
Ann Dillon and Jeanette Evans

Executive Summary

Purpose of usability inspection
The purpose of our usability inspection is to examine two issues of *Technical Communication* and provide the results with recommendations to its editor, Dr. George F. Hayhoe. *Technical Communication,* the professional journal of the Society for Technical Communication (STC), is considered by practitioners to be a primary source of information in the disciplines of document design, technical illustration, and education of technical communicators.

Dr. Hayhoe has recently guided the journal through a redesign of its layout and a redirection of its focus toward the concerns of technical communication practitioners rather than educators. His question to the teams conducting a usability inspection was whether or not the redesign met the goals he had established for it.

Scope of usability inspection
We conducted an inspection of the February and May 1998 issues of *Technical Communication;* at Dr. Hayhoe's recommendation, we also added the index from the November 1997 issue (the journal index is published yearly in the November issue).

Designing the inspection
We used the heuristic inspection model developed by Jakob Nielsen as the basis for our inspection of *Technical Communication.* In a heuristic inspection, usability specialists evaluate individual elements of a design according to established usability principles (i.e., "heuristics").

In researching Nielsen's work, we discovered that his heuristic principles applied to software user interface. We also discovered that there was not a defined set of heuristics that all information designers and evaluators use specifically for document design. A software program's screen appearance and the design of a journal, however, are each a form of user interface and have several objectives in common. Therefore, we have taken Nielsen's ideas and model and have applied or interpreted them to fit the inspection of a journal. We also examined the work of several expert practitioners who provided guidelines for selecting and combining the elements that make up a document.

We think it is important to point out that there are few hard and fast rules in the world of document design. This can be frustrating for someone who wants one quick answer, but in reality the lack of definite rules has a pragmatic basis. Audiences and situations are different, and document design has to be flexible enough to adapt to those differences. For the document designer, this requires skill, experience, judgment, and training to use design principles and techniques effectively for different audiences and situations. Again, we found few rules. We did find principles and guidelines and drew on those in preparing the measures for the heuristics we developed.

When developing our goals for the *Technical Communication* usability inspection, we recognized that the design of a journal is dynamic and must change periodically to meet the needs of its audience. We decided it was important that the editor be able to replicate our inspection in the future to evaluate other changes that might be made to the journal. We therefore sought to develop a usability inspection that could be used again; this would have the advantage of allowing the editor to compare similar studies and base decisions on comparable information.

Summary of inspection method

Based on Jakob Nielsen's usability heuristics for software interface, we developed a comparable set of heuristics for a professional journal and correlated them to the goals that Dr. Hayhoe had described for the journal in a request for proposals. We then took each heuristic and the journals and prepared a set of measures based on the needs of typical users and the guidelines of expert practitioners.

On an individual basis, each of us then examined the journals provided by Dr. Hayhoe and evaluated specific elements according to the measures we had established. We noted strong and weak points, offered recommendations in areas where we thought they would be beneficial, and assigned ratings of importance and severity to each measure. The ratings were primarily to assist the editor in setting priorities for any changes he would make.

Conclusion

In our estimation, *Technical Communication* easily meets the goals that Dr. Hayhoe has established for it. It combines visual appeal with the content necessary for a well-educated, experienced, practitioner-based audience and is a recognized resource for the profession of technical communication. We hope that our findings and recommendations will enhance an already outstanding publication.

Inspection Method

Preparation

Before beginning the usability inspection, we developed a set of heuristics for document design that compared with Jakob Nielsen's heuristics for software interface design. Based on the document design heuristics, we designated 17 design elements that we would examine as thoroughly as possible in *Technical Communication*. We prepared a test case for each of the 17 elements; the test cases assured that we would examine each measure separately and not overlook any important items.

In the test cases we also established measures that we used as the basis of evaluating the usability of each design element. In addition to the research we had conducted on heuristics and document design, we discussed the test cases' content with Dr. Hayhoe to make sure our inspections would be focused on the measures most meaningful to him in his role as editor. At his request we added several measures, primarily in the area of column format, index, content, and graphics.

Inspection

Up to this point the development of the usability inspection instrument had been intensely collaborative. For the inspection itself, however, we needed to work independently to assure that no bias would affect our findings and recommendations.

Each of us spent approximately a week examining specific pages and elements in the two issues of *Technical Communication* and the index in the November issue. As much as possible we eliminated any preferences we might have and examined the elements according to the measures we had established for usability. We then recorded our findings of strong and weak points; based on those, each of us prepared recommendations and assigned a rating of importance and severity according to how she perceived the usability of the element. We did not try to take into account the resources that might be necessary to carry out our recommendations; we focused strictly on usability.

After we finished the inspection, we compared our findings and prepared a set of consensus recommendations and ratings. For some elements, one of us might see no need for any changes, while the other might recommend modifications. In those instances, we elected to use the recommendations for change as the consensus. We knew that Dr. Hayhoe would use other evaluations and feedback as well as ours. In our estimation, it would be better to provide a recommendation that he could balance against others' feedback rather than omit a finding that might be important but was not examined by others.

The remaining sections of this report describe the heuristics we developed, our findings, and the resources we used in developing our usability inspection.

Developing the Document Design Heuristics

The Client's Goals

Before we could develop appropriate heuristics on which to base our usability inspection, we needed to identify the requirements of our client, Dr. George F. Hayhoe, the editor of *Technical Communication*. To do this, we used a request for proposal that Dr. Hayhoe had developed during the planning stage of the journal's redesign. The goals Dr. Hayhoe identified were:

- It is critically important that the document be visually inviting to the audience.
- Authors are increasingly relying on visual elements to help communicate their message, and this journal should be well-equipped to communicate both visual and verbal information.
- This journal is meant to serve as a primary source of continuing education for the audience.
- The design should identify STC and *Technical Communication* as leaders in the area of information design.
- The journal should be a model of technical publication design.
- The design should unify the journal's diverse content.
- The image should be modern but not avant garde.
- The image should be scholarly but not academic.
- The document should be timeless in legibility.

Our usability inspection needed to examine the elements of the journal that would provide the clearest picture of how close *Technical Communication's* new design came to the goals Dr. Hayhoe had articulated for it. Since our usability inspection had to be accomplished within an 8-week period, we needed a method that would yield the information we needed within the time we had available. We determined that the best means of accomplishing our task would be a heuristic evaluation based on the method developed by Jakob Nielsen.

The Method of Inspection

Usability expert Jakob Nielsen describes heuristics as "recognized usability principles" and offers ten heuristics as a guide for the development of a software user interface.

1. *Visibility of system status:* The system should always keep users informed about what is going on, through appropriate feedback within reasonable time.
2. *Match between system and the real world:* The system should speak the users' language, with words, phrases, and concepts familiar to the user, rather than system-oriented terms. Follow real-world conventions, making information appear in a natural and logical order.
3. *User control and freedom:* Users often choose system functions by mistake and will need a clearly marked "emergency exit" to leave the unwanted state without having to go through an extended dialogue. Support undo and redo.
4. *Consistency and standards:* Users should not have to wonder whether different words, situations, or actions mean the same thing. Follow platform conventions.
5. *Error prevention:* Even better than good error messages is a careful design which prevents a problem from occurring in the first place.
6. *Recognition rather than recall:* Make objects, actions, and options visible. The user should not have to remember information from one part of the dialogue to another. Instructions for use of the system should be visible or easily retrievable whenever appropriate.
7. *Flexibility and efficiency of use:* Accelerators—unseen by the novice user—may often speed up the interaction for the expert user such than the system can cater to both the inexperienced and experienced users. Allow users to tailor frequent actions.
8. *Aesthetic and minimalist design:* Dialogues should not contain information which is irrelevant or rarely needed. Every extra unit of information in a dialogue completes with the relevant units of information and diminishes their relative visibility.
9. *Help users recognize, diagnose, and recover from errors:* Error messages should be expressed in plain language (no codes), precisely indicate the problem, and constructively suggest a solution.
10. *Help and documentation:* Even though it is better if the system can be used without documentation, it may be necessary to provide help and documentation. Any such information should be easy to search, focused on the user's task, list concrete steps to be carried out, and not be too large.

(Nielsen, J. *Ten Usability Heuristics*)

The Heuristics for *Technical Communication*

With this list as a base, we developed a corresponding set of heuristics to use in evaluation of document design.

- *Aesthetics:* Aesthetic elements should contribute toward making the product visually inviting to the audience.

- *Communication of both visual and verbal information:* Design and format of the document should relay both visual and verbal information consistent with needs and expectations of the audience and users.
- *Content:* Content should meet the needs of the audience and the intended purpose of the document.
- *Design:* Solid design elements should be consistent with expectations of audience and purpose of document. Design elements should help readers navigate.
- *Image:* The document should project an image appropriate to the audience and purpose of the document.
- *Legibility:* Legibility is appropriate for the type of content and document, meeting the document's purpose and audience's needs.
- *Navigation:* Navigational elements should help the audience find and understand the information in the product.

To test the document design heuristics, we identified nine design elements in the issues of *Technical Communication* that we would examine. The nine elements can be divided into two general categories: User Interface and Aesthetics.

User Interface: The functional elements of the design that affect the ease and accuracy with which readers can progress through the journal and find the information they seek.

Subject of Test Case	Based on Heuristic
• Table of contents • Index • Page numbers • Summaries or abstracts of articles	• Communication of both visual and verbal information • Navigation

Aesthetics: The appeal of the journal's design and its ability to serve as a model for technical publication design.

Subject of Test Case	Based on Heuristic
• Layout • Type font and size • Headings • Column width • Content	• Aesthetics • Communication of both visual and verbal information • Content • Design • Image • Legibility

We expanded the nine test cases identified above to 17 test cases so that we could examine discrete aspects of the design elements. An example is the integration of graphics elements, which became four different test cases, thus allowing us to inspect cover art, article illustrations, department illustrations, and recurring illustrations in the level of detail they deserved. In addition to our conducting individual inspections, we prepared a set of consensus recommendations as part of our final report.

Definition of Terms

Document design
The field concerned with creating texts (broadly defined) that integrate words and pictures in ways that help people to achieve their specific goals for using texts at home, school, or work. (Schriver, K.A. *Dynamics in Document Design,* p. 10, 1997, John Wiley & Sons, Inc.)

Heuristics
Principles or guidelines for good design, general rules that describe common properties of usable interfaces and/or products. (Nielsen, J. *Summary of Usability Inspection Methods*)

Heuristic evaluation
A usability inspection method that involves having usability specialists judge whether each element follows established usability principles. The heuristic evaluation is done as a systematic inspection of a design for usability. The evaluation normally involves having a small set of evaluators examine the interface and judge its compliance with recognized usability principles. (Nielsen, J. *How to Conduct a Heuristic Evaluation*)

Test Case
An examination of an element of a product or service based on how a typical user is likely to use it, how the product or service works under those circumstances, what works correctly, and what performs incorrectly.

Reporting the Findings

The following tables provide the consensus ratings and recommendations from our two independent usability inspections of *Technical Communication*. The tables are separated according to User Interface and Aesthetics, which are the major heuristic categories we used. Each table then shows the test case, the element tested, its importance and severity rating, recommendation, and any external source (i.e., expert practitioner) if we were able to locate one for this inspection.

Ratings legend
Importance from standpoint of usability

A = High importance
B = Medium importance
C = Low importance

Severity from standpoint of usability

1 = Most severe
|
|
|
5 = Least severe

User Interface Findings

Test Case	Design Element	Importance	Severity	Recommendations	Reference to Expert Practitioner
1	Author's name	B	3	• Transpose title and author's name in header so that title in bold type face is an outside edge of header. Readers use titles as method of navigation, not author's name, and bold type face offers acceptable contrast with rest of text pages. • Continue practice of using on all feature and department pages.	N/A
2	Bulleted summary	B	4	• Use complete sentence for each bullet item since a complete sentence can best relay the sometimes complex ideas expressed in the summaries.	N/A
3	Index	B	2	• Offer more specific terms typical of ones readers would use. This would make the journal more usable for researchers as well as general readers. • Supply an index with each issue. Each issue would benefit from its own index with the fourth quarter index including titles of features as well as books and articles reviewed throughout the year.	N/A
4	Page numbers	A	2	• Place page number on every page, including the Table of Contents, where ads do not extend into the area normally allocated to the footer.	N/A
5	Table of contents	A	1	• Display continuation notice at bottom of first page when Table of Contents runs over into two pages. • Increase the weight of the type face under the reduced version of the cover to make it more legible. • Make column width of feature articles consistent (width of February issue is easier to read and therefore preferred). • Make Table of Contents the first page in the journal, if advertising contracts do not prevent.	N/A

Aesthetics Findings

Test Case	Design Element	Importance	Severity	Recommendations	Reference to Expert Practitioner
6	Body font	A	1	• Use a heavier weight of Garamond to increase readability of text • Use type face for bullets and list numbers that is more compatible with body text and does not offer such a strong contrast.	Schriver, Craig, Kostelnick and Roberts
7	Citations and references	B	2	• Use a heavier weight version of type font for references to increase readability. • Distinguish citations (i.e., usage of author name and date in article) from body text by using contrasting weight or slant. When several authors are cited close together, the citations and text are difficult to tell apart (example: pg. 180, first paragraph).	Schriver, Craig, Kostelnick and Roberts
8	Content	N/A	N/A	No changes recommended	N/A
9	Graphics integration: cover	N/A	N/A	No changes recommended	N/A
10	Graphics integration: articles	B	3	• Use consistency in format of titles and captions. • Reformat tables to use space more effectively, increase readability and visual appeal, and avoid breaks at awkward places. • Increase weight of figure captions to increase legibility. • In bar charts, use patterns or other devices as well as shading to make information easy to distinguish.	Schriver, Craig, Kostelnick and Roberts
11	Graphics integration: departments	B	3	• Use photo of book cover for each review. • Use mortar board as symbol for education in Recent and Relevant. • Use a standard drop-in piece of art to plug white space on first page of Book Reviews similar to the way the *New Yorker* fills extra space with pen-and-ink sketches.	Horton

Aesthetics Findings (continued)

Test Case	Design Element	Importance	Severity	Recommendations	Reference to Expert Practitioner
12	Graphics integration: recurring graphics	B	3	• Add rules to About the Authors and About the Book Reviewers. • Uses red for rules in headers, in COMMUNICATION in footers, and in summary box background throughout journal to add visual interest.	N/A
13	Headings: 1st level	A	1	• Use upper and lower case characters to improve readability. • Use same type face as 2nd-level heading, but in larger point size. • Increase amount of leading. • Add a return between heading and first line of paragraph.	Schriver, Horton, Kostelnick and Roberts, Wheildon
14	Headings: 2nd level	A	1	• Increase size and leading of 2nd-level heading to make it more prominent than 3rd-level heading. • Add a return between heading and first line of paragraph.	Schriver, Kostelnick and Roberts, Wheildon
15	Pull quotes	B	2	• Use a smaller type face, for example, 20 points. • Use primary short pull quotes, such as 17 words or fewer, for ease of readability.	Wheildon
16	Paragraphs: spacing and indention	B	1	• Add a line of space between the end of a list and beginning of a paragraph. • Maintain consistent indention of paragraph after breakhead.	Schriver
17	Column format	A	2	• Consider using 3-column format for feature articles. • Consider using vertical hairline rule between columns in features to distinguish them from department articles.	Schriver, Craig

Using Resources

Expert Practitioners

This provides a reference to the works we used in developing specific measures in several of the test cases. We also relied on them as we assessed elements within *Technical Communication* and in the choices we made when completing the test cases.

Test Case	Author	Reference Cited
1	Not Applicable	Not Applicable
2	Not Applicable	Not Applicable
3	Not Applicable	Not Applicable
4	Not Applicable	Not Applicable
5	Not Applicable	Not Applicable
6	Schriver	*Dynamics of Document Design,* pg. 258, 261–263, 274;
	Craig	*Basic Typography,* pg. 56;
	Kostelnick and Roberts	*Designing Visual Language,* pg. 143, 198
7	Schriver	*Dynamics of Document Design,* pg. 258, 261–263, 274;
	Craig	*Basic Typography,* pg. 56;
	Kostelnick and Roberts	*Designing Visual Language,* pg. 143, 198
8	Not Applicable	Not Applicable
9	Not Applicable	Not Applicable
10	Schriver	*Dynamics of Document Design,* pg. 263 margin note, 314;
	Kostelnick and Roberts	*Designing Visual Language,* pg. 279, 287, 293, 300
11	Horton	*The Icon Book,* pg. 244
12	Not Applicable	Not Applicable
13	Schriver	*Dynamics of Document Design,* pg. 263, 274;
	Horton	*Designing and Writing Online Documentation,* pg. 249;
	Kostelnick and Roberts	*Designing Visual Language,* pg. 144, 183;
	Wheildon	*Type & Layout,* pg. 125, 127
14	Schriver	*Dynamics of Document Design,* pg. 274;
	Kostelnick and Roberts	*Designing Visual Language,* pg. 183;
	Wheildon	*Type & Layout,* pg. 125
15	Wheildon	*Type & Layout,* pg. 123
16	Schriver	*Dynamics of Document Design,* pg. 275
17	Schriver	*Dynamics of Document Design,* pg. 263;
	Craig	*Basic Typography,* pg. 88

Bibliography

Craig, James. *Basic Typography: A Design Manual,* Watson-Guptill Publications, New York, 1990.

Horton, William. *Designing and Writing Online Documentation,* Second edition, John Wiley & Sons, New York, 1995.

Horton, William. *The Icon Book: Visual Symbols for Computer Systems and Documentation,* John Wiley & Sons, New York, 1994.

Kostelnick, Charles, and Roberts, David D. *Designing Visual Language: Strategies for Professional Communicators,* Allyn and Bacon, Boston, 1998.

Nielsen, Jakob. *Characteristics of Usability Problems Found by Heuristic Evaluation* <http://www.useit.com/papers>.

Nielsen, Jakob. *How to Conduct a Heuristic Evaluation* <http://www.useit.com/papers>.

Nielsen, Jakob. *Severity Ratings for Usability Problems* <http://www.useit.com/papers>.

Nielsen, Jakob. *Summary of Usability Inspection Methods* <http://www.useit.com/papers>.

Nielsen, Jakob. *Ten Usability Heuristics* <http://www.useit.com/papers>.

Schriver, Karen A. *Dynamics in Document Design,* John Wiley & Sons, New York, 1997.

Technical Communication, Journal of the Society for Technical Communication, February 1998, Volume 45, Number 1, published by the Society for Technical Communication, Arlington, VA.

Technical Communication, Journal of the Society for Technical Communication, May 1998, Volume 45, Number 2, published by the Society for Technical Communication, Arlington, VA.

Technical Communication, Journal of the Society for Technical Communication, November 1997, Volume 44, Number 4, published by the Society for Technical Communication, Arlington, VA.

Wheildon, Colin. *Type & Layout,* Strathmoor Press, Berkeley, 1996.

Source: Reprinted with permission from Ann Dillon and Jeanette Evans.

## CHAPTER 3

User and Task Analysis

 In Chapter 1, we talked about user-centered design as the process of developing products based on information learned from users. Usability testing is a cornerstone of user-centered design, as it provides essential information about users interacting with products. However, user-centered design does not begin with usability testing. It begins with an understanding of the users and the tasks they perform and the environments in which they perform these tasks. To learn about these critical elements—user, task, environment—you must collect data about users and their behaviors in *their* workplace or home. That means going to the users, not just bringing the users to you. This chapter addresses the methodology of *field studies*. Field studies are not to be confused with field testing, which refers to usability testing in the "field," or the user's workplace, as opposed to the lab (see Chapter 1). Field studies derive from social science and its reliance on *ethnographic* studies, such as the type conducted by Margaret Mead, who lived with people in their community to study their culture. Field studies, in the context of user-centered design, are not as intensive or long-lasting as ethnographic studies, but they can still provide rich data, which can be used as the starting place of user-centered design.

To understand the importance of field studies, we need to first explore the issues of conceptual design and the problems that result when the design of a product does not match the user's concept or experience. This understanding will establish the basis for our discussion of user and task analysis. We conclude by making some distinctions about users and tasks relevant to the World Wide Web.

Conceptual Design

Conceptual design provides the concept, or metaphor, that, if done well, allows the user to intuitively understand the meaning of the interface. No amount of brainstorming or attending meetings will tell developers whether a design concept will work for users. Nor will surveys or focus groups or any of the other methods for getting feedback from users, as discussed in Chapter 2. Getting the conceptual design right is critical for usability, as usability specialist Jeff Rubin explains: "The *conceptual model* or *metaphor* of a software user interface is the means by which it communicates the software's underlying operations and functionality to a user. It is the highest level of design, of communication, and is one of the prime determinants of the usability and ease of learning a software product" (130). Conceptual design is based on three premises about users and products (Rubinstein and Hersh):

1. Humans always form mental models, maps, or hypotheses about the underlying, invisible processes of a system or machine to help them operate it.
2. A product's conceptual model should match the user's existing mental model or, if a new product is being developed, should make sense to the user, such as the "desktop metaphor" did when Apple introduced the first commercially acceptable computer with a graphical user interface.
3. If the product's conceptual model matches the user's mental model or allows the user to create a mental model for use, then the product will be easier to learn and use.

Problems with Conceptual Models

When is a conceptual model difficult? According to Donald Norman, author of *The Invisible Computer*, difficulty arises with the model "when the controls and actions seem arbitrary, when the system can get itself into peculiar states, peculiar in the sense that the person using it does not know what it is doing, how it got there, or how to recover. When there is a lack of understanding" (174). Although Apple's desktop metaphor has been widely applauded as a usable concept, everyone in the development field knows the conceptual problem created by the Macintosh computer's "trash can," a part of its otherwise successful introduction of a graphical user interface. The concept of the trash can worked extremely well for discarding files that the user no longer wanted, because it matched the user's mental model of placing something in the trash that should be discarded. However, users were troubled and anxious when they had to drag a diskette to the trash can to eject it from the computer for future use, and the lines lit up at Apple's help desk as a result.

To give equal time to Microsoft, a more recent example of a concept that doesn't work is the Start command for Windows 95 and newer products, in which users must go to "start" in order to "stop." See the Abbott and Costello parody in the sidebar entitled "Who's on Start?" for a comical illustration of the problem this really presents to users, as it violates a conceptual model users have. Still another example is the concept of the cellular phone, which is not designed to look and act like a phone but rather like a two-way radio. Even when new users are told that the metaphor for the cellular phone is not a phone, but a radio, they are frequently confused about the requirement to press the "send" button to "receive" an incoming phone call. After all, the cell phone appears to be a phone and you use it like a phone to make and receive calls. So, why doesn't the interface look like a phone, a concept already clearly understood by users?

Who's on Start?

Costello: Hey, Abbott!

Abbott: Yes, Lou?

Costello: I just got my first computer.

Abbott: That's great, Lou. What did you get?

Costello: A Pentium II-22, with 40 Megs of RAM, a 2.1 Gig hard drive, and a 24X CD-ROM.

Abbott: That's terrific, Lou.

Costello: But I don't know what any of it means!

Abbott: You will in time.

Costello: That's exactly why I'm here to see you.

Abbott: Oh?

Costello: I heard that you're a real computer expert.

Abbott: Well, I don't know. . . .

Costello: Yes-sir-ee. You know your stuff. And you're going to train me.

Abbott: Really?

Costello: Uh huh. And I am here for my first lesson.

Abbott: O.K. Lou. What do you want to know?

Costello: I am having no trouble turning it on, but I heard that you should be very careful how you turn it off.

Abbott: That's true.

Costello: So, here I am working on my new computer and I want to turn it off. What do I do?

Abbott: Well, first you press the Start button, and then . . .

Costello: No, I told you I want to turn it off.

Abbott: I know, you press the Start button. . .

Costello: Wait a second. I want to turn it off. I know how to start it. So tell me what to do.

Abbott: I did.

Costello: When?

Abbott: When I told you to press the Start button.

Costello: Why should I press the Start button?

Abbott: To shut off the computer.

Costello: I press Start to stop?

Abbott: Well, Start doesn't actually stop the computer.

Costello: I knew it! So what do I press?

Abbott: Start.

Costello: Start what?

Abbott: Start button.

Costello: Start button to do what?

Abbott: Shut down.

Costello: You don't have to get rude!

Abbott: No, no, no! That's not what I meant.

Costello: Then say what you mean.

Abbott: To shut down the computer, press . . .

Costello: Don't say, "Start"!

Abbott: Then what do you want me to say?

Costello: Look, if I want to turn off the computer, I am willing to press the Stop button, the End button and Cease and Desist button, but no one in their right mind presses the Start to stop.

Abbott: But that's what you do.

Costello: And you probably Go at Stop signs, and Stop at green lights.

Abbott: Don't be ridiculous.

Costello: I'm being ridiculous? Well, I think it's about time we started this conversation.

Abbott: What are you talking about?

Costello: I am starting this conversation right now. Good bye.

Conceptual problems also occur with new Internet users, as the calls to technical support illustrated in Table 3.1 reveal (Kiesler; reported in Nielsen, "Tech Support Tales").

To design an effective conceptual model, which becomes the basis of the interface, developers have to study users at work or at home, observe what they actually do, see what they have created beyond what's available to help them perform

TABLE 3.1	Conceptual Problems for Novice Internet Users	
User's Question to Tech Support	**What Really Was Wrong**	**Nielsen's Comments**
My email freezes.	The user had never installed the modem (didn't know that it was part of the computer).	Reveals a fundamental flaw in the user's conceptual model of the system.
Modem won't dial.	Someone else was using the telephone.	One more problem caused by a fundamental error in the user's conceptual model of the system: the user would probably not have complained about not being able to use one of the telephones in the house while another member of the household was on the phone, but the user doesn't understand that using the modem is equivalent to making a telephone call. After all, a modem is a *computer* thing.

Source: Adapted from Jakob Nielsen, "Tech Support Tales: Internet Hard to Use for Novice Users" *Alertbox* (1 Apr. 1997) <http://www.useit.com/alertbox9704a.html>.

their tasks, and understand users' goals. In the next section, we discuss the importance of learning about users and their tasks where they work and live.

User and Task Analysis

The goal of user and task analysis is to understand:

- What users' goals are, not just the tasks they perform
- What processes they use to achieve their goals
- What characteristics shape the way they perform tasks and achieve goals (different groups of users may have different characteristics and goals)
- What previous experience shapes users' approaches to tasks
- What is most important to users or what is most helpful to them in performing tasks
- What impact the environment has on their ability to perform tasks

Two examples will illustrate the importance of conducting such user and task analyses, based on the experience of one company that did perform these up-front field studies and one company that did not. In the case of the company that did not perform a field study and therefore did not know the users' environment, the product was a documentation set for banking operations that was intended to be shelved in the workstation or office bookshelf of computer users in a banking center. The product was being developed for a customer based in Hong Kong. The technical communicators who worked on the project assumed that the environment would match that of typical U.S. banking centers. It wasn't until the senior technical communicator went to Hong Kong to initiate the training that she learned that everyone in the banking center worked together in an open room with no offices and no bookshelves. Thus, the document sets were stacked up precariously on top of a printer on a stand in the center of the room, which severely reduced their accessibility.

In the case of a company that did do field studies in anticipation of creating a product that would enter the market after a single competitor had already captured the marketplace, the company found that potential customers would only be interested in switching to the new product if they didn't have to learn new commands and could use the new product like the competitor's product. Still, new users, who hadn't used the competitor's product, wanted a product that was easier to learn than the one dominating the marketplace. With this understanding of the needs of two different user groups, the company developed two ways to use the product: one allowing users to select the competitor's keyboard commands and the other providing a new and simpler path. In addition, the company learned from the users of the competitor's product what they didn't like about the existing product as well as what they did like, which allowed the developers to design better features without sacrificing the features current users liked. The new product provided easier learnability for new users, while maintaining the "old" way for those already comfortable with the other product. The result was that the new product soon captured the major market share, dwarfing and then killing off the competing product.

What You Can Learn from Users

When you make site visits and listen to users, you can learn their vocabulary, observe the tools they use to perform tasks, and discern their mental models for how they perform tasks, frequently from the mistakes they make because the conceptual metaphor of the product they are using doesn't match their mental model. In *User and Task Analysis for Interface Design*, Hackos and Redish outline three broad categories of information that you can learn about users (35):

1. How they define themselves (jobs, tasks, tools, and mental models)
2. How they differ individually (personal, physical, and cultural characteristics, as well as motivation)
3. How they use products over time and the choices they make about the levels of expertise they want or need to achieve (stages of use)

By arranging to see and spend time with different levels of users, you can better appreciate the motivations and needs of novice users, as well as users who are comfortable with a process or product and those who are proficient with it. You can also learn what the motivation might be for users to learn how to use a new product or switch products or processes and how much control they have over such decisions.

Being able to see users of different skill levels is important in developing user-centered products because users' needs change over time, along with their motivation to learn new things or to make advances in their knowledge of a product. Hackos and Redish (79–87) divide any user population into four possible groups, with the characteristics shown in Table 3.2.

Most users will move beyond the novice stage in time, but few will become expert performers. It is critical, however, to understand what novices need as well as

TABLE 3.2	Characteristics of User Populations
Novices	• Fear of failure, fear of the unknown • Focus on accomplishing real work • Impatient with learning concepts rather than performing tasks • Theoretical understanding only—no practical experience
Advanced beginners	• Focus on accomplishing real work • Impatient with learning concepts rather than performing tasks • Randomly access tasks • By adding new and progressively more complicated tasks, begin to develop an empirically based mental model
Competent performers	• Focus on performing more complex tasks that require many coordinated actions • Ability to plan how to perform a complex series of tasks to achieve a goal • Willingness to learn how tasks fit into a consistent mental model of the interface as a whole • Interest in solving simple problems by applying a conceptual framework to diagnose and correct errors
Expert performers	• Focus on developing a comprehensive and consistent mental model of the product functionality and the interface • Ability to understand complex problems and find solutions • Interest in learning about concepts and theories behind a product's design and use • Interest in interacting with other expert users

Source: Adapted from JoAnn T. Hackos and Janice C. Redish, *User and Task Analysis for Interface Design.* New York: Wiley, 1998, pp. 79–87. © 1998 John Wiley & Sons, Inc. (Reprinted by permission of John Wiley & Sons, Inc.)

what competent performers need. For, as Hackos and Redish state, "products will succeed only if they facilitate users having successful first experiences, and only if they also allow for growth and learning and for a variety of patterns of use" (78–79). If developers lose sight of the novice users under the presumption that by now *everyone* must know something about the computer, they will restrict the desire or ability of new users to enter the market for their products. Although product development in the late 1980s and '90s focused on expert user performance to improve the efficiency of use of products in corporate settings, as Nielsen states, the Web has changed all that, putting the focus back on novice users ("Novice vs. Expert Users"). Terry Sullivan, in an online column about the Web, says much the same when he describes a change in the user population from a "more technically-minded and thus perhaps slightly more tolerant" audience to one that is now "increasingly impatient with and less tolerant of 'elaborate,' error-prone, overloaded designs" ("As Simple as Possible"). For an example of the problem in action, see the sidebar entitled "Not His Typing" on pages 92–93 (Laskas).

Stating a slightly different view in his book *The Inmates Are Running the Asylum,* Alan Cooper claims that most users are neither novices nor experts, although all users start as novices. The great middle group he calls the "perpetual intermediates." Although the novices and the experts are a fluid group, the perpetual intermediates tend to remain in this middle category for a long time (182–83). The question is, who are these users?

Since users are the great unknown for many developers, it would behoove developers to get in touch with users directly and learn from them about their needs, wants, and desires. When developers talk to users, observe them at work, ask questions about their goals and objectives, and analyze what they learn, they can begin to get an understanding of important issues that will affect design. Failure to do this can lead to disaster, as Norman explains, using the famous case of Thomas Edison's failed invention of the phonograph. Edison made decisions based on engineering principles and what he felt users would want. For engineering reasons, he decided to use the cylinder for recordings because it was the best technical solution. His competitor chose the disk, it being much easier to store, handle, stack, and label. However, when Edison later gave in to the preferred design, he made his needle track differently from that of the competitor's model, making their records incompatible (think of the Beta and VHS versions of VCRs in the early days). Edison also believed that buyers wouldn't be able to notice any real differences in sound quality between well-known performers and unknowns, so he saved money by making recordings of unknown performers. The customers, nevertheless, wanted to hear their favorite musicians, especially when the recordings of the unknown performers cost about the same as those of the famous ones. Edison failed because he miscalculated the needs, wants, and desires of his users. RCA Victor succeeded, and the rest is history.

For a more recent example of a problem caused by decisions made without learning the wishes of users, take the case of AuctionWatch.com, a site that attracts hundreds of thousands of visitors a month. When it redesigned its site, it faced a user revolt on the Monday the new site launched. As reported in the *San Jose Mercury News*, "Though AuctionWatch had warned users that changes were coming, the company didn't ask for their input or test any of the new additions—a slightly dangerous move for a firm whose business model rests on user loyalty" (Janah). Users complained that the advertising had gotten bigger at the expense of readability, that the new format was harder to use, and that some of their favorite features on the site had been eliminated. The company president said that the company "understands the importance of its users," but perhaps not well enough to understand the need to check with them before making major changes.

The point of these examples and all that we have discussed about users is that it is essential to adopt the following mantra: "Know thy user, for he is not thyself" (Rubinstein and Hersh 8). No one can speak for the user but the user. With this understanding of who the user is *not*, as well as a methodology for learning who the user is, we turn in the next section to a discussion of methods to learn about users' tasks and goals.

What You Can Learn About Users' Tasks and Goals

In addition to learning about the needs, wishes, and desires of users and the environments in which they work, you can also learn about the tasks they perform and the goals they have. Users' tasks are not necessarily users' goals. Tasks are things

Not His Typing

Jeanne Marie Laskas

MY FATHER CALLS. "Can you help me?" he says in an exasperated tone. "I'm trying to order a book for your mother on the computer."

"Of course," I say. "Where are you now?"

He's quiet for a moment. "Where am I?" he says. "I'm on the phone with you. I'm sitting here."

"No, I mean, where are you? On your computer."

"Oh," he says.

My mother picks up the phone. "IS THERE SOMETHING WRONG?" she asks me.

"Please don't shout!" my father says.

"Your father said he could get this book for me," she says. "But he's been at this an hour now and, oh, I don't know, can you help him?"

"Of course," I say. It's interesting to note that she has not asked me to help her, seeing as this is, after all, a book she wants. My father is my mother's link to the Internet. Technology is not her . . . thing. I don't think my father likes being my mother's link to the Internet. This brave new world is, to him, still very new. He feels anything but brave.

My mother hangs up, and my father tells me the history of his problem. He managed to find www.amazon.com. He even found the book. "And I clicked on 'order,'" he explains. "It said I needed to set up an account. I clicked on 'okay.' It asked me for my name and address. I put that in. And then it asked for 'company name.' I don't have a company name."

"Well, you just tab through that," I say.

"Tab through?"

"Yeah."

"What's tab through?"

"Push the tab button on your keyboard. It will skip to the next box."

"Oh. See, they don't tell you that."

No, they don't. Keyboard control is, by now, intuitive to those of us who spend our days with computers. So intuitive that it's hard to conceive of its not being intuitive.

"Well, where are you now?" I ask him.

Pause again.

"Dad, on the computer," I say. My father is an intelligent man. One of those people who skipped a couple of grades. He sailed through medical school. Computer literacy has nothing to do with intelligence, and he is living proof.

"I know that's what you meant," he says. "But I don't know where I am. I pushed 'help' and now the whole bookstore is gone."

---

that users do: steps they must take, processes they must complete, acts they must perform—to achieve a goal or objective. Developers sometimes focus on the tasks and lose sight of the users' goals. See the sidebar on page 94, a spoof on the General Motors Helpline, for a humorous example of the confusion that results when the task of "driving" is confused with the goal of "going places" in a car.

Users are primarily interested in attaining their goal; the task is the means to the end. When the task interferes with the users' goal or makes it hard to accomplish the goal, users become frustrated. By observing users performing their tasks and listening to them to learn what their goals are, you can understand ways to match what users want to accomplish, while minimizing those factors that delay or prevent them from reaching their goal.

"You must have pushed 'help' on your browser," I say. "That's not the help you need."

"I'm supposed to know what kind of help I need? Doesn't that say something is wrong with the help—not me?"

"It does."

"I mean help is . . . help. Or it should be."

"It should," I say. Everything he's saying makes sense. Just sense in a different realm. It's strange to think how two people can speak the same language, but not the same language at all. It's strange to think how this great era of telecommunications, the future that promised to bring people closer together, has put a chasm between my father and me.

And he, at least, owns a computer. He knows how to turn the thing on. He's an entire world ahead of my mother. My mother and I couldn't even begin the conversation my father and I are attempting to have.

"Okay, Dad," I say, "here's what I'm going to do. I'm going to go into amazon.com and I'm going to be you."

"You're going to be me?"

"Yeah, just give me your screen name and your password, and I'll be you, and I'll place the order."

"But ,— "

"It's okay, Dad."

I can tell he feels as though I'm asking him to cheat. My father is a man of integrity. He plays by the rules. He is a person who places a high value on never misrepresenting oneself to anyone, anywhere. How do I explain to him that there is no anyone, no anywhere, not even a oneself in this new land he's tiptoeing through?

My mother picks up the phone. "JOHN," she yells, "WHY DON'T WE JUST GO TO THE BOOKSTORE? I mean, if this is so . . . difficult."

"It's not difficult!" he says. "Please hang up the phone." Then, to me: "Okay, you go in and be me." It's ego pressure, pure and simple.

I click this, click that. "I'm just writing in your address," I say, narrating my every move like a surgeon trying to reassure the patient. When the order is complete, I give him his confirmation number. He thanks me. He says he'll call me again if he gets stuck.

"Oh, but as long as I have you," he says. "Can you just tell me how I double-space when I write a letter?"

"Sure," I say. "What are you using?"

Pause. "What am I using? The computer."

And so I settle in for what is going to be a long conversation, thinking how nice it is to spend some time with my dad.

Source: Originally published in the *Washington Post Magazine*, Oct. 10, 1999, by Jeanne Marie Laskas. Used with permission.

Cooper divides goals into four basic categories, with examples of each, as shown in Table 3.3 on page 95. He explains that a close parallel exists between corporate goals and personal goals, and both must be satisfied: "Software that fails to achieve either one will fail. Software that fails to achieve the personal goals of its user may not fail at first, but it won't earn loyalty from its customers, and will be very vulnerable to competition that does" ("Goal-Directed Design").

To learn about users' tasks, you need to understand how information or tasks flow for an individual user as well as what happens as the process moves across boundaries from one department to another. You can't get at users' goals merely by asking them, because they may not be able to tell you. Instead, you must first observe users, then talk to them, and match what they tell you with what you see

General Motors Helpline

Helpline: "General Motors Helpline, how can I help you?"
Customer: "Hi, I just bought my first car, and I chose your car because it has automatic transmission, cruise control, power steering, power brakes, and power door locks."
Helpline: "Thank you for buying our car. How can I help you?"
Customer: "How does it work?"
Helpline: "Do you know how to drive?"
Customer: "Do I know how to what?"
Helpline: "Do you know how to drive?"
Customer: "I'm not a technical person! I just want to go places in my car!"

and comprehend. For each task, you will want to gather information from the categories shown in Table 3.4 on page 96 (Faulkner 98).

This method of studying and learning from users about their goals and the tasks they perform to reach their goals not only produces products that satisfy and please users, but also products that contain the features they want and not the features they don't want. Products that fail to satisfy users' personal goals have led to the rise of the "Dummies" books, which generated $121 million in revenue in 1998.

Making the site visit meaningful requires planning and understanding which options you want to use to gather the information you need about users and their goals. In the next section, we look at planning and conducting the site visit.

Planning a Site Visit

When you plan a site visit, you have a number of options to choose from, some of which can be used in combination. These include:

- Shadowing a user for a day, which means following a user like his or her shadow to see where the user goes, what the user does, and how the user performs tasks to accomplish goals.
- Questioning users while they work, which involves watching and talking to users in their own work or home environment. Make notes about where users start and end tasks, what happens next, and whether users accomplish goals. Review these notes with the user to determine if you got it right from the user's point of view.
- Talking after the task, which allows the users to complete a task without interruption and then respond to questions you have about what you observed.
- Think aloud, which is a term you'll see most frequently associated with usability testing, but which can be used on site visits by asking users to speak their thoughts about what they are doing to help you understand what

TABLE 3.3	The Goal Stack
Goal	**Examples**
False goals: common in the software industry and easily achieved by programmers' ignoring the user and focusing on the requirements of the code	Save memory Save keystrokes Easy to learn Safeguard data integrity Speed up data entry Increase efficiency of program execution Use cool technology or features Increase graphic beauty Maintain consistency across platforms
Corporate goals: important to the corporation but not necessarily so for the people doing the work	Increase profit Increase market share Defeat our competition Hire more people Offer more products or services Go public
Practical goals: the bridge between the company's goals and the user's goals	Avoid meetings Handle client demands Record the client's order Create a paper model of the business
Personal goals: true for everyone; when users are made to feel stupid, their self-esteem drops and with it productivity drops	Not feel stupid Not make mistakes Get an adequate amount of work done Have fun (or at least not be too bored)

Source: Adapted from Alan Cooper, "Goal-Directed Design." 25 June 1996 <http://www.cooper.com/articles/drdobbs_goal_directed.html>.

they're thinking as they perform their jobs. This is very tiring for the user, and unnatural, so it is not the most common technique used.

- Critical incident technique, which asks users to explain everything they would do to perform a process or "critical incident." This technique is used when it isn't appropriate to observe the user performing the task, because of the sensitive nature of the task (privacy between doctor and patient, for instance) or because the task isn't performed everyday.
- Scenarios and role play, which provide another means, like the critical incident technique, of seeing what would happen in a particular situation. You might play the part of the customer or the patient, for instance. Critical incident information can be used to create a scenario or role play.
- Cued recall, which requires getting permission to videotape users performing tasks, so that you can review the tape with them afterward and discuss what they were doing or thinking at certain points. This technique can also

TABLE 3.4	Categories of Information to Learn About Tasks
Category of Information	Questions to Answer
The inputs to the task	What information is needed? What are the characteristics of the information sources? What is the availability of the information? What possible errors might occur? Who or what initiates the task?
The outputs from the task	What is the performance criteria? What happens to the output? How does the task performer get feedback about task performance?
The transformations	What is the nature of the decision making? What strategies exist for decision making? What skills are needed? What interruptions are likely to occur and when?
The task composition of the particular job	How often is the task done and when? Does the task depend on any other task? What is normal/abnormal work load? What controls does the task performer have over workload?

Source: Adapted from Christine Faulkner, *The Essence of Human-Computer Interaction*. Englewood Cliffs, NJ: Prentice Hall, 1998, p. 98.

be useful when it's not possible to interview the user immediately after observing the task being performed.

Figure 3.1 is a checklist for planning the materials to take on a site visit.

Asking Questions

Whenever you're using a technique in which you ask questions, you must be careful to ask questions that do not suggest an answer or that do not restrict the response.

Avoid asking "leading" questions, in which you suggest the response you want to get. For instance, leading questions might be, "Did you like the way the software performed?" or "Why didn't you use the online help?"

Instead ask, "What was your opinion about the way the software performed?" or "I noticed that you didn't use the online help. Can you tell me how you solve problems or find information?" By asking neutral questions, you allow the user to answer in his or her own words.

Ask open-ended questions, rather than closed questions. A closed question receives a limited response or a controlled (yes/no) response. Examples of closed questions are: "How many years have you been using this product?" or "Do you

Check	Material
Audio and videotape recording	
	equipment for video recording (perhaps a portable lab that includes camera, scan converter, recorder, microphones, cables, tripod)
	videotapes (check the correct format)
	power strip
	extension cord
	audio recorder
	tapes for audio recorder
	batteries for audio recorder
	extra batteries for microphones
	still camera, if you want photographs of environments, for example NOTE: Always ask permission before you take pictures.
	film for still camera
	extra batteries for still camera
Note taking	
	laptop with cables for plugging it in and extra battery
	diskettes for backing up files
	notebook if taking notes on paper
	pencils, pens
	portable printer with cords and cable if you want to print while on the road
	paper for the portable printer
Papers and other materials for working with users	
	folder for each participant
	copy of correspondence that went to that site
	release form for each participant at site (and extras)
	information from recruiting or screening questionnaire
	user profile questionnaires (take extras in case you talk to other users)
	other lists, questionnaires, forms, scenarios, or props for planned activities
	supplies for doing a group activity to capture a large process flow (for workflow analysis): poster paper, colored markers, color sticky notes (if you are going to use this technique)

Figure 3.1 Checklist for planning materials for a site visit

(From the work of Janice Redish, Redish and Associates, Inc., <http://www.stcsig.org/usability/resources>, or redish@ari.net.)

use the spreadsheet application of this product?" Open-ended questions allow the user to share information more broadly and freely. By asking open-ended questions, you frequently learn a lot more than you anticipated. Examples of open-ended questions include: "How would you describe your experience level using this product?" or "Which applications of this product do you use?"

Illustrations from Site Visits

Site visits can teach you a lot about what's important to users so that you don't eliminate something they need and want, while you're contemplating "improving" or upgrading a product. Several examples from site visits illustrate the value of learning what's important to users. For instance, what if your company is thinking of doing away with print documentation in favor of online documentation? How do you know whether this is a good decision? A site visit can show you. In one case, a company had two distinct groups of users of the documentation: system administrators and programmers. Documentation was a combination of print and online information. However, when these two groups were studied in the context of their work, the company learned that when the system administrators were troubleshooting problems, they would spread out half a dozen different books on their desk so that they were sure they were taking into account everything they needed to. Online help would have made it much more difficult for them to do the same thing. On the other hand, the programmers typically had a specific question about a particular function, which could be answered most quickly with the online help and which then enabled the programmers to get quickly back to making the changes in the code ("Making Online Information Usable").

In another situation, the design team was working on a network diagnostic system for a nationwide communications company. The team assumed that a nationwide map showing the network connections would be the appropriate display for the network. When they made their site visit, they learned that the company organizes the network according to customer accounts, not geographic location, because their first priority was to know who was experiencing a problem so that they could contact the customer, rather than where the problem was occurring (Wixon and Comstock). Of course, unexpected surprises can change your plans, as the sidebar by Robi Gunn, entitled "Field Trials: Trials and Tribulations of a Field Visit" shows (pages 100–101). However, even in those situations where everything does not go as planned, you can learn a lot.

So far, we've discussed ways to get information about users in the context of their workspace. A growing market is information appliances in the home. Some companies now make it a priority to conduct site visits in people's homes to learn about this environment and the user's needs. When they fail to learn what users want from information appliances, they may end up with products users may desire but can't use, as Dave Barry so aptly describes:

> ... Here is what really concerns me about these new "smart" appliances. Even if we like the features, we won't be able to use them. We can't use the appliance features we have *now*. I have a feature-packed telephone with 43 buttons, at least 20 of which I am afraid to touch. This phone probably can communicate with the dead, but I don't know how to operate it, just as I don't know how to operate my TV, which has features out the wazooty and requires *three* remote controls. ... And now the appliance manufacturers want to give us even *more* features. (D8)

If it isn't possible to see users in their home, a few techniques for getting feedback from them can add a lot to your understanding of their needs. You can set up phone surveys in advance and plan a task with the user, then phone the user and ask the user to tell you what he or she is doing while performing the task. With software or hardware that is already in use, this approach gives you information about the features people use and don't use, as well as what they like or dislike about the product. If the product is software, the user can send screen captures ahead to discuss problems, or you and the user can have the software open together so that you can see what the user is talking about.

Point-of-sale research is also an excellent source of information about consumer products. If you are planning to develop a product that will compete with others already in the marketplace, you can go to the place where shoppers would buy such a product and watch what they do. Using contextual inquiry, you can interview people at the point of a purchasing decision to find out what motivated them to buy a particular product. What did they find compelling? What expectations do they have for the product? For its documentation? If the product is available for practice, what did they try out?

Constraints on Doing Site Visits

It is easy to see the advantages of doing site visits. So, why aren't they a routine part of the development process? Well, for one, there is cost involved: the cost of traveling to the site, plus lodging and food while there, the cost of lost productivity at work while you're at the site, not to mention the cost of analyzing and presenting the mounds of data you'll take back to the office following a site visit. One consulting group estimates the time required to perform this analysis as four hours of analysis time for every one hour on site ("Contextual Enquiry"). Another reason that some companies don't do site visits is that designers frequently don't give sufficient credence to their value, thinking they already know about the users from other sources like marketing, surveys, and technical support, or worse, thinking that the users are like themselves.

In addition, many companies are slow to realize the full spectrum of activities that encompass user-centered design. Ehrlich and Rohn (76–78) describe four stages of acceptance of user-centered design: from skepticism to partnership (see Table 3.5 on page 102). Some companies are still stuck in Stage 1. Even companies that are in Stage 3 may include usability testing as part of their standard development process, but they have not yet attained Stage 4, where they understand the importance of involving customers or users before development begins.

Even with companies that have reached Stage 4, certain constraints have to be recognized when going into the field to do research about users and tasks:

- *Time constraints.* Users or customers can spare only a limited amount of time, and your company can spare only a limited amount of your time away from the office. Careful planning is critical to make a site visit a success, as time is of the essence.
- *Budget constraints.* Even with funding for site visits, the number of observations and interviews will be limited by both time and budget. Again, planning is the key to maximizing the opportunity.

Field Trials: Trials and Tribulations of a Field Visit
Robi Gunn

Both Feet First

I was excited. After two years of documenting an application, I was finally flying out to meet some real live users and observe how they used our product, and if I was lucky, how they used our documentation.

I dutifully and eagerly prepared myself for the visit. I read books and STC articles on field visits and questionnaires. I was on a quest, and dangerously close to realizing a dream. At last, I would be able to define my audience, and gage the usability of the online help and hard copy manual. I would finally get the answers to my questions directly from a group of users.

My goal has always been to write meaningful documentation, that is, meaningful from the users' perspective. At work I had asked questions and tried to determine who that elusive average user is, and what information the average user likely requires. I never got a sense that this had been previously defined, or that anyone could really give me that vital information. So I did what most of us do; I guessed. I tried to imagine what the average user was like, and then write for that person. Now that I was going to meet some users, they could confirm that my guesses had been correct, or provide me with the information I needed to refocus the documentation to fit their needs. This was the first and most important piece of the puzzle for me. From there, it would be smooth sailing with just a few adjustments and fine tuning (I hoped). I couldn't wait to hear what they thought of the documentation.

Ground Zero

"What do you mean you didn't know that there was documentation?" I said it calmly and politely, but that little voice inside my head was shrieking. How in the world had these people used our product for two years and not been aware that there was documentation?

Besides providing hard copy manuals and online help, we had just recently placed all our documentation on a web site and created a CD. It was a shock to me that they could have gone two years without realizing that there was documentation. More mysterious yet, they had documentation at their fingertips, literally one keystroke away. I would have thought that at some point during the two years, someone would have randomly (accidentally?) pressed the F1 key. In two years, no one was ever curious enough to wonder what that help menu was, or what that help icon on the screen might do if you clicked on it?

It felt like a bomb had been dropped. I had flown out to meet the users, observe them using the product, and interview them about the documentation to establish a baseline. I was acutely aware that I was now standing at ground zero. I put away my carefully prepared folder of questions and research. It no longer had any meaning. I quickly came to the conclusion that I would have to go backwards before I could go forward.

■ *Political and ethical constraints.* It's difficult to be in someone's workspace or home for very long, and you will never be invisible, so your presence puts a strain on the companies or families that agree to host you and on the individuals you'll be observing. You may also be observing sensitive information that will require your being discreet. You must also get permission to

Plan B

So instead, I began to demonstrate the online help. Prior to the visit, an agenda had been established that included meeting with various departments. During each meeting I gave a presentation of the basic features of the online help: Contents page, Index, Full Text Search feature, and context sensitivity. I indicated what procedures were documented and how they would typically (still just my best guess) use the online help to answer their questions. I got a great response. Most of the users seemed happy to find out that there was documentation, and the initial reaction was that it was "pretty good stuff." I also got the names and phone numbers of users that I could contact at a future date, and I promised to send copies of the manual and CD. I also gave them the URL for our web site, but found that there was some question if they had access to it because of security on their firewall. I thanked them for their time and interest, and headed back home.

Meanwhile, back at the ranch . . .

On the flight back, I mulled over how I would present this information to my boss. I concluded that it was a step in the right direction to find out the truth, regardless of how painful that truth turned out to be. I had established a baseline; it was just several hundred feet farther back than I had previously assumed. I had re-learned that valuable lesson: never assume anything. I also concluded that you have to start somewhere, and at least now we knew where that starting point was. A very important benefit from the trip: I had established contacts for the future. We could continue our mission to provide documentation that the users wanted.

Back at home, I sent copies of the manuals and CDs. I wrote thank you notes to our hosts. Then I began to follow up.

I verified how manuals are ordered and shipped. I confirmed that we had our processes in place, and that they were being followed. No problems there.

I collaborated with our Training Department. When the class for this product was taught, I made arrangements to provide pizza during a working lunch so that I had an opportunity to introduce and demonstrate the online help. Online help is now a regular part of the course. At the end of class for any product, all students now receive a copy of the documentation CD. In addition, the Publications Department is now registering documentation to get a handle on "who" has "what" documentation and we have started sending questionnaires.

I am planning to follow up with the contacts that I made now that they have had a chance to use the documentation. I will probably retool the questions that I had developed for the original visit into a questionnaire to send to them. A repeat trip to follow up and show our commitment to our users wouldn't be a bad idea either. What is more flattering to a user, or demonstrates more interest, than to seek input from them? And with that input, you really can write meaningful documentation, which is all I ever wanted to do.

Well, it's about six months since I made my field visit. I'm not where I want to be, and I'm not where I expected that I'd be, but I am hopeful about the future. I have an old plaque that says: "The longest journey starts with the first step." I have begun.

Source: Reprinted from *Usability Interface* (Oct. 1998). <http://www.stcsig.org/usability>.

take photographs, set up video cameras, or audiotape, and you must explain what you will do with the information you gather and record.

Although these constraints limit some direct access to users in their environments, an increasing number of companies that adopt a user-centered design

TABLE 3.5	Four States of Acceptance of User-Centered Design
Stage 1: Skepticism	Typifies organizations that have never been involved in user-centered design (UCD). They fear such processes will delay product development; they tend to focus on product features and schedule deadlines.
Stage 2: Curiosity	Companies recognize that their products need help and they become curious about what UCD can offer.
Stage 3: Acceptance	UCD people are on the development team.
Stage 4: Partnership	The organization has a high-level commitment to UCD, which includes getting customers involved early in the process.

Source: Adapted from Kate Ehrlich and Janice Anne Rohn, "Cost-Justification Usability of Engineering: A Vendor's Perspective," *Cost-Justifying Usability.* Eds. Randolph G. Bias and Deborah J. Mayhew. Boston: Academic Press, 1994, pp. 76–78.

process recognize the need for design team members to go on site. If you work for one of these companies, you may be overwhelmed with all the data you gather from a site visit and wonder what to do with it. In the next section, we examine your options for using the information.

What Happens After a Site Visit

When you return from a site visit, you will be armed with a rich load of information that has to be digested and shared with other members of the development group. If you received permission to record your site visits using audiotape, you can create a transcript of your interviews from the audiotapes. If you received permission to videotape, you can edit the videotapes into a highlights tape to show the development team the key issues discovered from the site visit. If you have taken photographs, they can be a useful reminder of the environment in which users work. In addition, you may have received permission to take *artifacts*, the objects that users create or assemble to help them perform their tasks. Artifacts may include sticky notes that users post as reminders to help them work with an existing product, self-created templates or quick reference cards, or books like the "Dummies" titles that users rely on when the documentation isn't clear or isn't available to them.

You will probably write a report to share your findings with the rest of the development team. In the report, you will want to include:

- User analysis, which leads to the creation of user profiles.
- Task analysis, which leads to task lists.
- Environment analysis, which leads to the development of constraints on how users work (such as noise levels, visibility, space requirements, interruptions, etc.).
- Methodology used for data-gathering.
- Recommendations for further research, which often includes a survey to get a larger response regarding issues learned from the site visit.

This report, along with the artifacts you bring back from the field, and the photographs, audio transcripts and video highlights, will prepare the team to begin the process of product development.

Cooper recommends using this information to create *personas* that bring users to life and thus help developers design products that truly match the goals of different levels of users. These personas do not represent the generic "user," which Cooper claims is so vague and loosely defined that it gives developers license to keep adding features and making decisions that the supposed user would want. Rather, Cooper's personas are intended to speak for specific users, each with a name, a car, a family, a job, a residence, and a life. To bring them to life, he purchases faces for each user from stock photo files or from the Web. According to Cooper, "Personas are the single most powerful design tool that we use" (*Inmates* 130). At every meeting, each member of the design team, as well as the client, is handed a sheet with the cast of these characters. All questions are posed in light of what Mary or Bill or Julio or Nobuku would want, not what the "user" wants. Some companies using this concept take it a step farther and make posters of their users, which they put up on the walls of the meeting room. One company makes t-shirts of the personas to be worn by different members of the development team. Others put up quotes received from users during site visits with pictures of the users working, as well as flowcharts of work processes.

In addition to creating personas, Cooper recommends creating *scenarios* to focus on the tasks users perform as they work to accomplish their goals. These scenarios are based on the personas, which are generated after studying users in the field. Scenarios are of two types:

- *Daily-use scenarios,* which reflect the primary actions users will perform most often.
- *Necessary-use scenarios,* which include all the actions that must be performed, although typically infrequently.

Because daily-use scenarios reflect uses that must be learned by all, they must be simple and intuitive for new users and they must also allow shortcuts and customization once users become more proficient. Necessary-use scenarios may be more numerous but they won't need customization, as they are used infrequently. Scenarios and personas provide a means to personalize both users and usage, based on what is learned from site visits. In this way, the knowledge from site visits isn't lost or generalized, but stays focused on developing products that match users doing real tasks to attain real goals.

Knowing about the users and the tasks they perform is the critical first step, but before we leave this subject, we must also establish a basis for product development that reflects the ways in which users learn. In the next section, we take up the subject of users' learning, so as to be able to apply this information in creating products that match users' learning styles as well as their goals.

How Users Learn

In addition to what you can learn from users by studying them in their environments, there is much that can be applied from research on how users learn new products. This research derives largely from the field of cognitive psychology, the science that studies the way people perceive and remember things, how they store information, and how they organize and retrieve that information when they need it. In this section, we look at some of the aspects of short- and long-term memory, followed by a discussion of learning styles, the specific needs of adult learners, and the research on minimalism and adult learners.

Short- and Long-Term Memory

As learners and users of information, we store information in either short-term memory for immediate use or long-term memory for later or continual use. A well-known outcome of cognitive research is the rule of 7, plus or minus 2, which holds that people can retain seven pieces of information in short-term memory, plus or minus two pieces (Miller). Thus, we can remember 5 to 9 numbers, 5 to 9 items in a list, 5 to 9 steps to perform a task, and so forth. When the U.S. Postal Service attempted to change zip codes from 5 digits to zip + 4, they reached the maximum number that the brain can store readily in short-term memory for immediate recall. Even at this upper limit, it is hard for many to remember the extra four numbers, so they don't use them. The same problem occurs in some large metropolitan areas, where users have to remember different areas codes for phone numbers in the same city. This requires users to dial 10 numbers to make a call, thereby exceeding the normal retention rate for short-term memory.

For long-term memory, research shows that we develop a *schema*, or pattern of action and behavior, that allows us to plug new information into one of our already familiar patterns or to modify the pattern as needed to fit the new information. When we find ourselves faced with a pattern that does not match one of our existing schema, we have to create a new mental model. With a new experience, however, we use as much as we can from what we already know to help us learn something new. When reading or hearing new information, one very important tool we use to fit the new information into a pre-existing mental model is vocabulary. Hearing or seeing words for which we know the meaning helps us use these to unlock new meaning. Of course, problems arise when familiar words are used in new or different ways or when words are misinterpreted because the user's schema does not match the new situation. The following humorous example points up the problem:

> A man and a woman walk into a bar and order a drink for every person in the bar. They are very happy. When the bartender asks them why they are so happy, they reply:
>
> "We finished a jigsaw puzzle in only two months."
>
> "Two months?" the bartender exclaimed, "it's not supposed to take that long."
>
> "That's not true," said the woman, "It said 2 to 4 years on the box."

For more in the same vein, see the sidebar entitled "Communication Gap."

Turning to real-world examples, take the case of the graduate student who was not a seasoned Web user, but who was required to study a Web site and report on its usability. He chose the Sony Web site, because he was interested in purchasing a camcorder. He hadn't purchased Sony products before and didn't know much about the features of its camcorders or any camcorder, for that matter, so he

Communication Gap

A judge was interviewing a woman regarding her pending divorce, and asked, "What are the grounds for the divorce?"

She replied, "About four acres and a nice little house in the middle of the property with a stream running by."

"No," he said, "I mean what is the foundation of this case?"

"It is made of concrete, with brick and mortar," she responded.

"I mean," he continued, "What are your relations like?"

"I have an aunt and an uncle living here in town, and so do my husband's parents."

He said, "Do you have a real grudge?"

"No," she replied, "We have a two-car carport and have never really needed one."

"Please," he tried again, "is there any infidelity in your marriage?"

"Yes, both my son and daughter have stereo sets. We don't necessarily like the music, but the answer to your question is yes."

"Ma'am, does your husband ever beat you up?"

"Yes," she responded, "about twice a week he gets up earlier than I do."

Finally, in frustration, the judge asked, "Lady, why do you want a divorce?"

"Oh, I don't want a divorce," she replied. "I've never wanted a divorce. My husband does. He said he can't communicate with me."

---

began his search by clicking on "My First Sony Products," reasoning that this would be the place to go for someone who hadn't bought Sony products before. Much to his surprise, but of no surprise to his classmates with children, he found himself at a page of children's products. Clearly, his mental model (and corresponding vocabulary) did not support Sony's model, which used its own marketing metaphor—"My First Sony"—on the assumption that visitors to the site would already be familiar with its meaning. For more examples of problems with vocabulary, see the sidebar on page 106 entitled "Computer Illiteracy," which has been widely circulated on the Internet (Carlton). Although some of these examples may be dated, they are still representative of the problems users typically experience when their schema does not match that of the product.

Experience affects how easily we may want to create new schema, based on our memory of previous pleasure or pain with similar situations. For instance, if we have a negative experience with learning a particular software product or trying to use a particular manual or online help system, we are likely to feel negative about learning how to use another similar product or going back to the manual or online help for future support. Thus, emotions play a significant role in our desire to learn about new products or have new experiences. Motivation also plays an important role in our enthusiasm for learning and our willingness to struggle through complex processes to gain knowledge of a tool or acquire a skill.

When it comes to readers of documentation, whether in print or online, we know from studies that readers:

- Use documents as tools
- Decide how much attention to pay to a document

Computer Illiteracy

- An exasperated caller to Dell Computer Tech Support couldn't get her new Dell computer turned on. After ensuring the computer was plugged in, the technician asked her what happened when she pushed the power button. Her response, "I've pushed and pushed on this foot pedal and nothing happens." The "foot pedal" turned out to be the computer's mouse.
- Another customer called Compaq Tech Support to say that her brand-new computer wouldn't work. She said she unpacked the unit, plugged it in, and sat there for 20 minutes waiting for something to happen. When asked what happened when she pressed the power switch, she asked, "What power switch?"
- Compaq is considering changing the command "Press Any Key" to "Press Return Key" because of the flood of calls asking where the "Any" key is.
- An AST customer was asked to send in a copy of her defective diskettes. A few days later a letter arrived from the customer, along with photocopies of the floppies.
- A Dell customer called to complain that his keyboard no longer worked. He cleaned it by filling up his tub with soap and water and soaking the keyboard for a day, then removing all the keys and washing them individually.
- A Dell technician received a call from a customer who was enraged because his computer had told him he was "bad and invalid." The technician explained that the computer's "bad command" and "invalid" response shouldn't be taken personally.

Source: Adapted from Jim Carlton, "Computers: Befuddled PC Users Flood Help Lines, and No Question Seems to Be Too Basic." *The Wall Street Journal*, 1 Mar. 1994, p. B1.

- Jump into documents (there is no shared "starting point") even when documents are labeled "read me first"
- Need to find information easily when they want it (navigation is critical to their success)
- Formulate a question
- Skim, skip, and read only as far as they think they must to get the answer to their question (even stopping mid-sentence)

On this last point, I have observed participants in usability tests of documentation reading only part of a sentence and then acting. The result is that the context of an additional chunk of information, which follows a command, is missed by the user. Because users will read only as far as they think they need to, they will tend to stop reading when they receive an instruction or command before they know what the result will be.

Writing documentation that is structured in this fashion is a violation of the *given-new* contract (Haviland and Clark; reported in Redish "Understanding Readers" 31). The given-new contract is the expectation people have that new information will be presented in a framework that is already known or has previously been given. At the sentence level, it means that readers get the contextual or known information first, followed by the new or resulting action. Using this pattern, the user can decide whether he or she wants to perform the step before doing so. One research study found that when readers get the new information before the given or contextual information, they can choose to do one of two things:

- Put the new information in a "buffer" until they get the context of use to understand it
- Guess at the context and act without waiting

The readers in the study jumped the gun and acted (Dixon 1987; reported in Redish "Understanding Readers" 33). From my observations of usability tests of the documentation, I can confirm that readers jump the gun frequently, as the following examples show:

- After apparently reading only the first five words of the instruction for inserting the diskette, the user said, "You don't tell me where."
- After apparently reading only the first six words of an instruction asking the user to click yes or no, the user clicked "no" and said, "Nothing's happening here. You need to tell me how long this is gonna take."
- After apparently reading the first seven words of an instruction to conclude a task, the user asked, "How do I know if I'm done?"

In all three cases, the information the user sought followed the command, but the users stopped reading and jumped the gun as soon as they identified an action they could take.

In screen design, the given-new contract applies to a consistent design, so that users will see new screens in the context of a familiar pattern from previous screens. For instance, boxes that contain choices should be presented in the same order on every screen. If users are accustomed to clicking in the lower left to go back and the lower right to go forward, they will be confused if the order changes or a different element is introduced. As well, screen design should match users' normal task flow. If tasks move from left to right, the screen should reflect that process. The Next or OK button should be on the far right as the logical place where the user ends up. If the task moves from top to bottom, the Next or OK button should be at the bottom of the screen.

In addition to these memory and consistency issues and the impact they have on learning, we must also consider the different ways in which people learn, a subject we explore in the next section.

Learning Styles

People are different, and so are the ways in which they learn. Learning styles can be characterized in the following four ways:

1. Doing
2. Imagining
3. Reasoning
4. Theorizing

The characteristics of each of these learning styles are presented in Table 3.6 (Coe 57).

TABLE 3.6	Characteristics of the Four Learning Styles		
Doing	**Imagining**	**Reasoning**	**Theorizing**
Relies on experiments and plans	Relies on imagination	Relies on deductive reasoning	Relies on theoretical models and inductive reasoning
Enjoys new experiences	Views experiences from multiple perspectives	Prefers hypothetical experiences	Tries to integrate disparate experiences
Takes risks	Brainstorms before acting	Acts in narrow, prescribed manner	Thinks of risks at an abstract level
Adapts to circumstances	Internalizes circumstances	Does not adapt well to changes in circumstances	Raises circumstances to theoretical level
Uses trial and error for problem solving	Relies on insight for problem solving	Uses hypotheses for problem solving	Relies on syllogistic reasoning for problem solving
Is at ease with people	Is people-oriented	Is not at ease with people	Is at ease with people on a theoretical level
Is impatient	Likes to counsel people	Has narrow technical interests	More concerned with sound logic than facts
Excels in marketing or sales	Excels in human resources and counseling	Excels in engineering	Excels in research and development

Source: Marlana Coe, *Human Factors for Technical Communicators*, 1996, p. 57. © 1996 John Wiley & Sons, Inc. (Reprinted by permission of John Wiley & Sons, Inc.)

Which learning style is yours? Which is your user's style? Obviously, one style does not fit all. Therefore, you must provide various ways for people to learn. Some want to learn by a tutorial or guided tour, some (although few) read the documentation first as a method of learning, some want to explore (using help when they need it), others like wizards (which present dialog boxes that ask questions or allow users to select options to perform a process). Still others want to be left alone, trusting that the interface will be understandable because it will match a mental model of previous action or will make sense intuitively.

When users skip the tutorial or don't read the manual, they are typically motivated by "the paradox of the active user" (based on research by Carroll and Rosson; reported in Nielsen, "Paradox"), which means that they are driven to be productive, to learn by doing, not by reading. Their goal is "throughput," the outcome, even if the method they choose to learn the product is less efficient than going through the manual or using the tutorial. Thus, the paradox. It does no good to instruct users to read the manual, as Figure 3.2, which represents a sticker on a VCR, does. Users make their own choices, based on their learning style.

> BE SMART!
> Read your MANUAL first.
> Save trouble later.

Figure 3.2 Sticker placed on new VCR

If help is available, active users rely on it, but the time spent getting to the right information when they need it is "downtime," not productive time, since it doesn't contribute to the completion of the task or the accomplishment of the goal. Because we know this about active users, we can decrease the downtime expended when we know the words they will use to search a help file to find the answers they seek. If the help topics are categorized by the features of the tool and not by the tasks that users want to accomplish, help will not be helpful, because the terminology of the tool is not known to the user. For instance, if the user wants to write an email message, "compose" (the word used by MSN's Hotmail) may not register as the place to go for this task.

Objects, particularly on-screen objects that are part of a graphical user interface (GUI), communicate to users by providing one or more of the following four "clues" about their use (Coe 167–68):

- *Affordances.* The actual and perceived properties of an object that suggest how we should interact with it. A chair's affordance is its "sitability."
- *Constraints.* The properties of an object that limit what we can do with it. We can stand in a chair to reach the top of the refrigerator (nothing in its design prevents this), but we can't use it to boil water (the design does not accommodate this objective).
- *Mappings.* The properties that suggest how we should interact with or use it. A door with a plate on it (and no handle) suggests that you push it open.
- *Visibility.* The degree to which the object conveys its affordances, constraints, and mappings. If the door has a handle, rather than a plate, can you tell how you should open the door? Does it want to be pushed away from you or pulled toward you? The degree of certainty the object conveys is its degree of visibility.

Donald Norman's classic book on this subject, The *Design of Everyday Things* (formerly *The Psychology of Everyday Things*) explains the problems that arise when a design does not match the user's mental model, using such common examples as doors that do not show how they should be opened, knobs on stoves that don't clearly suggest which knob turns on a particular burner, and faucets that don't suggest which way to turn the handle to get water. When objects communicate logically, intuitively, and consistently, users experience a high degree of success with the match to their mental models. When they do not, users are frustrated, frequently blaming themselves for failing to understand.

As the door and the stove knob problems illustrate, not all objects have good "visibility." However, objects should not be thought of as merely material. The characteristics of objects apply equally well to computer objects, or metaphorical concepts, such as the trash can object in the Macintosh GUI, which didn't suggest to users that it should be used to eject a diskette. Another object or concept that causes problems for users is *drag and drop*. A learnability issue is connected to the drag-and-drop concept whenever it is not transparent to users that this action is required to perform some tasks. Users must learn four concepts to use drag and drop ("Drag and Drop Has a Learning Problem"3):

1. What objects can I drag?
2. Where can I drop them?
3. What's it going to do when I let go?
4. If I don't like it, how do I undo it?

The first two problems relate to a lack of obvious affordances. Drag and drop isn't readily visible. It has to be "learned." The third problem results from a lack of consistency with the drag-and-drop feature. In many products, drag-and-drop will copy an object in one instance but delete it and replace it elsewhere in another instance. The user cannot intuitively determine which result will occur. Question 4 is related to question 3, in that if the user performs an action that doesn't achieve the desired result, the user needs to be able to undo it before it's too late. The undo feature may not serve as a real option, as the user may have already gone a step beyond the ability to undo some action. When this is a possibility, the system needs to provide verification questions to confirm the user's choice.

Adult Learners

Although learners of all ages may prefer different learning styles, adult learners have additional issues that must be given special consideration when designing products for them. These are largely based on adults' motivation for learning vs. that of children.

One theory of adult learning, called *andragogy*, emphasizes that adults are self-directed and expect to take responsibility for their actions. Andragogy presents the following conditions for adult learners (Knowles 55–61):

- Adults have a deep need to be self-directing.
- Adults need to know why they need to know something.
- Adults need to learn experientially.
- Adults need to approach learning as problem solving.
- Adults learn best when the topic is of immediate value.
- Adults enter into a learning situation with a task-centered orientation.
- Adults are motivated to learn by both external and internal stimuli.
- Because of life experiences (both pleasant and unpleasant), adults develop habits and biases that shape their approach to learning.

A survey of business professionals who were experienced computer users found that four of the six highest-rated usability characteristics (out of 21 choices) related to exploratory learning, which is the preferred mode of adult learners (Nielsen, "What Do Users Really Want?"). These findings support the research of John Carroll and his colleagues, which led them to prescribe a documentation approach called *minimalism*, a subject we address in the next section.

Minimalism for Adult Learners

As we presented in Chapter 2 in our discussion of heuristics, John Carroll and his colleagues at the Watson Research Center at IBM studied the ways in which adults learn new software, focusing their research on the documentation, particularly the tutorial, as a method of learning. The research began by watching people struggle with documentation and the task of learning how to operate a system or software tool. The description of the struggles of adult learners matches the issues adult learners experience when information is not presented in the way they want to learn it:

> Our interpretation of our subjects' struggles was that they were actually making rather systematic attempts to think and reason, to engage their prior knowledge and skill, to get something meaningful accomplished. They did not seem to be getting appropriate guidance and feedback from the systems and documentation they were using, even though they were being presented with a huge amount of information through these channels. For example, although they . . . made a great variety and number of errors, their materials did not support error recognition, diagnosis, or recovery, and the systems did not provide general undo functions. (Mack, Lewis, and Carroll; reported in Carroll, "Reconstructing" 2–3)

Based on these findings, Carroll and his colleagues pursued a different approach to the design of documentation, one that would give readers what they want in the way they want it. The approach, called minimalism, derives from two main principles of cognitive psychology:

1. Users construct their own mental models based on schema.
2. Users want to be actively involved in learning right away.

Even when users are learning a product for the first time, they still want to get started right away with tasks. A small group of users, perhaps 15% (Penrose and Seiford; reported in van der Meij and Carroll 42–43), will read a manual cover to cover. A second group begins at the beginning but then abandons the manual, returning to it only to look for some specific information. A third group uses the manual "as a last resort." The manual must support the needs of all these groups, and for all it must not look intimidating, which means it should take a minimalist approach. This concept gave rise to minimalist manuals, which have often been misunderstood and misinterpreted to mean brevity above all other considerations. Such a misinterpretation of minimalist principles has led to documentation with incomplete steps and insufficient or nonexistent overviews, which are needed to provide a context and outcome for action. Even when the minimalist principles are applied correctly to documentation, the minimalist model must be expanded to consider the different modes of learning (presented earlier in this chapter) and the different levels of understanding of the subject that users have when they learn a new product. Redish lists three considerations that have implications for documentation ("Minimalism in Technical Communication" 221):

1. Users come to documentation in different modes at different times (learning mode vs. doing mode).
2. Users differ in personality and learning style (risk takers, non-risk takers).
3. Users work in different problem domains (with different products, in different domains in one product).

Also to be considered are the needs of expert users. Hackos examines minimalism in light of the needs of these users, who have expertise in their field and with other software applications ("Choosing a Minimalist Approach for Expert Users"). She concludes that these "double experts" "need to know where to begin, where to go next, what the possibilities are, and how to get out of trouble. They do not need detailed task-oriented instructions to manipulate the interface objectives, nor do they need to consult instructional information to understand the primary purposes served by the software application" (152).

Because experts use online help frequently, if (and it's a big if) they can find what they want quickly when they consult help, the online help should be designed along minimalist lines to provide just enough information for experts to get started right away without training or instruction. As well, the words on the interface must match the expert users' vocabulary and the tasks must match the users' goals. For those who aren't experts, functions such as balloon help (Macintosh System 7.0 and above) can be turned on to explain the icons and features on a toolbar to those who need such explanations.

The influence of minimalism has been profound in its expansion of our understanding of adult learners in action and in its emphasis on understanding the tasks users want to perform as the basis for writing documentation and help to support their goals. Because the guiding principle of minimalism is task orientation, minimalism supports user-centered design.

Are Web users different? Do the principles discussed in this chapter apply to them as well? In the next section, we look at the special characteristics of Web users. For more information about usability and the Web, see Chapter 9.

Understanding Web Users

In many ways, Web users are the same as users of software or hardware. They have a goal and they are task-driven to accomplish it quickly. Although all the principles of usability apply equally to the usability of a Web site, one issue—learnability, or ease of learning—is more critical for Web users than the other issues, since Web users typically spend very little time on any individual Web site; so they need to be able to "learn" the site right away. What's more, the ever-increasing addition of new users to the Web means that there is always a large population of new learners. Approximately one in 15 visitors to a Web site has been using the Web for less than one month (Sullivan, "As Simple").

Web users have unique needs in several areas. One is speed: Web users demand fast download time. They're in a hurry to reach their goal. Users rarely *read* Web pages. Like most users of hardcopy and softcopy text, they skim, scan, and skip, but their tendency to do this when they use the Web. Thus, effective Web pages should use scannable text with highlighted keywords, bulleted lists, meaningful headings and subheadings, one idea per paragraph, and half the word count (or less) of conventional writing (Nielsen, "Changes") However, Web pages should be designed for readability first, not to show off complicated graphics or an array of colors. Too much of either can be "visually taxing" and "chaotic" (Sullivan, "The 'Vision Thing'"). A case can be made that bland sites are preferred when the customer is seeking information at high speed, as in banking transactions on the Web (Hurst).

Web sites also need to be predictable, as users coming to new sites bring the schema they have acquired from experience with familiar sites. Contrary to research on early users of the Web, at a time when its typical features were less well known or standardized, many users will now scroll "beneath the fold," the point below the visible portion of their screen ("For Whom the Page Scrolls" and Nielsen, "Changes"). Users scroll because they are looking for an appropriate link. How well they succeed in choosing the correct link depends on how well the site differentiates between links so that the user can predict which link to choose. Because users skim text in search of information, links are harder for users to see when they are embedded within text. When users click on a link and jump to a location, usability studies show that they will frequently go back, using the "back" button, and click on another link in pursuit of their goal. This phenomenon of *pogo sticking*, or jumping around on the site, can be a serious problem for users if their goal is to compare information. Their cognitive load may not be able to sustain the effort of remembering what they learned at the first link and then retaining that information for comparison when they locate the second link. Users become frustrated when the site forces them to jump back and forth or to write down information to compare to other information at a different link ("Pogo-sticking").

When users have a goal of obtaining information from a Web site, they will ignore banner ads (rendering them ineffective) if they interfere with the accomplishment of the goal. When the banner ad contains animation, users merely block out the ad when searching for content. Gratuitous animation, on the other hand, is a real distraction to users because it makes it harder for them to read or skim the site's content. Usability Web studies found that users put their hands over the animation as they tried to work to accomplish their goal (Spool et al.). However, according to these usability studies, users have "a seducible moment" that occurs after they have accomplished their goal. This is the point at which users can be lured from the path of their original goal to the site's goal of selling something. Users seem willing to be seduced away once their goal is met. Recognizing this, some successful e-commerce sites now place advertising below information items or embedded in information blocks at a point beyond which they determine users have satisfied enough of their goal to be lured away ("Creating Seducible Moments").

When users go to a Web site to shop, ease of use is the most critical factor in their ability to succeed in making a purchase and in their willingness and desire to return to the site. The Danish E-Commerce Association conducted a survey of 2,929

Internet users in Denmark, of which 61% had made purchases on the Web. Respondents were asked to list their top five reasons for shopping on the Web. The results are shown in Table 3.7 (reported in Nielsen, "Why People Shop on the Web").

Far and away, ease of purchase was the number one consideration. However, most Internet users do not visit a site to make a purchase. They go to the site for information. As the same Danish study shows, only 5% go to a site with the intent of buying something. Once there, if they feel confident about the ease of use of the site and usefulness of the information, they may make a purchase or they may return later to make a purchase. To gain the loyalty of Web users, Web sites should be designed so that visitors will return. For Web site designers, that means "provid[ing] useful content in a format that works the way people think" (Spool et al. xiii). *The Dotcom Survival Guide* (Creative Good) characterizes the customer as driven by a particular goal when visiting a Web site. Customers do not want to experience everything; rather, they want to experience the one thing they are seeking. Driven by this goal, their behavior fits the *page paradigm*, which means that users ask the following question about the page they choose (35):

Does the page take me closer to my goal?

- YES: Click to go closer to the goal.
- NO: Click Back to try again on the previous page.

In these ways, Web users may be different from users of other interfaces and products. In the next section, we continue to examine these differences, focusing on the specific needs of older users.

Web Sites and Older Users

Older users' needs must also be taken into consideration. One study, reported in *User Interface Design Update,* found that older users (ages 64–81), as compared to younger users (ages 19–36):

- Searched less efficiently
- Had the most trouble with tasks that required three or more mouse clicks
- Had more difficulty recalling previous moves and the location of previously viewed information

TABLE 3.7	Most Important Reasons People Shop on the Web
Easy to place an order	83%
Large selection of products	63%
Cheaper prices	63%
Faster service and delivery	52%
Detailed and clear information about what is being offered	40%
No sales pressure	39%
Easy payment procedures	36%

Source: Jakob Nielsen, "Why People Shop on The Web." *Alertbox* 7 Feb. 1999 <http://www.useit.com/alertbox/990207.html>.

- Were more likely to scroll a page at a time, vs. younger users who scanned a line at a time
- Searched less efficiently, making 81% more moves than younger users

Although the study may be flawed in that the younger group had much more familiarity with the Internet than the older group, still the findings about older users' differences seem to be "memory-related" rather than the choice of navigation strategy they adopted. More work needs to be done to understand the unique requirements of an aging population. In setting up usability tests of Web sites (or any graphical user interface) that attract an older user population, it may be important to include users with bifocals (or trifocals) to get information about what special issues they may have with screen visibility and readability. While the use of bifocals or trifocals is not restricted to an older population, it becomes increasingly common as the population ages. This, too, is an issue that needs further research.

Summary

In this chapter, we have examined the nature of field studies, especially contextual inquiry, to learn about users and their tasks and goals within their own environment. We placed field studies at the starting point of user-centered design. We looked at different techniques for conducting field studies, as well as the constraints placed on conducting such site visits. We also looked at users as learners, the discipline called cognitive psychology. As part of our discussion of this subject, we focused on schema theory or users' creation of mental models to help them shape new experiences to fit a previous mental model or to create a new mental model for future use. We then looked at the unique needs of users of documentation.

Next, we addressed learning styles to understand the different approaches that people employ. We examined how users view objects, particularly with regard to the objects in a graphical user interface (GUI). We discussed four clues that objects present:

- Affordances—the actual or perceived properties of an object
- Constraints—the properties that limit an object's use
- Mappings—the properties that suggest how we should interact with the object
- Visibility—the degree to which an object conveys its affordances, constraints, and mappings

With a general overview of learning theory, we focused on the unique needs of adult learners. For important contributions about adult learners and their needs regarding documentation, we looked to the findings of minimalism, as it was originally presented in 1980, as it has come to be understood (and misunderstood), and as it can be applied today to different audiences and different interfaces. Because the Web interface has become so important and poses unique challenges for users, we looked particularly at the research on Web users to see what similarities and differences Web users have, as compared to users of other media.

What the research shows, and what we have summarized in this chapter, is that users have a critical need to feel in control, they need a good mental model that makes sense to them, and they need to maintain a sense of certainty about what is happening to feel confident about the tool they are using to accomplish a task in keeping with a goal. Yet, users frequently feel out of control and frustrated, finding the experience more difficult than it ought to be.

Coming Up

The preparation for user-centered design begins with the principles established in this chapter. In the next chapter, we look at a methodology to increase the level of understanding we have of the user's world so that we design products that are user-centered rather than feature-centered. This methodology is called *iterative* testing, which allows a product to be tested and tested again, each time building into the product what we have learned about users. Through iterative testing, we maintain a continuing dialogue with the user to reaffirm that the design matches the user's world.

Questions/Topics for Discussion

1. Describe what *mental models* are and how they should factor into designing products for users.
2. What is the meaning of field studies and why are these studies the foundation for user-centered design?
3. What is the difference between users' tasks and users' goals? Which is the more critical aspect to focus on in developing user-centered products?
4. Describe some of the techniques that can be used to gather information about users and tasks during site visits. Which do you think would be easiest to do? Which would be hardest? Explain the reasons for your choices. Which technique would be most effective? Where does it fall within your easiest-to-hardest continuum?
5. List some of the factors that make site visits difficult to do. What impact would these problems then have on the use of site visits for data-gathering about users. Can you suggest any ways to overcome these problems to increase the frequency of use of site visits as part of a user-centered design process?
6. Cooper describes the personas that can be created after a site visit. What are these personas and what are their characteristics?
7. What is a *schema* and how does schema theory affect the design of usable products? Think of an example of a schema that is incorporated into the design of a product you use. How does it help you use the product?
8. How is the given-new principle violated in the following example? "Click on the red flower pot to take you to the landscape drawing page." As you

think of the given-new concept, what are users likely to do with this step in the instructions? How can you rearrange the information to put it into given-new order?

9. Using the table of learning styles presented on page 108, describe what learning style is yours. Based on your learning style, what approach do you take to learning how to use a new product?

10. How does the minimalist approach to documentation support adult learning theory?

11. In what ways are Web users different from users of products in other media? In what ways are they similar? How does information presented on the Web need to be designed to account for the differences?

Exercises

1. Requiring users to use the "trash can" to delete a diskette in the Macintosh interface and the "Start" option to locate "Shut down" in the Windows 95 interface violated mental models that users have. Identify another example of a violation of a mental model and describe the way in which it causes problems.

2. Vocabulary needs to be clear and match the user's vocabulary. What is wrong with the following three choices available to users in a computer program:

Log in
Open
Create

Describe how you think each command differs from the others. Now, redesign the commands to make the choices clearer to users.

3. Conduct a task analysis of a common task you perform but that others may not know how to perform. Examples include such common tasks as setting the alarm on your watch, picking up a message on your pager, or forwarding a phone call in a voice-mail system. Do the following to perform the task analysis:

- Write down each step in the task.
- Write down what each user would be expected to perform for each step in the task.
- What down a brief description of your primary user for this list of tasks.
- Are there any differences in the tasks for a different type of user? For instance, if your primary use is a novice, would some tasks be different for expert users? Write down a list of any of the steps that would be eliminated or done differently for expert users.

4. Using an available product in the classroom, such as an overhead projector or computer monitor or VCR, focus on one usability aspect of the prod-

uct, such as the location of a button or switch or the shape of a part of the product, and create a list of issues that need to be considered as part of user and task analysis. This activity can also be done in groups, with each group taking a different issue for the same product.

For Your Project

Plan a site visit to observe users working with the type of product you will be testing. The site could be someplace on campus or in the office or at home. For instance, you could observe someone using a word-processing program or spreadsheet. Or, you could observe someone using your type of product to cook a meal or to record a program using a VCR. Describe an objective for the site visit and your plan for the visit. Include a list of questions you will want to have answered, either through direct observation or an interview with the user, as part of the site visit.

References

Barry, Dave. "In any Tricky Battle of Wits with Appliances, I'm Toast." *Atlanta Journal-Constitution* 27 Feb. 2000: D8.

Carlton, Jim. "Computers: Befuddled PC Users Flood Help Lines, and No Question Seems to Be Too Basic." *The Wall Street Journal*, 1 Mar. 1994: B1.

Carroll, John M. "Reconstructing Minimalism." *Minimalism Beyond the Nurnberg Funnel*, Ed. John M. Carroll. Cambridge, MA: MIT Press, 1998. 1–17.

Carroll, John M., and Hans van der Meij. "Ten Misconceptions About Minimalism." *Minimalism Beyond the Nurnberg Funnel*, Ed. John M. Carroll. Cambridge, MA: MIT Press, 1998. 55–90.

Coe, Marlana. *Human Factors for Technical Communicators*. New York: Wiley, 1996.

"Contextual Enquiry." Usability Techniques series. Information & Design, 25 Nov. 1999 <www.infodesign.com.au>.

Cooper, Alan. "Goal-Directed Design." *Dr. Dobb's Journal* 25 June 1996. 21 June 1999 <http://www.cooper.com/articles/drdobbs_goal_directed.html>.

———. *The Inmates Are Running the Asylum: Why High-Tech Products Drive Us Crazy and How to Restore the Sanity*. Indianapolis, IN: SAMS, 1999.

"Creating Seducible Moments." *UIEtips* 25 Feb. 1999 User Interface Engineering <http://www.uie.com>.

Creative Good. *The Dotcom Survival Guide* 12 June 2000 <www.creativegood.com>.

"Drag and Drop Has a Learning Problem." User Interface Engineering's *Eye for Design*, Jan.–Feb. 1996: 3, 5.

Ehrlich, Kate, and Janice Anne Rohn. "Cost-Justification of Usability Engineering: A Vendor's Perspective." *Cost-Justifying Usability*. Eds. Randolph G. Bias and Deborah J. Mayhew. Boston: Academic Press, 1994: 73–110.

Faulkner, Christine. *The Essence of Human-Computer Interaction*. Englewood Cliffs, NJ: Prentice Hall, 1998.

"For Whom the Page Scrolls." *UIEtips* 20 Mar. 1998 User Interface Engineering <http://www.uie.com>.

Gunn, Robi. "Field Trials: Trials and Tribulations of a Field Visit." *Usability Interface*, Oct. 1998 <http://www.stcsig.org/usability>.

———. *User and Task Analysis for Interface Design*. New York: Wiley, 1998.

Hackos, JoAnn T. "Choosing a Minimalist Approach for Expert Users." *Minimalism Beyond the Nurnberg Funnel*, Ed. John M. Carroll. Cambridge, MA: MIT Press, 1998. 149–77.

Hackos, JoAnn T., and Janice C. Redish. *User and Task Analysis for Interface Design*. New York: Wiley, 1998.

Hurst, Mark. "The Web's Identity Crisis." 21 Jan. 2000 Creative Good <http://www.goodexperience.com/columns/012100.identify.htm>

Janah, Monua. "AuctionWatch Site Redesign Sets Off a Revolt." *San Jose Mercury News* 18 Aug. 1999 <http://www.mercurycenter.com/business/top/054559.htm>.

Knowles, Malcolm. *The Adult Learner: A Neglected Species*, 3rd ed. Houston: Gulf, 1984.

Laskas, Jeanne Marie. "Not His Typing." *Washington Post* 10 Oct. 1999: W31.

"Making Online Information Usable." 20 Oct. 2000 User Interface Engineering <http://www.uie.com/online.htm>.

Miller, George A. "The Magical Number Seven, Plus or Minus Two: Some Limits on Our Capacity for Processing Information." *Psychological Review* 63.2 (1956): 81–97.

Nielsen, Jakob. "Changes in Web Usability Since 1994." *Alertbox* 1 Dec. 1997 <http://www.useit.com/alertbox/9712a.html>.

———. "How Users Read on the Web." *Alertbox* 1 Oct. 1997 <http://www.useit.com/alertbox/9710a.html>.

———. "Novice vs. Expert Users." *Alertbox* 6 Feb. 2000 <http://www.useit.com/alertbox/20000206.html>.

———. "The Paradox of the Active User." Sidebar in "Personalization is Overrated" *Alertbox* 4 Oct. 1998 <http://www.useit.com/alertbox/activeuserparadox.html>.

———. "Tech Support Tales: Internet Hard to Use for Novice Users." *Alertbox* 1 Apr. 1997 <http://www.useit.com/alertbox9704a.html>.

———. "What Do Users Really Want?" *International Journal of Human-Computer Interaction* 1.1 (1989): 137–47.

———. "Why People Shop on the Web." *Alertbox* 7 Feb. 1999 <http://www.useit.com/alertbox/990207.html>.

Norman, Donald A. *The Design of Everyday Things*. New York: Doubleday, 1988.

———. *The Invisible Computer: Why Good Products Fail, the Personal Computer Is So Complex, and Information Appliances Are the Solution*. Cambridge, MA: MIT Press, 1998.

"Pogo-sticking: Downs and Ups." *UIEtips* 13 July 1998 User Interface Engineering <http://www.uie.com>.

Redish, Janice. Checklist for Planning Materials for a Site Visit <http://www.stcsig. org/usability/resources>.

———. "Minimalism in Technical Communication: Some Issues to Consider." *Minimalism Beyond the Nurnberg Funnel*. Ed. John M. Carroll. Cambridge, MA: MIT Press, 1998. 219–45.

———. "Understanding Readers." *Techniques for Technical Communicators*. Eds.

Carol M. Barnum and Saul Carliner. New York: Macmillan, 1993. 14–41.

Rubin, Jeffrey. "Conceptual Design: Cornerstone of Usability." *Technical Communication* 43.2 (1996): 130–38.

Rubinstein, Richard, and Harry M. Hersh. *The Human Factor: Designing Computer Systems for People.* Burlington, MA: Digital Press, 1984.

Spool, Jared, et al. *Web Site Usability: A Designer's Guide.* San Francisco: Morgan-Kaufman, 1999.

Sullivan, Terry. "As Simple as Possible." 28 Feb. 2000 *All Things Web* <http://www.pantos.org/atw/35504.html>.

———. "The 'Vision Thing.'" 28 Feb. 2000 *All Things Web* <http://www.pantos.org/atw/35396.html>

User Interface Design Update, Oct. 1998. Human Factors International <http://www.humanfactors.com>.

van der Meij, Hans, and John M. Carroll. "Principles and Heuristics for Designing Minimalist Instruction." *Minimalism Beyond the Nurnberg Funnel.* Ed. John M. Carroll. Cambridge, MA: MIT Press, 1998. 19–53.

Wixon, Dennis R., and Elizabeth M. Comstock. "Evolution of Usability at Digital Equipment Corporation." *Usability in Practice: How Companies Develop User-Friendly Products.* Ed. Michael E. Wiklund. Boston: Academic Press, 1994. 147–93.

## CHAPTER 4

Iterative Testing for User-Centered Design

 User-centered design (UCD) is the product development process based on learning about the user and applying what you learn to create products that match users' needs. In Chapter 3 we talked about the importance of going to the user's workplace or home to study users in their environment and to understand how they perform tasks. With this understanding, you can begin the process of user-centered design. But how do you know if the design you produce is what users really want? You could wait to see the reaction of users, once the product is released to market, and then correct the problems in the next release of the product. However, this approach risks alienating users who may not want to give your products another try after a bad first experience. Or you could test the product just before release, but this approach usually uncovers problems that are too costly to fix at such a late stage of development. Or you could test the product as it is being developed, and not once, but frequently. This process, called *iterative testing*, as illustrated in Figure 4.1, is a critical element in user-centered design. By incorporating what you learn from users and continuing to learn from users as the product moves through development, usability can be built into the product.

This chapter focuses on the approaches for conducting iterative testing during various phases of product development, but particularly in the earliest, or conceptual, phase. We begin by comparing testing that takes place during product development, called *formative* evaluation, to testing that occurs just before and after product release, called *summative* evaluation.

Summative Evaluation vs. Formative Evaluation

When usability testing first came to be understood as a method to learn how users would react to products, companies frequently agreed to do usability testing just before the product shipped to market. Typically, their motivation was to

Iterative Testing

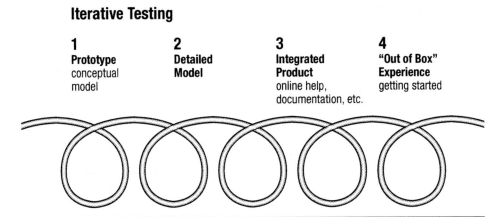

1	**2**	**3**	**4**
Prototype	**Detailed**	**Integrated**	**"Out of Box"**
conceptual	**Model**	**Product**	**Experience**
model		online help,	getting started
		documentation, etc.	

Figure 4.1   Iterative testing process
(Used with permission from Bev Arends.)

"confirm" a good design or to "validate" it for quality assurance. What they saw, when they observed users struggling with many features of the product, were problems that needed to be addressed but couldn't be fixed at such a late stage of development, unless they spent a lot of money in redesign and delayed the release date of the product. Most companies were not willing or able to do that, so products went to market with problems. Lessons learned from such late testing could be applied to the next release of the product, if customers who had experienced these problems were still interested in buying the next version after a bad first experience. This type of testing is called summative evaluation, because it is done at or near the completion of the development cycle. As is often the case when a product is tested this late in the development cycle, it falls to the technical communicators to "explain" the defects in the product through the documentation or to provide the appropriate troubleshooting notes to help users solve the inevitable problems they will experience.

Summative evaluation does have its uses. It can be used to measure how well the product performs against stated goals. If the testing takes place in the user's environment, it can add to the company's understanding of user and task analysis by seeing the actual product in use. It can help developers understand how users learn the new product and what support tools they use (documentation, tutorial, help desk). This kind of information can help the developers improve the design and development of the next version or the next product. When used as a part of iterative design, it is a critical step in following the product through the development cycle to see whether the final product matches users' expectations and goals.

Summative evaluation is also useful for testing competitors' products. When a company wants to enter an existing market, testing competitors' products will help designers learn what users like and dislike about the products currently available. Frequently such summative evaluations are conducted as comparative usability evaluations, in which each user may be asked to perform the same tasks using two or more products. Or, if a company already has a product in the marketplace but would like to get a better understanding of the competition, comparative evaluations can reveal much useful data. These types of evaluations are sometimes called usability *shootouts*, reflecting the idea of a "winner" in the showdown.

Where once it was common for companies to employ a one-shot summative evaluation of a product just before release, nowadays, a growing number of companies recognize that usability means adopting the user-centered design model. These companies understand that user-centered design is critical to the success of products in the marketplace. As the Standish Group's analysis of the factors that predict software products' success shows, user involvement is the number one factor in the success of software development. (See Table 4.1; as reported in Kreitzberg and Shneiderman 7.) Although nearly all these success factors are invoked when user-centered design is applied to product development, the top three factors are the basis of user-centered design. UCD cannot be implemented in an organization without executive management support. Once this is obtained, the other factors will naturally occur as part of the process.

User involvement contributes to successful product development, especially when users are involved throughout the product development process. Formative evaluation is one very important method to involve users and learn from them. Formative evaluation can begin even before there is a product to test, and it can continue late into the development process before the product is released. Generally, formative evaluation falls into three phases—early, middle, and late. The designation of the phase is typically characterized by the *fidelity* of the model

TABLE 4.1 **Top 10 Factors in Software Development Product Success**

Success Criteria	Points
1. User involvement	19
2. Executive management support	16
3. Clear statement of requirements	15
4. Proper planning	11
5. Realistic expectations	10
6. Smaller project milestones	9
7. Competent staff	8
8. Ownership	6
9. Clear vision and objectives	3
10. Hard-working, focused staff	3
	Total 100

Source: Charles B. Kreitzberg and Ben S. Shneiderman, "Making Computer and Internet Usability a National Priority," *Common Ground*, Jan., 1999, p. 7. (Used with permission from the Usability Professionals' Association.)

being tested, which refers to how closely the model reflects the actual finished product. The more the model being tested matches the actual product, the higher the fidelity of the test. Prototyping phases can move from low to high fidelity, using the following types of tools:

- *Paper.* Stickies, colored and plain paper, pencils, and scissors.
- *Word.* Boxes, tables, simple illustrations.
- *PowerPoint.* Creates the look of pages or screens.
- *Visio.* Creates an online prototype that allows users to move between screens in a more realistic representation of the product; integrates with Microsoft Office products.
- *Dreamweaver.* Creates HTML-based Web pages that have a high-level look and feel, very similar to the finished product.

We will discuss each of these phases, focusing on the first one (or lowest fidelity) as the easiest to include in the development cycle. More will also be said about the tools that can be used for each phase.

Paper Prototyping

Low-fidelity usability testing is frequently called *paper prototyping* because it is performed using prototypes of the product concept made from paper and other simple tools. Because it is cheap, fast, and easy, it can be used often to get users' reactions to any number of critical design issues about the product: the concept or metaphor, the look of the screen or page, the table of contents or index of the documentation, the navigation, terminology, and general task plan. Also because it is low-fidelity vs. high-fidelity, users are typically much more comfortable criticizing the product, and designers are frequently much more amenable to making changes for improvement. What's more, these changes can be made at very little cost to the development budget and in very little time, typically without any impact on the production schedule. Even in documented cases where more time is invested up front in iterative testing, as reported in *Usability in Practice: How Companies Develop User Friendly Products* (Wiklund), companies report that the savings are reaped in fewer user-assistance costs and cheaper revisions than if the testing took place after the code was written. Eliminating prototyping in the interests of speed to market can result in disaster, as the sidebar entitled "Low-Cost Dream Car Hits the Road, Pedestrians, Etc.," playfully demonstrates (Tognazzini).

In the next section, we look at the methods used to create and test paper prototypes.

Creating and Testing Paper Prototypes

Creating paper prototypes means using kindergarten technology: scissors, paper (white and colored), colored pens, sticky notes (various colors), note cards of various sizes, tape, glue sticks, rolls of correction tape, or sheets of colored dots and

Low-Cost Dream Car Hits the Road, Pedestrians, Etc.
Four Months from Concept to Reality

Dateline: Detroit Auto giant MegaMotors today introduced MegaDream 1.0, the first of an exciting new breed of production dream cars. Whereas typical cars are first prototyped, then tested, then redesigned, the MegaDream 1.0 went directly from the drawing board to production in under 5 months. Company spokesperson Clydesdale "Clyde" Snively credited the elimination of iterative design and testing with both the short time to market and a cost reduction in the $40,000 car of almost $300. "Consumers have always admired auto show concept cars. Now they have a chance to actually own one and save some cash to boot!"

We test-drove the new MegaDream and found the car just as exciting as all its Hollywood hype. With its smooth lines and distinctive design, heads are turned wherever you go. In fact, at least one head has to be turned: the driver's. The auto maker boldly attached the steering wheel to the left door, with the driver seated facing said door, "to make driving in reverse just as safe and comfortable as driving forward." (Company steering consultant Edward Harrow suggested they may change this side-saddle arrangement in the second release.)

The lack of user testing led to many of those endless and expensive meetings where groups of engineers close to the project sit around arguing over what naïve drivers will actually do, in the face of no evidence whatsoever. Arguments over the layout of the cockpit area were finally laid to rest by enabling the driver to decide his or her own configuration. Gas, brake, windshield wiper, and other functions are all easily switched around by a driver-preference function of the horn: one beep for brake on the left, two beeps for brake on the right, and so on.

This horn configuration system has so far caused eight fatalities this first week, as drivers in heavy traffic beep their horns to prevent collision, only to find the brake pedal they're stepping on has suddenly become the accelerator. An engineer close to the project admitted they had failed to consider that possibility but said they were planning an interim release that would instead tie the configuration to the current radio station. (No tests of this second design attempt are planned either: "Drivers have no business changing radio stations in heavy traffic, so they shouldn't have any more problems.")

We were impressed with the power of the new car, although the manual spark advance and choke, needed for every gear shift, were a bit daunting. Engineers pointed out, however, that bringing back driver-control over such features increased engine performance and versatility, and none of the engineers were having any problems adjusting them. (Spokesperson Snively admitted that making automatic spark advance a preference item is under consideration for version 2.0, "for the non-power-drivers.")

All in all, we found the MegaDream 1.0 to be a wonderful car, if a bit quirky. Even though it may have its critics, we feel the savings of $300 more than justifies the lack of testing. And for those few drivers who are unhappy with this first release, MegaDream 2.0 will be offered to surviving registered owners for only $36,000, with proof of purchase.

Source: Bruce Tognazzini, *Tog on Interface.* Reading, MA: Addison-Wesley, 1992, p. 80. © 1992 by Apple Computer, Inc. Reprinted by permission of Addison Wesley Longman.

labels. Acetate sheets are also frequently used, but this is probably moving just a bit beyond kindergarten. The materials for paper prototyping are probably already at hand; if not, they can be easily obtained from an office supply store or discount department store.

Once you've amassed these items, you're ready to create the paper prototype of whatever you want to test. You and your team can create a very low-fidelity prototype in as little as one hour or more typically in half a day or a day. You will need a team for this effort, because the testing will involve several people and the prototype requires the creativity and ideas of everyone involved in the development of the product. The team should include the developers (programmers and technical communicators) and usability or human factors experts, and may also include representatives from user support, training, and marketing.

A popular exercise that demonstrates how quickly paper prototyping can create concepts ready for testing was introduced by User Interface Engineering at the 1993 Usability Professionals' Association Conference. Conference participants signed up to join teams whose goal was to design the user interface for ordering fast-food at a kiosk. Team members were assigned to various roles on the product development team and all were to work together to create the interface. The scenario described a family that wants to order a list of items for no more than a certain total dollar amount. Each team worked to create the award-winning interface, which was tested by a user who had not participated in the process. Variations of this process have been presented at other conferences, but the concept is simple:

1. Create a problem or goal that the team wants to investigate with real users.
2. Create a scenario to test the concept or interaction in a typical transaction.
3. Observe the user performing the process, while a member of the team acts as the computer, producing new menus and screens as the user selects them. Other team members make notes of these transactions, as well as those places where the user is puzzled or unable to complete the task.
4. Following the completion of the task (or failure to complete the task), interview the user to learn more.

Using this process, a team can quickly build the learning from the first prototyping test into design changes, which can lead to the creation of another prototype to test again. Once the basic page design or screen design is drawn, multiple copies can be quickly produced using the photocopier. Likewise, multiple copies of icons, radio buttons, pull-down menus, and so forth can be made from an original.

Team Member Roles During Testing

After the completion of the prototype, potential users of the product are invited to participate in a test. To make the product "work" and to capture the findings from the test, team members take on the following roles during testing:

- *Facilitator.* This is the only member of the team who is allowed to speak with the user during the test. This person explains the test, answers questions, provides the scenario(s) of tasks, encourages the user to express his or her thinking process, and keeps track of the time during the test. The facilitator can also ask very general, open-ended questions to elicit responses from the user, such as, "What's on your mind now?" "What are you trying to do now?"
- *Computer.* This person is the "Wizard of Oz" behind the computer, who makes it respond to commands. When the user makes a selection, the computer responds with the appropriate screen or dialog box. If a pull-down menu is touched, the computer produces the list of items that would appear (on a sticky note, for instance). If the user "enters" some information (by writing or speaking), the computer can display the response (previously prepared) or "speak" the response. If a new screen is activated, the computer displays it. The computer needs to know the "architecture" of the design and be able to quickly locate all the pieces that have been created for the test.
- *Observer(s).* The remaining team member or members fulfill this role, which is to take notes on the actions of the user and any places where the user has problems. These notes can then be collated for team analysis.

Figure 4.2 shows a variation of this approach when the testing is conducted in a usability lab. Here, the prototype is created by taping paper to the computer screen. The sticky notes are then placed by Anupama, in her role as "the computer," in response to Mike's selection, indicated by his pencil pointing at a sticky note of a dialog box. The facilitator and the observers are in the room on the other side of the one-way mirror.

In a typical day of testing, the design team spends the morning creating a prototype and the afternoon working with users testing the prototype. For the best results, the users should match the profile of the people who will actually use the product, so in most cases they must be located and recruited in advance (see Chapters 5 and 6 for establishing the user profile and recruiting the users). Some companies recruit people down the hall in this early stage to get feedback on some basic issues that would likely affect all users of the product. By the end of the day following tests with only a few users, the team will have a rich set of notes from which to continue developing the product or go back to the drawing board.

What Teams Can Learn from Paper Prototyping

Because paper prototyping is fast and cheap, it allows the development team to get very early feedback on different concepts or metaphors of the product before it is developed. These can be based on the information gathered from site visits. What this type of exploratory testing tells you is how well the users understand the concepts or models proposed and which ones work best for them.

Figure 4.2   Paper prototyping in a usability lab
(Photo used with permission of Southern Polytechnic State University and the subjects.)

Prototype testing also provides opportunities to learn users' terminology and to determine where they will need documentation. Because you can observe users working with a paper prototype, hear when they ask questions, and witness where they just figure things out on their own, you'll learn where things will be intuitive, needing no documentation, as well as those places where online help or documentation will be needed. Here's a method William Horton suggests (44):

1. The users try to do a step. If they get stuck, they ask a question.
2. The expert answers the questions (but provides no information beyond the answer to the particular question).
3. An observer asks the user to paraphrase the answer.
4. If the expert agrees that the paraphrase is essentially correct,
   a. The observer writes down the paraphrase.
   b. The user performs the step and continues the process.
5. At the end of the process, the observer strings together the paraphrases in the user's own words. This becomes the outline for the first draft of the documentation or help file.
6. Through an iterative process, the developer can repeat the process with the next user, or give the "draft" to the next user and continue to modify it

and add to it, thereby capturing the terminology, vocabulary, and needs of the users for the documentation.

To determine the information users would expect to find in a pull-down menu or by clicking on a particular icon, a *matching* exercise can generate useful results. In this exercise, users are given a list of commands and asked to "match" them to a list of terms or a display of icons. They can do this on paper or they can verbalize this on a paper prototype of the screen display. This technique provides information about terminology and icon imagery, as well as navigation concepts.

To learn how users would want to use an index, you can give users "before" and "after" pictures of some task, like setting up a monthly calendar, and ask them to tell you what they would look up in an index to fill in the information to complete this task. Compile a list of all the users' terminology and build the index from there. Or you can test the index even before writing the outline by alphabetizing the key items that will be included and then showing users a picture of something and asking them to look up the things they would need to know to perform the task illustrated in the picture. In this case, users refer to a mock-up of the proposed index, while explaining what they're looking for. When they can't find what they're looking for, either because they use terminology that doesn't match index entries or because the entries are missing, appropriate changes can be made to the index and then to the subsequent documentation.

When you have multiple users of a complex product, you can use index cards, displaying numerous categories of documentation. By asking users to select and arrange the items from the index card collection, you can plan an online or paper document set for each of these different groups of users. Then you can write the documentation to include only what each group wants and not include information they don't want.

Developers at IBM (Fuccella and Pizzolato) describe a paper technique they use to get information about what content users want on a Web site. Using early data-gathering from focus groups and surveys to determine possible topics to include on the Web site, they create the topics and subtopics and place these on separate note cards, using pen and paper, sticky notes, or a word processor. Users are given a stack of these cards, each one containing a different topic, and asked to arrange the cards in the order that makes sense to them. They also provide blank cards for users to add anything they feel is missing from the stack. When users have completed this task, they are asked to explain how they have organized the cards and what each stack represents. The stacks are then collected and stapled together with the description written on top. After testing several users, the developers place similar stacks together and look for consistency in terminology and in items within the stacks.

Paper prototyping can also be used to test hardware or physical objects. In "The Third Dimension in Paper Prototypes," Säde and Battarbee describe how they created a three-dimensional, life-size, cardboard mock-up of an aluminum can recycling/refund machine. They then placed the model in a department store and got early design feedback very quickly from real users before going to a more expensive prototype.

Alternatives to Paper Prototyping

Prototyping doesn't have to be in paper if another material works better. A block of wood was the prototype for the Palm Pilot. The developer, Jeff Hawkins, cut a block of wood to fit in his shirt pocket. He then carried his prototype for the palm-sized computer with him, pulling it out of his pocket to "use" it as his personal daytimer, to access a phone number, or enter a reminder. He experimented with different interface designs by pasting them onto his block of wood. If a suggested feature wouldn't fit on the block of wood in a readable and usable way, it wasn't added to the design.

As with any tool, paper prototyping is effective in some applications, ineffective in others. In the next section, we discuss the advantages and disadvantages of this method.

Advantages and Disadvantages of Paper Prototyping

Advantages

Some of the advantages of paper prototyping have already been discussed: ease, speed, and low cost. But there are others, which, if not obvious from the previous discussion, bear mentioning here. Low-fidelity prototyping:

- Makes it possible to do user-centered design from the very beginning of the development cycle, fixing problems cheaply and easily.
- Makes it possible to not only test early, but also test often to get continuing feedback from users as the product moves through the development cycle.
- Makes it possible to manage risk, try new ideas and concepts, take chances, which can be corrected, changed, or scrapped if they don't work out.
- Provides a tangible object (the paper prototype), rather than a specification, that can be used in meetings and discussions about the product.
- Provides an excellent team-building activity that brings team members together quickly with "all hands being equal." Because coding is not involved, programmers do not have an edge over any other members of the team.

Research studies that have compared low-fidelity prototyping to higher-fidelity prototyping techniques (discussed in the next section of this chapter) show that in some cases the results are better and in other cases the results are similar to those of the higher-fidelity techniques. In one example, different development teams at UCLA (the University of California, Los Angeles) used either a standard development method or paper prototypes for a software product, with the following results (Boehm, Gray, and Seewaldt, 1984; reported in Hix and Harston 257–58):

- The groups using the paper prototyping approach appeared to be less affected by deadline pressure.

- The systems produced by the paper prototyping method were judged to be easier to learn and use.
- The code for the products developed following paper prototyping was 40% smaller than that of the products developed by conventional methods.
- The groups using paper prototyping completed their product development with 45% less effort than the groups using the conventional method.

In another study (Alavi, 1984; reported in Hix and Harston 258), groups using the paper prototyping system reported:

- A higher level of satisfaction
- Enhanced communication among team members
- Creation of a common baseline or point of reference for team members to discuss problems and opportunities in concrete terms
- A higher level of enthusiasm from users resulting from earlier involvement with users and greater product acceptance by users

A more recent study (Catani and Biers) compared low-, medium-, and high-fidelity prototyping to determine whether the findings were affected by the fidelity of the product tested. Users were asked to perform typical library searches using one of the three levels of prototypes. The results showed that there were no significant differences in the number of findings or the severity of problems identified and that similar findings were reported at each fidelity level.

Disadvantages

Paper prototyping does have some disadvantages, and it is not the best tool to use for some applications. For instance, when the product is complex, requiring a lot of screens and a lot of navigation, paper prototyping may make it too confusing for the users to figure out. And the person playing the "computer" may be overwhelmed by the number of choices at hand.

Other disadvantages of paper prototyping vs. more fully developed prototypes include the following:

- Cannot collect response times or data on the amount of time needed to complete tasks
- Cannot get user feedback about color, screen quality, look of graphics, sound, and so forth
- Requires teamwork, which may not always be an option
- Requires acceptance and understanding from management regarding the value of this throw-away medium

A study by Uceta, Dixon, and Resnick (1998) reported an additional disadvantage of paper prototyping as compared to a higher-fidelity, computer-based prototype. Although the results of the study demonstrated a similar number and type of usability issues, the paper prototyping tool required 30% more time for testing than the comparable computer-based tool. Thus, some usability groups prefer computer-based tools for prototyping. In the next section, we examine the methods and common tools for medium- and high-fidelity prototypes.

Medium- and High-Fidelity Prototyping

Medium-fidelity prototyping tools include HTML for a Web-based product, Lotus Notes for a Notes application, and PowerPoint, Paint, or a similar tool for a software product. High-fidelity tools include Director, Dreamweaver, Visual Basic, VisualAge, ScreenCam, or other similar tools. PowerPoint, a popular choice because of its widespread use (not just in the domain of developers), can be used for all levels of prototyping. For low-fidelity prototyping, it can replace pen and paper for screens and text production, which are then printed and cut up. For medium-fidelity prototyping, it can be run as a slide presentation, and for high-fidelity prototyping, it can be set up with links to simulate the software product concept and navigation scheme.

As part of the process of user-centered design, testing can begin with paper prototyping and continue as the product develops. Middle- and high-fidelity prototyping provides a means to continue to learn about how users work with the product so that the decisions are based on users' needs, not developers' guesses. In the middle stage of development, testing can get feedback from users when only a few modules are developed or when modules are only partially developed. Many of the issues learned from testing a portion of the software can be applied to the continuing development of the program. Issues such as navigation, terminology, organization of tasks and steps, and feedback can be understood in this middle phase.

Testing can be conducted with or without high-level "function" coding. Using HTML, for instance, a low-level coding tool, developers can quickly code user-interface prototypes that provide a more accurate sense of the look and feel of the interface than do paper prototypes. Prototypes created in HTML allow users to work with navigation as they would with the finished product. Changes can be made quickly, even during a usability testing session, and the tool is easy enough to learn so that all members of the team can contribute to the development process. Because a team member doesn't have to play "computer," the whole team can concentrate on what actually happens in the test. The user is less distracted as well, yet feels comfortable enough to suggest changes through recognition that the product is not finished.

Another technique that can be used in the middle stage of development provides a means of getting feedback from users about the documentation. Called *iterative reading protocol*, the method asks users to read aloud portions of a document under development. Users are also asked to think out loud, sharing their thoughts about what they are reading. This process answers the following types of questions:

- Can users find the information they need?
- Can they understand the information they find?
- Can they perform the tasks using the information they find?

This process can be repeated as the documentation is further developed. For examples of other ways to test the documentation and help while they're still under development, see the sidebar entitled "Six Slick Tests for Docs and Help" on pages 134–135.

In the later stages of product development, when the product is close to completion, testing should affirm that the design remains on track and the execution is pleasing to the intended users. In this late phase of testing, the team can learn whether the users' expectations have been met for speed and ease of use. This is the phase where quantitative data, such as time on tasks, number of errors, time to recover from errors, frequency of requests for help, and so forth, can be determined and matched against benchmarks established by the team from previous testing. You can also learn by observing what doesn't happen in these late-stage usability tests. These "non-events" can be discovered by watching for actions or behaviors that don't make sense or that surprise or puzzle you, next asking the users to describe what they were thinking about or doing at the time, and then building that knowledge into the product so that it becomes more intuitive for users ("Observing What Didn't Happen").

If prototyping is to be effective, it has to demonstrate a "payoff" in improving a product's usability. Michael Schrage suggests the following user's guide, or set of heuristics, for project managers to improve the likelihood that prototyping will pay off (201–13):

1. *Ask, who benefits?* The opposite is also true: ask who stands to lose. If a useful prototype is created, there can be political ramifications that need to be considered and addressed.
2. *Decide what the main paybacks should be and measure them rigorously.* Speed to market shouldn't outpace the customer's ability to absorb change.
3. *Fail early and often.* Rapid prototyping should mean rapid failure; however, the information learned in early prototyping captures vital data about design conflicts in time to correct them at little expense.
4. *Manage a diversified prototype portfolio.* Use inexpensive, informal prototyping tools to generate lots of ideas before settling on one approach.
5. *Commit to a migration path. Honor that commitment.* Follow through from the prototyping stage to the development stage to demonstrate commitment to the process.
6. *A prototype should be an invitation to play.* Prototypes should generate creativity and input from all involved. Prototypes should be viewed as conversation-starters for customers, vendors, and colleagues.
7. *Create markets around the prototypes.* Involve all parts of the organization to capture good ideas that can be incorporated into the prototype.
8. *Encourage role-playing.* Involve people in new and different roles as users. Have members of a cross-functional team adopt other members' positions during prototyping.
9. *Determine the points of diminishing returns.* Know and recognize when enough is enough.
10. *Record and review relentlessly and rigorously.* Videotape users working with prototypes; then hold lessons-learned sessions.

Six Slick Tests for Docs and Help

Usability testing isn't just for software and web sites. Testing documentation can ensure that it includes—and accurately conveys—all the information users expect and need.

Testing gives you accurate information on how well your documentation and help work. It can even uncover problems that are better solved by changing the interface.

As with most parts of the development, it's easier and less expensive to find and correct doc problems early in the process, so we try to test as soon as possible.

Choosing a method depends on what you want to learn, how much time you have, and where your greatest risks are.

1. Incredibly Intelligent Help

This technique lets you discover what information users actually need, before you've written anything.

We bring in test participants as soon as we have a version of the product that will let users do some of the tasks they'd do in the real world. This may be well before we've written the documentation, but this isn't a problem because a member of the development team simulates the documentation.

The incredibly intelligent part comes in when users get stuck or seem confused. At this point, the person simulating the docs asks, "What is your question right now?" When the user replies, the Help person provides a verbal clue, but gives as small a piece of information as possible. If this isn't enough, the user can ask another question.

By giving information only a bit at a time, we can find out exactly which piece is most important to the user. Knowing this helps teams provide appropriate documentation—not too much, not too little—or, better yet, to fix the interface itself.

2. Index Tests

You can determine whether users can get to the right topic in your index by having them work with the draft index. You can even test the index before you've written the documentation.

To test the index, we show users screen shots from the product and ask them to write down the first three terms they'd look up to find more information. This test lets you look inside users' heads and learn some of the terms they use—and expect to see. We write down all the terms they use; they could be words we've omitted or not referenced. The more of these we include, the better the index will work.

3. Summary Tests

By testing how well users comprehend conceptual material, you'll know how successfully you're communicating the information.

We ask users to read a section or examine a picture in the docs, then ask them to describe the three main points this element is trying to convey. (You should already know what you expect them to be!) If the users' answers match yours, you're probably getting your information across; if not, you may have some work to do.

4. Procedural Tests

This is a good way to test how accurately you've written the procedural details of your docs.

We give users the documentation or help, asking them to read a specific page or topic and then work with the software to complete the procedure this section describes.

We note where they have problems, where they get confused, or where steps are missing. Then we make the necessary changes in the next draft.

5. Lookup Tests

Lookup tests demonstrate if the docs or Help include the necessary information—and if users can get to the right topic and use it. They also let you find the users' biggest unanswered question.

To do a lookup test, we give users questions to answer or tasks to complete and see if the draft documentation helps them succeed. For example, when testing the documentation for a video product, we told users, "The picture you're getting isn't as clear as you'd like. Use the documentation and online help to find out what's wrong and how to fix it."

After conducting lookup tests, some teams have changed from printed to online help (or

vice versa), added index entries, or reorganized the information.

6. Rose in the Thorns Tests

It can be enlightening—and fascinating—to discover what experienced users don't know about a product. To do this, we've recently started experimenting with the Rose in the Thorns test.

We ask experienced users to look through the documentation or help until they find information about features they didn't know before.

Then we ask them if this new information is valuable to them. If there are important features users don't know about, we work with the interface designers to communicate them better.

Tips for Success

Three things help ensure successful tests of docs and help:

- These tests work best with a couple of users at a time. This increases the likelihood of brainstorming and lets us collect lots of information or keywords at once.
- We try to avoid product-specific terms in the task instructions.
- After the tests, we discuss with the team what we've seen and decide on next steps—including changes to the docs or more testing.

Source: This article appeared in the Sept./Oct. 1998 issue of *Eye For Design.*

Available at www.uie.com. Used with permission by User Interface Engineering.

Summary

In this chapter, we have continued the discussion of user-centered design, focusing on the method to build usability into the product development cycle through iterative testing. We looked at the differences between summative evaluation, which tests a product when it is complete, and formative evaluation, which tests a product in its developing stages. We then described the methodology for each phase of testing, placing greatest emphasis on early testing with paper prototypes, also called low-fidelity testing. We presented the method commonly used to create and test paper prototypes, the results that can be obtained, and the advantages and disadvantages of low-fidelity prototyping techniques. Next, we looked at the tools used for medium- and high-fidelity prototypes and the benefits to be derived from each of these methods.

Throughout this chapter, as in the previous chapters, we have emphasized that usability testing must be done often. Here we have added to that discussion by showing how it can be done *early* and often, as part of the process of creating products that deliver what users want.

Coming Up

Whether you are testing paper prototypes or higher-fidelity products up to and including the finished product, you need to plan the test so that it goes well and gives you good results. In the next chapter, we focus on the planning process. This process includes setting goals, establishing the user profile, determining the tasks, and documenting it all in a test plan.

Questions/Topics for Discussion

1. What's the difference between *summative* and *formative* evaluation? What's the usefulness of each type of testing?
2. Visit a university or business Web site and select one aspect of the site that seems confusing to you. How could paper prototyping be used to compare the current information on the site to some other models? What tools would you use to create the paper prototype? What would you ask users to do?
3. List the advantages and disadvantages of using paper prototyping as a method for gathering information about users and tasks.

Exercises

1. Card-stacking exercise: Working in groups, create a list of topics that you would use to design the interface for an information kiosk to assist visitors to your campus or office building or to a shopping mall or museum. What

kinds of information would they want to find there? Put each topic on a card for all of the areas that will be included in the kiosk. When you have completed this task, invite a user from another team to arrange the cards in the way that matches his or her mental model of topics. Provide blank cards for the user to add anything not included. Ask the user to explain his or her reason for grouping the cards in each stack. Then discuss this grouping with your team and decide on names for each of these groups.

2. Paper prototyping exercise: Working in groups, create a paper prototype for an information kiosk to assist visitors to your campus or office building or to a shopping mall or museum. If you did exercise 1, you can choose to use the groupings you have determined. The kiosk will be located in the lobby or in a central location. Visitors unfamiliar with the services or locations of departments would consult this kiosk to get a sense of where to go and how to get there. Consider both the types of visitors you need to help and the types of information they will want. Create a profile of your primary visitor and tasks. Then create the "interface," beginning with the main screen, from which the user can select other screens for information. Each member of the team should assume a role, as described in the chapter. When the task is complete (typically one hour), a representative from another group will become the target user for your kiosk to test the usability of your paper prototype. Discuss what you learned from this paper prototyping activity.

3. Bring in a picture of the completion of some task, such as creating a monthly calendar, planning a garden design, or arranging furniture in an office. You can find an example in a business or home improvement magazine or on the Web. If possible, find a before-and-after picture to show the task and the result. Ask a user to tell you what they would look up to complete this task. Compile a list of the words, phrases, and topics the user uses. This procedure will provide suggestions for the table of contents, index, or help requirements. Discuss how you would arrange this information, using a card-sorting or paper prototyping technique.

4. If you performed the user and task analysis of a common task, described in Chapter 3, you can now conduct a test to determine the documentation you will need and the terminology you should use to match the user's vocabulary. Ask your volunteer user to perform the steps in the process, following the procedure described on page 128. When the user gets stuck, provide information to help the user. Then ask the user to repeat the information. Write down what the user says in the user's own words.

For Your Project

Create a new feature for the product you will be testing or redesign a part of the product that you believe will cause problems for users in its present design. Set up a paper prototyping exercise to test your new feature or redesign, and test it with a user who is not a member of your team. You may want to use the results of this paper prototyping exercise to create a middle- or high-end prototype to include in your usability test plan.

References

Catani, Michael B., and David W. Biers. "Usability Evaluation and Prototype Fidelity: Users and Usability Professionals." *Proceedings of the Human Factors and Ergonomics Society 42nd Annual Meeting*, Chicago, IL, 5–9 Oct. 1998. 1331–35.

Fuccella, Jeanette, and Jack Pizzolato. "Giving People What They Want: How to Involve Users in Site Design." June 1999 IBM <http://www–106.ibm.com/developerworks/library/design-by-feedback/expectations.html>.

Hix, Deborah, and H. Rex Harston. *Developing User Interfaces: Ensuring Usability Through Product and Process*. New York: Wiley, 1993.

Horton, William. *Secrets of User-Seductive Documents: Wooing and Winning the Reluctant Reader*, 2nd ed. Arlington, VA: STC Press, 1997.

Kreitzberg, Charles B., and Ben S. Shneiderman. "Making Computer and Internet Usability a National Priority." *Common Ground* Jan. 1999: 6–8.

"Observing What Didn't Happen." *Eye for Design*, Jan.–Feb. 1999 User Interface Engineering <http://www.uie.com/observng.htm>.

Säde, Simo, and Katja Battarbee. "The Third Dimension in Paper Prototypes." *Common Ground* Oct. 1998: 15–18.

Schrage, Michael. *Serious Play: How the World's Best Companies Simulate to Innovate*. Boston: Harvard Business School Press, 2000.

"Six Slick Tests for Docs and Help." *Eye For Design* Sept.–Oct. 1998 User Interface Engineering <http://www.uie.com/sixslick.htm>.

Tognazzini, Bruce. *Tog on Interface*. Reading, MA: Addison-Wesley, 1992.

Uceta, Fernando A., Max A. Dixon, and Marc L. Resnick. "Adding Interactivity to Paper Prototypes." *Proceedings of the Human Factors and Ergonomics Society 42nd Annual Meeting*, Chicago, IL, Oct. 5–9 1998. 506–11.

Wiklund, Michael E., ed. *Usability in Practice: How Companies Develop User-Friendly Products*. Boston: AP Professional, 1994.

CHAPTER **5**

Planning for Usability Testing

If you're developing a product by applying the user-centered design approach described in the previous chapters, you have been planning for usability testing throughout the development process. If, however, you have just been given the assignment or you have just received approval for the usability test of a product, you may not have done any previous planning about issues affecting usability. Now's your chance. The product you are testing may be in the early stages of development or it may be near completion. Perhaps you will be asked to do a comparison of products to determine what to include in a new product or to see how your product measures up against a competitor's product. Or, if you're a student, you may be asked to perform a usability test of an existing product or one that you have designed. In any event, you have the opportunity to learn a great deal about the product and the process of usability testing, if you plan the test well.

This chapter focuses on the planning process. Planning for usability testing involves the following steps:

- Establishing the team
- Defining the product issues and the audience
- Setting goals and measurements for the test
- Establishing the user profile
- Selecting the tasks to include in the test
- Determining how to categorize the results
- Writing the test plan

We begin with the first task—establishing the team—and move through the process sequentially. Although the process is described as sequential, many of the tasks can be done simultaneously, with the final task—the test plan—summarizing everyone's efforts in the planning process.

Establishing the Team

Some companies take a team approach to user-centered design, which includes members of the team conducting usability testing. Other companies adopt a user-centered design process but do not use a team approach to usability testing, preferring to establish usability centers where experts in human factors and usability perform testing services for internal clients on their products. Typically, companies using this latter approach invite interested developers to sit as observers during testing. When this isn't possible, a video-highlights tape and a report become the vehicle to communicate the results of testing. In other cases, a company may hire a usability consulting firm to conduct the test and deliver the results. Companies with executive viewing rooms provide a way for visitors from the client company to observe the test administrator at work during testing. Such an approach using external evaluation has the advantage of assuring that the tests are well run and expertly performed. Tester bias is eliminated, as the test administrator does not have a stake in the outcome of the test and can therefore conduct the test and interpret the results impartially.

Although this approach has its proponents, we present the team approach. Not only does the team approach support user-centered design, but it also creates a learning opportunity for the team that can improve future product development, as well as the current product being tested. This benefit of learning should not be undervalued because, as Peter Senge states in *The Fifth Discipline*: "The organizations that will truly excel in the future will be the organizations that discover how to tap people's commitment and capacity to learn. . . . [and] teams, not individuals, are the fundamental learning unit in modern organizations" (4, 10). In addition to the value derived from team learning, there is much to be gained from the shared experience of seeing real users struggle, repeatedly, with real problems associated with your product, your creation, your masterpiece. Because "seeing is believing," the most rapid way to effect change is through the process of seeing not one, but user after user struggle over the same tasks. As frequently happens in usability testing, the developers on the team move from an initial condemnation of "that stupid user" to the realization that "we definitely have a problem here" and finally to "I know how to fix that!" Using the team approach, all stakeholders become committed to the success of the usability test from the beginning, with success measured by the number of issues or problems uncovered.

If the team has not had experience in usability testing, it may be helpful to obtain guidance from an outside expert: your instructor, if you are doing this as a class project, or a human factors expert, if your company has one, or if your company does not, an outside usability consultant who specializes in a team approach. If an outside expert is used, this person should both guide and facilitate the process, allowing team members to direct their own project, while providing support to maintain the validity of the test. If you find that you lack the support of an expert, you can use this book as your "facilitator." The main goal is to do a test with the support of your team members; then learn from it and do it again. Many organizations find that the sheer act of doing a usability test for the first time is so energizing to the team that it establishes the momentum to do it again, and earlier, in the development cycle.

Team Structure and Size

Who should be on the team? When putting together a cross-functional team, all those with a common goal of learning about the product should be included. In a corporate setting, these "stakeholders" naturally come from development—both information and systems developers—but they can also come from marketing, sales, training, quality assurance, and technical support.

What's the right size for a team? An effective team needs to include at least three people who represent different viewpoints and who can expend effort to perform the many planning and preparation tasks efficiently. The upper limit may be determined, in part, by the size and location of the facility where testing will be done. How much room will the team have to work in? Will team members be in a usability lab behind a one-way mirror, or will they be sitting in the room with the participant? Or will they be doing testing in the field? Our teams comprise up to six people, as our lab can accommodate that number in the observation room. For more information about team formation and dynamics of teams, see the end-of-book appendix, Making It Work as a Team.

Once the team is in place, its first task is to define the issues and the audience for the test. In the next section, we look at how to define these issues and, once defined, how they shape the planning for a test.

Defining the Issues and Audience

As is frequently the case when you begin planning a usability test, you want to learn *everything* about the usability of the product. As a result, the wish list from team members (or their managers) can be quite lengthy. Nevertheless, you've got a limited budget and a limited time to get results. So, what do you do?

If your organization has done site visits to learn about users and their tasks, you already have a rich source of data to help determine what to test. If marketing has done focus groups, this also provides very useful data for testing. If technical support has a log of issues and problems with previous releases of a product, again, you have rich data to use for testing. Likewise, surveys, response cards, information from sales, and other avenues for gathering data make an excellent starting place for determining what to test. But the first thing to realize is that you cannot test everything. Usability testing, as defined in Chapter 1, is not validation testing and it's not quality assurance testing. Rather, usability testing is typically exploratory: a tool to learn about user preferences, satisfaction, and problems. It should not be the only tool, as the data gathered from focus groups, surveys, contextual inquiry, technical support logs, and so forth also provide excellent insight into users' preferences, satisfaction, and problems.

This may be your only test, however, and so much is riding on the results. So, how does the team determine what to test? You begin by determining the answers to the following questions:

- How much time do you have for the test?
- How much money do you have for the test?
- Where will the testing be done and under what conditions?
- Who wants to know the results? (or who is sponsoring the test?)
- What is best learned from usability testing, and what would be more effectively learned from other methods?

Let's look at each of these questions to understand how the answers affect the test you will plan.

How Much Time Do You Have for the Test?

In companies that practice user-centered design, usability testing is included in the development cycle, typically more than once, as part of the iterative design process. In other situations, usability testing has to be sandwiched into development, with the greatest obstacle being the perception held by management that testing will delay product release. Thus, testing frequently has to be done quickly, which a team approach can support. Because the research on usability testing supports a "discount" approach that produces effective results with four or five test participants (see Chapter 1), usability testing can be done within a very short timeframe, if needed.

Some companies routinely use more than four or five participants, recommending a higher number to provide greater assurance that they're seeing a realistic pattern of use. However, even with a very small number of participants, you're likely to see a clear pattern of problems emerge with very little variation, which is why testing beyond a small number is usually considered unnecessary. There may be circumstances, however, where no clear pattern emerges, which usually indicates that the test is flawed in some way: the user profile may not be specific enough, or the tasks may be too loosely defined, or there may be an inherent problem with the product that results in numerous and varying issues for users. In any case, when a "'non-pattern' pattern" emerges, it is generally not useful to keep testing with more participants (Prekeges). Instead, the test should be re-evaluated.

Sometimes if the budget is really large, the client or company may want to test a large number of participants, using the "safety in numbers" approach. When customers say, "Our product has more than a million users; how can we expect to get reasonable results if we test only eight," User Interface Engineering, a usability consulting company, tells clients that "eight is more than enough," asserting that it takes only four or five, but that with eight you get some "breathing room" in case there are problems with one of the tests or a participant doesn't show up ("Eight Is More Than Enough").

Determining a Testing Schedule

Whether you have the luxury to plan testing over a long period of time or the more realistic situation of having to plan, conduct, and evaluate the results of testing in a very short period of time, certain parts of the planning and testing process must be scheduled. The schedule needs to include dates for the following activities:

- Testing dates
  - Number of participants needed
  - Length of each session
  - Number of days needed for all participants
- Test report or follow-up results meeting
- Pilot test, which precedes the full test dates to allow for a dry-run and repairs to any parts
- Walkthrough, which can be done with or without a user, but is more effective with a "tolerant" user who can understand glitches and interruptions
- Recruiting participants, with back-ups
- Delivery of parts of the test
- Completion of the test plan
- Approval of the test plan

Although the order of these tasks may seem a bit odd at first, experience proves that the most important dates to schedule are the testing dates, followed by the date for the follow-up report, as these mark the end of the cycle. Once these dates are established, the team can see how much room they have to back up from these dates to deliver the other items and schedule the other events needed to conduct the test.

As a minimum, a typical planning process for the schedule might look like this:

1. *Initial team meeting.* Team meets, discusses general approach to testing, defines tasks, sets date for planning meeting.
2. *Half-day planning meeting.* Team meets to set objectives for the test, plan the parts of the product to test, create the user profile and screening questionnaire, determine the tasks to test, the evaluation instruments, the testing environment, the roles for the team, and the schedule for deliverables and testing.

Figure 5.1 illustrates the agenda for this planning meeting.

How Much Money Do You Have for the Test?

Because "time is money," it is somewhat arbitrary to consider how much time you have to test separately from how much money you have budgeted for testing. But the budget does have an impact on how you test, aside from the impact of how much time you have for testing. A major issue that affects budget is how you recruit the participants. Companies with a very small or perhaps no budget for testing frequently solve the problem of how to obtain participants for the test by

NCR and Southern Polytechnic
Agenda for Planning Meeting
April 2, 200__, 9 A.M.–noon

1. Define goals and concerns for the test:
   - Concerns raise the issues of usability testing that the test should be designed to uncover.
   - Goals establish the objectives to measure for usability.

2. Establish the parts of the product to test.

3. Create the user profile and screening questionnaire.

4. Create the task scenarios.

5. Decide how to measure usability (quantitative and qualitative measures).

6. Assign roles for the team members.

7. Establish method for analysis of data.

8. Establish equipment needed for the test and configuration of the evaluator room.

9. Establish dates for the following:
   - Delivery of draft of test materials for review
   - Delivery of final test materials
   - Walkthrough with tolerant user
   - Pilot test
   - Testing dates
   - Findings/recommendations meeting
   - Test report

Figure 5.1 Agenda for planning meeting
(Used with permission of NCR. NCR is a registered trademark of NCR Corporation.)

recruiting people from down the hall. This is a fatal flaw of testing, as someone down the hall or even on the other side of the building may not represent the user *unless the user is truly someone down the hall*. That is, if the user profile is an internal user in the organization, then, of course, you will want to recruit people for the test from inside the organization. More commonly, however, employees in the organization, no matter how removed they are from the product development team, cannot correctly represent the user because *they are not the user*. The temptation to save money by using participants inside the company is not an issue for small companies only. When a very large computer company used internal participants in a test, it failed to take into account that insiders, no matter how far removed from the developers, still have an understanding of terminology that may not be shared by the product's real users. In the case of this company, it wasn't until after the product launched and the help calls started to come in that they learned about the terminology issues, which hadn't shown up in usability testing. The lesson here is that if budget is an issue for recruiting participants, the team must work hard to come up with a solution that solves the problem of how to recruit real users for the test.

Some possible solutions are to offer small gifts as incentive, such as mugs, t-shirts, mousepads, keychains, and the like; or you may be able to provide something more substantive, such as software. Recruiting friends or even family members, *if* they match the user profile, can work. Providing food frequently works, even if the team members have to prepare it or pay for it themselves, as it offers a small reward to participants who volunteer. Some companies go into a shopping mall or busy pedestrian area and recruit participants on the spot. Using the company's customer base can also work, especially if the customer-users are persuaded that they will be helping to improve a product that they use or will want to use.

Of course, if your team has sufficient budget to recruit users and pay them, then other methods for identifying users can be employed, as we discuss in Chapter 6. Another issue that has budget implications is where and how the testing will be done and under what conditions. We consider this issue next.

Where Will Testing Be Done and Under What Conditions?

When planning a usability test, you must first decide whether you want to do field testing, lab testing, or the newest approach, remote testing. Your decision may be based, in part, on the stage of development of the product being tested, as well as the location of the users. Field testing, for instance, works best for summative evaluation (see Chapter 1), to determine how well the product works in the real world for which it has been created. Lab testing (or testing without an actual lab) works best for formative evaluation, to diagnose problems with the product while it is still under development and can be changed. Remote testing is now also becoming an option because of the technology that can support it. Remote testing works best when the users are in far-flung locations, even in other countries. It has its most common use in testing Web sites. In planning for remote testing, a unique issue that may have to be addressed in remote testing of international sites is the choice of language for the test. Should the test be run in one language or multiple languages? If multiple languages, translators have to be recruited. If the test is conducted in one language, questions of misunderstandings related to language differences may arise. See Chapter 9 for more information on planning remote testing for the Web.

Once the decision is made about the type of testing that is best for the situation, the next question to address is the set-up for testing. In field testing, the team probably has little control over the set-up; however, being in the real world of the user and experiencing it as he or she does is the advantage of this type of test. In remote testing, the same may be true when the testing environment is the real world of the user. However, as most testing is done in a laboratory setting, whether or not an actual lab is used, the team needs to decide how the lab will be set up, how the team will interact with the participant, and whether one or more participants will be doing the evaluation at the same time.

The "lab" set-up can simulate an office or home or an assembly line, or it can reflect a commercial setting like a hotel front desk or a checkout stand. If, for instance, the product being tested is to be used in a grocery store checkout stand, the team needs to determine how to simulate this. Should the test include "customers" as they go through the checkout procedure? Can an actual checkout stand be brought in for the test, or does the team need to build a mock-up of one? Does the customer need a cart full of groceries for the test? Should there be music, announcements, or other types of background noise typically found in a grocery store? If the product you're testing is software, is the user expected to install the product in a noisy and distracting situation? If so, how can this be simulated? Or is the person frequently interrupted while performing the task? Should a member of the test team be assigned the role of the one who interrupts, and what would be the nature of the interruption? Should it be a phone call or the arrival of a delivery person? Because issues such as these can affect performance, the team needs to consider ways to simulate a real-world situation if it is critical to gaining an understanding of the product in use.

If you're conducting the test in a room in which the team will be present, where will they sit? Where will the facilitator sit and what role will he or she assume? Will the facilitator sit quietly until each scenario is complete and interact with the participant only at those stopping points? Or will the facilitator sit beside the participant, using a technique called *active intervention*? With active intervention, the facilitator asks questions, probes the user for the rationale behind choices, and poses questions to get the user's reactions to certain aspects of the product. This technique works well in the early stages of product development when testing prototypes, as it provides rich data about user preferences, but little or no data about time on tasks and the user's normal flow of tasks.

In addition to considering the role and position of the team in the testing environment, the team also needs to determine how many participants to test at once. The typical approach is to use one participant at a time. However, another technique, called *co-discovery* or *co-participation*, employs two users who talk to each other while they're solving a problem together. With co-discovery, the participants can talk naturally to each other, which eliminates the need for the unnatural thinking-aloud protocol.

The main reasons to use co-discovery are:

1. You are testing early in the development lifecycle and can learn a great deal about the problem-solving approach that participants use and related usability issues.

2. The real-world situation supports two people helping each other perform a task.
3. It tends to promote more comments than think-aloud sessions.

The major drawbacks to co-discovery are:

1. You have to recruit twice as many users, as each pair generally counts as a single user.
2. You minimize the collection of quantitative data, relying more on qualitative data results, thus making the results harder to collate.
3. One person may dominate, thus affecting the feedback from both users.

In addition to the options of active intervention, think-aloud protocol, and co-discovery, a fourth option to consider when planning a test is called *retrospective recall*. With this option, the user is asked to perform the task in the normal fashion, and after completion of the test, the user and facilitator (or the entire team) review the videotape together. The user explains what motivated action or why problems occurred. The facilitator or team can interrupt and ask questions to get additional insight. Although this technique makes the testing situation much more natural and allows for accurate time on tasks, the process of reviewing the videotape can double or even triple the time for each test. Thus, determining the technique to use is an important part of planning the test.

At the same time that the team is deciding on the testing approach and the type of test to conduct, the team also needs to consider the aspects of the product to test to reflect the needs of the sponsor, as described in the next section.

Who Wants to Know the Results?

Because the list of possible issues to learn from any usability test is typically much longer than can be addressed in any one test, the deciding factor about what to focus on may be based on who wants to know. Another way of putting this is to consider the needs of the sponsor of the test. Is the test being sponsored by the product documentation group? If so, then the focus of the test will be how and when the users seek help from the documentation. With such a focus, the team has two approaches it can use:

1. *Direct users to the documentation or online help* to see whether they find what they need and whether it is useful. Other questions such as how long it takes them to find information and the search strategies they use (index, table of contents, query) can also be observed. Instructing users to use the documentation may not follow the natural inclinations of the users, but if the objective is to see what happens when users use the documentation, you get better results.
2. *Don't direct users to the documentation or online help*. Instead, see whether (or when) they use the documentation or help. This may be a more natural approach, but the team may find that they learn little about the help or documentation because some users never use it.

In some of our tests of documentation, we have instructed users to use the documentation and even put it in their hands, along with the scenario. Then we have observed users staring at the screen and the scenario and saying, "I don't know how to do this" or "This is confusing to me." Yet, they do not use the documentation, which is provided to help them with the specific tasks outlined in the scenarios. In post-test interviews, when we ask them if they used the documentation, they say, "Oh, I guess I should have used this," as they pick it up and thumb through it for the first time, saying, "Yes, this would have been helpful." What we learn, however, is that their natural inclination is to explore and *do*, not read to learn to do. Thus, the team can focus on how to make their desire to act more intuitive so there is less need for documentation.

The same observation of users not using the documentation was reported in the test of the help system for chemists who query very large databases to get information about chemical compounds. The sponsor of the test wanted to learn whether the users could:

- Find the information they needed to query the database
- Retrieve all the information they needed
- Avoid retrieving any information they did not need

See the sidebar entitled "Does Help Help Users" for an explanation of the issues in the test (Grayling).

What if the sponsor for the usability test is from training and wants to know how well a computer-based training program prepares the users for on-site training? What if the sponsor is from the admissions office of a university and wants to know whether users will be able to locate and print the online application for admissions? What if the sponsor is from sales and wants to know whether the Web site motivates the users to complete the transaction for purchase? In each of these situations, the needs of the sponsor shape the focus of the test. If the sponsorship for a test is shared among several departments and the list of issues is long, the team will have to decide what can best be learned from testing and what can be obtained more effectively from other methods. We look at this issue in the next section.

What Is Best Learned from Usability Testing vs. Other Methods?

Because usability testing is most effective as a diagnostic tool to learn problems that users experience with a product, quantitative data gathered from testing of four to five users can shed much light on users' problems. However, usability testing is not the answer to many questions that designers or sponsors may have about a product. Questions such as color preference, font size, use of particular graphics, array of products available, and so forth are matters of personal preference of particular users. Getting feedback from four to five users will not provide valid data. Other more reliable measures can be gained from market research, including focus groups and surveys and questionnaires, which can get larger num-

Does Help Help Users?

In creating a test of an online help system for chemists who query very large databases to get information about chemical compounds, the test team decided to ask the users to use help just as they normally would, rather than instruct them to go to help menus if this was not their normal use. To try to get them to use the online help, however, they created scenarios that they believed would be sufficiently challenging to steer the users to the help for answers. The team relied on customer service to give them suggestions about how to create these complex scenarios.

Knowing that adult users typically prefer trial and error as a problem-solving approach, they expected users to employ this strategy before going to the online help. What they were not expecting were "the extreme lengths to which our test subjects would go to avoid using the Help menu" (Grayling 170). Even when the users searched all the user-interface elements for assistance, they "preferred to revert to the as-yet-unsuccessful trial and error strategy rather than go to the Help menu and review the very material that was designed to assist them" (171). Although this finding did not tell the team what it wanted to know about the online help, it did provide a finding that they would not have learned if they had set up the test to require the users to use online help. From a testing standpoint, the usability test described here failed to give the results the sponsor wanted. From a usability standpoint, however, it provided rich data to change the interface so as to provide the information that users were searching for and not finding.

Source: Trevor Grayling. "Fear and Loathing of the Help Menu: A Usability Test of Online Help." *Technical Communication* 45.2 (1998): 168–79. Reprinted with permission from *Technical Communication,* the journal of the Society for Technical Communication, Arlington, VA, U.S.A.

bers of responses and probe more deeply into users' preferences. Questions such as how users reach a Web site, how they feel about the speed of download, and whether they prefer one method of access over another also fall in the category of information that can best be determined by means other than usability testing. For instance, when a Web-based service for employers and job seekers in the computer industry decided to test its Web site, it first decided to conduct focus groups to learn about certain issues regarding users' preferences and expectations that wouldn't be easy to document in a usability test. Among the questions they wanted marketing to learn from focus groups were the following:

- What motivates users to put their résumés online?
- What are their expectations when they put their résumé online?
- How much time do they expect this process to take?
- How much time are they willing to spend performing this process?
- After what amount of time would they give up?

The answers to these questions allowed the usability testing team to establish a baseline for quantitative measures to determine success rates for users performing tasks, followed by questionnaires to confirm users' satisfaction with the time expended on tasks. Gathering information like this from other sources provides a baseline from which to measure results from usability testing, especially when the team is interested in learning users' preferences and expectations. For more information on focus groups, see Chapter 2.

Another method of getting information about usability issues is through a heuristic evaluation (see Chapter 2). If another group has not already done this, the test team can perform its own heuristic evaluation in preparation for the test. The information that the team gathers from each person's list of problems or potential problems can be used to set priorities for testing hunches or confirming the presence of problems. Of course, if a heuristic evaluation is done early enough in the design of the product, obvious problems can be corrected before usability test planning begins. Others may become part of the issues list for test planning.

Putting Planning into Practice: Hotmail Example

Up to this point, we have been discussing the principles of the planning process. Now, we want to shift to an example of the planning process put into practice. This example comes from a usability test of Hotmail, the popular, free email service provided by Microsoft. Here we introduce the background behind this test and the criteria presented from the test sponsor. In subsequent chapters we will continue to present aspects of the Hotmail test. Although other examples are also used in this book, the Hotmail test will be fully developed to let you see "inside" the planning and preparation process used by the team and to learn what they learned as they received information from their sponsor and used it to plan, prepare, conduct, evaluate, and report the results of usability testing.

Case Problem: Usability Test of Hotmail

Background

In 1999, a student team in a graduate course on usability testing at Southern Polytechnic State University (SPSU) participated in a comparative usability evaluation (CUE) organized by Rolf Molich, a usability specialist at DialogDesign in Denmark. This one, called CUE-2, was the second such comparative evaluation performed. CUE-1 had been conducted the previous year and the results presented at the 1998 Usability Professionals' Association meeting. For information about both evaluations, see <www.dialogdesign.dk/cue.html>. Because CUE-1 teams were not given any information about the sponsor's concerns and issues, the rules for CUE-2 were changed to provide information about the sponsor's concerns and a mechanism for asking questions about the product. In addition, the sponsor would participate in the presentation of the results at CHI 99 (the annual conference of the Computer-Human Interaction Special Interest Group of the Association of Computing Machinery). One further addition to CUE-2 was allowing student teams to participate along with the professional teams, all of whom submitted reports anonymously. The Southern Polytechnic test team·was the only student team that did all the work of planning, conducting, and analyzing the results of testing themselves.

The scenario given to all the teams participating in CUE-2 is presented in the sidebar on pages 152–153.

SPSU Team Analysis

At this point, the question for the usability team was to decide which issues from the sponsor (management) could best be learned from a usability test and which issues would be better understood using other methods. The team determined that the following would best be learned from usability testing:

- Registration
- Login
- Logout
- Customization
- Compose
- Password retrieval
- Sending and receiving attachments
- Reminders
- Hotmail member directory and email look-up
- Sorting messages in your InBox
- Reading a message
- Address book
- Folders
- POP
- Accessing help

However, because marketing and engineering submitted such a long list of concerns, but presented them in priority of interest to product marketing (the sponsor), the team had to decide how many of these issues could be addressed in one test. If the team wanted to do comparison testing of users, they could add the following issue:

- Viewing Hotmail with or without frames (do users have a preference?)

Other issues that management was interested in learning about were better understood through focus groups or tracking software on Web usage or with a larger number of participants than is typical in the discount usability model with four to five participants. For instance, focus groups could be used most effectively to determine the answers to the following questions:

- Which avenue do users of Hotmail choose to reach the Web site?
- Are users' perceptions of Hotmail influenced by the avenue they choose to reach the Web site?
- Is there any distinction in the kinds of users who choose one avenue of access over another?
- Because Hotmail defaults users to a frames version if the users' browser supports frames, do users prefer the non-frames version?
- How do users currently use email?
- If users use the competitors' products—Yahoo Mail and Netscape Web-Mail—how satisfied are they with these products?
- If users use Hotmail, how satisfied are they with the product?
- Would users recommend Hotmail to a friend?

CUE-2 Scenario for Hotmail Test

Scenario (Version 18, January 1999)
You've been hired to evaluate Hotmail.com, the world's free email service you can access from any Internet connected personal computer. The marketing management at Hotmail has sent you the following information which identifies their goals and objectives for this evaluation.

Part One: Hotmail was recently acquired by Microsoft and can now be accessed from both of the following URL's:

<www.home.microsoft.com>

and

<www.hotmail.com>.

Management is very interested in knowing which avenue users are taking to reach their site, and whether or not users' perceptions of Hotmail (and MSN) are influenced by the avenue they choose. [Note: The original Hotmail.com home page and the logo in the top left corner of the navigation bar within the site will most likely change branding in early October. You are required to take a screen shot of the state of the Hotmail.com home page you evaluate for the CUE comparison so we can know if different teams evaluated different branding designs.]

If users are already familiar with Hotmail, how do they choose to access it? Is it easier for new users to locate Hotmail from one URL over the other? Is there any distinction in the kinds of users that tend to use the various avenues?

Additionally, Hotmail defaults you to the frames version of their site (if your browser is capable of interpreting frames). Management is very interested in knowing whether users prefer the non-frames version.

Hotmail's biggest competitors are: Yahoo Mail and Netscape WebMail.

Do NOT test the localized versions of Hotmail, like <www.Hotmail.dk>.

Part Two: Management is also very interested in the general usability of their product and has identified some specific areas of concern. Below is a list of features that Marketing and Engineering have identified as benefiting from user feedback: (Listed in order of importance to Product Marketing):

1. Registration
2. Login
3. Logout (what do users expect after hitting the logout button?)
4. Viewing Hotmail with or without frames—do users have a preference?
5. Customization (under the "Options" section, particularly "Preferences" for viewing style)
6. Performance issues (speed, etc.)
7. Compose
8. Password retrieval

- Would users recommend one of Hotmail's competitors to a friend?
- How reliable do users think Hotmail is? Would they want to use it for urgent or time-sensitive information?
- What are users' general attitudes toward advertisements? Do they click on them? Why or why not?

In addition, the team determined that performance issues connected with speed of download could not be determined in the usability lab, as the lab has a T1 line for fast access to the Internet, whereas individual users' access around the world could vary greatly, depending on the method of access (modem and modem speed, DSL line, or other method) and the type of computer used. Experimental design tests, using a large number of participants, would be a better method to obtain information about performance issues, especially comparisons of speed using different browsers such as Yahoo and Netscape. Tracking software could determine where users go on a site, such as whether they use the POP option and whether they click on any advertisements.

9. Sending and receiving attachments
10. Reminders
11. Hotmail member directory and email look-up
12. Sorting messages in your InBox (by Subject, Date, etc.)
13. Reading a message (related issues: Screen resolution and size; URL recognition when a message has a URL in it)
14. Address book
15. Folders
16. POP (under "Options")
17. Advertisements (general attitude, do users click on them? Why, why not?)
18. When do users try to access help (do not test help system, just identify when users feel they need help)

General questions which management is interested in addressing are:

1. How do users currently do email?
2. Generally, how much effort do users have to expend to interact with and use Hotmail effectively?
3. How satisfied are users with Hotmail?
4. If a first time user, do users think they will continue using Hotmail on their own?

5. Would user recommend Hotmail to others?
6. How reliable do users think Hotmail is? Would they want to use it for urgent or time sensitive information?

Hotmail management wants to focus only on the mail features and functions, and not the other services now offered from the site. They are *not* interested in the following areas:

Classifieds

Web Courier

News and Links

or other general portal features.

User Profile: Hotmail is a world-wide free email service targeted towards anyone who would like the convenience of managing their email online through a Web browser. Hotmail can be accessed from any computer or kiosk that provides Internet access, making it easy to access your mail from anywhere. Hotmail also allows you to manage all your own personal email without it being recorded on your employer's servers.

Source: <www.dialogdesign.dk/cue.html>.

Once these types of issues are sorted out by the team, the next aspect of planning a test is to set test goals and methods of measurement. We examine that aspect of planning in the next section.

Setting Goals and Measurements

Setting goals for a test means determining two things:

1. What do you want to learn from the test?
2. How do you want to measure the results you receive?

To answer these two questions, the team needs to learn how its members see the issues, especially since team members probably view the product from different perspectives. Knowing what each member wants to learn and determining how to measure the results are important for achieving results that the team can use.

Ill-defined questions will result in lost time and effort. Team meetings, email exchanges, and conversations will be needed to establish clear goals that can be measured. Here's a list of questions team members should ask themselves and each other (Rojek and Kanerva 150):

- What do you want to learn from this test?
- What are your greatest fears about this product?
- Are there different points of view in the group about this issue?
- What are you willing to change as a result of this test?
- Have you made assumptions about users or their strategies?
- Is a particular feature targeted at all your users or a subset of users?
- How will you know when the product is good?

Once the team understands its goal for testing, it can turn its attention to the users' goals.

Users' goals are based on tasks, but users' tasks are not the same thing as users' goals. For instance, the user's task may be to complete a registration form for a workshop on a Web site, but the goal is to attend the workshop. So, the objective of a test of this task is to determine the ease of use of the form, the amount of time required to complete it, the number of steps involved, and the user's assessment of the simplicity or difficulty of the task to accomplish the goal.

Defining clear objectives makes test planning easier because all decisions about what to test, how to test, who to test, and what measures to use to evaluate data from the test derive from the test objectives. Test objectives should be measurable and task-based. Typically, developers will say that they want to know if a product is intuitive, user-friendly, better than the competitor's product, or appropriate for the novice user. But what is meant by "intuitive," "user-friendly," "better," and "novice user," and how will you know if the product achieves these values for this user? The best way to determine this is to set a general goal, then *operationalize* it. When you operationalize a goal, you are defining it in specific, measurable terms. Here's how James Prekeges, a usability specialist, describes an operationalized goal of making files in a software application "easier" to open and close:

> All users tested will be able to open and close a file within 3 tries the first time they try each action during the course of using the product, and 80% of users will be able to successfully open and close a file in one try by the third time the user attempts to do each action. Further, the overall satisfaction with ease of use of these features must be an average of at least 4 on a scale of 5, with no users reporting less than 3 out of a possible 5.

Measurable goals determine not only that users can perform tasks, but also that they can perform them in a specified time that matches their expectations. So, what can you measure in a usability test? The most common measurements include:

- Time on task
- Percentage of tasks completed (correctly without help, correctly after help)
- Percentage of tasks not completed

- Number of errors (recoverable or not)
- Time to recover from an error
- Number of repetitions or failed commands
- Number of commands or features not used
- Time spent navigating (on paper or on line) in search of information
- Number of steps to complete a task
- Number of assists (calls to help or use of online help or print documentation)
- Number of clicks (optimum path to correct information)
- Quantity of information found
- In comparison testing, which of two products performs better when users have to locate information or perform tasks

In addition to establishing measurable goals about tasks and actions, you can also establish measurable goals about users' satisfaction. Although user perceptions and satisfaction are subjective (or qualitative) data, you can quantify their views through questionnaires and then compare the results from all your users to establish average user responses. Survey questions can be formulated that ask users to rate their satisfaction with:

- Ease of use
- Ease of navigation
- Usefulness
- Ease of learning
- Ease of recovery from errors
- Helpfulness of help and other support
- Number of positive features they can recall

Quantitative data can also be gathered about preferences when users are comparing products or versions of a product in development, or when they are asked to compare the product being tested to the way they are currently performing tasks.

Your team needs to establish the ratings it will accept as measures of success in the task areas (performance measures) as well as in the subjective areas. Does the team want a maximum level of performance or a minimum acceptable level? What would be an acceptable number of attempts to succeed? What percentage of users should rate the experience at a certain satisfaction level? As an example, a goal may be operationalized that 100% of users should rate the ease of use of the product at 4 or 5 on a 5-point scale.

Goals vs. Concerns

Dumas and Redish define a concern as a question and a goal as a statement resulting from the question (110). The concerns come from the questions raised by the team, as we discussed earlier in this chapter. The goals become concrete statements in answer to these questions, which then shape the nature of the usability test.

For example, if you are planning a test of some new data input forms to be used in a computerized banking procedure, you might establish the goals, based on the process of moving from a general goal to specific concerns and then to a usability goal that can be measured (see Table 5.1).

For the test of a software tool to be used by homeowners to create garden designs, the team established the following concerns and goals, focusing on the documentation and tutorial:

- *Installation concern.* Will a user be able to install the program quickly and easily?
- *Installation goal.* The user will install the program, using the written documentation, within 5 minutes.
- *Tutorial concern.* Will the user be able to identify and use the key tools quickly and easily?
- *Tutorial goal.* The user will be able to identify the key tools and use them within 15 minutes of receiving the tutorial document.
- *Task concern.* Will the user be able to quickly and easily develop a landscape plan for a home garden based on a written description?
- *Task goal.* The user will develop a landscape plan for a home garden based on a written description within 30 minutes.

Establishing Qualitative Goals

In addition to quantifying goals and establishing benchmarks or objective measurements, you should also plan to capture qualitative data, which can be a rich source of information about users' satisfaction and problems with the product.

TABLE 5.1	Progression from General Goal to Concerns to Usability Goal
General goal	Create input forms that users will want to use.
Specific concern	Will the users want to work with the input forms, or will they avoid the forms?
Specific concern	Will users attempt to update the data records by opening the form in a data sheet view instead of in a form view, effectively bypassing the input form?
Quantitative usability goal	Each user will switch to the database view of a form no more than once per session.
General goal	Design input forms through which users can navigate quickly and easily.
General concern	Will users be able to navigate through the forms?
Quantitative usability goals	1. The user will be able to locate the correct form for the task in 2 minutes or less. 2. The user will be able to locate a blank form to enter a new record in 2 minutes or less.
	3. Time needed to locate the correct form should be less for the last task than it was for the first attempted task by each user.
General goal	Create input form that users will prefer over previous procedure.
Specific concern	Will users find greater satisfaction in using the new input form vs. the previous input procedure?
Qualitative usability goal	Users will rank the new form with at least a 4 (on a 5-point scale, with 5 being the best) when asked their satisfaction level with the form.

(Used with permission of Susan E. Reu.)

Although quantitative data can tell you that *something* is wrong, qualitative data can tell you *what* is wrong from the user's point of view. You can capture qualitative data from the things that users say when they think out loud, from their body language and facial expression, even from their sounds, such as sighing, moaning, or perhaps even screaming. In addition, post-task, open-ended questions and especially the more in-depth post-test questionnaire provide opportunities to get qualitative data from users. To capture and study this information, teams frequently videotape the interview of the post-test questionnaire session.

Once you've established the objectives of the test, as well as the ways of measuring the results, you are now ready to determine the users for the test. This is a critical step, as you must carefully define a profile for the user in order to get consistent results with a small number of participants. We take up the method for establishing the user profile in the next section.

Establishing the User Profile

When thinking about the users of your product, you will likely come up with a number of categories of "typical" users. The more specific you can make your descriptions of your users, the better you will be at identifying people who match your user profile. As Alan Cooper advocates, you can establish personas of users by creating detailed descriptions, including photos, to fix in your minds what a particular user would want. For more on this topic, see Chapter 3.

Within a potentially large group of users, you can define subgroups of users by their familiarity with your product, familiarity with similar products, and general level of technical or computer expertise (if the product requires technical or computer competence). Still further, you can subdivide users by the ways in which they will use the product. Jared Spool of User Interface Engineering uses *core vs. ring theory* to characterize users on the basis of the way in which the product fulfills the user's needs. For instance, a user called Chip has the following characteristics:

- Runs a $2.5 million auto-repair business
- Bought two applications
  - car diagnosis package
  - business finance package

Although he uses both packages, Chip is a "core" user of the car diagnosis package, in which he has subject matter expertise; however, he is a "ring" user of the business finance package. As a core user, Chip customized the car diagnostic package to streamline his business, was familiar with the jargon, and didn't use the wizards available to help him learn the system. As a ring user of the financial package, he did not understand the jargon, considered himself a novice, and relied on the wizards to help him. He also was not comfortable making changes, so the package shaped how he ran that aspect of the business, vs. the other way around, in which he shaped the package to match his business practices.

If the four or five participants brought into a usability test included both ring and core users, it would be extremely difficult to correlate the results from testing to draw conclusions about either population, as there would be too few users on which to base assumptions. Thus, it is critical to the success of a "discount" usability test to identify the specific characteristics of a subgroup of users for each test. If you want to learn about more than one subgroup, you need to establish more than one user profile, and then test with at least three participants per subgroup.

Chauncey Wilson, a usability specialist, recommends considering the following factors* in establishing a user profile:

- Motivation—how motivated are users to use the product?
- Typing skills—critical for some jobs.
- Task experience—familiarity with the task that the product supports.
- Turnover rates—high turnover rates would indicate that ease of learning issues is critical.
- General education.
- Learning style.
- Computer background.
- Software applications used.
- Expected training support for the product.
- Age ranges.
- Stress level when performing tasks.
- Domain (subject matter) knowledge.
- Number of people involved in performing the tasks.
- Job category.
- Level of automation.
- Attitude toward the job.
- Location of use (home, office).
- Physical characteristics.
- Disabilities—what percentage of the user population has disabilities that could affect product use?
- Number of people in user population with English as a second language.

Although one of the most valuable benefits of usability testing is learning about the first-time user's experience, you want to be careful about designing tests (and products) that capture the experience only for novice users, unless you are confident that a majority of your users will be novice users or that this is the particular group you want to understand. Even with a large population of novice users, many of these users will likely become more proficient in time, so you need to consider whether the product will continue to support their needs when they mature as users.

Defining the Characteristics of a Subgroup

Because there are so many variables regarding potential users of your product, each subgroup of users must be carefully identified to match the characteristics of the users within that group. If you know that you have both experienced and

---

*Used with permission of Chauncey Wilson.

inexperienced users of your product, you can probably create several categories within each of those groups. How do you define inexperienced users? Are they inexperienced with your product or with all products like yours? Or are they experienced with other products but not your products? Or are they inexperienced with the tool and technology of your product, but experienced in the process that your product supports? As you can see, there are many ways to define the word "experience." If you ask the users to rate their own proficiency or experience with a product, you can get wildly varying interpretations. So, you must ask specific questions that provide a range of responses, such as:

- Length of time using the product
- Number of times per week they use a product
- Number of hours per week they use a product
- Specific tasks they perform with the product (this could be a list or it could be open-ended to see how they respond)

This line of questioning can be used for other types of skills required as well, such as a particular software or hardware proficiency users may (or may not) have.

One way to characterize your subgroups is to determine the percentage of users who match a particular subgroup. For instance, if you learn from site visits, surveys, and other methods that 50% or more of your user population will have between six months and two years of experience with a particular computer application critical to understanding your product, you can begin to define your subgroup using this information. You will then need to add other characteristics from the list above to narrowly define the user profile and avoid "the wild-card effect," which means that "random variability among participants can result in highly variable outcomes, making the comparison of techniques difficult" (Gray and Salzman 237). Rubin recommends making one subgroup out of those who have the least competent proficiency with the product. These least competent users, although they may not represent a large percentage of the population, can teach you a lot about the "novice" experience with the product, particularly as it relates to ease of learning, intuitiveness, and product design (129). Dumas and Redish recommend that when you cannot select three to five users from each subgroup, you should select users from both ends of the spectrum of users, leaving out the middle of the range. They argue that if, for instance, you include novice users and experienced users and leave out the intermediate group, whatever problems you see for both novice and experienced users will likely be true for intermediate users (125–26). When mixing your groups, however, you want to be sure that your test includes at least three users from each group, rather than trying to test six users of varying experience. In this way, you can validate your results more easily and avoid the wild-card effect. Of course, if you test a larger number with varying experience and you sort the results according to users' specific experience, you should be able to account for differences (and similarities) between the experience levels.

Other factors that are important to consider in your user population are age and gender, particularly according to the potential effect they may have on users' experience with computer products. Although there is much research that still needs to be done about the impact of these two factors on product use, we do have some research results. In Chapter 3, we reported on the impact of age on memory-based tasks and click rate using the Web. Another study of older users found that time of day affects performance. Using the preferences of their audience, with more younger people preferring afternoon times for tasks and more older people preferring morning times for tasks, the study tested users' optimal and non-optimal times for tasks. Not surprisingly, both groups performed better at their preferred time of day (Intons-Peterson, et al. "Aging, Optional Testing"). In a second study to clarify issues raised in the first study, results showed that older adults demonstrated poorer performance on recall when tested at their less preferred time of day. Younger adults were not significantly affected by time-of-day issues (Intons-Peterson, et al. "Age Testing"). In addition, issues may arise when users wear eyeglasses, particularly when they wear bifocals or trifocals, which are more commonly worn by older users; thus, you may need to test some users who wear glasses.

Gender can also be a factor in usability, although studies of this issue are scant. It was recently reported, for instance, that researchers at the University of Ulm in Germany scanned the brains of men and women as they performed the task of escaping from a three-dimensional virtual reality maze. The researchers found that the brains of men and women process directions differently: men relied on the left hippocampus and used geometry to find their way out of the maze; women used the right frontal cortex, relying on memory to recall landmarks they had passed ("Which Way Out?"). When the question of whether to include women in Web testing was posed to subscribers of a usability listserv, respondents suggested that there are likely gender issues to be learned from comparing women and men, but that the problems with most Web sites are so pervasive that no one has gotten down to fine-tuning the differences between men's and women's preferences or use. However, whenever your user population includes both men and women, it is a very good idea to include both in your user profile, as the differences can be noteworthy.

See the sidebar entitled "Hotmail User Analysis" on pages 162–163 and the appendix entitled "Hotmail Usability Test Plan" at the end of this chapter for the Hotmail user profile, based on this analysis.

Once the user profile is established, the next step in planning is to create the list of tasks to test, which we take up in the next section of this chapter.

Selecting the Tasks to Test

The list of tasks you want to test typically far exceeds the time and budget you have for testing. So, the choice of tasks to test should be based on your operationalized goals (as discussed earlier in this chapter) and the needs of the users you have identified. Other considerations that might affect the tasks are the amount of time you have for testing, coupled with the number of participants you can use in the test. If, for instance, you want to test two subgroups of three users each and you have two days for testing, you may decide that you can test three users per day for two hours per user, total time, including pre-test and post-test questionnaires. If you have more time, you can test more users or test the same number of users performing more tasks. We have found that users tire after an hour of testing, so we design our tests typically to last one hour with a total time for each participant of one and one half hours. Some test groups use longer time periods per user, ranging from several hours to all day. If you want to test for longer periods, you have to include breaks or a meal for the user, as well as for the team. More about scheduling users will be discussed in Chapter 6.

With a general understanding of the amount of time you want to allow for each user, you can establish priorities for the tasks you want each user to do. These tasks may be the same for all users, or you may want to begin with the same tasks for all users and then add more advanced tasks for the more proficient users. To maximize the amount of time you have with each user, it's a good idea to prepare some optional tasks for any users who complete the tasks in less time than anticipated.

The biggest mistake some people make in creating the task list is to try to learn the answer to every question anyone has about the product. Instead, you should simplify the tasks to keep the test focused on specific goals. Because a usability test is typically exploratory, you can't expect to "validate" all phases or features of the product. As well, you want to avoid the "might as well" syndrome, which goes something like this: "While you're at it, you might as well ask users to . . . "

Tasks are frequently determined by using the following criteria:

- First impressions (look and feel of the product)
- First tasks (so important in fixing in users' minds whether they will consider the product easy or difficult to use)
- Tasks most frequently performed
- Critical tasks (even if performed less frequently)
- Specific problem areas (typically identified by sponsor or heuristic evaluation)
- New tasks added to a product or changes made from an earlier version of the product (including changes made after an earlier usability test of a prototype)

Organizing Tasks

Once you've created a list of the tasks you want to test, you need to arrange them in some order. The best way to begin testing is with a short and simple task.

If you want to get users' first impressions of your Web site, for instance, you can begin with a task that has them look at the homepage without clicking on anything and give their impression of what type of a site it is and what their feelings are about the site (or as compared to other sites). Another task may be to ask the users to explain (again without clicking anywhere) where they think they would go on the site to find different kinds of information (based on a list you provide).

(continued on page 164)

Hotmail User Analysis

The Hotmail sponsor submitted the following user profile:

> Hotmail is a worldwide, free email service targeted toward anyone who would like the convenience of managing their email online through a Web browser. Hotmail can be accessed from any computer or kiosk that provides Internet access, making it easy to access your mail from anywhere. Hotmail also allows you to manage all your own personal email without it being recorded on your employer's servers.

SPSU team's issues with the profile

The Southern Polytechnic State University (SPSU) team noted that the sponsor's user profile "leaves much to be desired. If it sounds like a marketing piece, it probably is, and it probably came from the marketing group, which is a frequent source of information about a product's users. However, this information will not lead to a user profile that can be used to screen participants for a test because it says only that the product has universal appeal, which does little or nothing to help identify target users, let alone specific subgroups of target users for this test."

Questions presented to the sponsor from the team

As the user profile was inadequate for their purpose, the SPSU team presented a list of questions to their contact person (a member of the advisory committee for CUE-2, not a member of the client organization). What follows are their questions, and the responses they received from the advisory committee member.

Question: What information, if any, do you currently have on your users? Demographics would be helpful!

Answer:
- Hotmail is intended for anyone who wants a free email account which they can access from a Web browser. Of course, this means that users have to have access to the Internet already. So, typically, Hotmail users are people who have Web access at work, but who want a free, personal email account to use from work that is not maintained by their employer. Most businesses frown on employees using their company email accounts for personal email. Also, using a separate Web-based email account ensures that your personal email is never on your company's servers.
- Hotmail users are also business people who travel a lot. It's often easier for business people at remote client sites to find a terminal with a browser running than it is to dial into an ISP and download mail. With Hotmail, you just need any browser running on any computer anywhere.
- Hotmail users are also students who get Web access for free on terminals in the school library, in student lounges, or in cyber-cafes.
- Hotmail is for users who would rather not have to deal with setting up a third party email client in order to have their ISP host a mail account for them. With Hotmail, all you need to do is configure your browser.
- Hotmail is for anybody who might already have an ISP mail account, but has a need for a second email address.
- Hotmail can also be used to corral many accounts . . . say, you're a user with accounts from many different providers because you want to have multiple Web personas (i.e., several businesses) . . . you can have all the mail forwarded to a Hotmail account so that you don't have to go

to each account separately to read the mail.
- Hotmail users are international users and international travelers.
- Hotmail users are households/small business with a single ISP account—everyone in the household/small business can use the same computer to access individual Hotmail accounts from the browser without having to have separate ISP accounts.

Question: What level of computer expertise does Hotmail expect users to have?

Answer: They are expected to know how to turn on their computer, connect to the Internet and launch their Web browser. They are not necessarily the ones who configure their Web browser or their TCPIP configurations. That may have been done by a system administrator or a friend or colleague.

Question: What level of Internet experience does Hotmail expect users to have?

Answer: They are expected to be familiar with a Web browser and know how to click links in a Web page and enter URLs, but extensive browser experience should not be necessary to get started. Hotmail could be the reason they attempt to use a browser in the first place.

Question: Which expertise levels does Hotmail think are most important to target in our study?

Answer: A cross-range of novice and expert Web users and novice and expert email users (people may be expert email users, but novice Web users; or expert Web users but novice email users, etc.). Hotmail has a special interest in determining whether or not Hotmail meets the needs of people who use email on a regular basis with moderate to heavy use.

Question: How many of the current Hotmail users have used other email software, and how do they compare it to Hotmail?

Answer: Assume that this varies across our user base. The usability study hopefully will determine these attitudes (as well as others); that's why we engaged usability consultants :)

Question: Do you have any data regarding Hotmail users outside of the IT [information technology] world? How many people not familiar with technology have a Hotmail account?

Answer: Don't have this exact data, but again, Hotmail *is* intended for people outside the IT world.

Question: Does Hotmail currently have more male or female users? Students or professionals? Younger or older people? Any information on income of current Hotmail users, since the site is free? Any information that would fall into other categories not listed would be most helpful!

Answer: Sorry, I can't supply you with any specific demographics. Again, Hotmail is intended for *anybody* who wants a free email account.

Question: What companies are your biggest advertising clients?

Answer: Sorry, I can't provide this information.

Question: Does Hotmail have any big "company" accounts?

Answer: Sorry, I can't provide this information.

Question: What types of complaints or compliments does Hotmail receive from its customers? How are they related to human factors and usability?

Answer: I wouldn't want to bias the observations you gather from your study :) You're the usability specialists.

(continued)

Question: Because of the limitations on attachments, is this perceived as an inconvenience?

Answer: That's what we want you to find out for us :) You're the usability specialists.

Team analysis of responses

Although this information was certainly helpful to the team, it didn't supply them with everything they would have been able to learn from the client (or sponsor) of the test if they had been able to address these questions directly to the client. The team discussed what they learned about the user population from the responses to the questions. One member's analysis for her teammates was as follows:

Question: What information, if any, do you currently have on your users. Demographics would be helpful!

Analysis: Translation: no answers really given here. They're telling us what they *want* their users to be, not necessarily who their users actually are. What something is intended for and what it's actually used for can be two different things.

Question: What level of computer expertise does Hotmail expect its users to have? What level do they have, if known?

Analysis: Useful information, although the answers to these two questions

were nearly the same. They seem to see computer and Internet experience as equivalent. So a novice user for Hotmail would be one that already knows a little bit about their computer and a bit about surfing the Web. A novice user would not be someone who knows absolutely nothing about computers.

Question: Which expertise levels does Hotmail think are most important to target in our study?

Response: I think that the first group will be hard to come by (expert email, novice Web). The Web is really what brought most people to the Internet. The second group (expert Web users and novice email users) should be much easier.

Although the team still had some unanswered questions, they felt that the responses from the Hotmail advisor provided enough information to identify some of the subgroups of users and to create user profiles for these. The team created two user profiles: one for a novice and another for an expert user. These are included in the appendix entitled "Hotmail Usability Test Plan" at the end of this chapter.

Note: At the conclusion of the CUE-2 evaluation, it was learned that the SPSU team was the only one involved in the evaluation that submitted questions to the sponsor.

Source: Questions from SPSU student team used with permission of Michael Quinby. Responses from Hotmail "sponsor" used with permission of Erika Kindlund, a member of the CUE-2 advisory committee acting as a representative from Hotmail. Analysis of sponsor's responses used with permission of SPSU team member Nadyne Mielke.

If you're testing a software product that needs to be installed, the typical first task is to ask users to install the product, as this will be the first place users will interact with the product and form impressions about it. Or you might describe a typical first task as "browsing": asking the user to explore the software and documentation of a product. This is quite often a normal first task for users, so it feels natural to be asked to do it. Judy Ramey, a usability professor and consultant, calls this basic task of exploration "fishing" as opposed to more specific tasks to expose problems, which she calls "trapping."

For each of these tasks, you can plan the amount of time the task should take and you can establish ways to measure the results, using both quantitative and qualitative measures, as discussed earlier in this chapter. The first task or tasks, which will be developed into the first scenario, should be designed to be short for the following reasons:

- You want to make the user feel at ease by beginning with a simple task.
- Because many tests ask the user to think out loud, the test administrator will be able to remind the user to think out loud after the completion of the first task.
- A short first task provides the team with the opportunity to ask questions and also to make any adjustments needed to the equipment or in response to the user's needs.

A typical list of tasks we use when testing software and documentation is as follows:

Task 1. Install the software and give first impressions of the product once installed. Time: 5 minutes.

Task 2. Using the quick reference card and a tutorial, practice with the tools users will need to perform typical tasks with the product. Time: 15 minutes.

Task 3. Perform a typical task or series of tasks with the product (using the quick reference card, knowledge gained from the tutorial, and documentation, as needed). Time: 30 minutes.

Here's an example from a software product called "Better Working Desktop." The Spinn Team* created the following set of user characteristics:

- Use computer with Windows or DOS operating systems in their business or personal lives, with the following levels of experience:
  - Novice: 0–3 months
  - Intermediate: 3–12 months
  - Skilled: more than one year
- Education—high-school diploma or higher
- No experience with similar computer products
- Currently use a paper-based organizer to perform similar tasks
- Use the computer to make more productive use of their time

The Spinn Team's task plan for Better Working Desktop incorporates the goals of the test with the measurement criteria and the tasks.

Scenario 1: Install

Goals

- Test the usability of the instructions and procedures provided on the Quick Reference Card (QRC) developed for the installation.

---

*Used with permission of the Spinn Team: Barbara Delano, Sean Romer, William McClain, and Jim Mattingly.

- Determine whether the user can successfully install and access the program using the QRC.

Measurement Criteria

- The user should be able to install the program to the hard disk and access the program successfully within 5 minutes.
- The user should be able to install the program to the hard disk drive using the information on the QRC without calling the help desk.

Tasks

1. Remove the disk from the product box and install it in the computer.
2. Use the QRC, if needed, with the installation procedure.
3. When the installation is complete, open the program.

Scenario 2: Tutorial

Goals

- Test the usability of the QRC in learning how to use the tools to perform tasks.
- Determine whether the user can successfully perform the tasks, using the QRC, without assistance from the help desk.

Measurement Criteria

- The user can complete the tutorial, using the QRC, in 15 minutes.
- The user can complete the tutorial without calling the help desk.

Tasks

Use the tools in the software to:

- Find the address book.
- Find where you would enter information into the address book.
- Find how you would enter information into the address book.
- Find the memo pad.
- Find out how to write a note and save it in the memo pad.
- Find out how to access a note that you have saved to the memo pad.
- Find the calendar.
- Find the calendar reminders feature.
- Enter a reminder and close the calendar.
- Access your reminder entry.

Scenario 3: Application

Goals

- Test the usability of instructions and procedures provided on the QRC developed for typical tasks.
- Determine whether users can successfully perform each task using the instructions on the QRC.

Measurement Criteria
- The user will be able to successfully perform all tasks within 30 minutes.
- The user should be able to successfully complete all tasks using the QRC without calling the help desk.

Tasks
1. Open the address book. Enter two addresses. Close the address book.
2. Open the calendar. Enter the week's schedule. Close the calendar.
3. Open the calendar. Enter a new appointment. Close the calendar.
4. Open the to-do list. Make an entry in the to-do list. Close the to-do list.

This list of tasks for each scenario will be more fully developed in the preparation for testing. Creating scenarios from a task list is described in Chapter 6. The sidebar (below) describes the way in which the SPSU team created the task list for Hotmail.

Task List for Hotmail

As we presented earlier in this chapter, management's wish list of the tasks to be tested for Hotmail was far greater than could be accomplished in a typical test. Also, as the team sorted through the list, they determined that quite a few areas where management wanted information could be better obtained from other data-gathering methods, such as focus groups, heuristic evaluation, surveys, and tracking software. Management did list the items in order of priority, so that helped the team plan the tasks to include in the test. Because they decided to test two groups of users—novices and advanced users—they also decided to sort out which tasks would be performed by both groups (with results compared) and which tasks would be performed by the advanced users only, as shown in Table 1 from their test plan. See their test plan at the end of this chapter for more information about the characteristics of these two user groups, as well as the time for each task.

Table 1 Test Participants and Tasks to Be Tested

Tasks to Be Tested	Advanced User Task	Novice User Task
Registration	X	X
Logging in to Hotmail	X	X
Logging out from Hotmail	X	X
Reading messages	X	X
Composing (writing) a message	X	X
Sending and receiving messages	X	X
Sending attachments	X	
Creating and using folders	X	
Creating and using address book	X	

Source: Used with permission of the SPSU Hotmail team: Marji Schumann, Benjamin Speaks, Melany Porter, Arlene Nadyne Mielke, Michael Quinby, and Anusuya Mukherjee.

Once you have established the tasks for the test, matched to the users and the test objectives, the next item to plan is the way in which results will be categorized.

Determining How to Categorize the Results

As part of planning, you need to plan what you will do with the data you collect and how you will analyze it. Earlier in this chapter, we talked about the need, in most cases, to collect both quantitative and qualitative data. But you will find, once you begin collecting this information, that you have many, many findings. So, how can you organize them to interpret what you have collected and to report this information to others? Two approaches are typically used: top-down and bottom-up. Both get you to the same place, but as the labels suggest, they go about it in opposite ways. By understanding the methodology of both approaches, your team can choose the approach that works best in your situation.

Top-Down Approach

The top-down approach begins with an established set of categories for potential findings from a usability test. These are typically based on a set of heuristics for usability. Whenever you observe a violation of a heuristic, you can place it in one of the categories. In Chapter 2, we discussed various heuristic models, with the most popular one being Nielsen's 10 heuristics for usability. Using Nielsen's heuristics, you can look for violations of any of these heuristics, such as "visibility of system status" or "consistency and standards." Findings from a usability test can be plugged into these 10 heuristics. However, these heuristics are intended for evaluation by experts, rather than for observations of users in a usability test, so they may not always apply to what you see in a usability test.

The Usability Group has created its own list of heuristics, called a Yardstick™, which is based on principles of user interface design. Table 5.2 shows each element in the Yardstick and the relevant questions that define the design principles associated with each element.

The advantage of using a system like this one is that the team has a common vocabulary for talking about the issues that arise in usability testing. The person who logs the findings can set up a code to match these usability principles to the findings for fast team analysis after each user completes a test. In addition, being aware of the types of findings that occur in most usability tests alerts the team to be on the lookout for some they might otherwise overlook. If the test is being administered by one or perhaps two people, using this system can improve the likelihood of capturing a variety of findings, rather than focusing on one or two of the most obvious issues. Finally, if testing is conducted over time and by different teams or individuals, the top-down method provides consistency of analysis and interpretation, regardless of who is doing the testing or reporting the findings.

TABLE 5.2	Usability Yardstick to Measure Findings
1. Clarify the core concepts	Does the design match the user's mental model (e.g., the desktop metaphor)?
2. Fit content to customers who use the product	Does the content fit the user's expectations? Is the information organized or mapped properly and at the right level for the audience? Are there any missing parts?
3. Plan and maintain consistency	Is there consistency from program to program (external consistency) and within a program (internal consistency)?
4. Provide reassuring feedback	How does the system provide feedback or information to the user (dialog boxes, time to complete tasks, etc.)?
5. Clarify interaction rules	Does the system follow a standard set of rules for interacting with the product from a design point of view (e.g., drag and drop or buttons)?
6. Structure navigation clearly	Does the user understand how to get from point A to point B (menu, icon, keyboard use)?
7. Use plain terminology	Does the language match the user's own vocabulary of use?
8. Optimize user assistance	Can users get help when they need it (online help or performance support)?
9. Optimize visual design	Is the visual design effective and pleasing (e.g., do radio buttons look like radio buttons; are the icons intuitive in design)?
10. Design for the context of use	Can the product be used as designed (are there "bugs" in the system that prevent it or is the context of use poorly conceived)?

Source: Courtesy of The Usability Group, LLC <www.usability.com>.

The disadvantage of using such a system is that it establishes a prescribed method for responding to observations of users, as opposed to the next method we'll discuss, which works without any predetermined terminology to allow for collective interpretations, based on individual observations.

Bottom-Up Approach

Using the bottom-up approach, the team works together to incorporate everyone's individual findings and determine how they should be grouped into categories with descriptive labels for each category. This approach is called *affinity matching* or *affinity diagramming,* as it matches items that have an affinity or similarity. It is bottom-up because the team collaborates to determine what should be matched and what each group of matched items should be called. Here's how it typically works (Scanlon):

1. Each member of the team puts one thought/observation/idea per sticky note (or 3" × 5" card).
2. In a room designated for the analysis, each member organizes his or her own sticky notes (or swaps with another team member) to group items that seem to go together, without designating any pre-defined categories.

3. While this is going on or when it is done, any member can move any of the notes to other groupings if they see a better match. If a note keeps getting moved back and forth, then it's all right to duplicate it to put in both places.
4. Categories that get bigger than five items should be broken up into new groups.
5. When this process is complete, the team works together to label the categories.

For a fuller discussion of this process, see Chapter 7.

The advantages to using this bottom-up method of analysis are that it equalizes the involvement of all members of the team and allows for the possibility of seeing observations from testing in new and refreshing ways. It also brings the team together in a consensus-building activity to decide what items belong together and what they should be called. Another advantage is that it allows for more discussion as part of the analysis, whereas the top-down method puts a label immediately on an observation. As a result, this method may produce much finer groupings than the top-down method using preset groupings. Or this method can produce subgroupings under larger groupings.

The disadvantages to using this method are that it requires a bit of learning (and practice) to understand how it works, and it requires a room and a team meeting to do it. For those trying the process for the first time, it can be confusing and even overwhelming, so a good facilitator is needed to involve everyone and keep the process moving forward. Another disadvantage is that inconsistency may creep into this process, as team members may record different kinds of observations from user to user, because there is no standard method for labeling findings.

As you can see, each of these methods has its advantages and disadvantages, so deciding which method to use is an important part of the planning process, which is why we discuss it here. When you get to Chapter 8, you will see how either method becomes the basis for interpreting the findings and reporting the results. First, however, you need to document your plans so that your team and your management or sponsor understand what you are planning to do and how you are planning to do it. This information goes into the test plan, which we discuss in the next section.

Writing the Test Plan

Throughout this discussion of the planning process, references have been made to the test plan. The test plan, as you might well imagine, contains the decisions made by the team or test facilitator about the elements of the usability test. But, you may also be asking, why bother with the test plan when you've already decided these issues and there's no one else to inform? As Rubin explains, there are many important reasons why you should make the extra effort to document your decisions in the test plan (81–82):

1. *It serves as the blueprint for the test.* Whether the readers are your team members who have been in on all the planning, or management or your sponsor who has not, the test plan puts everything in writing for all to confirm what was decided.
2. *It serves as the main communication vehicle.* In so doing, it provides a mechanism to clarify any differences of opinion about what was agreed to. In stating test objectives and the test process, it presents a permanent record of what will be done.
3. *It describes or implies required resources.* Resources might include the location of the space for testing plus the commitment of the time of the test team and the resources for recruiting the participants. When these resource requirements are documented, they can more easily be justified and allocated.
4. *It provides a focal point for the test and a milestone for the product being tested.* The test plan serves as a project planning document for the test. Once documented in the test plan, the dates for delivery of material, as well as the dates for testing, can be coordinated and scheduled. Commitments of time to prepare for testing, such as recruiting participants, can also be documented, so that they don't get left out of the process.

How to Format the Test Plan

The format of the test plan may be dependent on the expectations of your audience, the level of readership, and the formality or informality of your group or organization. The test plan could be as informal as a memorandum or the minutes of a planning meeting. Figure 5.2 is an example of planning meeting minutes that serve as the test plan. Once such an informal plan has been approved without further changes by the team, everyone has a record of what was decided. Then, the test administrator or team leader can use the test plan as a reminder of the follow-up actions that various team members will deliver. These can be shared by email attachments until all members of the team have agreed to the documents that support the usability test.

In more formal situations, particularly when the usability test is being sponsored by someone else in the organization, the test plan should be a formal report that documents major elements of the test, including the goals and objectives of the test, the user profile, the task list, the evaluation methods to be used, and the dates for testing. Additional items that can be included, if relevant, are the testing environment and the testing methodology. If an organization has standardized these two aspects already, there is no need to repeat them in every test plan.

As you can see, a test plan, whether formal or informal, captures the planning process described in this chapter. The "Hotmail Usability Test Plan" in the chapter appendix is an example of a formal test plan. It includes the following elements:

- *Title page.* Identifies who the sponsor is (if applicable) and who the team (or usability facilitator) is. Includes the date of submission of the test plan.

Minutes of Meeting: NCR and Usability Center, SPSU
April 2, 2000   9 A.M.–noon

Present
Adrienne Forzese, NCR; Phil Hilliard, NCR; Carol Barnum, Usability Center; Laura Jones, Usability Center

Purpose
Plan Usability Test for Retail Concepts Tutorial

Accomplishments and Assignments

Primary focus of the product: Developed to support instructor-led training class, but reduce time of training.

Audience: Software engineers/programmers and store managers. Primary audience for tutorial is people who don't have background in retail because they are:

- new programmers at NCR
- worked at NCR but not on retail products
- new programmers hired by the customer (not familiar with retail)

Secondary audience: anyone who wants to learn retail concepts on the Web.

Concerns for the usability test:
- Does the tutorial test accurately measure the learning?
- Do the users understand the terminology?
  - POS workstation equipment
  - POS workstation functions
  - Back office functions
- Is the interface intuitive?
  - Do the users know where they are?
  - Can they get back to where they want to be?
  - Is the sequence intuitive? (Do they follow it?)
  - If not sequential, how do they navigate? Does the navigation path matter?
- Are there any page design/graphics issues?
  - Resolution?
  - Mixture of graphics and clip art?
  - Do the graphics/clip art detract or enhance learning objectives?
- Do they succeed?
  - Do they get a passing score?
  - Is the length appropriate for learning?
  - Did they complete the tutorial?

Goals of the usability test (listed in reverse order of concerns):
1. Each lesson will be completed in 5 minutes.
2. The test will be completed in 15 minutes.
3. The graphics will help support learning objectives.
4. 100% of users can successfully navigate through the lessons.
5. 100% of users know where they are and can get where they want to go.
6. 100% of users can go to the test when ready.
7. 100% of users will pass the test (demonstrating mastery of terminology and concepts).

Figure 5.2 Planning meeting minutes—informal test plan *(continued)*

(Used with permission of NCR. NCR is a registered trademark of NCR Corporation.)

Parts of the product to test: The entire tutorial, plus the test. Time: 45 minutes. 1 hour/participant.

Assignments for test and responsibilities:
- User profile/screening questionnaires/recruit participants—Carol (test facilitator)
- Task scenarios—Adrienne (narrator)
- Post-task questionnaires—Laura (logger)
- Post-test questionnaires—Laura, then Phil (camera/video operator)

Dates:
- User profile draft to team by 4/7. Return comments by 4/9. Screening questionnaire to follow.
- Scenarios draft to team by 4/16
- Post-task/post-test questionnaires to team by 4/23
- Delivery of final test materials by 5/2
- Walkthrough for test (no participant)—9 A.M.–10 A.M., Wed., 5/7
- Pilot with participant—10 A.M.–11:30 A.M., Wed., 5/7
- Day 1 test (3 participants), Tues., May 20
- Day 2 test (2 participants), Thurs., May 22

Figure 5.2

- *Table of contents.* Reflects the first- and second-level headings in the test plan, with corresponding page numbers.
- *Purpose.* Provides an overview of the test plan and the purpose of the test.
- *Problem statement and test objectives.* Establishes the issues of importance for the test, framed as goals and objectives. It may also provide the scope and limitations of the test: what will be included in the test and what will not.
- *User profile.* The specific description of the user for this test. If the test will address two or more types of users, then each one needs a profile of specific characteristics. A detailed description or list of these characteristics will specify who should be recruited for the test.
- *Methodology and task list.* Describes the dates for testing, the length of each session, the issues to be addressed in each session, the tasks each user will be asked to perform, and the number of participants. If the planning process has progressed to the point of creating the actual scenarios (discussed in the next chapter), these can be included in the test plan. If this hasn't been formalized, a list of tasks is appropriate.
- *Evaluation methods.* Describes the data-collection methods, including the types of data that will be collected (quantitative and qualitative). If pre-test, post-task, and post-test questionnaires have been developed at this point, they can be included in the test plan.

Optional topics that can be included in the test plan, if determined at this point and if appropriate to the intended audience, include the following:

- *Test environment and equipment.* If the equipment to be used in testing or the capabilities of the facility for testing are known, they can be described here. In the Hotmail test plan, for instance, it was important to document the type of computer equipment being used in order to account for possible issues related to response times of the product. Also, if the testing environment needs to be configured in a certain way, this should be documented. For example, in a usability test of NCR's checkout stand with a scanner, we needed to determine how we would build a mock-up of the checkout stand and how we would set it up in the lab.
- *Roles of the team.* These can be presented in the test plan or determined later in the preparation stage.
- *Report elements.* Describes the information that will be contained in a report following testing. Also describes the method of delivery and type of report: formal or informal; paper or electronic delivery. If other deliverables are expected, such as a presentation or a video-highlights tape, these should be described, along with their delivery dates.

For more examples of test reports see the companion Web site for this book, <www.ablongman.com/barnum>.

Summary

Because usability testing is an intense, fascinating, and exhausting process, which frequently takes place over several fast-paced days, the success of the usability test is largely dependent on the thoroughness of the planning process. In this chapter, we have reviewed that process, which includes planning for team activities and responsibilities; defining the product issues and the needs of the audience or sponsor; settings goals, objectives, and measurements; establishing the user profile, especially the narrow band of the user population that will be recruited for the test; selecting the tasks to test based on the goals and objectives for the test; determining the method to be used to collect the data and categorize the results; and finally documenting the whole process in a test plan. If the effort is made up front to put the plans in place, the rewards will follow with an efficient and productive testing process.

Coming Up

Although it is somewhat arbitrary to separate planning for usability testing from preparing for usability testing, a distinction can be made according to those elements that have to be planned (as covered in this chapter) and those elements that have to be produced in preparation for testing. In the next chapter, we take up the aspects of the test that follow planning but precede testing. These include the production of the screening questionnaire and pre-test questionnaires for users, the recruitment of the users, the creation of scenarios, and the post-task and post-test questionnaires for the scenarios and the overall test. In addition, the team has to designate the roles of its members and create the checklists and scripts that team members will use during the practice sessions and test sessions.

Questions/Topics for Discussion

1. Describe several different options for setting up a usability test. Consider the availability of space, the number and type of users, the placement of the test administrator or team in relation to the participants, and the time factors involved. Compare the advantages and disadvantages of each option.
2. When would co-discovery be a good option? What are the advantages and disadvantages of co-discovery?
3. If you are testing the documentation, describe the two approaches you can choose. What are the advantages and disadvantages of each approach?
4. For what kinds of information-gathering is usability testing the best option? For what kinds of information-gathering are other methods better suited? Name some of these other methods and the types of data they would be most effective in gathering.
5. How can you determine which group of users you will want to select for a particular test? Describe some of the approaches you can use to create a user profile for the group you select. How many participants do you need, as a minimum, in each group or subgroup?
6. List several of the criteria you would use to establish the tasks you want to test. If you're testing software documentation, what might the tasks be?
7. Describe the two approaches for collecting and analyzing the data you will gather in a usability test. What are the advantages and disadvantages of each approach? Which one is more appealing to you? Be prepared to explain the reasons for your choice of methods.
8. What are the reasons for writing a test plan? Who should receive the plan? Describe the main elements of a test plan.

Exercises

1. Using the following list of vague goals, operationalize them by stating them as measurable goals:

    a. The online documentation is easy to use.

    _____

    b. Users will find the manual helpful.

    _____

   c. The table of contents allows users to navigate through the document.

---

   d. Online help is better than paper-based help.

---

   e. Online help is helpful.

---

2. Describe the types of typical tasks you would expect users to perform when using a software product for the first time.

For Your Project

1. If you are going to be working as a team to plan and conduct a test, use the agenda shown in Figure 5.1 as a guide to develop an agenda for your team's planning meeting. Include the goal of the meeting, the list of people who should attend, and the time to be allotted to plan the team's usability test. This activity can be done by all members of the team with the ideas merged for one agenda, or it can be performed by the team leader, if one is designated.
2. Create a list of concerns (stated as questions) for your product to be tested. Operationalize these as goals so that the results can be measured.
3. Create a persona of your main users. If you intend to test more than one type of user, create a persona for each type.
4. Using the list of factors (shown on page 158) for establishing the user profile, complete all the relevant information about your user group. If you have identified more than one group, complete a profile for each group.
5. Create a task list for the product you plan to test. Arrange the items on the list. Assign times for each task. Eliminate any items for which there will not be enough time to test.
6. Determine the method you will use to collect data and analyze your results. If you're working as a team, discuss the advantages and disadvantages of each approach and arrive at a consensus on the team's preference.
7. Write the test plan, using the appropriate level of formality or informality required in the testing situation. Also choose the correct format, depending on whether the readers of the report are internal or external.

References

Cooper, Alan. *The Inmates Are Running the Asylum: Why High-Tech Products Drive Us Crazy and How to Restore the Sanity.* Indianapolis, IN: SAMS, 1999.

"CUE 2 Scenario Version 18. January 1999." <www.dialogdesign.dk/cue.html>.

Dumas, Joseph S., and Janice C. Redish. *A Practical Guide to Usability Testing.* Norwood, NJ: Ablex, 1993.

"Eight Is More Than Enough." *Eye For Design*, May–June 1998. User Interface Engineering <http://www.uie.com>.

Gray, Wayne D., and Marilyn C. Salzman. "Damaged Merchandise? A Review of Experiments that Compare Usability Evaluation Methods." *Human-Computer Interaction* 13 (1998): 203–61.

Grayling, Trevor. "Fear and Loathing of the Help Menu: A Usability Test of Online Help." *Technical Communication* 45.2 (1998): 168–79.

Intons-Peterson, Margaret J., et al. "Age, Testing at Preferred or Nonpreferred Times (Testing Optimality), and False Memory." *Journal of Experimental Psychology: Learning, Memory, and Cognition* 25.1 (1999): 23–40.

Intons-Peterson, Margaret J., et al. "Aging, Optimal Testing Times, and Negative Priming." *Journal of Experimental Psychology: Learning, Memory, and Cognition* 24.2 (1998): 362–76.

Prekeges, James G. "Usability Testing for Non-Testers." STC 40th Annual Conference, Dallas, TX, 6–9 June 1993.

Ramey, Judy. "Usability Testing." STC Region 7 Conference, Beaverton, OR, 19–20 Oct. 1995.

Rojek, Jill, and Amy Kanerva. "A Data-Collection Strategy for Usability Tests." *IEEE Transactions on Professional Communication* 37.3 (1994): 149–56.

Rubin, Jeffrey. *Handbook of Usability Testing*. New York: Wiley, 1994.

Scanlon, Tara. "Affinity Analysis: Tips and Tricks." Usability Progression, STC 43rd Annual Conference, Washington, DC, 5–9 May 1996.

Senge, Peter M. *The Fifth Discipline: The Art and Practice of the Learning Organization*. New York: Doubleday, 1990.

Spool, Jared. "Darwinian Design." STC 45th Annual Conference, Anaheim, CA, 17–20 May 1998.

The Usability Group. "Usability Yardstick." 7 Apr. 2000 <http://www.usability.com>.

"Which Way Out?" *Time* 10 April 2000.

Wilson, Chauncey. "User Profile." Online posting. 21 Sept. 2000. Used with permission of author.

Wilson, Chauncey, and Judy Blostein, ed. "Pros and Cons of Co-Participation in Usability Studies." *Usability Interface* 4.4 (April 1998). 21 June 1999 <http:www.stcsig.org/usability/>.

Hotmail Usability Test Plan
Evaluation of Hotmail Internet Email Service

March 1, 1999

Professor Carol Barnum
Southern Polytechnic State University

Anusuya Mukherjee, Nadyne Mielke,
Melany Porter, Marji Schumann,
Benjamin Speaks, Michael Quinby

Table of Contents

Purpose of the Hotmail Usability Test

The purpose of the Hotmail usability test is to collect information about how users are using this Web-based email product and whether they experience difficulties performing simple and more complex tasks using the product.

Microsoft management is interested in learning about how users use and perceive Hotmail and whether they experience any difficulties with the site, so that improvements in usability can be made.

This test plan describes:

- The problems to be tested and our strategies for addressing them
- The users we will select for our test groups
- Our test methods
- The tasks to be tested
- The test environment
- The roles of our team members
- The evaluation measures we will use
- The materials and other deliverables we plan to provide with the final report describing the usability test results

Problem Statement and Test Objectives

This usability test of Hotmail hopes to gain quantifiable data addressing Hotmail developers' specific concerns about Hotmail's usability. We will assess the ease or difficulty of the following Hotmail tasks:

- Registering for Hotmail
- Logging in and logging out of Hotmail
- Composing an email
- Sending and retrieving email (to include sending attachments)
- Using the Hotmail member directory to look up member email addresses
- Sorting messages in the Hotmail InBox
- Creating an address book that contains frequently used addresses
- Setting up folders to store messages by category

Other items in which developers expressed an interest are more general in nature. Developers want to collect information about Hotmail user perceptions. These include:

- How users currently use email
- The level of effort required to use Hotmail
- Satisfaction with Hotmail (determining whether users continue using it, recommend it to others, etc.)
- Perceived reliability of Hotmail
- Perceived speed of Hotmail

The focus of the research will be task-oriented and directed toward how the user subjectively responds to the issues listed above. The test planning activities will include several meetings of the test team to decide the best ways to test the issues and to narrow down the list of characteristics we will look for in potential test participants.

The test will be designed to allow us to extract mostly quantifiable, verifiable data. Participants will be given a pre-test questionnaire, scenarios that direct them to perform specific tasks, post-task questionnaires designed to extract detailed and specific feedback about Hotmail features, and post-test surveys to rate the usability of the product overall.

The test will be conducted in a full-scale usability lab. Novice users will be given 40 minutes to complete three of the four test scenarios we designed. Advanced or expert users will be given 1 hour and 5 minutes to complete all four of the test scenarios.

The test team has decided to exclude five issues based on a consensus that they would be best addressed by a focus group.

1. **What users think of Hotmail's performance**. Because of the wide variety of equipment choices, modem speeds, and other factors affecting this issue, it is difficult to compare these factors. It might be preferable to use a post-test questionnaire to assess the test participants' impressions about system performance.
2. **The password retrieval process**. We omitted a study of the password retrieval process because it requires setting up password "prompts" that would require time to elapse for users to forget their passwords or password clues.
3. **Reminders**. We excluded a study of "reminders" because they would be used by only a small subset of advanced users.
4. **Accessing other email through a POP account**. We will not test POP account access because this issue is too difficult to test, given the proprietary nature of other email accounts.

Our objectives are to test two user groups in the following task areas, as shown in Table 1.

Table 1   User Groups and Tasks to Be Tested

Tasks to Be Tested	Advanced User Task	Novice User Task
Registration	X	X
Logging in to Hotmail	X	X
Logging out from Hotmail	X	X
Reading messages	X	X
Composing (writing) a message	X	X
Sending and receiving messages	X	X
Sending attachments	X	
Creating and using folders	X	
Creating and using address books	X	

User Profile

According to the information received from Hotmail contacts, the product's current users consist of anyone who wants a personal, free email account that can be accessed from any Web browser from any location. This means current Hotmail users are people who have access to the Web from home, work, or even from a remote location in another country.

Business people, even those who have access to company-owned and managed email systems, are one of the main groups currently using Hotmail. Hotmail allows these users to avoid potential conflicts with employers who discourage employees from using company email accounts for personal mail. Because Hotmail is Web-based, employees are better able to preserve their privacy when sending personal mail, as most employers do not track traffic on Web-based email accounts. Business people who travel are especially likely to use products such as Hotmail, because it allows them to access Hotmail from any remote site with a Web browser.

Students who may or may not own personal computers are common users of Hotmail, because it is free and can be accessed from any campus Web site.

International travelers may use Hotmail while on the road, accessing it from hotel rooms or commercial Internet kiosks.

Users within households and small businesses may use Hotmail, as it is available at low cost and allows multiple persons using a single computer to hold separate private accounts.

Required Level of Computer Expertise
The level of computer expertise Hotmail requires of its users is that they know how to turn on a computer, connect to the Internet, and launch a Web browser. Hotmail also expects its customers to be familiar with basic Web navigation techniques, including how to move forward and backward through pages, how to click links in a Web page, and how to enter URLs. However, using Hotmail does not require extensive Internet and browser experience. Hotmail has suggested that the minimal skill required to use products like Hotmail may be one factor explaining why its customers choose to use Web-based email systems in the first place.

Because the spectrum of Hotmail users is very broad, we decided to test two groups of users: novice and advanced users. In this way, we hope to capture the broadest range of feedback concerning Hotmail's usability. Both user profiles are described below.

Novice Users
We assumed that even novice users would have to have basic computer experience, including keyboarding skills, Windows experience, and basic abilities in accessing and navigating a Web browser. To keep the delineation between novice and advanced users as "clean" as possible, we decided to select only people for this group who have NO email experience. (It will be challenging to recruit a test user base of people who have experience with the Internet but no previous email experience, but we believe our pretest questionnaire will assist in this matter.)

Advanced Users
Advanced users will have all of the capabilities of the novice users, and many more. In addition to having computer experience, keyboarding skills, and experience using the World Wide Web, these users will have previous experience using other email programs

5

(except for Hotmail). We will select a group of participants who have extensive Web experience (6 mos +), and who use email frequently.

To screen test participants' skill levels, we will ask questions such as "How often do you access email?", "Where and when do you use email?", and "Do you attach messages routinely to your email?"

Potential questions for focus groups related to this matter might be questions addressing preferences around advanced user functions, such as "Do you want anonymous email capabilities?"

Method (Test Design) and Task List

The test scenarios for each participant will be centered on several users' specified tasks. We will provide the participant with descriptions of each task. However, we will not provide specific, step-by-step instructions on how to accomplish the designated task.

Novice Test Design
Hotmail asked for testing of the following features and tasks, which we divided into simple and more complex tasks. Of the four scenarios we created in total, we allocated three scenarios to novice users. The scenario list for novice users omits Scenario 3, which covers tasks that advanced users typically perform. Although Scenario 3 is optional, we may ask select novice users to complete it if testing time allows. For information about Scenario 3, see the section "Advanced User Test Design."

Scenario 1:
    Register for Hotmail.

Scenario 2:
    a. Read messages in the mailbox.
    b. Write a new message (Compose).
    c. Reply to a sender's message.

Scenario 4:
    a. Delete some messages.
    b. Leave Hotmail.

We will ground the novice test participants in user-based task scenarios that make use of neutral language when providing instruction. The use of neutral language will limit any biases or cues that could aid or deter the test participant. The novice task list will be outlined as follows.

Novice Scenario/Task List
Scenario 1: Allocated time, 15 minutes
You have recently decided to sign up for email using a service called Hotmail. Using your Web browser, go to the following address:
    www.Hotmail.com

Once you are at the Hotmail Web site, go ahead and sign up for a free email account. If you need any assistance, feel free to use the online help provided by Hotmail.

When you finish signing up for Hotmail, take some time to look around the site and explore its features—but for now, don't try to look at or send any email.

Scenario 2: Total allocated time, 25 minutes
Task A   Check for any email messages that you may have received in Hotmail. Open one of them, and close it when you finish reading it.

Task B   Send a message to the following email address:
   Bill.smith@i-solutions.com
Be sure to tell the recipient that you are sending out this message to test your new Hotmail account.

Task C   Check to see if you have received any new email messages while you've been working in Hotmail. Look for a message with the subject line "Usability," and respond to it with a message telling the sender that you got the email.

Scenario 4: Total allocated time, 15 minutes
Task A   Erase all of the messages in your mailbox.

Task B   Sign off from Hotmail.

Advanced User Test Design
The advanced user test includes all of the novice scenarios described previously and an additional scenario (Scenario 3) that requires the users to perform more sophisticated file management and organizational tasks. All of the scenarios that will be performed by advanced users are listed below.

Scenario 1:
   Register for Hotmail.

Scenario 2:
   a. Read messages in the mailbox.
   b. Write a new message (Compose).
   c. Reply to a sender's message.

Scenario 3:
   a. Search Hotmail to find a sender who has a Hotmail account.
   b. Send a message to this person, and attach a file to the message.
   c. Create a place to store messages.
   d. Create an address book to store the email addresses of people who write to you.

Scenario 4:
   c. Delete some messages.
   d. Leave Hotmail.

Advanced User Task List

As explained above, the advanced tasks are the same as the tasks performed by novice users, with one exception: After they complete Scenario 2 and before going on to Scenario 4, advanced users will be given a scenario in which they perform more sophisticated email tasks, as explained below:

Scenario 3: Total allocated time, 25 minutes

TASK A   You just realized you want to tell a friend you have a new Hotmail account. You know your friend also has a Hotmail account, but you don't know his email address. Using Hotmail, look up your friend using his first and last name:

- First: Freddy
- Last: Kruger
- City: Smyrna
- State: Georgia

TASK B   You decide that you want to send Freddy a message to tell him about your new Hotmail account. You also decide to send Freddy a file he's been asking for along with your message. Go ahead and write Freddy an email telling him you have a Hotmail account, and attach the file to it. The file you are sending is located on the A drive and is titled "Test.doc."

TASK C   Check to see if you have any new email messages. Go ahead and place one of the emails you received in a holding area called "My Stuff." If this holding area isn't there, create it.

TASK D   You just realized that you would like to keep Freddy's email address accessible for future correspondence. Create a place in Hotmail to store his address for other mailings.

Novice and Advanced Users—Pre-Test Questionnaire
- Does anyone in your family use the Internet? For what?
- What do you think of the Internet?
- What is your impression of the speediness of Hotmail?

Novice and Advanced Users—Post-Test Questionnaire
- What is your impression of the speediness of Hotmail?
- What task did you find the most difficult to do? What other tasks were difficult?
- What tasks were easy to complete?
- Would you recommend Hotmail to a friend?
- Would you recommend Hotmail since it is for free?
- Did you click on any of the advertisement banners at Hotmail? Why or why not?

Test Environment/Equipment

The usability evaluator room (where participants will work) is furnished with the following equipment:

- Three wall-mounted video cameras, allowing filming of test participants from various perspectives and angles
- Desk on which a computer can be set up to simulate a work environment
- Pentium computer running Windows 95 with Netscape Communicator and Internet Explorer software
- Ethernet connection to a T–1 Internet connection

The evaluator room is separated from the observation room by a one-way mirror. The observation room contains the following equipment:

- Audio/visual console
- Audio channel mixer
- VHS recorder
- VHS recorder equipped for editing
- Special effects generator
- Microphone
- Speaker (with a pickup to the evaluator room)
- Computer running Windows 95 and U-Loggit software (to log and categorize test observations)
- Printer
- Screen video pickup

Roles of the Team

Our team consists of six members. Five of the members will perform specific tasks and one member will be a "floater," performing varied duties as required.

Briefer: A briefer will explain the usability test activities to the participants and will administer the pre-test and post-test questionnaires.

Camera operator: One team member will operate all the cameras.

Logger (data recorder): One team member will be responsible for typing in observations and logging data using U-Loggit.

Narrator: One member will serve as a narrator. The narrator's role is to make verbal observations about test events. This process gives the logger an opportunity to capture information about events that the she may miss while entering and logging data.

Test administrator: One team member will be responsible for overall coordination and troubleshooting duties.

Evaluation Measures (Data Collection)

The evaluation measures will be a combination of quantitative measurements and subjective observations. The quantitative and qualitative data measures are listed below.

Quantitative Data
The following data will be recorded when carrying out the Hotmail usability test:

- Time to completion of each task
- Number of participants completing tasks within allocated time
- Number of participants completing tasks with extra time
- Number of problems encountered
- Number of errors (unsuccessful tries)
- Number of local problems
- Number of times each participant uses "help" menu
- Number of times each participant accesses advertising sites
- Length of time each participant spends on browsing advertisements

Qualitative Data

- Facial expressions
- Verbal comments when they think out loud
- Spontaneous verbal expressions (comments)
- Interviews before the test
- Interviews after the test
- Miscellaneous activities (stretching, wanting breaks, etc.)

Report Contents and Preparation

The report will be presented in a formal report format with the following sections:

- Cover letter
- Title page
- Executive summary
- Contents
- Discussion on the background of the project
- User profile
- Description of the planning phase with estimated and actual work hours
- Description of the test (methods and tasks)
- Collected data (both quantitative and qualitative)
- Analysis of the collected data
- Recommendations on the basis of analyzed data
- Appendices (questionnaires, etc.)

The formal report will be presented with the following supports:

- A formal oral presentation on the results of the report
- A video highlights tape showing the important aspects of the test conducted

Finally, we feel that the previously mentioned format will provide a detailed and comprehensive summary of our usability findings and test methodologies.

Source: Used with permission of the SPSU Hotmail team: Marji Schumann, Anusuya Mukherjee, Nadyne Mielke, Melany Porter, Benjamin Speaks, and Michael Quinby.

## CHAPTER 6

Preparing for Usability Testing

 If you have followed the planning process described in the previous chapter, you have already defined the goals for your usability test, established the user profile, determined the tasks you will test, and your method of data collection and analysis, all of which you have documented in the test plan. You are now ready to produce the documents needed to recruit the participants and conduct usability testing, as well as the documents needed by each member of the team. This chapter covers both of these topics. We will first address the documents for the participants, along with strategies for recruiting qualified participants, as these activities need to get under way early. Next we will describe the roles for each team member and the documents needed to support the activities of the test team. Finally, we will discuss the importance of a walkthrough to test the materials and the process, followed by a pilot test to make sure that everything works according to plan.

To recruit participants and get feedback from them during a usability test, you will need to create the following documents:

- Screening questionnaire(s) to recruit participants for testing
- Pre-test questionnaire to further qualify participants
- Post-task questionnaires for each scenario
- Post-test questionnaire at completion of the test
- Consent/release forms

In the next section, we describe how to create the screening questionnaire, which will be used to recruit the participants.

Creating the Screening Questionnaire

To create the screening questionnaire, you need to devise questions that identify the characteristics of your user, based on your user profile. If you determine that you want to test more than one type of user, you will, of course, need to create a screening questionnaire for each type of user and be sure to recruit at least three users (preferably four or five) for each user profile. In the previous chapter, we talked about all the possible characteristics you might want to learn about your user. Because the recruitment of a very specific type of user is so important to validating the results of testing, the screening questionnaire is only the first of two forms you will use to identify the match between each user and your profile of the subgroup of the user population you are involving in this particular test.

The most common types of information to include in a screening questionnaire focus on the proficiency of each user regarding the product and the skill level of the user regarding the tasks to be performed using the product. The specific information you want to learn will come from questions that include phrases like "how much?", "how often?", "how long?", and "in what ways?" Asking users to identify their own level of knowledge or proficiency rarely produces consistent (or accurate) results. Using ranges is more effective. A sample of a detailed screening questionnaire used by Xerox is shown in Figure 6.1. It uses close-ended questions that ask potential participants to choose the closest match to rate their level of experience regarding "how much," "how many," and "what type" of computer experience they have.

A different approach, shown in Figure 6.2, uses open-ended questions that asks users to supply the specifics about their level of expertise. The questionnaire was developed to recruit participants for a usability test of an NCR scanner product, in which a certain level of technical expertise was sought. In this case, the team wanted to see how potential participants characterized their experience and expertise in their own words.

In the next section, we look at the ways to recruit participants for a test.

Recruiting Participants

Recruiting participants can be a very labor-intensive activity, so be prepared to set aside the appropriate amount of time needed, if a member of your team is doing it, or the appropriate amount of money needed, if an outside agency is doing it. Stephanie Rosenbaum, President of Tech-Ed, a usability consulting firm, states that you should budget at least two hours to recruit one participant, with the expectation of making five or six phone calls on a customer list before finding someone willing and able to participate (69). Dumas and Redish say that you should anticipate making between four and fifteen calls to qualify each user (145).

Recruiting Directly

When recruiting the participants yourself, you need to determine the likely places to find them. If you have a database of pre-qualified users, obviously this is the

Usability Participant Questionnaire

| Please fill in the ovals like ● not ☑ or ⊗ |

I. Participant Information

Name: _____   Intelnet #: _____

Email: _____   Mailstop: _____

Your current position: _____

Number of years in this position: ○ 0–1 years   ○ 1–3 years   ○ over 3 years

If you are a manager of people, how many people are in your group? ○ 0–5 people ○ 5–10 people ○ 10 or more

---

II. Computer Experience

How much experience have you had with the following types of computers and computer devices?

	Never used	1–6 months	6–12 months	1–3 years	3+ years
IBM or compatible:	○	○	○	○	○
Mac:	○	○	○	○	○
6085:	○	○	○	○	○

About how many hours a day do you use a computer?

At home   ○ 1–3 hours   At work: ○ 1–3 hours
               ○ 3–8 hours   ○ 3–8 hours
               ○ more than 8 hours   ○ more than 8 hours

What type of computer do you use?

At home   ○ IBM or compatible   At work: ○ IBM or compatible
               ○ Mac   ○ Mac
               ○ Laptop   ○ Laptop
               ○ Mainframe   ○ Mainframe

Do you use Microsoft Windows?   ○ Yes   ○ No

What type of applications do you use?

○ Word Processing (like Word)   ○ Project Management (like MS Project)
○ Spreadsheet (like Excel)   ○ Desktop Publishing (like Pagemaker)
○ Database (like Access)   ○ CD-ROM/Multimedia
○ Presentation (like PowerPoint)   ○ Other _____

What do you typically use your computer for?

○ Games and Pleasure   ○ Word Processing
○ Graphics   ○ Decision Support
○ Accounting/Finance   ○ Programming
○ Data Storage (i.e., databases)   ○ Other _____

Please return this questionnaire to Usability & Technical Documentation at mailstop: 810-01A by 4/26/95.

Figure 6.1   Xerox screening questionnaire, using close-ended questions

Source: This information was developed by Usability & Technical Documentation, Xerox Corporation, and was based on a similar survey from Microsoft Corporation. Compiled for the UPA Conference, July 1995. Available at <http://www.stcsig.org/usability/>

1. Have you ever used a scanner on the job?

   Yes _____   No _____

2. Have you used Windows 3.1 or Windows '95 on a PC?

   Yes _____   No _____

   If yes, tell us which program you've used and the length of time you have used this program.

   _____
   Program   Length of time used

3. Have you ever opened up the back of a PC and changed out a board or added a component?

   Yes _____   No _____

   If yes, was it successful? Yes _____   No _____

   If it was successful, tell us what component or components you have changed out.

   _____

4. Have you ever worked as a computer technician?

   Yes _____   No _____

   If yes, describe the type of work you have done and the length of time you have done it.

   _____
   Type of work

   _____
   Length of time

5. List your major here at Southern Polytechnic. _____

6. List your class rank (freshman, sophomore, etc.). _____

7. Check the appropriate categories for the following:

   _____ Male   _____ Female

   _____ Right-handed   _____ Left-handed

Figure 6.2   Screening questionnaire, using open-ended questions
(Used with permission of NCR. NCR is a registered trademark of NCR Corporation.)

place to start. If, however, you need to go out and find the users, the typical places to look include:

- Customer lists, obtained from sales and marketing. Make sure, however, that the customer is the user. Frequently, the customer is the purchaser, but not the actual user of the product.
- Potential customers, where such information exists, who have shown an interest in the product, but have not purchased it.
- User groups or professional organizations.

- Newspaper advertisements.
- College or university campuses/placement offices.
- Qualified friends.

Whichever method you use, the people you recruit must match the user profile and must provide the appropriate answers to the questions in the screening questionnaire to qualify as a participant. Some people use the questionnaire to solicit participants by phone, filling in the answers to the questions as the participant responds to each question. Others mail, email, or fax the questionnaire to prospective participants. Still others post the questionnaire on their Web site, soliciting interested participants to complete the form if they would like to join a database of potential future users. Each choice will produce different results.

Telephone recruiting is the most time-consuming approach but yields the most direct and fastest results. You find out immediately whether someone is qualified and available. Email is more efficient but produces fewer responses, requiring follow-up or a larger database of addresses to work from. Faxing is fast and can provide for quick turnaround with a fax-back number for responses, but there can be legibility problems with some fax machines. Regular mail eliminates the problems of email attachments going astray or losing formatting because of software incompatibility, but it takes the longest time for delivery and response and requires a postage-paid return envelope for the best results.

Whatever you do, do not be tempted to recruit people at work, unless, of course, the user is someone at work. No matter how removed some people at work may be from your department and your product, the fact that they work for your organization gives them access to information and company terminology, which places them within the "milieu" of understanding that the real users won't have. When there seems no choice but to recruit people at work because of budget or time restrictions, recruit friends instead, as they will at least be closer to the real user population than insiders at work.

However you recruit participants, you will need to offer them some incentive for their participation. Incentives range from money to small gifts (such as company mugs or mousepads) to food. Your team will have to consider what will work in each case. Figure 6.3 shows the cover sheet for the screening questionnaire used to recruit university students for the NCR scanner product. Because the students were already on campus and available for a 2-hour block of time, we felt, correctly, that we could recruit the number of participants needed with a $20 incentive.

If you are a student trying to recruit participants for your usability test, food generally works as a sufficient incentive, especially since you're likely to recruit people you know: friends, family, and co-workers.

Recruiting Indirectly Through Agencies

Outside agencies, such as employment agencies or marketing research firms, can be used to recruit participants. When using an outside agency, you should supply the screening questionnaire, which the agency then uses to recruit participants who qualify. Market research firms tend to produce better participants because

Question: How would you like to earn a fast 20 bucks in under 2 hours?

If you match our user profile, you can earn a fast $20 for less than 2 hours' work and help us learn about a new product that is about to go on the market.

If you're interested AND if you have 2 hours available on campus on one of the following days, please complete the questionnaire.

Check availability (place a checkmark by any day and time that you are available).

Wednesday, December 4   _____ 9–11 A.M.

Friday, December 6   _____ 8:45–10:45 A.M.
                                         10:45 A.M.–12:45 P.M.
                                         1:45–3:45 P.M.

Tuesday, December 10   _____ 8:45–10:45 A.M.
                                         10:45 A.M.–12:45 P.M.

Include your name and a phone number where you can be reached.

Name   Phone

Figure 6.3 Incentive to recruit students for a test, sponsored by client
(Used with permission of NCR. NCR is a registered trademark of NCR Corporation.)

they already have databases they can search, which contain information on participants they have used for focus groups and product surveys. Employment or temporary agencies can be effective when you are looking for specific computer skills, as they typically have this information on their applicants. When you use an outside agency, you will also want to produce a script for the recruiter to read that explains the type of work to be done by qualified participants and the reason for the test. With this script, you provide a way to minimize possible bias that could be introduced by an outside agency, and you also increase the likelihood that participants aren't misinformed about what they'll be doing, if hired.

Companies that use outside agencies find that the regular use of the same agency tends to improve their results, as the agency comes to understand the process involved in recruiting participants for a usability test. Typically, the recruiting agency will pay the compensation for the user's time, either at the agency's hourly rate or at a rate determined by you. Several companies report the typical pay for a 2-hour test at $50.00. This amount generally provides sufficient incentive for someone to take the time to participate without making the task seem like a job, which doesn't create the right atmosphere for usability testing.

Scheduling Participants

Once you have selected the participants you want to include in the test, you need to schedule them for a specific day and time. The more contact you can have with the participants before they are supposed to participate, the more likely they will appear as scheduled. As a minimum, you should call a day or two in advance to

(continued on page 195)

Thank you for considering being a volunteer for our usability test. We will work to make sure the test environment is pleasant and fun for you, with a casual dinner being served. The results from our usability test will be used to help improve a computer software product's ease of use.

Please answer the following questions. We will use your answers to determine if you will be a participant in our usability test.

The testing will take place on March 22 and March 29 from 6–8 P.M. The usability test will require $1\frac{1}{2}$ hours of your time.

Please place a check next to the dates on which you are available, if any.

March 22 _____ March 29 _____ Either date _____ Neither date _____

Please disregard the rest of the questionnaire if you are not able to attend one of the dates. Thank you again for your consideration.

Note: The top part of this questionnaire would not be used for the second screening.

Name: _____ Age: ☐ 15–20 ☐ 21–30 ☐ 31–40 ☐ 41–50 ☐ 51 or above

Home Phone: _____ Sex: ☐ Male ☐ Female

Work Phone: _____ ☐ Right-handed ☐ Left-handed

Please answer the following questions about your computer experience:

1. Do you use an IBM or compatible personal computer?

   ☐ Yes
   ☐ No

   If you answered "no," please disregard the remaining parts of the questionnaire.

2. What kind(s) of programs have you worked with? Check all that apply.

   ☐ Word processing
   ☐ Spreadsheets
   ☐ Graphics
   ☐ Other(s) specify _____

3. How long have you been using personal computers?

   ☐ 0–3 months
   ☐ 4–6 months
   ☐ 7–9 months
   ☐ 10–12 months
   ☐ More than 12 months

4. Have you ever used a Web browser?

   ☐ Yes
   ☐ No

   If you answered "no," please proceed to question 7.

5. Which Web browser have you used? Check all that apply.

   ☐ Microsoft Internet Explorer
   ☐ Netscape Navigator
   ☐ Other(s) specify _____

6. How long have you been browsing the Web?

   ☐ 0–3 months
   ☐ 4–6 months
   ☐ 7–9 months
   ☐ 10–12 months
   ☐ More than 12 months

7. Which Internet Service Provider(s) do you use? Check all that apply.

   ☐ AOL
   ☐ Prodigy
   ☐ CompuServe
   ☐ Mindspring
   ☐ Other (specify) _____
   ☐ I do not use/have an Internet Service Provider.

Figure 6.4   Pre-test questionnaire for Hotmail test *(continued)*

(Used with permission of SPSU Hotmail team: Marji Schumann, Anusuya Mukherjee, Nadyne Mielke, Melany Porter, Benjamin Speaks, and Michael Quinby.)

8. Does your Internet Service Provider (ISP) OR your work/school location provide an email program?

ISP   ☐ Yes   ☐ No
               ☐ Not applicable: I have no ISP.

Work/School ☐ Yes   ☐ No
               ☐ Not applicable: I don't use email from work/school.

If you answered "no" or "not applicable" to BOTH of the categories in this question, please proceed to question 11.

9. Which email program does your Internet Service Provider OR your work/school location provide?

	ISP	Work/ School
Microsoft Outlook Express	☐	☐
Express	☐	☐
Eudora	☐	☐
Other (specify)	☐	☐
_____		
I do not know.	☐	☐

10. How long have you been using your Internet Service Provider's OR your work/school location's email program? (If you use multiple programs, indicate the time period corresponding to the program for which you have the MOST experience.)

☐ 0–3 months
☐ 4–6 months
☐ 7–9 month
☐ 10–12 months
☐ More than 12 months

11. Do you use the World Wide Web for email?

☐ Yes
☐ No

If you answered "no," please proceed to question 14.

12. Which World Wide Web email program(s) do you use? Check all that apply.

☐ Yahoo!
☐ Hotmail
☐ Netscape
☐ Other (specify) _____

13. How long have you been using your World Wide Web email program(s)?

☐ 0–3 months
☐ 4–6 months
☐ 7–9 months
☐ 10–12 months
☐ More than 12 months

14. Where do you use email? Check all that apply.

☐ From a personal home account
☐ From an account at work
☐ From a public access terminal (library, Internet cafe, other)
☐ From school
☐ Other (specify) _____

15. What do you use email for? Check all that apply.

☐ Work
☐ Personal
☐ Other (specify) _____

16. Do you know how to send attachments to someone via email?

☐ Yes
☐ No

17. Do you know how to make files for the email you receive so similar emails can be grouped?

☐ Yes
☐ No

18. Do you know how to create and send a simple email message?

☐ Yes
☐ No

Figure 6.4

remind them of their scheduled day and time and to confirm their participation. Calling works better than emailing because it's more personal, but you can also email a reminder, perhaps with directions and any other needed information, a few days before you call.

Even with such efforts, you can anticipate at least 10% no-shows (Rosenbaum 69; Dumas and Redish 149). When you're doing "discount" usability testing with only a few users, these no-shows can have an adverse effect on your results, so you will need a back-up plan for the no-shows. Here are some options:

1. *Double-book.* Although double-booking can increase the time for recruiting and the cost, as well as disappoint the person who doesn't get to participate in the test, it eliminates the problem of no-shows. We used double-booking when recruiting students for the NCR scanner product. Because they were already on campus and were informed that they would be paid whether or not they participated in the test, they didn't seem to mind showing up to find out. Of course, if two people are making a special effort and have an interest in the product being tested, the disappointment of not being selected may cause problems you would want to avoid.
2. *Have a back-up nearby.* If possible, recruit a back-up who can be available all day and who is nearby. If a participant doesn't show up, you can call the back-up person, who can arrive quickly to participate.
3. *Schedule an extra person or two.* If you are planning to test five participants, schedule a sixth person just in case someone doesn't show up. You can then cancel the sixth person (but compensate him or her for the willingness to participate) or go ahead and use that person as an added participant. This works especially well when you can schedule the extra person or two without adding a day to the testing schedule. The only possible impact resulting from scheduling another person is that it makes for a longer day, and you will need a plan to use the block of time that didn't get filled earlier in the day because of a no-show.

The screening questionnaire is your first assessment of a participant's suitability for a particular test. You will want to reaffirm each person's suitability on arrival for the test with a second questionnaire, which we discuss in the next section.

Further Screening on Arrival

If you have given the screening questionnaire by phone or email or have hired an external agency to record this information, you can use the same questionnaire to confirm that the participant has the criteria needed to match the user profile. An example of such a form, used for the Hotmail test, is shown in Figure 6.4 on pages 194–195.

Better still, you can create an additional form to learn more about the participant, now that he or she has qualified for the test and is willing to participate. This second form is typically called a pre-test questionnaire. An example of a brief, open-ended form, which was used in the NCR scanner test to select a participant from the two who arrived for the test, is shown in Figure 6.5. The information provided by both potential participants, along with the pre-screening ques-

Instructions: Please complete the following questionnaire before starting the usability test. And thanks for your help!

Name and mailing address (for sending the check):

_____

_____

_____

Your social security number (to get the check):

_____

Your major _____   Number of years in major _____

Right-handed _____   Left-handed _____

Male _____   Female _____

Technical ability: Describe the types of software, hardware, or add-ons you have added to a PC computer.

Experience with Windows 3.0 or '95 on a PC: Please tell us how long you have used Windows 3.0 or '95. If you have used both, tell us how long you have used each one.

Work as a computer technician: No _____   Yes _____

If yes, how long? _____

If yes, please describe the type of work you have done as a computer technician.

Figure 6.5   Pre-test questionnaire for NCR scanner product
(Used with permission of NCR. NCR is a registered trademark of NCR Corporation.)

tionnaire for both, was given to the subject matter expert to select the participant who most closely matched the intended user.

A more detailed example, used to further qualify participants for a usability test of a college Web site, is shown in Figure 6.6. Having additional information about participants, which this second form provides, will add to the team's understanding of the user's actions and can also shed light on unique findings by a particular user.

Please complete the following questionnaire before starting the usability evaluation. And thanks for your help!

Your name _____

Social Security Number _____

Mailing address:

As a student considering college, what information do you look for about a college?

What are your top criteria in choosing a college? Please list at least three items.

1.
2.
3.
4.
5.

What colleges are you considering? Please explain for each college the thing about it that appeals most to you.

College   Most appealing aspect

1.
2.
3.
4.
5.

What majors or subjects are you interested in studying in college?

1.
2.
3.
4.

What college Web sites have you visited? Name at least three.

1.
2.
3.
4.
5.

What do you know about the college whose Web site is being tested today?

Have you ever visited this college's Web site?

_____ Yes   _____ No

Figure 6.6   Pre-test questionnaire for college Web site
(Used with permission.)

A note of caution here. What if you determine through the pre-test questionnaire that the person who has arrived for the test does not, in fact, match the user profile? Should you go ahead with the test and not include the results, or should you politely thank the participant for coming, provide the compensation offered, and go to plan B (your back-up)? In most cases, it is more productive to choose the second option of thanking and dismissing the person, rather than wasting the time of observing someone who doesn't match your intended user.

Although the importance of preparing the questionnaires to recruit and schedule participants cannot be underestimated, this activity shouldn't take all the team's time and effort. At the same time that this activity is underway, another team member or members can be creating the scenarios, which will provide the typical tasks users will be asked to perform. We present strategies for creating these scenarios in the next section.

Creating Scenarios

Scenarios are descriptions of the typical tasks you want the participants to perform. These tasks should be based on your objectives for the test, as well as the description of tasks in your test plan (see Chapter 5). While it's relatively easy to come up with a list of tasks you want users to perform, it's a bit tricky to translate these tasks into scenarios. The two challenges are to:

1. *Avoid creating steps or instructions.* Focus on the process, not the steps needed to complete the process.
2. *Avoid using the language of the product.* If you tell users where to look for information or what a button or icon is called, you direct them in a way that they might not otherwise determine on their own. So, you need to use their vocabulary, not yours.

The example in Figure 6.7 shows what a procedure or set of instructions would look like (a task plan), followed by a scenario for the participant, based on the objective of completing the task.

What if you want to test the documentation? There are two approaches you can consider:

1. You can instruct the users to work the way they normally work, then observe *whether* users consult the documentation.
2. Or, you can *direct* users to the documentation to learn what issues they may have when they use it.

In a series of scenarios created to test the online documentation for the NCR scanner product (Figure 6.8 on page 201), NCR wanted to learn about two potential users of the documentation: a grocery store clerk learning to use the scanner (scenario 1a) and a technician who would be responsible for setting up and servicing the scanner (scenarios 1b, 2, and 3). The team reasoned that if the user profile identified participants with the appropriate technical background who had not

Task Plan

The task: Undergraduate students can use a graphical user interface to petition to graduate (called Admission to Candidacy).

The goal: Complete the three sections of the Admission to Candidacy for a degree.

Task 1: Complete Section 1.
From the Welcome Screen click the <Next> button.
Fill out all the fields for the student information.

Task 2: Complete Section 2.
From the Section 1 screen click the <Next> button.
Complete the "Current Schedule."
Complete the "Proposed Final Semester Scheduler."
List any special information pertaining to the petition and/or scheduler.

Task 3: Complete Section 3.
From the Section 2 screen, click the <Next> button.
Read the agreement and agree to it by selecting the graduation semester.
Click the <Next> button.

Scenario

You are close to graduating from this university and you need to complete a petition to graduate, which will be approved by your department head and the registrar. The form is now online. Locate the petition and, using the information provided about your current and proposed final schedule, complete the form and submit it.

Notes

a. The scenario will provide the information needed about the student's current and proposed final schedule so that the participant doesn't have to create this information on the spot.

b. The scenario does not identify the name of the form to avoid using specific terminology that the participant might not have.

c. The scenario does not specify how many parts there are on the form.

d. The language of the scenario is goal-directed, focusing on the completion of a task to satisfy a goal.

Figure 6.7   Example of task plan as basis for scenario
(Used with permission of Barbara Thomas, Southern Polytechnic State University.)

used a retail scanner before, they would be able to perform all scenarios. For these scenarios, participants were *directed* to use the documentation.

Although we have stressed the need to avoid using terminology that users may not know or use themselves, what if you are testing internal users who will understand product-specific terminology? In a test of a banking software package being introduced as a replacement for paper forms, the scenarios shown in Figure 6.9 on page 202 used terminology (jargon, in this case) that was already known by the participants. This is appropriate because terminology was not the issue. Instead, the test needed to determine whether the software was more efficient than the manual method.

For an examination of the scenarios prepared for two groups of users in our continuing example of the Hotmail test, see the sidebar on pages 204–205 entitled "Scenarios for Hotmail User Groups."

Scenario 1

Scenario 1a: You have been hired as a grocery store clerk. Part of your training involves learning how to use a specific scanner, called an NCR 7875 Scanner/ Scale.

Task: Using the online information document:

1. Locate the information that tells you how to scan an item.

2. Scan two items. *Note:* You can only scan twice in this set-up.

Scenario 1b:

Task: Using the online information document, locate the following:

• Servicing information

• Programming information

• Laser safety label

   Now, take a few minutes to relax and explore the documentation. For instance, click on various icons and buttons. Tell us what you are looking at and why.

Scenario 2

You are an NCR Customer Engineer who services the 7875 scanner/scale. You have been called to a local grocery store because a scanner is not working.

Assumptions: Assume the scanner has already been turned off.

Task 1: Using the information document on the PC, remove the following component: Front Bezel.

   Note: Try to avoid touching any other component inside the unit.

Task 2: Using the online information document on the PC, replace the same component.

Scenario 3

You are an NCR Customer Engineer responsible for installing and servicing the 7875 scanner/scale. A local grocery store has just received its new 7875 scanner/ scale and you have been asked to install it and verify that it is ready for use.

Task: Install the NCR 7875 scanner/scale. Use the online document on the PC to find the information you need to:

1. Verify that the unit is ready to install.

2. Install the unit in the checkstand.

3. Determine if the unit is operational.

   Note: Do not calibrate the scale.

Test restriction: Since we do not actually have an NCR 7450 to connect to the scanner, we're using a box to represent the NCR 7450.

Figure 6.8   Scenarios for NCR scanner

(Used with permission of NCR. NCR is a registered trademark of NCR Corporation.)

Field Account Managers (FAM) List

- You will use the four scenarios below [only two are shown here] to enter data about FAMs into the Access database.

- Please stop after completing each scenario. Let me know when you have finished.

- Do not continue to the next scenario until instructed to do so.

Scenario 1

—The new FAM for Unique Corp. in Brazil is named Juan Hernandez. He has replaced the previous account manager in the city of Porto Alegre. Juan's telephone number is 55-51-222-6666 and his fax number is 55-51-222-6667.

—Your job is to locate the appropriate input form and update the Unique Corp. FAM list.

Let me know when you have finished this task.

Scenario 2

—You have just learned the name of the Solar Systems, Inc. subsidiary in Singapore; it's Solar (Singapore) Ltd. You need to go to the appropriate input form and add the subsidiary name to the Solar Systems, Inc. FAM list.

—While you are working on this, you notice that the Solar Systems FAM in Singapore is listed as "Tan Hood Nan," but you know her name is "Nan Hood Tan." Also make this correction to the data.

Return to the main database when you have finished.

Figure 6.9 Scenarios for testing banking software to create field account managers (FAM) list
(Used with permission of Susan Reu.)

For each scenario that you create, which can contain a single task or several grouped tasks, you will also want to create a post-task questionnaire to get immediate feedback from the participant. The next section addresses the ways to create this type of questionnaire, as well as the final questionnaire, called a post-test questionnaire.

Creating Post-Task and Post-Test Questionnaires

It is outside the scope of this book to go into detail about the pitfalls to avoid in creating questionnaires so that you do not bias responses. Entire courses and any number of books address the subject, which we discuss only briefly in Chapter 2 when addressing the issue of surveys. The main point to keep in mind when creating post-task and post-test questionnaires is to write neutral questions that do not suggest a desired response and to provide a choice of responses that is consistent. A Likert scale, in which participants register the extent to which they agree or disagree with a statement, is commonly used, as in the following example:

The terminology was easy to understand.

_____ Strongly agree   _____ Agree   _____ Neither agree nor disagree
_____ Disagree   _____ Strongly disagree

Another approach is to make a neutral statement and ask participants to select the appropriate response, as in the following example:

How easy or difficult was it to use the online help?

1	2	3	4	5
Very easy	Somewhat easy	Neither easy nor difficult	Somewhat difficult	Very difficult

Still another approach is to ask participants to rate their level of satisfaction on an issue, as in the following example:

Rate your level of satisfaction with the toolbar.

1	2	3	4	5
Very satisfied	Somewhat satisfied	Neither satisfied nor dissatisfied	Somewhat dissatisfied	Very dissatisfied

Or you can list a category or present a topic and ask participants to respond, as in the following example:

Navigation

1	2	3	4	5
Very easy	Easy	Neither easy nor difficult	Difficult	Very difficult

An example of this last approach is shown in Figure 6.10 on page 206, a post-task questionnaire for the NCR scanner product, used after scenario 1. Similar questionnaires would be used after scenarios 2 and 3, followed by a post-test questionnaire, illustrated in Figure 6.11 on page 207.

The post-test questionnaire frequently asks for both quantitative and qualitative responses, taking a more comprehensive overview of the product after the participant completes the test. An example of a more comprehensive questionnaire is shown in Figure 6.12 on pages 208–209. It was used at the conclusion of the test of a college Web site, directed at high-school students who might be potential applicants for admission.

With the completion of the post-task and post-test questionnaires, you will have prepared all the documents that participants will use. But you're not done yet. You also need to prepare the documents the team will use to perform their roles during the test. In the next section, we present the roles for the team members, followed by the checklists each team member needs for his or her role.

Scenarios for Hotmail User Groups

Novice Scenario/Task List

Scenario 1: Allocated time, 15 minutes
You have recently decided to sign up for email using a service called Hotmail. Using your Web browser, go to the following address:

www.Hotmail.com

Once you are at the Hotmail Web site, go ahead and sign up for a free email account. If you need any assistance, feel free to use the online help provided by Hotmail.

When you finish signing up for Hotmail, take some time to look around the site and explore its features—but for now, don't try to look at or send any email.

Scenario 2: Total allocated time, 25 minutes
Task A Check for any email messages that you may have received in Hotmail. Open one of them, and close it when you finish reading it.

Task B Send a message to the following email address:

Bill.smith@i-solutions.com

Be sure to tell the recipient that you are sending out this message to test your new Hotmail account.

Task C Check to see if you have received any new email messages while you've been working in Hotmail. Look for a message with the subject line "Usability," and respond to it with a message telling the sender that you got the email.

Scenario 4: Total allocated time, 15 minutes
Task A Erase all of the messages in your mailbox.

Task B Sign off from Hotmail.

Advanced User Test Design

The advanced user test includes all of the novice scenarios described previously and an additional scenario (Scenario 3) that requires the users to perform more sophisticated file management and organizational tasks. All of the scenarios that will be performed by advanced users are listed below.

Scenario 1
Register for Hotmail.

Scenario 2
  a. Read messages in the mailbox.
  b. Write a new message (Compose).
  c. Reply to a sender's message.

Scenario 3
  a. Search Hotmail to find a sender who has a Hotmail account.

Defining Team Members' Roles

Planning for a usability test includes planning for each team member's role during the test. When the team is conducting the test, each member should have a clearly defined role, best suited to that person's expertise. For consistency, each person should maintain the same role throughout the test. A team needs a minimum of three people to fulfill the following essential roles:

■ *Facilitator.* This is the person who has direct interaction with the participant, so this must be the most people-oriented member of the team. Sometimes this person is called the *briefer,* as this person briefs the user on the testing situation and the tasks to be performed. Typically, this person also debriefs the user at the completion of the test. This is perhaps the most challenging role on the team, as the facilitator must avoid biasing the participant during his or her interaction with the participant.

b. Send a message to this person, and attach a file to the message.

c. Create a place to store messages.

d. Create an address book to store the email addresses of people who write to you.

Scenario 4

c. Delete some messages.

d. Leave Hotmail.

Advanced User Task List

As explained above, the advanced tasks are the same as the tasks performed by novice users, with one exception: After they complete Scenario 2 and before going on to Scenario 4, advanced users will be asked to perform more sophisticated email tasks, as explained below:

Scenario 3: Total allocated time, 25 minutes
Task A   You just realized you want tell a friend you have a new Hotmail account. You know your friend also has a Hotmail account, but you don't know his email address. Using Hotmail, look up your friend, using his first and last name:

- First: Freddy
- Last: Kruger
- City: Smyrna
- State: Georgia

Task B   You decide that you want to send Freddy a message to tell him about your new Hotmail account. You also decide to send Freddy a file he's been asking for along with your message. Go ahead and write Freddy an email telling him you have a Hotmail account, and attach the file to it. The file you are sending is located on the A drive and is titled "Test.doc."

Task C   Check to see if you have any new email messages. Go ahead and place one of the emails you received in a holding area called "My Stuff." If this holding area isn't there, create it.

Task D   You just realized that you would like to keep Freddy's email address accessible for future correspondence. Create a place in Hotmail to store his address for other mailings.

Source: Used with permission of the SPSU Hotmail team: Marji Schumann, Anusuya Mukherjee, Nadyne Mielke, Melany Porter, Benjamin Speaks, and Michael Quinby.

- *Logger.* If the team has logging software or creates a macro in word-processing software to capture observations and times on a task via computer, the logger should be the fastest typist on the team and should also be knowledgeable about the product so as to understand what happens. Frequently, this person doesn't get to directly observe as much as the other team members, so the team passes on comments to the logger or writes them on sticky notes. If the team is not in a separate room but sits in the same room with the user, then the logger function may be shared by several team members, who use clipboards with forms for logging findings. One person may be assigned the timing function, using a stopwatch.
- *Camera/video operator.* This person has the responsibility for the equipment set-up in the control room or in the room with the participant, if a control room is not used. This person sets the cameras in position and makes sure the video recorder is working properly. If the equipment supports it, this person can make changes to the camera views or use the split screen or

This questionnaire is designed to tell us how you feel about the product based on the tasks you just performed. Please circle the number that most clearly expresses how you feel about a particular topic.

1. Using the software was:

1	2	3	4	5
Very easy	Easy	Neither easy nor difficult	Difficult	Very difficult

2. Navigating through the software was:

1	2	3	4	5
Very easy	Easy	Neither easy nor difficult	Difficult	Very difficult

3. Finding desired menu choices was:

1	2	3	4	5
Very easy	Easy	Neither easy nor difficult	Difficult	Very difficult

4. Locating the information needed in the software was:

1	2	3	4	5
Very easy	Easy	Neither easy nor difficult	Difficult	Very difficult

Comments:_____

_____

_____

_____

Figure 6.10   Post-task questionnaire for NCR scanner product
(Used with permission of NCR. NCR is a registered trademark of NCR Corporation.)

picture-in-picture effects to record different actions from the user, the product, or both. If there is no camera or video equipment, this person may assume the role of the timekeeper, recording start and stop times for each of the tasks.

Other useful roles include the following:

- *Narrator.* If the team is large and is conducting the test in a control room, the narrator can assist the logger in capturing findings, including verbal and nonverbal communication issues. The narrator can also pass along comments from the other team members to the logger. When a narrator is used, this person sits next to the logger.
- *Help desk operator.* This role is typically assumed by the subject matter expert on the product or the person on the team who has become most famil-

This questionnaire is designed to tell us how you feel about the product you used today. Please circle the number that most clearly expresses how you feel about a particular statement.

1. How do you rate the overall ease of use of the online information document?

1	2	3	4	5
Very easy	Easy	Neither easy nor difficult	Difficult	Very difficult

2. How easy or difficult was it to find information in the online information document?

1	2	3	4	5
Very easy	Easy	Neither easy nor difficult	Difficult	Very difficult

3. What did you like least about the online information document?

_____

_____

_____

4. What did you like most about the online information document?

_____

_____

_____

5. What one thing would you tell the designers to change about the online information document?

_____

_____

_____

Comments:_____

_____

_____

Figure 6.11 Post-test questionnaire for NCR scanner product
(Used with permission of NCR. NCR is a registered trademark of NCR Corporation.)

iar with the product. This person is needed when the product has technical support available to users or if the scenarios instruct participants to call the help desk if they get stuck. This role can be combined with another role, such as narrator or camera operator.

■ *Test administrator.* This person assumes responsibility for managing all phases of the project and keeping things on schedule. This person is typically the team leader. In smaller teams, the test administrator and facilitator roles are frequently combined.

This questionnaire is designed to tell us more about your experience using the Web site today. Please circle the number that most clearly expresses how you feel about each topic.

As compared to other college Web sites you have visited, rate the Web site in the areas described below.

Ease of navigation

1	2	3	4	5
Very easy	Easy	Neither easy nor difficult	Difficult	Very difficult

Usefulness of the information

1	2	3	4	5
Very useful	Useful	Neither useful nor useless	Not very useful	Not useful at all

The look and feel of the pages

1	2	3	4	5
Excellent	Good	Neutral— no opinion	Not very appealing	Not appealing at all

Explain the basis for your rating.

Can you recall how different sections of the Web site are identified?

_____ Yes

_____ No

If yes, please explain how different sections of the site are identified.

After visiting the Web site, would you be interested in revisiting the site?

_____ Yes

_____ No

Please explain the basis for your answer.

Figure 6.12   Post-test questionnaire for college Web site *(continued)*
(Used with permission.)

If you would be interested in visiting this Web site again, what information would you look for the next time you visited?

What information would you want to have that you didn't see on the Web site?

List the three most interesting things you learned about the college.

1.

2.

3.

As a result of using the Web site, rate your overall level of satisfaction or dissatisfaction with the site.

1	2	3	4	5
Very Satisfied	Satisfied	Neither satisfied nor dissatisfied	Somewhat dissatisfied	Very dissatisfied

Please explain the reason for your rating.

After visiting the Web site, would you consider applying to this college?

_____ Yes

_____ No

Please explain the reason for your answer.

Would you recommend that a friend check out this Web site?

_____ Yes

_____ No

Please explain the reason for your response.

Figure 6.12

What Makes a Good Moderator

Chauncey Wilson

1. A successful test session starts when you meet the person and take him/her to the testing facility. A relaxed, warm (but not overly friendly) first meeting is important. The trip up the elevator is often a place to begin establishing rapport.

2. A moderator should make a list and practice neutral "prods" that can be used to elicit information, get more detail, etc. Making a list of neutral questions or statements and practicing with them can help remove bias from the session.

3. When I first started lab testing, I found it very useful to videotape myself in some pilot and real sessions. I discovered little tics and some poor verbal habits. You can also note nonverbal cues that you may be giving the participant.

4. Avoid the use of loaded words like "test" (study is probably fine), "subjects" (colleagues or something less negative is probably better).

5. I like to use the rule adopted from the American Psychological Association (APA) that a participant in a study (of any kind) should leave the situation in no worse shape than when he/she arrived and, if possible, should leave with some positive reaction to their participation.

6. A good moderator should ensure that any observers follow a set of guidelines like never talk about a participant in the hallway or restrooms (this can be very embarrassing), no laughing in "soundproof" observation rooms, etc.

7. There are occasions where a participant is really not appropriate. This can be a very touchy situation, especially if they have traveled some distance to participate. There are graceful ways to end a session with a person who will add no value.

8. A test moderator should always, always run a pilot session or two to verify that the hardware and software and tasks are appropriate. I know some people who have been in the field a long time who jump right into a study without doing a pilot, but I think that even experts need to do this. I also think a good moderator uses himself/herself as a pilot and goes through all the tasks, even if help is needed from a domain expert. Knowing the tasks well allows more subtle observation.

9. A good moderator schedules enough time between sessions to allow time for resetting the system, finishing up with a late participant, etc. I like to have an hour

In the next section, we look more closely at the responsibilities of the facilitator or briefer, as this person has direct contact with the user and therefore must take special care in preparing to handle this role successfully.

Facilitator/Briefer

Because the facilitator or briefer/debriefer (also called the moderator) has the most direct contact with the participant, this person's task is to be cordial (even soothing), consistent in all statements and actions, and unbiased. That's a tough

between sessions, which means a maximum of 3–4 sessions a day.

10. A good moderator is extremely careful to protect the person's privacy and never uses the person's name. This is just as important for internal users as external users. Many companies are a bit cavalier about internal users, but an internal user who does poorly in a study might have some severe self-esteem issues.

11. It is good to prepare a checklist to remind yourself of all the procedures, forms, etc. Again, this is useful even for experts. Something as simple as forgetting to have pens for the participants can be a bit unsettling.

12. It is useful to put together a script for a study. If you are going to read a script verbatim, tell the user and explain that you are doing this for consistency, but also note that you will answer any procedural questions (though not product questions) at any time. Even if you don't need a detailed script (for an informal study, for example), writing one up helps make for smooth sessions.

13. You might want to wear clothing that is similar to the style generally worn by your participants. If the participants are senior VPs, then a suit would be appropriate. If the participants are students, then jeans might even be appropriate.

14. If you have more than one participant at a time, you might need to develop methods for getting feedback from shy participants. The co-participation method where two users think aloud as they work together is a method where someone with a dominant personality can overwhelm the other participant.

15. A good moderator knows when to end a task or when to ask the person to move on after struggling for a long time. If a user tries the same flawed method to complete a task six times in a row, you may not learn anything further and you may want to provide a series of "hints" to see if the user will find the path to success. You may also have a time limit per task. If they don't finish a task in, say, 10 minutes, then you ask the user to move on to the next one. The method to do this has to be gentle, and you may want to have some catch phrases ready when this occurs.

16. At the end of the study in which you are testing a product that is important to your users, you might want to give them some tips on how to use the software more effectively. You wouldn't want to do this if you plan to have them back in some type of longitudinal study, but giving them some gentle tips is one way to make the participation a positive experience.

Source: Used with permission of Chauncey Wilson.

job and it takes practice to understand how to handle it, which the walkthrough and the pilot will provide before full testing begins. Chauncey Wilson, a usability specialist, offers sage advice about what makes a good moderator (in the sidebar shown above).

To maintain consistency, the briefer (or moderator) needs to create a checklist of tasks and reminders, as well as a script or outline of the briefer's overview and orientation for each participant. Figure 6.13 is a checklist used by the Blade Group, which tested Southern Polytechnic State University's Web site. A script provides a consistent orientation for each participant. Even experienced briefers recommend using a script. If you feel awkward reading from a script, you can

(continued on page 213)

Checklist for the Briefer

Welcome

_____ Introductions

_____ Show participant the restroom, offer a drink

_____ Settle him/her with some reading materials (magazines/catalogues)

_____ Explain there will be a short wait while everything is prepared, tell exact time testing will begin

Consent Form, Pre-Test Questionnaire, Instructions

_____ On the way to testing, share about concept of usability testing, school's grant and lab facilities

_____ Seat in evaluator room

_____ Show cameras, computer, phone, microphone

_____ Explain testing the usability of the material, NOT the user

_____ Go over consent form, allow time to read and sign

_____ Give pre-test questionnaire

Instructions

_____ Explain working through scenarios while thinking out loud and calling when done

_____ Demonstrate calling the help desk

_____ Stress thinking out loud

_____ Have user practice thinking out loud with the stapler

_____ Reiterate thinking out loud and reassure participant that they are not being tested

Equipment

_____ Clear objects in front of microphone

_____ Make sure participant knows how to call on the telephone

_____ Be sure software is loaded properly

During Testing, Post-Task Questionnaire

_____ Interrupt if unable to complete task

_____ Offer plenty of reassurance, especially when tasks prove difficult

_____ Give feedback on the quality of the thinking-out-loud procedure

_____ Ask participant to clarify any questionable thoughts or actions

_____ Give post-task questionnaire to fill out

_____ Return screen to the homepage for the next scenario

Upon Completion, Post-Test Questionnaire

_____ Give post-test questionnaire

_____ Show participant the lab facilities and the team

_____ Give gift, thank profusely

Figure 6.13 Briefer checklist

(Used with permission of the Blade Group: Betty Owen, Loretta Joslin, Ardenna Morton, Diana Mason, and Elizabeth Wong Mark.)

explain, as part of the script, that you are doing this to maintain consistency with all the participants. In less formal tests, when a script isn't used, a separate checklist of the topics you want to cover with each participant will do. Whether you create a script or a detailed checklist, you will want to use it to welcome participants, explain the procedure for the test, and any unusual requirements or expectations, such as asking the participant to "think out loud." You will also want to describe the room and the equipment and assure the participant that you are conducting a test of a product, not the user.

The briefer script shown in Figure 6.14 was used by Team Inertia for a usability test of the Southern Polytechnic State University Web site. It indicates not only what the briefer will say but also what the anticipated response will be from the participant.

A briefer's script outline, used in less formal testing situations, combines checklists, reminders, and procedures, as shown in Figure 6.15 on page 216.

Consent or Release Forms

As noted in the briefer's checklist, you will need to provide one or more legal forms to obtain participants' consent to conduct testing and to protect the information learned if the product has not yet gone to market. If these forms already exist in your organization, the test administrator or briefer will need to obtain them. If the forms do not exist, they will need to be created. There are two types you may need:

1. *Nondisclosure agreement.* Secures agreement from the participant to keep secret the information learned about a product in development. If the product is on the market already or otherwise available to the public (as in a Web site), then this form is generally not needed.
2. *Consent form.* Secures permission from the participant to be tested, and, if taped, to be videotaped or audiotaped during testing. Called *informed consent*, this form describes the nature of the test as well as the use of the information obtained (and videotaped) during the test. It also informs participants that they can choose to stop the test at any time for any reason. Figures 6.16 and 6.17 on pages 217 and 218 are examples of consent forms created for participants testing the Southern Polytechnic Web site for the Humanities and Technical Communication Department.

Some companies obtain permission to use the names of the participants, or, in other cases, the first names only of the participants. Other companies promise not to reveal participants' names, referring to them instead as participant A, B, C or 1, 2, 3.

Checklists for the Hotmail test team's narrator, logger, test administrator, camera operator, briefer, and test assistant are provided in the appendix at the end of this chapter.

If the test is not being conducted in a lab, then several of the roles described earlier will not be needed, including narrator, logger, and help desk. The test administrator/briefer will still be the only team member interacting with the

(continued on page 215)

B = indicates briefer comments
P = participant response expected

B: I would like to thank you on behalf of the team and welcome you to our usability test of the Southern Polytechnic Web site. We REALLY appreciate your coming in today to help us out. Your input is going to be very valuable to us as we evaluate the Web site and see how easy or how difficult you find it to use.

As you can see, we have cameras here in the room with you. We will be looking at the computer screen with one of the cameras, so that as you work, we can see what you are clicking on, and where you are going. That will be very helpful to us. Also, we are going to be recording your facial expressions to see if things seem to be going just as you expected, or if you seem surprised at where a button takes you. We will also be able to see if you seem to be getting frustrated with what we've asked you to do, and just how things go for you. All this will REALLY help us to evaluate the Web site that you'll be working with today.

Please take a look at this little black object next to the computer. It is a sensitive microphone that will pick up everything you are saying. We would like for you to think out loud during this session. It would help us so much if you could tell us what you are thinking. For example, "I am clicking on this button because I want to look at courses in the biology department." So if you could just think out loud, that would really help us out a lot. You don't have to speak loudly because this microphone is very sensitive. Just speak in your normal tone of voice and the tape will be able to record your thoughts. Do you think you can do that for us?

P: Participant responds.

B: OK, so that you can practice thinking out loud, I would like for you to take this stapler and load some staples into it. While you are doing that, if you would, please tell us exactly what you are doing each step of the way, as well as what you're thinking about. OK? Great.

P: Participant loads stapler while thinking out loud. Briefer praises his/her efforts for thinking out loud.

B: Please remember, we are testing this Web site. We are not testing you. So don't be nervous. There are no right or wrong answers. We just want to see how things go for you. Does that sound all right?

P: Participant acknowledges.

B: All right, if you will please, just sign our release form here. It says:

"I, the undersigned, agree to be part of a usability study being conducted at Southern Polytechnic State University. As a participant, I agree to be videotaped. I allow my comments and observations about my experiences to become part of the findings of the usability study."

P: Participant signs release form.

B: All right, great. Now do you have any questions for me?

B: OK, let me ask you this, "Did you know that there is a career field called technical writing?"

P: Yes or No.

B: What do you think technical writing is?

P: Participant answers will vary.

Figure 6.14 Briefer script *(continued)*

(Used with permission of Team Inertia: Anita Carpenter, Henri Dongieux, Cindy Ravenna, Diane Rhone, Diana Samuels, and Lynn Smith.)

B: All right, if you will, read this first task over and let me know if you have any questions.

P: Participant may answer.

B: Now, when you have finished this task, please push line 1, intercom, and page on the phone here. Also, if you get completely stuck, where you don't have any idea at all how to proceed any further, you can call the help desk, using this phone the same way. OK?

P: Participant responds.

B: Now then, do you have any questions at all?

P: Participant answers.

B: Great, well, I'll leave you for now. Call me when you're finished. Please remember to think out loud for us. That would really be helpful. Thanks.

Briefer leaves the room and leaves participant to complete scenario one. After the completion of each scenario, the briefer returns to the lab.

B: How was that task for you?

P: Participant responds.

B: Briefer asks any questions handed to her by team members during the task.

B: All right, now we are going to take a look at the departmental page for the Humanities and Technical Communication Department. You will start your next task here.

After each of the tasks, the briefer enters the room to ask the participant how that task was. She also asks any questions handed to her by team members who noted things on sticky notes.

Following completion of each questionnaire, the briefer questions any responses that are on the low side of the rating scale to get a better understanding of the reason(s) for the ratings.

At the completion of the test, the briefer asks the following questions so the interview can be recorded on camera. These answers become part of the qualitative data gathered.

B: What was your favorite thing about this site?

P: Participant gives response.

B: What was your least favorite thing about this site?

P: Participant gives response.

B: What impressions of the department did you get from this site?

P: Participant gives response.

B: Would you return to this site?

P: Participant gives response.

B: Would you recommend this site to others?

P: Participant gives response.

Figure 6.14

participant, while other members of the team sit within the peripheral vision of the participant and take notes on their observations. For this task, an observation form needs to be created, as shown in Figure 6.18 on page 219. It can be a simple form that includes the name of the participant or number, the start and stop times for each task or scenario (this can be recorded by one member of the team only), the type of observation or task, and the observer's comments.

1. Welcome

2. Filled out questionnaire?

3. Filled out release?

4. Describe usability lab (cameras, one-way mirror, microphone).

5. Tell participant that we are testing the ONLINE DOCUMENTATION, not the product itself, and especially *not you.*

6. Describe think-out-loud procedure.

7. Practice with a stapler. [bring stapler, with staples unloaded]

8. Talk about the scenarios.

9. Talk about calling for help and telling us when finished with task.

10. Tell about post-task questionnaires.

11. Ask if there are any questions.

12. Thank participant for help.

13. Give participant first scenario.

Notes: After Scenario 1, turn power off. After Scenario 2, ask participant to leave room so we can set up Scenario 3.

For Scenario 3, tell participant about the box, the interface cable in the box, the mock-up box behind the computer, the scenario, and the assumptions.

"Assumptions will make it easier for you to do the task by telling you what to skip in the instructions and other useful information about the set-up of the equipment today."

Figure 6.15   Briefer script outline
(Used with permission of NCR. NCR is a registered trademark of NCR Corporation.)

With the completion of these forms and checklists, you are ready to rehearse your roles in a walkthrough, then go to the dress rehearsal, called the pilot test. We conclude the chapter with a discussion of these last two components of the preparation process.

Conducting the Walkthrough and the Pilot

Just as a play would not be performed without a "reading," followed by a dress rehearsal, usability testing should not be performed without the same preparation. The walkthrough is the equivalent of a reading of the script for the play, whereas the pilot is like the dress rehearsal. The walkthrough is the team's first chance to test the materials and the parts given to each member of the team. The pilot is a quality check to make sure that the final version will work when the curtain goes up on a full day of testing.

Purpose	A student group at Southern Polytechnic State University (SPSU) has asked you to participate in a study of a departmental Web site. By participating in this study, you will help us make the Web site easy to use.
Study Environment	The study takes place at SPSU's usability laboratory, where you will be observed as you use the site.
Information Collected	We will record information about how you use the Web site. We will ask you to fill out questionnaires, and we will interview you. We will use the information you give us, along with the information we collect from other people, to recommend ways to improve the site.
Videotape Waiver	All or some of your work with the site and the interviews will be videotaped. By signing this form, you give your consent to SPSU to use your voice, verbal statements, and videotaped pictures, but not your name for the purpose of evaluating the site and showing the results of our testing.
Comfort	You may take a break at any time you wish. Simply inform the test administrator that you would like to do so.
Freedom to Withdraw	You may withdraw from this study at any time.
Freedom to Ask Questions	If you have any questions, you may ask the test administrator now or at any time during the study.

If you agree with these terms, please indicate your acceptance by signing below.

Signature: _____

Printed name: _____

Date: _____

Figure 6.16 Legal disclosure form
(Used with permission of Team Inertia: Anita Carpenter, Henri Dongieux, Cindy Ravenna, Diane Rhone, Diana Samuels, and Lynn Smith.)

Conducting the Walkthrough

The walkthrough is a chance to test the equipment, the scenarios, the questionnaires, and the checklists for the team members. It gives team members their first chance to practice their parts. It provides the initial feedback on the length of the scenarios, the problems a user may have in understanding the tasks, the terminology, the questions asked, or the nature of the test. It should be scheduled far enough in advance to rework any and all parts of the test before the pilot.

A *tolerant user* should be recruited for the walkthrough. "Tolerant" means that the person can deal with mistakes, computer crashes, delays, and confusion. The tolerant user can be recruited from inside the company or through friends or

I agree to participate in the research titled Graduate Student Usability Testing of the Humanities and Technical Communication (HTC) Web Site, which is being conducted by Elizabeth Wong Mark, Betty Owen, Loretta Joslin, Ardenna Morton, and Diana Mason, under the direction of Dr. Carol Barnum, Humanities and Technical Communication Department, Southern Polytechnic State University (SPSU). I understand that this participation is entirely voluntary; I can withdraw my consent at any time without penalty and have the results of the participation, to the extent that it can be identified as mine, returned to me, removed from the research records, or destroyed.

The research has been explained to me as follows:

- The purpose of the study is to evaluate the usability of a certain portion of the SPSU Web site. The researchers wish to determine the ease of use of the site and how users perceive it.

- Participants will work at a computer that has access to the specified Web site and be given tasks related to accessing the site. While the participant tries these tasks, he or she will be directly observed and/or videotaped so that the research team can review the participant's interactions with the instruction and the participant's comments during this interaction. The entire activity will take approximately 2 hours.

- The participant's identity will be kept confidential in any transcriptions and reports generated from this research. Any comments or expressions made during the usability test may be used for the purpose of evaluating the Web site and showing the results of this research. The videotape will be included as part of the final report submitted to the course instructor. All videotapes related to this research project will be turned over to the Humanities and Technical Communication Department.

The researcher will answer any further questions about the research, now or during the course of the project.

Please sign both copies of this form. Keep one and return the other to the researcher.

_____
Signature of Participant/Date

Figure 6.17 Consent form
(Used with permission of the Blade Group: Betty Owen, Loretta Joslin, Ardenna Morton, Diana Mason, and Elizabeth Wong Mark.)

family, as this person does not have to exactly match the user profile. Of course, the more closely this person matches the user profile, the more applicable the information obtained will be. But here, the emphasis should be on tolerant, for the team is going through role training, a functional check of the system and the equipment, and the effectiveness of the usability plan.

The team should adopt the attitude that the walkthrough is intended to find the flaws in the plan. It is a data-gathering session, in which the tape should roll,

Participant name:	Date:	
Task	**Start/stop time**	**Observer's comments**

Figure 6.18 Template for observation form

the checklists should be tested, the script delivered, and the highlighter pens employed to track all the problems that need attention. The tolerant user can be asked to share his or her views of the scenarios and questionnaires to help the team understand issues that may cause problems for future participants. Although it may be difficult to time the scenarios if there are frequent interruptions, the walkthrough can still be used to determine if the scenarios are about the right length for the time allotted. Frequently, scenarios have to be shortened, as the goals for the test are often more ambitious than can be accomplished in a typical test session.

During the walkthrough, the logger or data recorder may find that this is his or her first opportunity to work with the logging software or data sheets to record findings. Ideally, the logger should become familiar with the logging software in advance, but if this isn't possible, the walkthrough provides this chance. Likewise, the camera operator may find that this is his or her first time manipulating the cameras and working the video equipment. For the briefer or narrator, the walkthrough is clearly his or her first opportunity to practice friendliness, thoroughness, and the neutral posture required when interacting with a participant. Using the script and checklist, the briefer will likely need to add notes and make changes about things that couldn't be anticipated before going "live."

Other tasks to test during the walkthrough may include testing sound and light levels in the evaluator room and in the control room, the use of the phone, intercom, or microphone systems, the location of tables and chairs before and during testing, and the configuration of the computer or the product to be tested. Upon completion of the walkthrough, the team will want to conduct a debriefing to plan the changes that need to occur before the pilot. These changes are frequently numerous, in which case review dates may need to be set to approve all the changes, including script and checklist changes for team members.

Conducting the Pilot

The pilot is the test of the test. It should be scheduled two or three days before full testing begins, which gives the team enough time to make additional changes, as needed, but is still close enough to the testing days that team members will be clear about their roles and responsibilities without further training. The participant in the pilot should be someone from the actual pool recruited for the test. There are two reasons for this. If the walkthrough has correctly uncovered the problems and they have been corrected, the pilot can frequently go quite smoothly. In these cases, the team can add the pilot's results to those of the other participants, increasing the number of participants by one. If, however, the pilot uncovers problems not previously seen in the walkthrough (because the tolerant user was not an exact match for the user profile), then the team still has time to make the corrections and can use the data gathered from this participant to improve the testing process. Either way, the pilot participant must match the user profile to make the pilot effective.

The results from the pilot, whether or not they will be used in the final report, give the team the chance to practice the approach they will use to analyze the findings and anticipate the types of findings they're likely to get in the subsequent sessions. If the team has agreed on some common terminology for the findings (top-down approach discussed in Chapter 5), they can try out the terminology to see if they understand how to apply it to observations.

Summary

Finally, you're ready. You've prepared all the materials you need for usability testing, determined the roles of team members, and created the script and checklists needed for each member to do his or her job. You've recruited the participants and put yourself and two users through the paces in a walkthrough and a pilot. You've made all the final adjustments needed, checked with your participants to be sure they're available, and checked to make sure the room is reserved and the equipment is operational. And, by now, you're no doubt fired up, especially since you've just finished the pilot, which is the closest thing to the real thing.

Coming Up

In the next chapter, we guide you through the actual testing day. This includes your arrival before testing begins to go through the checklists one more time and take your place on the team in preparation for the arrival of the first participant. It also includes information on conducting the test session, collating the results from the participant, and planning for the next one, and so on, until the testing is completed. You'll need a good night's sleep, which you should have earned by taking all the right steps to get here. Usability testing is both exhausting and exhilarating, at times frustrating but always fascinating, as you'll experience (vicariously) in the next chapter.

Questions/Topics for Discussion

1. Discuss the ways in which a screening questionnaire can be used to get information about potential users for a usability test. What are the advantages and disadvantages of each method?
2. For your project, create a list of places where you will be able to recruit participants for usability testing. What method will be most effective to use to screen participants in each of these locations? What incentive will you use to get them to agree to participate? What method will you use to provide a back-up participant?
3. Describe the difference between a task plan and a scenario. In creating a scenario, what two issues do you want to avoid?
4. In creating post-task and post-test questionnaires, what issues do you want to avoid so as to create questions that do not bias the reader? List several questions you would like to ask participants. Include questions to gather both quantitative and qualitative data.
5. List the various roles your team will need to assume. Describe the responsibilities for each role assumed by a team member.
6. Describe the types of checklists you will need to create. What is the purpose of these checklists?
7. Describe the purpose of the walkthrough and the type of participant you should recruit for this phase of preparation. What is the difference between the walkthrough and the pilot? How is the participant different for the pilot?

Exercises

For Your Project

1. Create the pre-screening and pre-test questionnaires. Because these questionnaires are such an important tool in recruiting the right participants for the test, all team members should participate in the process or review the drafts created by one team member.
2. Determine the team roles for each member, depending upon the set-up of the usability test and the conditions under which the team will be conducting the test.
3. Create checklists (either by each team member or as a group) for each team member. Also create a script or outline for the briefer. If the team is observing in the same room as the participant, create observer sheets.
4. Create or obtain consent/release forms for participants.

5. Create post-task and post-test questionnaires. This task can be done by one team member (to be reviewed by the group) or as an activity by the group.
6. Schedule the walkthrough and the pilot. Schedule a tolerant user for the walkthrough and a participant for the pilot. Schedule the days and times for testing. Schedule the participants for the test days and times.

References

Dumas, Joseph S., and Janice C. Redish. *A Practical Guide to Usability Testing.* Norwood, NJ: Ablex, 1993.

Rosenbaum, Stephanie. "Chapter 3: Selecting Appropriate Participants for Usability Testing." *Practical Approaches to Usability Testing for Technical Documentation.* Ed. Chris Velotta. Arlington, VA: STC Press, 1995. 63–72.

Wilson, Chauncey. "What Makes a Good Moderator." Online posting. 18 May 2000. Used with permission of author.

"Xerox Participant Questionnaire" <http://www.stcsig.org/usability>.

Hotmail Evaluation Team Checklists

The following checklists were prepared for each key testing role:

- **Narrator**
- **Logger**
- **Test administrator**
- **Camera operator**
- **Briefer**
- **Test assistant**

Checklist for the Narrator

Before each test participant comes:

_____ Know the product/system well.

_____ Know the objectives of each task.

_____ Know the steps related to each task scenario.

_____ Know the team's objectives as related to video and data captures.

_____ Coordinate efforts with the data recorder to ensure results are captured.

During each task session:

_____ Provide information to the data recorder.

_____ Work with the data recorder to verify the accuracy of actions and comments.

Checklist for Scenario 1
Scenario 1
You have recently decided to sign up for email using a service called Hotmail. Using your Web browser, go to the following address:
www.Hotmail.com
Once you are at the Hotmail Web site, go ahead and sign up for a free email account. If you need any assistance, feel free to use the online help provided by Hotmail.
When you finish signing up for Hotmail, take some time to look around the site and explore its features—but for now, don't try to look at or send any email.

_____ How does the user enter the URL for hotmail.com?

_____ Pay attention to how the user navigates the page (mouse versus tab).

_____ How does the user navigate information forms (mouse versus tab)?

_____ Does the user access the online help?

_____ Does the user click on any banner ads?

_____ Note any facial expressions to the logger.

_____ Note any verbal comments to the logger.

_____ Note any body gestures to the logger.

Checklist for Scenario 2
Scenario 2

Task A Check for any email messages that you may have received in Hotmail. Open one of them, and close it when you finish reading it.

Task B Send a message to the following email address:
  Bill.smith@i-solutions.com
Be sure to tell the recipient that you are sending out this message to test your new Hotmail account.

Task C Check to see if you have received any new email messages while you've been working in Hotmail. Look for a message with the subject line "Usability," and respond to it with a message telling the sender that you got the email.

_____ Note to the logger how the user navigates the Inbox Screen.

_____ Can the user understand the radio box concept?

_____ Pay attention to how the user navigates the page (mouse versus tab).

_____ How does the user navigate information forms (mouse versus tab)?

_____ Does the user access the online help?

_____ Does the user click on any banner ads?

_____ Note any facial expressions to the logger.

_____ Note any verbal comments to the logger.

_____ Note any body gestures to the logger.

Checklist for Scenario 3
Scenario 3

Task A (discontinued)

Task B You decide that you want to send your friend Marji a message to tell her about your new Hotmail account. Along with your message, you also decide to send her a file she's been asking for. Go ahead and write Marji an email telling her you have a Hotmail account, and attach the file to it. The file you are sending is located on the A drive and is titled "Test.doc." Marji's Hotmail address is
  marji_miller@hotmail.com

Task C Place one of the emails you have received in a holding area called "My Stuff." If this holding area isn't there, create it.

Task D You just realized that you would like to keep Marji's email address accessible for future correspondence. Create a place in Hotmail to store her address for other mailings.

_____ Note to the logger how the user navigates the Attachment page.

_____ Note to the logger how the user navigates the Folders page.

_____ Note to the logger how the user navigates the Address Book page.

_____ Pay attention to how the user navigates the page (mouse versus tab).

_____ How does the user navigate information forms (mouse versus tab)?

_____ Does the user access the online help?

_____ Does the user click on any banner ads?

_____ Note any facial expressions to the logger.

_____ Note any verbal comments to the logger.

_____ Note any body gestures to the logger.

Checklist for Scenario 4
Scenario 4
Task A Erase all of the messages in your mailbox.

Task B Sign off from Hotmail.

_____ Note how the user interacts with the radio box/pull down deletion menu.

_____ Note the user's facial expressions when logging off from Hotmail.

_____ Pay attention to how the user navigates the page (mouse versus tab).

_____ Does the user access the online help?

_____ Does the user click on any banner ads?

_____ Note any facial expressions to the logger.

_____ Note any verbal comments to the logger.

_____ Note any body gestures to the logger.

Checklist for the Logger

Before the test:

_____ Turn on logging computer.

_____ Check error codes in logging software.

_____ Enter new test information into logging software.

_____ Check headphones and microphones for logger and narrator.

_____ Test logging software.

_____ Check video feeds.

_____ Check logger's monitor.

_____ Change monitor views as necessary.

_____ Check cable from logging computer to printer.

_____ Check paper and ink in printer.

_____ Do a test print from logging software.

_____ Check paper and toner in copy machine.

_____ Do a test copy.

After each test participant:

_____ Print report.

_____ Copy report.

_____ Distribute copies to evaluation team members.

_____ Place original in test participant's folder.

_____ Set up logging software for next test participant (if any).

At end of day:

_____ Print final report.

_____ Make sure all members of team have copies.

_____ Have logging software ready for next team.

_____ Turn off computer.

_____ Refill printer (if necessary).

_____ Turn off printer.

_____ Refill copier (if necessary).

_____ Turn off copy machine.

_____ Order paper (if necessary).

_____ Back up logging software data files.

Checklist for the Test Administrator

Before each test participant comes:

_____ Make sure each evaluation team member has a copy of the scenarios, questionnaires, etc.

_____ Monitor the evaluation team members to confirm they are using their checklists.

_____ Greet the test observers.

During each test session:

_____ Manage any problems that arise.

_____ Observe and take notes, noting real problems and "big picture" issues.

_____ Collect follow-up questions to review with the test participants.

After each test session:

_____ Collect test paperwork (questionnaires, notes, etc.).

_____ Make sure the computer is set up for the next test participant and clear the room of any materials left behind by the test participant or briefer.

_____ Bring test participants into the observation room and describe the testing process from the evaluation team's point of view.

_____ Lead the team in a brief session to catalog results and identify any usability issues discovered during the test.

After each day of testing:

_____ Conduct a brief review with the other members of the evaluation team to summarize the test day's findings.

Checklist for the Camera Operator

Before each test participant comes:

_____ Turn on the equipment.

_____ Adjust the cameras to the proper setting for taping.

_____ Check the sound both in and out of the monitoring booth.

_____ Label the tapes for the session.

_____ Load the tape into the VCR.

During each test session:

_____ Synchronize starting times with the data recorder.

_____ Run the equipment.

_____ Select the picture to record and handle the recording.

_____ Adjust the sound as needed.

_____ Change the videotapes when necessary.

After the test participant leaves:

_____ Rewind the tapes used during the session.

_____ Check to make certain the tapes are labeled properly.

_____ Turn off the equipment.

Checklist for the Briefer

Before each test participant comes:

_____ Make sure the evaluation room is properly set up. Turn on the computer equipment. Get the product ready.

_____ Make sure the documentation is in place, if appropriate.

_____ Have a pad and pens or pencils for taking notes.

_____ Have an ink pen ready for the test participant to use in signing the Consent form.

_____ Check the folder for that test participant. Make sure all of the forms are in the folder.

At the beginning of each test session:

_____ Greet the test participant.

_____ Check the test participant's name to be sure that this is the person whom you expect.

_____ Make the test participant comfortable. Offer food and beverage.

_____ Bring the test participant into the evaluation room.

_____ Let the test participant see the cameras and other equipment.

_____ Show the test participant where to sit.

_____ Give the test participant a brief introduction to the test session.

_____ Ask if the test participant has any questions.

_____ Remind the test participant to think out loud.

_____ Remind the test participant to tell you when he or she has completed each task.

_____ Put the "Testing in Progress" sign on the door.

At the end of each test session:

_____ Ask the test participant to fill out the post-test questionnaire.

_____ Go in to the evaluation room and thank the test participant for his or her help.

_____ Debrief the test participant. Go over the test participant's responses to the post-test questionnaire.

_____ Give the test participant the payment or other incentive.

_____ Offer to show the test participant the observation room. Show the equipment and introduce the team.

_____ Thank the test participant and show him or her out.

After the test participant leaves:

_____ Put all the forms in the test participant's folder.

_____ Turn off the equipment in the evaluation room.

Checklist for the Test Assistant

Before each test participant comes:

_____ Make sure that there is sufficient paper and that all of the evaluation team members have writing instruments to take notes.

_____ Label each page of the notes with the project name, test participant's number/name, date, and time.

During each test session:

_____ Take notes on problems and other observations.

After each test participant leaves:

_____ Review and edit notes so that they are legible and clear.

_____ Put notes in that test participant's folder.

Source: Used with permission of the SPSU Hotmail team: Marji Schumann, Anusuya Mukherjee, Nadyne Mielke, Melany Porter, Benjamin Speaks, and Michael Quinby.

Conducting the Usability Test

 It's testing day and you're ready. You've planned your test, prepared the forms for participants and the team, tested the process in a walkthrough and a pilot, reconfirmed the availability of your participants, and now there's nothing left to do but conduct the test. This chapter walks you through the process of conducting a usability test. It begins by describing a typical test day, although there can be many varieties and models. Then, we look at the challenges of putting the planning process into practice. These include:

- Greeting and setting the participant at ease
- Administering forms
- Briefing the participant on the process
- Using think-aloud protocol
- Being an unbiased briefer/debriefer
- Processing help calls
- Handling visitors (observers)
- Collecting and organizing data
- Collating data into findings

A Typical Test Day

Although there may be no such thing as a typical test day, because the length of each test varies with the product and the goals of the test, a typical test day can be presented as a working model, using a timeframe of 1.5 hours per participant (see Figure 7.1). A reference to this model was presented in Chapter 5 (Figure 5.2, on pages 172–173), with three participants on the first day and two participants on the second day. This plan allows for the end of the second day to be used for analysis and recommendations.

230

Day 1

Team arrives/prepares	8:00–8:45 A.M.
Participant 1 arrives	8:45 A.M.
Participant 1 session	9:00–10:30 A.M.
Analysis/set-up for next session	10:30–11:00 A.M.
Participant 2 arrives	10:45 A.M.
Participant 2 session	11:00–12:30 P.M.
Lunch	12:30–1:30 P.M.
Analysis/set-up for next session	1:30–2:00 P.M.
Participant 3 arrives	1:45 P.M.
Participant 3 session	2:00–3:30 P.M.
Analysis/review	3:30–5:00 P.M.

Day 2

Team arrives/prepares	8:00–8:45 A.M.
Participant 4 arrives	8:45 A.M.
Participant 4 session	9–10:30 A.M.
Analysis/set-up for next session	10:30–11:00 A.M.
Participant 5 arrives	10:45 A.M.
Participant 5 session	11:00–12:30 P.M.
Lunch	12:30–1:30 P.M.
Analysis	1:30–2:00 P.M.
Summary of findings	2:00–4:00 P.M.

Figure 7.1   Usability testing sessions (90 minutes each, a total of 5 sessions)

An alternative plan, shown in Figure 7.2, presents a typical test at Xerox Corporation, in which six participants will evaluate the product over the 2-day period. If analysis and recommendations take place at the end of the second day, it makes for a very long day. Most likely, in the Xerox example, detailed analysis and recommendations would occur on another day. In both plans, you will notice that it is a tight schedule, which will work only if everyone knows what is supposed to happen and the team follows its checklists to make sure nothing is forgotten and everything is consistent from participant to participant.

Some usability experts schedule even more time between participants to allow time to collate data following each participant. If an hour or more is provided between participants, the tradeoffs are one of the following: (1) the test days become longer, (2) more test days are required, or (3) fewer participants evaluate the product. Regardless of the test schedule you use, you need to focus on a good methodology to make each participant's experience meaningful and satisfying. In the next section, we look at how to meet, greet, and make the participant feel welcome.

Greeting the Participant

The participant should have interaction primarily or exclusively with the facilitator (also called briefer). Thus, the facilitator's first job is to be ready to meet and greet the participant on arrival. Frequently, the participant will arrive early, so the

Monday, March 6th

1:00–3:00 P.M.	Overview presentation scheduled

Tuesday, March 7th

7:30 A.M.	Arrive at site Power up lab and do prep testing
9:00 A.M.	**First** participant arrives Run through test session checklist
9:15 A.M.	Begin test
10:30 A.M.	End test Debrief user and post-test questionnaire filled out
11:00 A.M.	**Second** participant arrives Run through test session checklist
11:15 A.M.	Begin test
1:00 P.M.	End test Debrief user and post-test questionnaire filled out
1:15–2:00 P.M.	LUNCH
2:00 P.M.	**Third** participant arrives Run through test session checklist
2:15 P.M.	Begin test
3:30 P.M.	End test Debrief user and post-test questionnaire filled out
4:00 P.M.	Compile notes and identify any outstanding problems to communicate immediately Check and supply new batteries for test equipment Label all test materials and store Prepare test materials for next test day

Wednesday, March 8th

7:30 A.M.	Arrive at site Power up lab and do prep testing
9:00 A.M.	**Fourth** participant arrives Run through test session checklist
9:15 A.M.	Begin test
10:30 A.M.	End test Debrief user and post-test questionnaire filled out
11:00 A.M.	**Fifth** participant arrives Run through test session checklist
11:15 A.M.	Begin test
1:00 P.M.	End test Debrief user and post-test questionnaire filled out
1:15–2:00 P.M.	LUNCH
2:00 P.M.	**Sixth** participant arrives Run through test session checklist
2:15 P.M.	Begin test
3:30 P.M.	End test Debrief user and post-test questionnaire filled out
4:00 P.M.	Compile notes and identify any outstanding problems to communicate immediately Check and supply new batteries for test equipment Label all test materials and store Pack up lab for transportation

Figure 7.2 Test schedule of daily events with six participants

(Information created by Wendy W. Naughton, Usability & Technical Documentation Group, Xerox Corporation, July 1995. Available at <http://www.stcsig.org/usability/>.)

facilitator needs to know what to do with the participant while the team is getting ready. Will the participant be asked to wait in the hall? Let's hope not. As well, the participant should never be allowed to just roam around when the team is getting set up. The team should avoid contact with the participant, which means that the evaluation and control room doors need to be closed. If the participant sees the hubbub of activities that precede a test, it could make the participant nervous, even more nervous than he or she is likely to be at the prospect of doing something unknown and unfamiliar. The ideal situation is to have a separate area where the participant can relax, have some refreshments, and peruse reading material of interest. If a separate area cannot be provided, then the participant needs to be escorted to an area out of sight of the test team, where relative calm prevails. It could be a part of the hallway that has been set up with refreshments, table and chairs, or the lobby or waiting area of an office building.

When the participant is made comfortable and the facilitator has exchanged greetings and perhaps engaged in some small talk, the facilitator should explain what forms the participant will need to fill out and why. This may or may not be part of the briefing for the test, but the forms need to be completed and the briefing conducted before the participant begins to work with the product. We cover both of these topics—the required forms and the nature of the briefing—in the next section.

Briefing the Participant

After the participant is made comfortable, the facilitator may begin the briefing in the waiting room, asking the participant what he or she has been told by the recruiter (if the participant has been recruited by someone other than a team member). Any misconceptions can be clarified at this point. For instance, in a recent test we conducted with high-school girls evaluating a Web site for a women's college, one of the participants said, "So, I'm to be the guinea pig." This statement provided the opportunity to turn a negative view of the participant's role into something more positive and productive. Another participant said, "So, you must be having problems with the Web site that you want me to help correct." Again, this statement provided the chance to explain that the client was interested in learning the effectiveness of the Web site when used by people who might be interested in attending the college, which is why she had been recruited for the evaluation.

Once the facilitator has moved beyond the initial stage of welcoming the participant, he or she should give the participant the forms to fill out and explain why and how these forms are being used. See Chapter 6 for a discussion of these forms. If more than one participant is recruited for the same time slot, but only one will be selected, the facilitator needs to explain the selection process. To keep up with these forms and all the other paperwork associated with each participant, the facilitator needs a file folder for each participant. A method to minimize the paper shuffling that can occur when looking for the right piece of paper to give the participant is to file the completed forms and parts of the test at the back of the file as each one is used, so the next form needed is always on top and the forms already used are arranged in chronological order. With the paperwork completed and filed, the facilitator then begins the pre-test briefing, which we discuss in the next section.

Pre-Test Briefing

The pre-test briefing should follow the script or outline prepared by the briefer, as described in the previous chapter. The main areas of the briefing are typically the following:

- Description of the room, including camera equipment used to record the actions and words of the evaluator.
- Description of the observers, either in the room or behind a one-way mirror in the control room. If the observers are in the room, they should be briefly introduced (first names will do).
- Explanation of the product being evaluated.
- Explanation of the process of the evaluation, including scenarios, questionnaires, and the use of the telephone (if appropriate).
- Explanation of think-out-loud protocol, if used.
- Demonstration of the think-out-loud process.
- Reminder that you are asking them to help you evaluate the product: you are testing the product, not the user.

Some companies prepare a videotape to inform the participant about the nature of usability testing and to brief the participant on the aspects of the test. This videotape accomplishes two goals: (1) it frees up some time for the briefer to continue preparing for the session, and (2) it provides consistency in the briefing so that all participants are assured of hearing the same information. The main disadvantage of using a videotape is that it reduces the personal time between the briefer and participant, thereby minimizing the initial opportunity to establish rapport and set the participant at ease.

A Note About Terminology

It is important to say a word about terminology here. When usability testing was viewed as being like any other "scientific experiment" using "human subjects" (as opposed to rats, for example), participants were called *test subjects*. Now that usability testing has come to be understood as a diagnostic and exploratory tool, the somewhat frightening use of "test subject" has been dropped in favor of more appropriate terms like *participant, evaluator* or *user*. In the spirit of this change, some recommend not calling the usability test a "test" in the presence of the participant, preferring to use *evaluation* in keeping with the participant's role as an *evaluator*. Using this preferred terminology, a sample briefing might begin as follows:

"We call this room the evaluator room, and you are the evaluator. I'm going to give you some tasks to do with the product and ask you to help us understand how these processes work for you. . . ."

Others call the evaluation a *study*, in keeping with the idea that the evaluator is a partner in studying or exploring the usability of the product. As these terminology issues arise, the goal in choosing the terminology you will use is to set the participant at ease in the potentially uncomfortable, and usually unnatural, setting of a laboratory. Not only does the laboratory setting have the potential to make the participant uncomfortable, but the participant may also feel uncomfortable when asked to "think out loud," the subject of the next section of this chapter.

"Thinking-Out-Loud" Procedure

Although observers or a well-directed video camera or cameras can capture much or all of what a user does when performing tasks, these techniques will shed no light on why a user does these things. Encouraging the user to use a the technique called *thinking out loud*, in which the user verbalizes his or her thoughts, shows the test team what is behind the user's actions or inactions each step along the way. Although some participants may spontaneously respond aloud to something they see or do, it is more likely that most will work in silence, as they would at home or on the job. Getting them to think out loud is asking them to perform a somewhat unnatural act, so it may take a bit of coaching and some reminders along the way. In our lab, we post several reminders—on the computer monitor, on the desk top, on top of the printer, beside the phone, and on each scenario. We also reinforce the concept with a little practice exercise, in which we ask the user to load staples into a stapler or tape into a dispenser while thinking out loud. (As a side note, thinking out loud should not be confused with "talking out loud," which the process is frequently called in error.) In presenting the process to the user, the facilitator should emphasize that the team is very interested in understanding what the user is *thinking about* when performing the task, not just the user's description of the task itself. For instance, the briefer might say:

"We want to know what you expect to happen when you make a choice and whether it meets with your expectations or not. We want to know what surprises, what delights, what confuses, or even frustrates you, and why. When you share with us what you're thinking as you go along, we get a better understanding of how the process works for you."

See the sidebar entitled "Methods for Successful 'Thinking-Out-Loud' Procedures" for additional information related to the thinking-out-loud procedure. It covers not only preparing the participant, but also techniques for the briefer to use when interacting with the participant during the test. This technique is most frequently used in exploratory testing during the earlier phases of product development when information about the user's thoughts and actions is more useful to the team than the time on task or the process of having the user work without interruption.

(*continued on page 238*)

Methods for Successful "Thinking-Out-Loud" Procedures

Judy Ramey, University of Washington, with Additions by Usability Analysis & Design, Xerox Corporation

In General

- When you are screening the participants for a study, notice how they respond to your questions. Decide on a strategy for engaging the participant before they arrive for the usability study.
- Be careful of the social dynamics you set up with the participant.

  Don't joke, indulge in sarcasm, flirt, or betray your own nervousness.

  Maintain a professional, neutral persona.

  Keep yourself "small" in relationship to the participant. Sit slightly back from the participant, in a chair that is lower.

  Avoid wearing heavy perfume or aftershave. The participant may have allergies to the odor or find it distracting.

  Don't wear suggestive, revealing, or tight, uncomfortable clothes.

- Don't bias the participant.

  Don't betray your own views or opinions of the participant's level of skill.

  Don't let the participant become aware of any bias you may have about the product.

- Avoid interactions with the user that can shift the focus from the user's domain to the designer's.

  Don't expect the user to tell you how to fix problems.

  Don't expect the user to answer other design questions.

  Always keep the focus of attention on the user, not yourself. Avoid "I" statements and long explanations of how the system works.

  Stay in the relationship with the participant. Don't worry about the next question you are going to ask.

  Write down design ideas so that you don't need to worry about forgetting them after the test.

- Don't let yourself get impatient!

  When the participant seems to have a problem, they can often unravel it without your help.

  When you feel you should jump in, count to ten first.

  If you jump in too soon, you lose valuable data and they become dependent on your help.

- Learn to probe in a neutral way to get information on which to base your design improvements

Techniques that encourage thinking out loud

- Prompting
- Echoing
- "Conversational disequilibrium"
- Summarizing at key junctions

Prompting

- Focus on tasks, not features.

  Don't ask, "Do you like that dialog box?" but, "Did that dialog box help you reach your goal?"

- Focus on questions, not answers.
- Explore user thinking in a neutral way.

  Don't be too quick to assume that the user is lost or having a problem.

  Don't say, "What is your problem here?" but ask, "What is your goal?" or "What are you thinking you should do here?"

- Don't betray your own interests or point of view by your comments, emphasis, "waking up" and getting interested, showing in facial expression or vocal tones that you disagree.
- Good user-focused questions:

  What is your goal?

  What did you expect when you did that?

  How did you expect that to work?

  Can you tell me what you were thinking?

  What do you want to accomplish here?

  Describe the steps you are going through here.

  How did you feel about that process?

  Tell me about your thinking here.

  What did you expect to happen when you . . . ?

Echoing

- Repeat their own word or phrase back to them as a question: "That message is confusing?"

  Echoing sets up a social dialog and reinforces social conversation expectations: they say something, you repeat it, they say the next thing because that is what is expected in conversation.

- Don't put words in their mouth or offer interpretations.

  If they say, "I'm not sure what to do here," don't say, "So you are confused because the menu bar is unclear?"

  If they say, "That didn't happen like I expected," don't ask, "So you thought that the task menu would be displayed here?"

- Signal that you're listening (mmm hmm . . .).

"Conversational disequilibrium"

- Let your statements trail off and end in an upswing, as if you were asking a question. The participant will usually complete your statement.

  "And you were expecting . . . ?"

  "And your goal is . . . ?"

- Signal that you are there, you are interested, but that it is still their turn to talk (mmm hmm).
- Speak softly.

Summarizing at key junctions

- When you have learned something new that is key to understanding, summarize the event and the thinking that the user explored, very briefly. Users may offer more detail about their thought process.
- Keep the recorder on or keep taking notes after you think that the test session is finished. Users will often make interesting reflections about their processes during the casual remarks at the end of the session.

Source: Available at <http://www.stcsig.org/usability>.

Issues of time on task have been debated when using the think-out-loud process, so we address this topic next.

Effect of Thinking Out Loud on Timed Tasks

Some research suggests that thinking out loud slows down the response time for users and therefore does not provide for accurate data regarding time on task (Rhenius and Deffner; van der Meij). Even for those who believe that this is the case, the research shows that thinking out loud "do[es] not change the sequence of their thoughts" and "slow[s] them down only moderately" (Ericsson and Simon, reported in van der Meij 210). Others cite evidence showing that thinking out loud does not affect time on task "except for very low-level tasks that occur in a very short time (a few seconds)" (Hix and Hartson 307).

If absolutely accurate time on task is an issue, you should probably choose a method other than thinking out loud, such as retrospective review, in which you ask the participant to review the videotape after the test to tell you what he or she was thinking. In most cases, however, especially when testing is for diagnostic or exploratory purposes, thinking out loud provides a rich source of additional information about the user's perceptions of the product's usability.

Being an Unbiased Briefer/Debriefer

As stated earlier, the briefer has perhaps the hardest job on the team because of the possibility of inadvertently introducing bias into the test by the briefer's actions or words. If you have the job of briefer, learning to minimize such bias takes time, but watching yourself interacting with a participant on videotape can help a lot in improving your effectiveness. Watch your body language and tone of voice. Although you want to establish rapport with the participant, you don't want to become too chummy. Briefers should avoid physical contact with the participant, even when well intentioned, such as a pat on the shoulder to show encouragement, which can be interpreted as condescending or too friendly by a stranger. Briefers should also avoid biasing the participant with a remark like, "So, how did you like that?" and with eager, hopeful, or puzzled facial expressions.

Because the participant is eager to please, the participant's response can easily be influenced by the desire to assure the briefer that the experience was just fine, even when the team has observed that it was anything but fine. In fact, it is quite common for test teams to observe a user struggle mightily with a task, only to report that it was "no problem." Anything the briefer can do to minimize the participant's tendency to give the briefer the answer he or she thinks is wanted will improve the results of testing. Instead of a query like, "How did you like that?" the briefer might say, "How was that for you?" or "What did you think of that?"

Some interesting research supports the lengths to which a participant will go to indicate pleasure, rather than displeasure, when reporting the experience to the one thought responsible for the product. Reeves and Nass report in their book, *The Media Equation*, that not only are people polite to those who ask questions about their experience, but they are also polite to the computer when given a questionnaire on the computer's performance. In their experiment involving this hypothesis, the authors found that people responded more positively to a computer if the questionnaire was on the same computer as the task performed. If, however, the questionnaire was on a different computer, the responses were more harsh. In other words, *"people are polite to computers, too"* (5; italics added for emphasis). Knowing this, you can see how careful you must be to avoid biasing the responses you receive from participants generally eager to please.

In an effort to perform the tasks described in the scenarios, the participant may ask you questions. The way you respond is different from the usual way, as we describe in the next section.

Handling Questions

If the participant asks you a question, try to avoid answering it. Of course, you don't want to be rude and just ignore the question, but you will also learn more if you politely respond by asking a return question to get the participant to share his or her thoughts with you. For instance, if the participant says, "Did I do that right?" you can say, "What do you think should have happened?" Another approach is to elicit further information from the participant, saying something like, "Tell me what makes you wonder whether you did it right."

Sometimes, the team will have a question for the participant that they want the briefer to ask. Let's say that the team wants to know why the participant used the back button rather than the home button to return to the homepage on a Web site. The briefer needs to avoid biasing the possible response by saying, "Why didn't you use the home button?" or "Didn't you see the home button?" Instead, the briefer might say, "Tell me how you navigated back to the homepage." Or, if you want to see whether the participant missed the home button at the bottom of the page, you might ask the participant to scroll down the page and tell you what he or she sees. However, if you have observed that the participant did not scroll down the page, you might ask, "Where do you think you might look for a more direct route back to the homepage?"

If you are in the same room with the participant, he or she may be more inclined to talk to you. When the participant talks to you, you should avoid reacting positively or negatively. Nondescript responses like, "um hm," "OK," and even head nodding to show that you're listening will keep the participant talking without influencing the direction of the responses. In addition, you want to avoid comments like "That was great!" when you observe the successful completion of a task. Such a comment may make the participant feel that "success" is the object of the exercise. Likewise, when the participant has problems, you should avoid comments that suggest the participant has failed in some way. A comment like, "Don't worry—lots of people have trouble with that task" can have a negative influence on the participant. When the participant is clearly frustrated and feels like a failure (which they frequently say that they do!), you can respond by thanking them for allowing you to see how the product worked for them and identifying the important issues for you. See the earlier sidebar, "Methods for Successful 'Thinking-Out-Loud' Procedures," for additional suggestions on how to get the participant to talk and how to avoid biasing the participant's responses.

In addition to the contact you have with the participant at the beginning and after each of the scenarios, there may be other times in which you will need or want to intervene during the test. We discuss these situations in the next section.

How (and When) to Intervene

The most likely situation in which the briefer may need to intervene is when the team sees the participant struggle repeatedly without being able to solve a problem or conclude a task. Certainly, it's useful to see the strategies a participant uses to escape from or solve a problem, but there comes a point when the struggle is counterproductive and the team recognizes that the participant is clearly lost and needs help. At these times, you will want to stop the participant. Or, if you are in the room with the participant, you will want to move toward the participant or speak up to stop the participant. You may decide to do this on your own or you may get a signal (pre-arranged) from the team to do this. In either case, the method you use to intervene or stop a participant needs to be applied with care. If mishandled, the participant may feel a sense of failure or embarrassment.

Another situation that typically requires intervention occurs when the participant doesn't know that he or she is struggling but is clearly far off the task. For instance, we have seen users leave the Web site during a Web usability test and not realize it. In another situation, the computer froze up (a technical difficulty) and the participant didn't realize it and couldn't figure out why the system wasn't responding. Or, in still another instance, the participant was trying to access information that wasn't yet developed (which frequently happens in testing a product in the early stages of development). In any of these cases, swift intervention may be needed. By asking open-ended questions, you can learn from the participant's responses what he or she thinks is happening and how the participant might solve the problem, once he or she is made aware of it. Questions like, "What are you trying to do now?" or "What do you think the system is doing now?" get at the user's view of the problem. If the user can't solve the problem, you may need to intervene with a quick fix to get the user back to where he or she was before or to take the user where he or she needs to be.

In addition to the strategies a facilitator needs to employ when interacting with a participant, the help desk operator also needs to function a bit differently from the norm in the interest of learning about what causes the participant to call for help. We take up this topic in the next section.

Handling Help Calls

As we've seen, most, if not all, of the interaction between the participant and the team falls to the job of the facilitator. However, calls to the help desk are typically handled by another member of the team. Although some aspects of the interaction between the help desk and the participant are similar to those between the facilitator and the participant, others are different. In addition, some of the techniques of supplying help comply with typical help desk procedures; others do not.

When a participant calls for help, the team member designated as the help desk operator should respond as though he or she is really in another location. Although, in reality, the help desk operator can see what the participant is doing, it's useful to get the participant to describe where he or she is and what the problem is. In this way, the situation matches the real world of calling the help desk and explaining the problem fully so that the help desk operator can understand the problem from the user's perspective.

However, what the help desk operator does next is not quite the same thing that a real help desk operator does. Whereas the help desk operator would normally describe possible solutions to the problem, the team member performing the help desk function during a usability test should take a less direct approach to see whether the user can work through the problem with little help. This approach provides information about the user's problem-solving strategies. The help desk operator might ask the participant what he or she has tried, question whether the user has consulted online help or the documentation (if these are available), or ask where the participant thinks the answer to the question might be found. If these approaches don't solve the problem, the next step is to offer a helpful hint. For instance, if the participant is on the wrong screen and can't figure out that part, the help desk operator might suggest going back to the homepage or scrolling to the bottom of the page for other options. If there's a navigation bar that the participant isn't noticing, the help desk operator might ask whether the participant has looked at that place on the screen. Or, if the participant says that he or she has consulted the documentation and can't find the information needed, the help desk operator might ask what other words the participant could try to search the index or table of contents. If that doesn't work, the help desk operator can suggest a word to get the participant going again.

Still another approach is to respond to a question with a question. If the participant asks, "How do I create a new form?" the help desk operator might respond with, "What do you think you would want to try first to create the form?" Although this approach may sound a bit like playing "20 Questions" (a game in which the participants can only ask questions of the "expert" that can be answered with "yes" or "no"), the rationale behind this strategy is to understand the problem-solving approach the participant uses so that the product can be configured to match the user's mental model. As these examples show, the usability help desk person should provide the least amount of information needed to get the user back on track and then encourage the user to call again if more help is needed. In this way, help in a usability test is different from help in the real world.

Now that we have covered the ways in which team members will interact with the participant, we need to explore what can happen when the team has visitors who can interact with *them* during the test. We take up this subject in the next section.

Handling Visitors

If you're using the cross-functional team approach advocated in this book, you may wonder who else, beyond your team, would want to see the test. The answer is "management." It's in your best interests to encourage management to view some of the testing because, as we've said earlier, there's nothing that can replace the experience of viewing a real user struggling with your product. However, you need to be prepared for some shock and disbelief on the part of your visitors, and you'll be better able to handle the situation if you understand why this is a common reaction when a visitor who has responsibility for the product comes to observe a test.

The Good, the Bad, and the Ugly

When a visitor or visitors come to observe a usability session, they may or may not have much knowledge of the usability testing process. Most likely, if they are visiting, they have come to "check it out." This offers you both an opportunity and a challenge. The opportunity is that you can and should coach them on the process and the objectives. You can tell them what kinds of issues you are investigating and, if you've already conducted one or more sessions, you can share some of the findings. Here is your opportunity to be a usability advocate for the process, for its learning potential, and for its usefulness as a first step or critical part of a user-centered design process. The nature of your advocacy role will be dependent on how enlightened or unenlightened your visitors are about usability testing and user-centered design.

Although the opportunity that visitors provide to advocate usability is good, here's the bad part of having visitors. If they're in the control room with you, they can be disruptive to the team. Disruption takes many forms. They can converse with you or with other visitors. Typically, they will most likely sit quietly at first, but as they become more comfortable with the process, they may start making suggestions and even try to solve the problems they see, something you will want to avoid doing, as we discuss later in this chapter. Worse yet, if you do not have a control room and the visitors are part of the observers in the room with the participant, they can spontaneously suggest some advice to the participant, or worse, blurt out "oh, no!" or some similar remark when they see the user make a "mistake."

The ideal solution is to place observers in another room with a member of the team there to facilitate their understanding of the process. Some labs have an *executive viewing room* for this purpose, as described in Chapter 1. In other situations, observers are placed in another room with a TV monitor connected to the lab so that they can see what the participant is doing, well out of earshot of the action. Or in a more sophisticated set-up, the TV monitor displays exactly the same images that are being videotaped, which might include a small image of the user and an undistorted image of the computer screen, provided by direct feed from the participant's computer to the control room and from the control room to the viewing room monitor.

So far, we've covered the "good" and the "bad" aspects of having visitors. There's still the problem of the "ugly." This has two manifestations: calling the user stupid and seeing that "my baby is ugly." The problem of calling the user stupid occurs when the visitor first sees the participant struggle with the product. The typical reaction to the uninitiated visitor is, "Where did you get that stupid user?" followed by comments about how that user couldn't possibly represent the real user, and so forth. When you get this kind of reaction from a visitor, it helps to understand the psychology of the situation: a manager or developer—in fact anyone with a vested interest in the success of the product—will naturally want to blame the user first. Here you have the opportunity to show the visitor the screening and pre-test questionnaires for this user and to explain how this user matches the user profile. You will also need to encourage the visitor to stay for the next user or explain, if you have already done several sessions, how many times you have seen a user struggle with this problem before. Ideally, if the visitor stays to see a second and perhaps even a third user struggle with the same problems, a change of attitude takes place, in which the visitor no longer blames the user but accepts the fact that there's a problem. Then, of course, the visitor's inclination is to say, "We have a problem and I know how to fix it!"

Perhaps at the same time that visitors are calling the user stupid, they're also experiencing the shock of seeing the user call their "baby" ugly, metaphorically, that is, because of the problems the user experiences. And, of course, if the participant is using the think-out-loud technique, he or she may, in fact, *say* ugly things about the product. In a recent test we conducted on a Web site, one of the participants got so frustrated that she blurted out, "This is the worst Web site I have ever seen!" That's an extreme example, but a real one, of calling the baby ugly. Again, you will have to help your visitors get past this feeling of rejection to understand that a good usability test *should* find problems so that the baby can be treated before it leaves the "hospital."

Forewarned is forearmed about the potential benefits and hazards of having visitors observe your usability test. In the next section, we discuss what to do on the completion of each test session to collect, organize, and catalog the information you have gathered.

Organizing the Data

During each test session, your team will collect a lot of data in the following forms:

- Screening questionnaire
- Pre-test questionnaire
- Post-task questionnaires for each scenario
- Post-test questionnaire
- Observation sheets or log of observations

- Additional notes from team members
- Videotape of session

How best to organize all this information and then make sense of it quickly? For starters, the checklists for each team member should describe the ways in which the various parts of the information packet are to be organized and assembled. For instance, as described earlier, the test materials need to be put into folders or a notebook for each session. In addition, the videotape needs to be rewound and labeled. The data-logging forms or notes need to be collected and, if the team uses logging software, the logger needs to clean up the information, save it, print it, and make copies for everyone for analysis later. The computer may need to be reset to the starting point and any information entered by the previous user needs to be cleared.

All these activities must be done very quickly because the room needs to be set up for the start of another session. Ideally, the schedule will allow time not only for preparation for the next session, but also for analysis of the findings from this session. We discuss how to review and make sense of your findings in the next section.

Collating Data Into Findings

So much data and so little time. It can be overwhelming. To make sense of it, you should first take a quick look at your major findings. If you have used forms to log your observations, you can see how much correlation and consistency you have among the team members. Using a flip chart or sticky notes or a spreadsheet on a laptop computer, you can collate the findings into one centralized document. Some people use a tape recorder to talk through this review of the findings and capture this discussion for later transcription. If you have logging software or you have created a macro in word-processing software, the task is made easier, in that all the findings are already centralized and can be printed out in a single document, but harder in that the detail is generally much greater than can be captured manually on logging sheets. Figure 7.3 is the log recorded for one participant evaluating part of the Southern Polytechnic Web site. It was created using a macro in Microsoft Word and provides a line number for the team's reference, a time stamp to locate it on the videotape, a coded category for the type of finding, and a description of the finding. Working from copies of the printout of the log, the team can quickly discuss and categorize the findings. For an example of a log created with a commercial logging software product, see the Hotmail events report in the chapter appendix.

Using Top-Down or Bottom-Up Process

In Chapter 5, we discussed two approaches to categorize findings: top-down or bottom-up. If you are using a top-down method, you will already have determined the categories of findings (and tested this system during the pilot).

(continued on page 248)

Log #	Time	Code	Description of Events
1			
2	7:36:32	P1	Reading scenario. She says, 'Academic Dept.' and clicked on
3		(Rachel)	'Academic Dept.' Says, 'Writing, Editing . . . I don't see anything on
4			list,' going down each one individually. Alphabetical order no writing.
5			Clicked on 'Degree Program.'
6			
7	7:37:53	P1	Working with Multimedia. Still can't find anything. Have to go back to
8			'Academic Dept.' Scrolling down again. Reading question again. Says, I
9			can't find it. Reading question again . . . thinks it might be 'Computer
10			Science.' Starting to read down list and thinks it possibly could be it.
11			
12	7:38:59	P1	Reading left frame again, starting from bottom doing the same thing to
13			make association. Clicked on 'Degree Programs' . . . 'Academic Depts.'
14			Clicked on 'Quality Assurance' . . . reading 'Masters Program
15			Description.' She says, 'No, got to try them all.' Hesitating over each
16			one.
17			
18	7:40:10	P1	Reading over 'Civil Service.' Checking out Construction, picture
19			doesn't come up, backed up, Back to 'Academic Dept.' Clicked on
20			HTC.
21			
22	7:40:45	P1	Reading text at left of frame. Says, 'would that be, what question says,
23			clicked Back button, now click 'Electrical and Computer Engineering.'
24			Picture doesn't come up, clicked on Back button again. Clicked on
25			'Industrial Engineering Technology.' Takes a look at that page and goes
26			to 'School of Management' Reading, scrolling around, reading, looking
27			at big paragraph . . . reading a bit out loud.
28			
29	7:42:12	P1	Expression blank . . . Back at 'Academic Dept.' Hesitates over math,
30			clicked on . . . eyebrows furrow . . . goes back to 'Degree Programs',
31			running mouse over all 'Degree Programs.' Scrolling to the bottom;
32			appears pain over instructions . . . going over the instructions again.
33			Clicked on 'Engineering Technology.'
34			
35	7:43:42	P1	Says, 'No.' Scrolls up list of 'Graduate Programs,' and now is at
36			Undergrad again. Clicks on 'Computer Science,' 'Undergraduate.' Says,
37			'Or on an international level.' She thinks multimedia means computer
38			science. Looking at Course Requirements for Undergraduate Computer
39			Science . . . scrolling back up . . . book marked 'Computer Science
40			Degree Program.'
41			
42	7:45:29	P1	Ah, ha, read second question and said ah ha . . . 'Careers in Technical
43			Communication.' She found it and book marked it. . . . Reading the 3rd
44			question, Back at 'Graduate Program' and is about to click on MSTPC.
45			
46	7:46:23	P1	Reading it and scrolling down . . . she says 'I guess that one' and puts a
47			bookmark there.
48			
49	7:46:23	P1	Telephoned to say, 'I'm done with the first one.'
50			
51	7:48:12	*B/D	Diane: 'I like the way you were thinking out loud, that was great!'
52			
53	7:50:13	P1	Wasn't sure what to do or look for initially. I had to look around . . . I
54			couldn't find anything on . . . I found a page that had looked like what I
55			was looking for, so I clicked it.

Figure 7.3 Log of usability evaluation, created with a Word macro (*continued*)

(Used with permission of Team Inertia: Anita Carpenter, Henri Dongieux, Cynthia Ravenna, Diane Rhone, Diana Samuels, and Lynn Smith.)

Log #	Time	Code	Description of Events
56			
57	7:52:17	B/D	I'm going to get you to where you need to be, here . . .
58			
59	7:53:34	P1	Reading first question in Scenario II. At 'HTC' . . . clicked on
60			'Prospective Students,' looking for 'Graduate Courses', clicks on
61			'Undergraduate Courses,' reading over courses, is book marking,
62			scrolling to the bottom and backup . . . reading re foreign languages,
63			looking but won't find foreign language . . .
64			
65	7:55:11	P1	She says she doesn't see it . . . reading course title one by one . . . clicks
66			on courses, then undergraduate, back where she started. She's running
67			mouse over button, reading. She says, 'Oh wait' and clicks on specifics
68			of BAITC . . .
69			
70	7:56:39	P1	She's looking, scrolling very slowly, she finds 'Foreign Languages and
71			International Studies.' Says, '18 hours of foreign languages' scrolling
72			backwards at 'Bachelor of Arts Program.' She's reading next question,
73			'Who should you contact?' Clicks on BAITC, finds Dr. Smith's name
74			on Contact info . . . finds picture of one of the HTC faculty members,
75			clicks on 'Faculty Bios,' and selects Dr. Carol Barnum's picture.
76			
77	7:58:38	P1	Finished Scenario II.
78			
79	7:59:22	B/D	Diane says, 'Another questionnaire about that experience for you.'
80			
81	8:01:22	P1	I thought that I was in the right place, then I found things for
82			undergraduate courses, then I found . . . the rest of it was very easy. In
83			comparison between the two I like this one a lot better.
84			
85	8:02:57	B/D	Now we're onto our third scenario.
86			
87	8:03:09	P1	Clicks on 'Prospective Students,' 'Admission Requirements.' She says
88			and clicks on 'Freshman Admissions' . . . reading . . . Found number 1
89			already and is working on number 2 which is the Deadline Date . . . now
90			clicking on 'Deadline Date'.
91			
92	8:04:14	P1	She says, 'Semester Deadline Dates?' She writes the answer on the
93			post-it notes. Reading the third question . . . Clicks back in Admission
94			in frame, clicks on 'Undergraduate Admission' . . . clicks on 'Additional
95			Information', then 'Application Instruction Checklist.' Is going through
96			titles of that page . . . reading . . . clicked on Freshman . . .
97			
98	8:05:42	P1	Scrolling down and back up same page . . . clicks to return to
99			'Admission', clicks on 'Apply Online' and then 'Directions and Info.'
100			Clicks on 'Establish your Account.' Clicks continue and is on the
101			'Create Your Account' page . . . reading question and thinks this is the
102			page . . .
103			
104	8:07:10	P1	On tuition question, which is #4, clicks on tuition financial aid, student
105			fees, reading . . . scrolling back and forth . . . says, 'blah, blah, blah, blah.'
106			
107	8:08:19	P1	Still scrolling back and forth for awhile, then says, 'blah, blah, blah . . . !'
108			
109	8:08:53	P1	'What is the tuition per year?' Clicks the Back button, clicks on Fee
110			Payment not realizing it's the same page . . . clicks the Back button
111			again, clicks on Undergraduate Admissions . . . there's a sigh in there . . .
112			on Financial Information screen . . .

Figure 7.3   Log of usability evaluation, created with a Word macro *(continued)*

Log #	Time	Code	Description of Events
113 114 115 116 117	8:09:57	P1	Says, 'I've already read all these . . .' At bottom of Financial Info screen, clicked on 'Financial Aid' . . . says, 'what about the tuition!'' Says, 'what about the tuition' again. 'I don't care what you can borrow, she growls . . . expression of frustration . . .
118 119 120 121 122	8:11:07	P1	'It doesn't say . . .' 'No' she says, 'Financial Info, it shouldn't be there . . .' on Admissions page, clicked on 'General Info Instructions', scrolling downward . . . says 'how much does it cost?'
123 124 125 126	8:12:06	P1	Back at HTC home page . . . she says, 'I'm a prospective student?' 'I'd like to know about . . .' clicked on Admissions and says, 'I've been here!'
127 128	8:12:48	P1	She's at 'Financial Info' reading student fees . . . she's reading fast.
129 130 131	8:13:44	P1	Still reading . . . she's scanning text . . . she stopped navigating for awhile and continues to read.
132 133 134 135 136 137 138 139	8:14:34	P1	Still reading 'I don't want to refund my fees, I don't care about illegal parking . . . how can I graduate if I can't pay the tuition . . . Hits the Back button and is now at 'Matriculation and Non-Resident Tuition' . . . She's growling . . . says, 'credit hours,' but that doesn't help her either . . . sighing and growling, back down page, says, 'I don't care . . .' scrolling, 'I see no fee, I see hours at 'General Info', now back to Financial Info.' Clicks on 'Scholarship and Financial Aid' page.
140 141	8:17:15	P1	At 'Graduate Courses,' now 'Undergraduate Admissions Record' page.
142 143	8:17:50	B/D	Skip to the next page, you're doing great!
144 145 146 147 148 149 150	8:18:04	P1	Book marked 'Financial Aid' page . . . did financial aid question. She's looking for 'Undergraduate Catalog' and is searching the left hand frame; reading the pop ups and is looking under Admission . . . is at 'Undergraduate Admissions', clicked on HTC homepage . . . scrolling that page . . . clicks on 'Prospective Students' . . . says 'I want an undergraduate catalog'; clicks on 'Program Descriptions,' then 'Bachelor of Arts' . . .
151 152	8:19:51	P1	Scrolling at Tech . . . At 'Undergraduate Admissions,' scrolling at . . .
153 154 155 156 157 158	8:20:50	P1	At 'Undergraduate Admission Requirements' . . . clicks on 'Additional Information' at bottom of frame; Back to Admissions, then 'Graduate Courses.' Scrolling back and forth, now TCOM, now at 'Bachelor of Arts' on the Specific Requirements for that; looking over buttons on frame, clicks on 'Peers and Professionals' . . .
159 160 161 162	8:22:15	P1	Back to HTC homepage, looking at 'Current Students,' 'Guidelines,' 'Procedures', scrolling down and back up page . . . Back at 'Current Students,' Back at HTC homepage, checking out everything . . .
163 164 165 166 167	8:24:33	P1	At Admissions page, scrolled down and back up. Stopped at 'Undergrad Admissions' clicked on 'Getting More Info' 'I guess that would be it', she says. 'I didn't see catalog.' Scrolling up page, back at Admissions, looking under 'Online Application.' Book marked 'Request more information . . .'
168	8:26:20	P1	Called to say, 'OK, I'm done.'

* Briefer/Debriefer

Figure 7.3

Categories include such areas as conceptual issues, feedback, navigation, terminology, design issues, and so forth.

You can easily capture these findings across all of your users by using a flip chart or white board. As Figure 7.4 shows, you can divide the flip chart or board into columns, in which you identify the finding number (column 1), the line number for quick reference to the log if needed later (column 2), your description of the finding (column 3), the category label (column 4), and the user who experienced the problem. Findings are numbered consecutively down the flip chart or board. If you observe more than three users, you add columns for additional users.

Here's how it works. Going through the log for user 1, the team captures any issue that might be a usability "hit." The first issue is listed as finding number 1, with its line number recorded, followed by a description (and label). A checkmark is placed in the user 1 box to indicate that the problem occurred with user 1. Later, if the problem also occurs with user 2, all that needs to be added is the line number for user 2 and a corresponding checkmark in the box for user 2. If user 2 doesn't experience this problem, but has a problem not experienced by user 1, a number is added to the list at the bottom of column 1 and the description of the problem is noted, with a checkmark in the user 2 box. Figure 7.5 is a summary of the findings collated from one scenario, in which participants searched the Southern Polytechnic University Web site to locate information about the International Technical Communication degree program. As you can see, this method shows how many participants experienced the problem, ranging from four out of five to one out of five.

If you're using a bottom-up method of affinity matching, you will take a different approach, working from sticky notes or notecards to sort observations and then decide on labels for them. See the sidebar entitled "Affinity Analysis: Tips and Tricks" for a fuller explanation of how this process works.

1	2	3	4	5	6	7
Finding number	Line number	Description	Label	User 1	User 2	User 3

Figure 7.4 Method for capturing findings

Issue List from All Usability Evaluations: HTC Web Site

Issue	Participant				
	Rachel	Alia	Adrienne	Anthony	Steven
Scenario 2					
Used mouseovers: "could see what was there. I didn't have to click on it."	67	17			
Willing to scroll through curriculum to find foreign language	70				
Looked for foreign langage within TCOM course descriptions	62		15		
Shouldn't have to scroll through curriculum to find unique courses	x				
Used Peers and Professionals button immediately to find faculty	75	15	15	14–16	
Trouble distinguishing between courses and curriculum		17	14	16	16
Lost 1 minute searching around in the Writing Center pages			13		
Had difficulty finding foreign language requirement		19	13		
Eventually looked in admissions requirements for foreign language			13		
Never found foreign language because convinced it was within TCOM course listing			15		
Used Donna's name for contact information			14		
Never found BAITC-specific information throughout entire test			x		
Stated on brief that "nothing jumped out at her" (foreign language requirement)			17		
Didn't immediately scroll to bottom of curriculum to find foreign language. Assumed the requirement was 3 hours from the courses above					13
By Scenario 2, settled down to read the mouse-overs					12
Didn't understand differences between BA & BS		18	14		
Expected a faculty button in left frame				18	
Expected a link to "Contacts" or a navigation button on it					13
Missed links at top of Freshman admission requirements page (for appl. Deadline)				20	
Didn't scroll far enough to see appl deadline (visible at bottom of screen) information				20	

Each number is the number of the log where the issue appeared.

Figure 7.5 Summary of findings from one scenario

(Used with permission of Team Inertia: Anita Carpenter, Henri Dongieux, Cynthia Ravenna, Diane Rhone, Diana Samuels, and Lynn Smith.)

249

Affinity Analysis: Tips and Tricks

Tara Scanlon

Affinity analysis, also called affinity diagramming, is a technique for organizing qualitative data into coherent patterns or themes. I've found it most useful for helping teams analyze and learn from large amounts of data, particularly from Contextual Inquiry (CI). I've also used it to analyze brainstorming ideas and usability test feedback and as a tool for organizing technical documentation.

Steps

1. Extract the data, ideas, or information you want to analyze. Write one thought per Post-It™, and, if you are working from a transcript, note where in the transcript the idea came from.
2. Give each participant in the affinity analysis 15 or 20 completed Post-Its. Make sure everyone understands their Post-Its.
3. Ask participants to start organizing all the Post-Its into groups that seem to go together. Set some ground rules:

- No talking. If you think a note belongs someplace else, just move it.
- If a note seems to be moving back and forth, it's okay to duplicate it and put it in both places.
- Avoid predefined categories.
- If you see something that prompts a new idea or question, make a new Post-It.
- Categories should contain no more than five Post-Its. It is okay to have categories that contain only one Post-It.

4. When the grouping has finished, gather the team together to label the categories. These labels should capture the theme of the grouping.
5. Affinitize the groupings, thus creating a hierarchy.

Tips for Making the Affinity Analysis Process Work Smoothly

The tips outlined here can help you streamline and optimize your affinity analysis process.

Focus the Analysis with a Question
- Focus the analysis. Use a question as the theme for the analysis, and let the titles of the categories become answers to that question.

Data Is More than Words
- Data doesn't have to be words. Use pictures, objects, photographs, etc.

Whichever method you use, the objective is to locate usability "hits." The more hits, the better, since the goal of usability testing is to uncover issues (or hits) affecting the usability of the product from the perspective of the user. You will need to count these hits, or instances of occurrences of usability issues. These constitute one type of quantitative data. In the next section, we discuss other ways of measuring quantitative data.

"Post-It" Alternatives Are Available—See if They Work for You

- Create your own "post-its" with a word processor, scissors, and double-sided adhesive.
- Take a walk through your local office supply store. There are always new gadgets or gizmos to help with the mechanics of affinity analysis.
- If you're going to use spray adhesive, spray outside. (It takes a long time for the smell to dissipate.)

Make Post-Its Readable

- No fine-point pens or markers.
- The bigger the Post-Its, the easier they are to read.
- Use a different color ink or Post-It for labels.

Open Post-Its by Snapping

- To open Post-Its, grab the package on either side and twist to snap the packaging.

Make Categories and Names Meaningful

- If you have more than five items in a category, you really have two categories.
- Avoid predefined categories.
- If you have a category called "Miscellaneous," you're doing something wrong.

Make the Affinity Diagram Moveable

- Post flip-chart paper on the walls before the affinity analysis begins to make the analysis transportable.
- Once the categories are set, run a strip of tape over them to keep them from falling off the wall.

Re-use the Analysis to Continue Learning

- Do it twice. Once you've organized the data, ask "How else can we re-organize this to learn something different?"
- Keep the analysis posted for as long as possible. People will come to new insights or remember new details if they look at the affinity diagram a week after the analysis.

Facilitate the Process Effectively

- To help new people, start with a simple affinity exercise, such as shapes.
- Keep the Post-It-to-people ratio reasonable. People disengage if they have fewer than about 20 Post-Its each to organize.
- Remember that participants go through different stages during the affinity process. These roughly include:
  - Being overwhelmed, not sure where or how to begin
  - Getting into the groove and doing the gross categorization
  - Getting frustrated with the details of categorization, not sure where the process is leading
  - Seeing the magic of data transformed into information

You'll need to offer different types of suggestions and encouragement during each of these.

- When facilitating the analysis, be directive. If people seem to be standing around, ask them to break down a category, start labeling, etc.
- Use the labeling process as a way to spark group discussion.

Source: Used with permission of Tara Scanlon, an independent usability consultant (tara@ultranet.com).

Measuring Quantitative Data

Quantitative measurements can be either objective or subjective. Objective measurements come from your observations of user performance on tasks, as discussed in the previous section. Measuring the users' performance on these *benchmark tasks* provides an *objective usability metric* (Hix and Hartson 225). Subjective measurements come from quantifying the users' opinions expressed on post-task and post-test questionnaires.

When two or more participants experience the same problem or express the same opinion about a problem, you know you need to address it. The more people who experience the problem, the more obvious is the need for change. Now, however, is not the time to decide on the changes. You want to stay in a problem-solving mode while you are conducting the usability sessions, so that you're able to remain open to understanding the problem as you continue to observe the participants. If you arrive too quickly at solutions for the problems, you may be jumping to the wrong conclusions.

However, when your qualitative findings from observations don't match up with your quantitative data from the post-task and post-test questionnaires, you face the dilemma of trying to determine what accounts for the differences and which data to accept as having more credibility. For instance, as frequently occurs in usability testing, the team may observe users struggle with a task or fail to complete a task, but then the participants report that the task was "easy." What's going on here? As you might have guessed from our earlier discussion of research by Reeves and Nass, the participants are eager to please, so they rate the experience higher than it might have been. In addition, participants tend to blame themselves for problems. They'll make comments like, "I can't believe I didn't see that." Or, "If I had read the documentation, as I was supposed to, I would have been able to do the task." So, when you have conflicting data, believe what you see more than what the user tells you about the experience. At the same time, probe for more information from the user in the post-test questionnaire to get beyond "the pleasure principle" that motivates a false-positive response from the user.

As stated earlier, it's reasonable to assume that if two or more users have a problem, it needs to be addressed. But what do you do when only one participant has a problem? We discuss this issue in the next section.

How to Measure Outlier Data

Outlier data represent findings from one participant only. Should you dismiss such findings as unique and not representative? If you're testing a large number of users and only one in the large group experiences a problem, you may be able to conclude that this person had a peculiar problem that wasn't representative of the normal use of the product. However, if you're testing a small number of participants, then every person's issues are potentially important because they might represent problems for many other users. One person's issue out of five participants represents 20% of the user experience you observed. For each unique finding, you need to take a close look at what happened and try to determine why. It may very well indicate a usability issue that needs attention, even though only one person experienced it. Figure 7.6 shows the findings from the test of input forms for a new database program in a marketing organization. The problems or concerns are divided into categories of findings and the number of participants experiencing the problem. When you study the outlier data experienced by only one of the six participants, you see that these concerns represent problems that will very likely be experienced by others and should therefore be addressed.

Outlier data can also arise from time-on-task measurements. For instance, if all users but one are within a specific range for acceptable time on task, what does the team do with one participant's excessive time on a task? Again, the team should study the reason one user took much longer than the others and determine whether there's a usability issue involved. Figure 7.7 presents time-on-task data from the Hotmail test. It also explains the outlier data for user 3 (advanced user) and user 5 (novice user) in scenario 1 and for user 2 (advanced user) in scenario 3.

In addition to quantifying the findings regarding tasks, you will also want to analyze the qualitative data you get in comments from users, plus the team's observations of body language and other nonverbal and verbal expressions of frustration or confusion. We discuss this topic in the next section.

Interpreting Qualitative Data

In the same way that you go through the logging sheets or the printout from the software log to catalog data that can be quantified, you will want to make a separate (or simultaneous) pass through the logs to capture qualitative data. In addition, you will want to go through the post-task and post-test questionnaires to catalog the written comments made by participants. Finally, if you videotaped the post-test interview, you may also want to review the comments made by participants here, if the team's notes need clarification. Gathering together all this information is an important part of compiling the data from each session. Figure 7.8 on page 256 presents a table of qualitative findings, taken from unstructured user comments following scenarios 1 through 3 of a usability test of Southern Polytechnic's Web site and responses to specific questions in the post-test questionnaire.

Finally, lest they be forgotten, positive findings need to be collated and documented. We discuss why and how to do this in the next section.

Recording Positive Findings

There are two very important reasons to capture and collate positive findings:

1. *Everyone likes to hear good news.* Although usability testing has the goal of uncovering problems that users experience, it should not overlook the value of relating what users like about the product. Even though stakeholders may be able to move past the phenomenon explained earlier where they see the user "call their baby ugly," it is important psychologically to demonstrate that users also "call their baby pretty." These kinds of comments can be spontaneous or they can be gathered from the responses to open-ended questions.
2. *If you don't document the positive findings, they could be changed.* Because changes are likely to occur to a product based on recommendations from the team, there is always a danger that the things that work well for users could end up being changed along with the things that cause problems. Documenting the positive findings makes it clear what shouldn't be changed.

(continued on page 257)

This problem encountered by user number:	1	2	3	4	5	6
Navigating/Locating						
1. Can't find the record she needs without switching to Datasheet view; doesn't want to page through the records until locating the right one.	X			X		
2. Not sure how to find a "new" (blank) record form.	X			X	X	X
3. Couldn't find address fields when first looking at screen (needed to maximize screen).		X				
4. Wanted to be able to pull up the correct record by typing in the country name, rather than by paging through all the forms until the desired record came up.			X	X		
5. Needs the FAM records to sort upon opening the form. (Customer records have been programmed to do this already.)						X
On-Screen Instruction						
1. Doesn't realize the difference between saving the file, and saving the record.	X					
2. Tried to sort (in form view) without specifying which field to sort by. No sort is possible until you specify a field.		X				X
3. Wanted instructions re/FAM name entry, i.e., "First Name, Last name" or split this field into two fields.			X			
4. Wasn't sure how to type a person's name (all caps?, type the period after the middle initial?) or a company name (all caps?). Needs instructions on screen.		X	X	X	X	
5. Unsure about phone numbers—use ( ) or – within?		X	X			
6. Wanted to know how to create a new line within an address field so that it shows up as a two-line address.		X				
7. Needed instructions to draw attention to paging arrows at bottom left screen area.			X			
8. Couldn't "save" the new record because had forgotten to enter data into the key field.			X		X	
9. Would like a "Quick Tips" list or quick reference card, including, for example, use CTRL/" to copy data from the corresponding field in the previous record.					X	X
Form Design						
1. How will you know if you create a duplicate record?		X				
2. If using this for a mailing list, how would you indicate formal name vs. informal ("Dear Dave")? Need field for salutation.		X				
3. Needed more space in the address field.		X				
4. Would like a spell check feature.		X		X		
5. Frustrated because when she highlighted a field and pressed "END," she expected the cursor to go to the end of the field, but it went to the last field of the record.				X		

Figure 7.6 Concerns grid showing data from six users *(continued)*
(Used with permission of Susan Reu.)

This problem encountered by user number:	1	2	3	4	5	6
6. Wants the customer (company) name to pre-fill when you bring up a blank form. Right now only the customer number pre-fills.				X	X	
7. Would like common titles to pre-fill as you begin to type them: "President" or "Treasurer."				X	X	
8. In the database menu, form list, wants to be able to type the first letter of the form name and jump there rather than scrolling.				X		
9. Change field label "Short Name" to something like "Legal Name" or "Subsidiary Name."					X	
10. Wants to have all the open windows shifted to the right so that the Database window (serving as a menu) is visible at the left. Each time she has to move the other windows over to see the form listing.						X

Figure 7.6

	Scenario 1 (10 min)	Scenario 2 (15 min)	Scenario 3 (15 min)	Scenario 4 (10 min)	Total Time (50 min)
Test participant 1 (Novice)	9:29	4:34	14:25	3:36	**32:04**
Test participant 2 (Advanced)	1:04	5:52	17:33	1:24	**25:53**
Test participant 3 (Advanced)	13:43	6:13	9:42	1:12	**30:50**
Test participant 4 (Advanced)	5:40	5:57	6:50	0:49	**19:16**
Test participant 5 (Novice)	17:03	6:56	10:12	1:02	**35:13**
Test participant 6 (Advanced)	6:35	5:43	8:11	1:03	**21:22**
Explanation for exceeded time limits	The time limits presented few difficulties for the participants, with the following exceptions. **Scenario 1:** Participant 3 exceeded the time limit on Scenario 1 because she thoroughly read the terms of service agreement and the mail group descriptions. Participant 5, a novice, exceeded the time limit primarily because system response time was very slow at the time of testing. **Scenario 3:** Participant 2 exceeded the time limit primarily because he tried several times without success to use the non-operating Hotmail search feature.				

Figure 7.7 Timing results from Hotmail test

(Used with permission of the SPSU Hotmail team: Marji Schumann, Anusuya Mukherjee, Nadyne Mielke, Melany Porter, Benjamin Speaks, and Michael Quinby.)

Questions	Participant 1 (Rachel)	Participant 2 (Alia)	Participant 3 (Adrienne)	Participant 4 (Anthony)	Participant 5 (Steven)
Comments (Scenario 1):	The first task was a lot more difficult because I didn't see anything that said exactly what I was looking for, but it got a lot easier.			I'm going crazy	I think that the page was set up well and I like it that you have links in the text and not just in the Navigation Bar.
Comments (Scenario 2):	I liked the info that popped up when I ran the mouse over a link. It was very helpful because it told me what was there without having to click to find out that's not what I wanted and have to go back.			Why me?	This scenario was a lot easier than the other one.
Comments (Scenario 3):	I clicked on things that said tuition but I couldn't find what I was looking for and it got frustrating, finding all this information I didn't need.			I'm going to Disneyland!	This area I felt I was jumping around quite a bit and that on the tuition part that if you would move it with all the requirements then it would be easier to find.
What information was difficult to locate?	Tuition fees	How many semester hours of foreign language was needed & "money figures"	Some tuition stuff, catalog, the first thing (on the whole program)	Half of it	The tuition and where the catalog was.
What information was easy to locate?	Admission information	admission requirements, application, undergraduate courses	Admission stuff, most things with direct links	Half of it	The catalog link is too small.
Enough information about BAITC?	Yes, I think so	Yes	Mostly, yes	Yes	Yes
Any other information	No. Not that I can think of	No	Things explaining the undergraduate catalog	No	No
Anything confusing	I couldn't find the tuition fees even when I clicked on Tuition.	Nothing really, I just couldn't find some things I was looking for.	The catalog & where to find a few things	Yes, everything	I think that if you have been there quite a few times then it would be easy.
How does it compare to other sites?	it was easy to navigate, but I couldn't find what I was looking for. There was a lot of information, but it wasn't what I wanted.	Pretty alike. I normally don't use college Web sites but it worked like several other sites I have been to.	About as easy to get around mostly.	Harder	A lot of information

Figure 7.8 Qualitative findings from post-task and post-test questionnaires

(Used with permission of Team Inertia: Anita Carpenter, Henri Dongieux, Cynthia Ravenna, Diane Rhone, Diana Samuels, and Lynn Smith.)

Positive findings should be included in the test report, as well as on the video-highlights tape, as we will discuss in the next chapter. To capture this information, you need to collate the positive findings as part of your data collation. An example of a list of positive findings from a usability test of a Web site for a women's college includes the following unsolicited comments or observations from users:

1. *Use of color.* Students commented that they thought the site was colorful and professional and included nice pictures.
2. *News events.* Students noticed and were impressed by the inclusion of news events on the homepage.
3. *Site search.* The site search feature worked each time it was used. The feature allowed some students to overcome problems they had finding certain information by providing direct links to the content for which they were searching.
4. *Information.* One student commented that she liked the fact that there was a lot of information presented on the site.
5. *Contact information.* Students noticed that they could send emails to the college using the email address at the bottom of the pages. Students recognized that there was contact information at the bottom of each page on the site.
6. *Video.* Students thought finding out how to order a copy of the admission video was easy.

See the sidebar on pp. 258–260, which presents the findings from the Hotmail test, including quantitative, qualitative, and positive findings based on questionnaires and interviews with the participants.

Summary

In this chapter, we have taken you through a typical day of testing, including strategies for meeting and greeting the participant, preparing the participant for the test session, processing help calls and handling visitors. Next we described strategies for making sense of all the data you collect from the participants. With the focus on collating the data, both quantitative and qualitative, we emphasized the importance of resisting the temptation to jump to conclusions about how to solve the problems observed at this point. Instead, the team should employ a strategy (top-down or bottom-up) to catalog the findings, including positive findings, so as to make sense of them for further analysis later.

Coming Up

In the next chapter, we describe the ways in which you will share the results of testing with others. To begin this process, the team will first need to analyze and interpret the meaning of the data, then recommend improvements that should be made now and improvements that can be saved for later, and report these findings and recommendations in the appropriate way to the appropriate people.

Hotmail Test Findings: Qualitative and Quantitative

Feedback from questionnaires and interviews

On the following scale, rate your need for/interest in having anonymous email capabilities.

Participant	No interest /need	Low interest /need	Don't feel strongly either way	Moderate interest /need	High interest /need
#1				X	
#2					X
#3	X				
#4				X	
#5			X		
#6				X	

On the following scale, rate your impression of Hotmail's speed and responsiveness.

Participant	Very slow	Moderately slow	Neither fast nor slow	Moderately fast	Very fast
#1					X
#2				X	
#3		X			
#4				X	
#5		X			
#6			X		

Will you use Hotmail in the future?

Participant	Never	Rarely	Sometimes	Fairly frequently	Very frequently
#1				X	
#2		X			
#3	X				
#4		X			
#5					X
#6			X		

On the following scale, rate how you would recommend Hotmail to your friends and associates.

Participant	Would not recommend	Would recommend with reservations	Don't feel strongly either way	Would probably recommend	Would strongly recommend
#1					X
#2	X				
#3	X				
#4			X		
#5		X			
#6				X	

If you plan to use Hotmail at all in the future, please indicate how you might use it:

Participant	While traveling for pleasure	While traveling for business	At work for business use	At work for personal use	At home	Not applicable —will not use
#1	X				X	
#2					X	
#3						X
#4						X
#5		X				
#6					X	

Following are free-form comments from the participants.
What did you like MOST about Hotmail?

1. Participant #1: It's fast and pretty easy to use.
2. Participant #2: Easy to send email to another Hotmail member, easy to delete messages.
3. Participant #3: Log off.
4. Participant #4: It's very fast. Also, the screens aren't cluttered.
5. Participant #5: The in-box (once you are familiar with it) was fairly straightforward—nice to know how many messages you had (new and unopened).
6. Participant #6: Fairly easy to follow without printed instruction sheet or manual.

What did you like LEAST about Hotmail?

1. Participant #1: There's not confirmation for signing off and sending messages sometimes.
2. Participant #2: File attachment difficult and not clear.
3. Participant #3: Attaching files, moving email to folders.
4. Participant #4: I don't think people who've never used email will find it easy to use—at least initially.
5. Participant #5: It seemed to take a long time to get from one section to another.
6. Participant #6: Didn't see a button to allow review of "sent" messages.

What would you change about Hotmail?

1. Participant #1: Get good pictures on the homepage.
2. Participant #2: Clarify and simplify file attachment process.
3. Participant #3: Lose the horizontal toolbar with Reply, Reply All, etc. Add drop-down menus. Allow right-click shortcut menus.
4. Participant #4: The OK button after sending email. The lack of instructions for moving and deleting mail.
5. Participant #5: Maybe the layout and design.
6. Participant #6: Need an obvious outbox.

Please add any other comments about Hotmail that might be useful in helping Hotmail improve this email product.

1. Participant #2: Reduce amount of options—high percentage of PC users very seldom use more than sending/receiving messages in home environment. Perhaps if you target businesses, they will have more use for various options.
2. Participant #3: Make it look like Outlook Express.
3. Participant #5: The flow (or ease of going from one section to another) could use some improvement. Not all sections seemed as easy to maneuver as others did. The address book was a nice feature because it stored quite a bit of useful information that may not always be easily accessible.
4. Participant #6: File attachment seems to take longer than either Lotus Notes or Eudora.

Positive feedback summary
Participants offered several positive comments about Hotmail. They liked:

*   The ability to log into Hotmail from any location—noted as a plus when traveling on business.
*   The ease of sending and deleting messages.
*   Hotmail's overall simplicity of use: "I didn't need an instruction manual to use it."
*   The uncluttered, simple layout of the site.
*   The thoroughness of the address book feature—it lets you add considerable biographical information about people.
*   The quick responsiveness of Hotmail (this from users using Hotmail at low-traffic times).

Critical feedback summary
Some of the participants commented on issues they would like to see improved in Hotmail. They criticized:

*   The wordiness of the terms of service text.
*   The limited amount of graphics. Some users commented that the site should be made more visually attractive.
*   The slow response time (this from users using Hotmail during high-traffic times).
*   The excessive number of "clicks" required to attach a file.
*   The inconsistent location of options. Sometimes options are placed in the left frame of the window, sometimes in the middle of the window, and sometimes at the bottom of the screen.
*   The "wordiness" of the online help text.
*   The fact that Hotmail quizzes new users for demographic information about themselves although it touts itself as an anonymous email product.
*   The spell check feature. It does not provide you with feedback to confirm it is checking words.

Source: Used with permission of the SPSU Hotmail team: Marji Schumann, Anusuya Mukherjee, Nadyne Mielke, Melany Porter, Benjamin Speaks, and Michael Quinby.

Questions/Topics for Discussion

1. Describe the activities of the facilitator in interacting with the participant before, during, and after a usability test. Why should the facilitator be the only team member who has personal contact with the participant?
2. List the items that should be covered in a typical briefing.
3. Describe the think-out-loud protocol and a technique you would use to familiarize the participant with this procedure. What are the advantages and disadvantages of using this procedure during a test?
4. Because the facilitator can inadvertently influence the participant by his or her interactions with the participant, what are some ways that the facilitator can work to minimize these potential influences?
5. Discuss the strategies a facilitator (or help desk operator) can use to avoid answering direct questions.
6. Name some situations in which the facilitator or the team might decide to intervene to stop the participant during a test.
7. Describe the options for handling visitors and the ways in which to minimize potential problems when visitors observe part or all of the testing.
8. Discuss the implications of the research conducted by Reeves and Nass on responses you might get from users, following their completion of a usability test.
9. Discuss the meaning of *outlier* data and methods for interpreting such findings.
10. Discuss the reasons to include positive findings and the ways in which to present this information.

Exercises

For Your Project

1. After your first test session, meet with your team and debrief the process. Analyze each team member's role. Make any additions or changes needed to the checklists or scenarios (but don't change any of the questionnaires so that the data analysis will be consistent). Study the video, if needed, for clarification of any actions by the user. Check the testing schedule to confirm that the timing for each task is appropriate and the spacing between users is adequate. Make any adjustments needed before the next test session.
2. Conduct a team findings meeting as soon as possible after the first testing session, using a printout from the logging software or the observer sheets. If you're using the top-down analysis method, work with a flip chart to create the list of categories as shown in Figure 7.4. Fill in the findings for the first participant. If you're using the bottom-up method and have a wall space available for the whole testing period, begin the affinity matching process with the findings from the first participant.

References

Hix, Deborah, and H. Rex Hartson. *Developing User Interfaces: Ensuring Usability Through Product & Process*. New York: Wiley, 1993.

Reeves, Byron, and Clifford Nass. *The Media Equation: How People Treat Computers, Television, and New Media Like Real People and Places*. New York: Cambridge UP, 1996.

Rhenius, Detlef, and Gerhard Deffner. "Evaluation of Concurrent Thinking Aloud Using Eye-Tracking Data." *Proceedings of the Human Factors Society 34th Annual Meeting*, 8–12 Oct. 1990. Orlando, FL. 1265–69.

van der Meij, Hans. "The ISTE Approach to Usability Testing." *IEEE Transactions on Professional Communication* 40.3 (1997): 209–23.

Events Report for Hotmail #6, User 1

Event	Cat	Description	Task #	Task Time	Tape Time Mark In	Mark Out
1	O	User uses mouse to navigate; clicking in URL window and typing www.hotmail.com	1	00:00:41	00:01:40	00:01:46
2	R	User reads screen; Hotmail login screen	1	00:00:52	00:01:54	00:01:57
3	C	User is confused; trying to type a login name	1	00:01:19	00:02:19	00:02:24
4	E	User encountered an error; hit enter, ping!	1	00:01:28	00:02:24	00:02:33
5	R	User reads screen; found "register"	1	00:01:36	00:02:34	00:02:41
6	O	User uses mouse to navigate; clicked sign in	1	00:01:52	00:02:52	00:02:57
7	A	User is angry; sighed deeply	1	00:02:00	00:03:01	00:03:05
8	A	User is angry; "this program is taking a long time"	1	00:02:07	00:03:07	00:03:12
9	E	User encountered an error; no response	1	00:02:17	00:03:18	00:03:22
10	O	User uses mouse to navigate; clicked okay	1	00:02:25	00:03:28	00:03:30
11	O	User uses mouse to navigate; clicked register again	1	00:02:28	00:03:30	00:03:33
12	R	User reads screen; reading TOS	1	00:02:44	00:03:44	00:03:49
13	O	User uses mouse to navigate; scrolling down with mouse clicks	1	00:02:49	00:03:49	00:03:54
14	R	User reads screen; still reading TOS	1	00:04:50	00:05:53	00:05:55
15	A	User is angry; "gosh, this is long"	1	00:05:16	00:06:19	00:06:21
16	A	User is angry; "I hope I'm not supposed to remember all this"	1	00:06:17	00:07:12	00:07:22
17	O	User uses mouse to navigate; clicked "I accept"	1	00:06:23	00:07:24	00:07:28
18	R	User reads screen; at password/ personal info screen	1	00:06:34	00:07:34	00:07:39
19	K	Choosing screenname	1	00:07:11	00:08:06	00:08:16
20	T	User navigates with tab; using tab to navigate menus	1	00:07:14	00:08:26	00:08:19
21	R	User reads screen; reading password requirements	1	00:07:29	00:08:29	00:08:34
22	O	User uses mouse to navigate; to scroll down the screen	1	00:07:37	00:08:37	00:08:42
23	O	User uses mouse to navigate; no problem with pulldown	1	00:07:41	00:08:43	00:08:46

| | | | | | Tape Time | |
Event	Cat	Description	Task #	Task Time	Mark In	Mark Out
24	K	Entering demographic info	1	00:07:57	00:08:58	00:09:02
25	R	User reads screen; reading boilerplate	1	00:08:44	00:09:44	00:09:49
26	O	User uses mouse to navigate; hit submit	1	00:09:14	00:10:17	00:10:19
27	E	User encountered an error; "this I don't believe" name is already chosen	1	00:09:32	00:10:28	00:10:37
28	A	User is angry; "this is very frustrating"	1	00:09:58	00:10:55	00:11:03
29	E	User encountered an error; internal error	1	00:10:01	00:11:03	00:11:06
30	H	User calls for help	1	00:10:32	00:11:13	00:11:37
31	E	User encountered an error; "due to an internal error, we cannot process your request"	1	00:10:47	00:11:41	00:11:52
32	A	User is angry; "this is rather annoying"	1	00:10:59	00:11:59	00:12:04
33	O	User uses mouse to navigate; clicked submit with Ben's help	1	00:11:39	00:12:41	00:12:44
34	R	User reads screen; password retrieval screen	1	00:12:00	00:12:58	00:13:05
35	E	User encountered an error; hit enter to submit information, 'ping!'	1	00:12:26	00:13:23	00:13:31
36	C	User is confused; "what is that" re: password hint question	1	00:12:55	00:13:50	00:14:00
37	A	User is angry; "blah blah blah"	1	00:13:51	00:14:52	00:14:56
38	O	User uses mouse to navigate; clicked submit	1	00:13:54	00:14:56	00:14:59
39	R	User reads screen; "welcome to Hotmail"	1	00:14:39	00:15:04	00:15:44
40	O	User uses mouse to navigate; clicking on scrollbar	1	00:14:44	00:15:44	00:15:49
41	R	User reads screen; reading faster	1	00:15:09	00:16:11	00:16:14
42	K	Didn't choose any mailing lists	1	00:15:37	00:16:38	00:16:42
43	O	User uses mouse to navigate; scrolling back up, pulling scrollbar (not clicking)	1	00:15:46	00:16:42	00:16:51
44	O	User uses mouse to navigate; clicked submit	1	00:16:17	00:17:14	00:17:22
45	R	User reads screen; email login screen	1	00:16:25	00:17:25	00:17:30
46	R	User reads screen	2	00:00:16	00:25:46	00:25:48

Event	Cat	Description	Task #	Task Time	Tape Time	
					Mark In	Mark Out
47	E	User encountered an error; document contained no error	2	00:00:41	00:26:07	00:26:13
48	B	User goes back one screen	2	00:00:44	00:26:13	00:26:16
49	E	User encountered an error; same	2	00:01:02	00:26:30	00:26:34
50	B	User goes back one screen; uses right mouse button	2	00:01:07	00:26:34	00:26:39
51	R	User reads screen; reading Steve Miller message	2	00:01:35	00:27:03	00:27:07
52	A	User is angry; banging mouse	2	00:01:50	00:27:19	00:27:22
53	R	User reads screen; laughing	2	00:02:06	00:27:28	00:27:38
54	O	User uses mouse to navigate; clicked close	2	00:02:17	00:27:47	00:27:49
55	R	User reads screen; back in inbox	2	00:02:21	00:27:51	00:27:53
56	O	User uses mouse to navigate; clicked on compose	2	00:02:47	00:28:16	00:28:19
57	R	User reads screen; email screen	2	00:02:52	00:28:22	00:28:24
58	T	User navigates with tab; between fields	2	00:02:18	00:28:47	00:28:50
59	O	User uses mouse to navigate; clicked send	2	00:04:44	00:30:13	00:30:16
60	R	User reads screen; confirmation screen	2	00:04:47	00:30:16	00:30:19
61	O	User uses mouse to navigate; clicked okay	2	00:04:49	00:30:19	00:30:21
62	R	User reads screen; back at inbox	2	00:05:00	00:30:30	00:30:32
63	O	User uses mouse to navigate; clicked on Steve Miller hot link	2	00:04:22	00:30:47	00:30:54
64	A	User is angry; exasperated	2	00:05:29	00:30:59	00:31:01
65	R	User reads screen; responding to email, typing above quoted material	2	00:05:51	00:31:16	00:31:23
66	A	User is angry; "this takes a long time"	2	00:06:35	00:32:04	00:32:07
67	A	User is angry; deep sigh	2	00:06:45	00:32:15	00:32:17
68	R	User reads screen; confirmation screen	2	00:06:51	00:32:21	00:32:23
69	O	User uses mouse to navigate; clicked okay	2	00:07:01	00:32:32	00:32:33
70	E	User encountered an error; network error	3	00:01:18	00:37:31	00:37:34
71	A	User is angry; "and wait even longer"	3	00:01:30	00:37:43	00:37:46
72	R	User reads screen; back at inbox	3	00:01:36	00:37:50	00:37:52

Event	Cat	Description	Task #	Task Time	Tape Time Mark In	Mark Out
73	O	User uses mouse to navigate; clicked on compose button	3	00:01:51	00:38:04	00:38:07
74	C	User is confused; looking for attach file	3	00:03:37	00:39:50	00:39:53
75	O	User uses mouse to navigate; clicked on attachments	3	00:03:40	00:39:53	00:39:56
76	R	User reads screen; reading instructions	3	00:03:56	00:40:09	00:40:12
77	T	User navigates with tab; typing test .doc inpath window	3	00:04:07	00:40:19	00:40:23
78	R	User reads screen; reading instructions	3	00:04:17	00:40:31	00:40:33
79	O	User uses mouse to navigate; clicked attach to button	3	00:04:22	00:40:33	00:40:38
80	O	User uses mouse to navigate; clicked ok	3	00:04:33	00:40:44	00:40:49
81	R	User reads screen; back at email compose screen	3	00:04:39	00:40:53	00:40:55
82	E	User encountered error; "where does it say I have an attachment?"	3	00:04:47	00:40:58	00:41:03
83	O	User uses mouse to navigate; clicked send	3	00:04:54	00:41:08	00:41:10
84	R	User reads screen; confirmation screen	3	00:05:00	00:41:14	00:41:16
85	O	User uses mouse to navigate; clicked okay	3	00:05:04	00:41:19	00:41:20
86	R	User reads screen; email inbox	3	00:05:15	00:41:29	00:41:31
87	C	User is confused; looking for my stuff	3	00:05:22	00:41:36	00:41:38
88	O	User uses mouse to navigate	3	00:05:59	00:42:05	00:42:15
89	O	User uses mouse to navigate; clicked on folders, looking for one called my stuff	3	00:06:22	00:42:31	00:42:38
90	O	User uses mouse to navigate; clicked on options image map	3	00:06:26	00:42:38	00:42:42
91	O	User uses mouse to navigate; clicked on folders again	3	00:06:43	00:42:56	00:42:59
92	R	User reads screen; back at folders menu	3	00:06:48	00:43:02	00:43:04
93	O	User uses mouse to navigate; clicked on create	3	00:06:54	00:43:08	00:43:10
94	O	User uses mouse to navigate; typing folder name	3	00:07:00	00:43:10	00:43:16
95	O	User uses mouse to navigate; clicked submit	3	00:07:03	00:43:16	00:43:19

Event	Cat	Description	Task #	Task Time	Tape Time Mark In	Tape Time Mark Out
96	R	User reads screen; has a folder called My Stuff	3	00:07:14	00:43:26	00:43:30
97	O	User uses mouse to navigate; back at email box	3	00:07:25	00:43:39	00:43:41
98	C	User is confused; trying to figure out how to move items into folder	3	00:07:39	00:43:49	00:43:55
99	O	User uses mouse to navigate; checked radio box next to Steve Miller	3	00:07:57	00:44:06	00:44:13
100	O	User uses mouse to navigate; selected My Stuff folder	3	00:08:01	00:44:13	00:44:17
101	T	User navigates with tab: hit enter	3	00:08:12	00:44:26	00:44:28
102	C	User is confused; "how do I do this?"	3	00:08:16	00:44:28	00:44:32
103	O	User uses mouse to navigate; clicked Move to	3	00:08:25	00:44:37	00:44:41
104	O	User uses mouse to navigate; submit	3	00:08:27	00:44:41	00:44:43
105	A	User is angry; deep sigh	3	00:08:37	00:44:51	00:44:53
106	R	User reads screen; back at email inbox	3	00:08:44	00:44:56	00:45:00
107	O	User uses mouse to navigate; clicked on addresses image map	3	00:09:07	00:45:19	00:45:23
108	R	User reads screen	3	00:09:17	00:45:32	00:45:33
109	O	User uses mouse to navigate; clicked create	3	00:09:27	00:45:41	00:45:43
110	R	User reads screen; typing Marji's info	3	00:09:47	00:46:00	00:46:03
111	T	User navigates with tab	3	00:10:06	00:46:19	00:46:22
112	O	User uses mouse to navigate	3	00:10:06	00:46:22	00:46:22
113	O	User uses mouse to navigate; clicked submit	3	00:10:23	00:46:34	00:46:39
114	R	User reads screen	3	00:10:31	00:46:47	00:46:47
115	R	User reads screen	4	00:00:18	00:52:55	00:53:11
116	O	User uses mouse to navigate; clicked radio boxes	4	00:00:29	00:53:18	00:53:22
117	O	User uses mouse to navigate; clicked delete	4	00:00:32	00:53:24	00:53:25
118	R	User reads screen; signoff from, Hotmail, "how do you do that?"	4	00:00:58	00:53:44	00:53:51

Source: Used with permission of the SPSU Hotmail team: Marji Schumann, Anusuya Mukherjee, Nadyne Mielke, Melany Porter, Benjamin Speaks, and Michael Quinby.

Analyzing and Reporting Results

 As a member of the usability test team or even as an observer, you've probably seen things you didn't expect to see (as well as things you did expect to see), and you've probably wanted to fix the problems right away. In the last chapter, we cautioned against jumping too quickly to conclusions abut the nature of the problem and the solution required. Now that the testing is complete, you can begin to make sense of what you have observed and what the participants have reported in questionnaires. This chapter presents a method for interpreting the data you have collected, making recommendations based on your interpretations, and reporting the results of testing in the appropriate media to the appropriate audiences.

Analyzing the Findings

If you followed the process described in the previous chapter, you have already collated the findings from each session. You have captured the issues you observed in each session and you have determined the number of times each participant experienced the same problem. You have used pre-determined labels to categorize these problems, or you have used affinity-matching to determine what these categories should be. You are now ready to analyze the findings. In this analysis, you will determine the cause of the problems, evaluate their impact on the usability of the product (scope and severity of each problem), and recommend solutions for fixing the problems. We discuss each of these topics in the upcoming sections of this chapter, beginning with the method to determine the causes of problems.

Determining the Causes of Problems

Identifying a problem is one thing. You do this when you state that a problem is of a particular type or category, such as *navigation*, *concept*, or *terminology*. Identifying the cause of the problem may not be as simple. If the problem is one of navigation, for instance, the cause of the problem could be many things: poor design of the information on the page, inconsistency, unfamiliar terminology, a concept that doesn't match the user's mental model, and so forth. Because the team brings different perspectives to bear on the cause of the problem observed, it can work together to determine the most likely cause as well as the most appropriate solution. This is where a team is far more effective than a single individual in interpreting usability observations. For more information on the benefits of team analysis, see the end-of-book appendix, Making It Work as a Team.

Listening to the user can also be very instructive. By going back to the videotapes to observe what the user does and listen to what the user says, the team can focus on the user's view of the problem. Some users offer solutions, which should also be taken into consideration, although not necessarily adopted outright. As a side note, but an important one, any proposed solution should be tested to see whether, in fact, it is an improvement. Otherwise, you can never be sure that the solution doesn't create some other problem or make the situation worse.

In some cases, however, the solution is obvious and easy to fix. If users use a term that's different from the term used in the product, the users have provided the solution to the problem, which is to make the system's terminology match the user's vocabulary. Likewise, if users are confused about a lack of response from the computer or they are unsure whether they have completed a task successfully, the solution is to provide this feedback information.

In most cases, however, the solution will require some study of the data. Studying the data means looking at what users did, what they said, what they recorded in questionnaires, and what you observed. This approach of analyzing multiple sources of data is called *triangulation*, which provides an excellent way to confirm suppositions. When you study the collated data, you want to see what similarities there are among the sources of data collected from one user and from among the users as a group. When participants experience the same problem performing a task, do they have the problem for the same reason? Are their attempted solutions to the problem similar or different? If similar, they may be suggesting the solution to the problem. If different, the team will have to analyze the strategies employed by users to determine the best solution to recommend.

In addition, the team should return to the test goals, as these goals are frequently based on anticipated or known problems uncovered from heuristic evaluation, from calls to the help desk, from contextual inquiry, or from other sources. A return to the goals of the test can be a good cross-reference to see what problems occurred and how well or poorly the product performed for users against the test goals. For instance, how many participants were able to install the product within the timeframe of acceptable use? And did their comments, your direct observations of their actions, and their responses on questionnaires confirm that this timeframe of performance was acceptable to them?

In addition to analyzing the meaning of the data you have collated, you will also need to determine the scope of each problem and its severity, or impact, on usability.

Determining the Scope and Severity of Problems

The scope of the problem refers to how narrowly or how widely the problem occurs in the product. Scope can be characterized as *local* or *global* (Dumas and Redish 322–23). A local problem affects only one page of the documentation, one error message or one screen or menu in a software product, or one page in a Web site. A global problem occurs in more than one place, usually indicating a broad-based problem within the product. Although global problems tend to be more severe and require more immediate attention, a local problem can be equally severe in its impact on performing a specific task. When that task is frequently performed or critical, even if seldom performed, a local problem can be assigned the highest priority for improvement. In addition, a grouping of local problems can suggest a global problem that needs to be addressed. In fact, one of the key benefits of usability testing is that the information learned from a single test of parts of a product can be applied to other parts of the product and can also be educational for the developers of future products.

Once you agree on the types of problems that result from a test and can categorize them as local or global, you need to determine the severity of the problems, as a way of measuring how quickly each problem needs to be fixed. Severity codes or scales vary, but each includes an extreme at one end, indicating a problem that prevents completion of the task, and the opposite extreme, indicating an enhancement that would be nice to do, but mostly for cosmetic value. One such scale, suggested by Dumas and Redish, uses four levels (324–25):

- *Level 1:* prevents completion of a task
- *Level 2:* creates significant delay and frustration
- *Level 3:* has a minor effect on usability
- *Level 4:* subtle problem; points to a future enhancement

Rubin uses a different four-point scale, with the following designations (278):

- 4: unusable; the user cannot or will not use the part of the product
- 3: severe; the user will attempt to use the product but will be severely hampered
- 2: moderate; the user will be able to use the product with moderate effort to get around the problem
- 1: irritant; the problem occurs occasionally or can be avoided or is cosmetic

Others rank the severity more succinctly, using labels that need no explanation:

- Disaster
- Serious
- Cosmetic

Or, a 5-point scale:

- 1: Catastrophic
- 2: Major
- 3: Medium

- 4: Minor
- 5: Cosmetic

Some scales also include a rating for the marketing implications of a problem.

At this point in your analysis, you have identified a finding, placed it in a category, determined whether the finding is global or local, and assigned a severity code to it. Compiling your findings in a table, as shown in the Hotmail example (Figure 8.1), clarifies the scope and severity of the problem and prepares the team for a discussion of recommendations.

Making Recommendations

The last step in the analysis process is to recommend a solution for each problem or several possible solutions. Factors affecting the implementation of recommended solutions may be beyond the team's ability to control. One factor may involve the amount of time and resources that can be expended on implementing the recommendations. Another factor relates to the development stage of the product at the time of testing. If the testing is done early in product development, the recommendations can generally be made quickly and inexpensively. If, however, testing takes place late in the development cycle, then few changes may be permitted before the product releases. Still, the recommendations should be made and the arguments put forth for improving the usability of the product. One of the benefits of usability testing is to document improvements that should be made to increase the user's satisfaction with the product. If the changes cannot be made to the current product, seize the opportunity to make the case for earlier product testing next time to allow for faster, cheaper changes. Of course, the argument should also be made that any recommended changes be tested to confirm that the improvements do, in fact, increase the usability of the product. Typically, follow-up testing can be done at far less expense than initial testing because much, if not all, of the planning has already taken place: you know the user profile, the tasks you want to test, and the objectives of the test. You may even be able to bring in fewer participants to test, as the objective is to confirm improvements over previous data collected from testing.

In any event, you will want to present your findings and your recommendations in the appropriate form to the right people. In the remaining sections of this chapter, we discuss the options you have in the media and method of your presentation of results.

Reporting the Results

Just as audience analysis is the basis for decisions you make about your users and their level of experience and understanding, so, too, is audience analysis the basis of decisions you make about how and to whom to report your results. At a very minimum, you may be reporting only to your own team, in which case a summary of findings and actions with the names of the people assigned to do follow-

Usability Problems	Number of participants affected	Severity level	Scope
1. Participants were unable to find users in Hotmail's directory.[1]	2	1	local
2. The process for sending attachments confused participants. (Four participants thought they had successfully attached a document when they had not.)	4	2	local
3. Participants were unsure if items had been moved into the selected folder.	2	2	local
4. Participants received internal and network errors.	2	2	local
5. Participants expected to be able to press the Enter key to submit information, but this worked only in isolated instances.	3	3	global
6. Participants were unsure whether to click on the radio box or the link to reply to email.	4	3	local
7. Participants had problems finding the "create folder" icon.	3	3	local
8. Participants were unsure if they had signed off from Hotmail successfully.	2	3	local
9. Participants were unsure which button allowed them to compose an email.	1	3	local
10. Participants had trouble navigating between inbox screen and folder screen.	2	3	local
11. Participants were confused about the password hint question.	4	3	local
12. International participants were unsure of the terminology "first name" and "last name."[2]	W	3	local
13. Participants complained about excessive amount of reading materials in the Terms of Service.	4	4	local
14. Participants were unable to find messages they had sent.	1	4	local
15. Participants disliked the Compose window.	1	4	local

[1]We removed this task from our scenarios after the first two test participants were unable to complete the task and the evaluation team confirmed that the task could not be completed.

[2]This finding was collected from our walkthrough participant, whose other testing results are not recorded in this report. We included this finding because it may be of special interest to developers interested in internationalization and localization issues.

Figure 8.1 Collated findings, rated by scope and severity (Hotmail)

(Used with permission of the SPSU Hotmail team: Marji Schumann, Anusuya Mukerjee, Nadyne Mielke, Melany Porter, Benjamin Speaks, and Michael Quinby.)

up revisions may be sufficient. This report can be sent via email as an attachment. It serves as the group's memory of the results of testing and the actions taken, and it can be used as a starting place for future testing.

Generally, however, an audience exists beyond the team, and this audience will have differing levels of understanding of the test and the testing process. Your need to address this audience also provides you with the opportunity to advocate more usability testing, more often, and earlier, as part of a user-centered design process, if this isn't the current practice. Your change-making potential should not be underestimated, nor the opportunity lost as part of your reporting on the results of testing. How best to report? You have several options, including a written report (formal or informal), a presentation, an edited videotape of highlights, and a multimedia presentation. We discuss each of these methods of reporting in the following sections.

Preparing a Written Report

If you want the message from usability testing to be that it makes the product more usable, then any report you write must be a reflection of good usability principles: useful, usable, and desirable. Even when developing such a report under time constraints, every effort should be made to make the report an effective communication tool.

At its most basic level, the report should communicate the goals of the test, the structure of the test, and the outcomes from testing to a general audience, which could include management-level up to executive-level readers and people in other departments with an interest in the results of testing. The report should present information of a general nature in non-technical terms, so that those without formal training or experience in usability testing can understand the five W's and H of basic journalistic practice: who, what, when, where, why, and how.

At the same time, you want to communicate to insiders, those in the know about usability testing, who want to learn what you did and how you did it as much as they want to know what resulted. These people are interested in the methodology of testing. They want to know the particulars regarding:

- Criteria or goals for the test and the basis for these
- User profile
- Number of users
- Tasks created (with rationale for the order of tasks)
- Length of sessions
- When, where, and how testing was conducted
- Type of testing done (think-out-loud, co-discovery, exploratory)
- System specifics that could have an impact on results (operating system, Web browser, or connection speed)
- State of the product (prototype, partial product, full product)
- Measurement instruments (quantitative and qualitative)
- Severity scale

Of course, management and executive readers will want to know about some of these same areas, but in less detail, and certainly in less technical detail. Management or executive readers will also be the audience for the change-making argument you will make to sell the benefits of usability testing as part of a user-centered design process.

As you can see from this discussion, you will need to plan your report by thinking about the different groups of potential users of the information and your purpose in communicating with each group. Naturally, the more effective the organization and structure of the report, the more readily the readers will be able to access the information they seek. Therefore, document design is a critical concern. The report should employ good technical writing principles, using headings, subheadings, lists, tables, white space, and graphics to communicate clearly to different audiences simultaneously. And let's not forget pictures. Screen captures to show the problems in a software product, sample pages from the documentation or help files, a download of Web pages—all use the show-and-tell principle to demonstrate what the issues are as you describe your findings. In the next section, we talk about the essential parts of the formal report. Informal reports may contain fewer parts.

The Essential Parts of the Formal Report

The report should contain the following parts in the following order:

- Cover memo or cover letter
- Executive summary
- Introduction
- Methodology
- Results
- Recommendations/actions
- Appendices

In the following discussion of each of these parts, we show examples from two usability test reports of certain aspects of Southern Polytechnic State University's (SPSU) Web site: (1) Team Inertia's report, which focused on the B.A. degree in International Technical Communication, and (2) the Blade Group's report, which focused on the M.S. degree in Technical and Professional Communication.

Cover Memo or Letter

Write a cover memo (for an internal sponsor) or a cover letter (for an external client) to explain the nature of the report, the results, and the next steps to be taken. This one-page letter or memo is also an excellent place to press for more usability testing for this or future products by emphasizing the value derived from learning about the user's experience. Figure 8.2 is Team Inertia's cover memo, directed at the internal sponsors of the test.

Executive Summary

Directed primarily at non-technical readers such as executives, but generally read by all, this part of the report provides an overview of the project scope and results. Because it is a summary, it should be short (generally one to three pages for

1 May 2000

Dr. Ron Koger, Vice President of Enrollment Management
Dr. Ed Vizzini, Dean, College of Arts and Sciences

Dr. William Pfeiffer, Department Head, HTC
Dr. Herbert Smith, Associate Professor, HTC
Dr. Carol Barnum, Professor, HTC

Attached is the Usability Test Report for Team Inertia, which signifies the completion of our usability test of the HTC Web pages and the SPSU Web site. Our test evaluated the usability and quality of the information available within the Web pages, with a specific emphasis on information relating to the new BAITC degree to be offered this coming fall.

First, we performed a heuristic evaluation of the HTC Web pages and the SPSU Web site, basing much of our work on the state of the art as defined by Nielsen. Then, we redesigned portions of the site based on what we found to be the most obvious usability problems. After testing four participants, we made more changes to the Web pages and finished the testing with two additional participants. A number of different types of data were compiled and analyzed, and the report you are now reading is the result.

We were concerned with usability issues such as the level of integration between the HTC Web pages and the SPSU Web site, the level of information available to users, and the ease with which prospective BAITC students could be led into the application process and other administrative procedures.

We found that moving between the HTC Web pages and the SPSU Web site is often a disjunctive and disruptive experience. We also found that information on Technical Communication, notably the BAITC, is scarce within the pages. Several problems were identified in leading the prospective student into the application process, the most important of which are difficulties in locating contact and tuition information.

We recommend that future redesigns of both the HTC Web pages and the SPSU Web site as a whole take into consideration the problems we identified. And we would like to take this opportunity to reiterate the importance of usability testing as a means of uncovering the most important problems and issues affecting the performance of a user interface.

Thank you for the opportunity to evaluate such a new product. If you have any questions about the project not adequately addressed here, please do not hesitate to contact us. We would be happy to address any and all concerns you might have.

Anita Carpenter   Henri Dongieux   Cynthia Ravenna

Diane Rhone   Diana Samuels   Lynn Smith

Figure 8.2   Cover memo (Team Inertia)

(Used with permission of Team Inertia: Anita Carpenter, Henri Dongieux, Cynthia Ravenna, Diane Rhone, Diana Samuels, and Lynn Smith.)

a formal report; one to two paragraphs for an informal report). Its purpose is to brief readers on the goals for the test, the nature of the test, the results, the recommendations for improvements, and the rationale for making these improvements. Figure 8.3 is the executive summary for Team Inertia's usability test report.

Introduction

This section can be skipped by those in the know, but will provide essential information to those unfamiliar with the usability testing process. It presents the background needed to understand the issues and may also include information about

---

The Humanities and Technical Communication (HTC) department recently completed a comprehensive redesign of the departmental Web pages within the SPSU Web site. Among the goals of the site are to represent the HTC faculty nationally as well as to persuade greater numbers of students—and especially greater numbers of academically high-achieving students—to apply to and enroll in SPSU's degree programs in Technical Communication.

Team Inertia conducted a usability test of the HTC's departmental Web pages, paying especially close attention to the information presented within these pages on the new Bachelor of Arts degree in International Technical Communication. Initial evaluation of the Web product and other test preparation was carried out in January and February 2000, while testing with participants took place through March and April.

The goals of the test included providing answers to the following questions:

- How well do the HTC Web pages integrate within the larger SPSU Web site?
- How well does the information in the HTC Web pages educate prospective students about the fields of technical communication and international technical communication?
- How smoothly do the HTC Web pages and the SPSU Web site guide a prospective student from the phase of initial interest in the program and the university all the way to the application process?

Test participants were high-school students who were comfortable using the Web and interested in writing and communication. Most had also studied a foreign language. These participants were intended to approximate the real users who would approach the HTC Web pages, seek information on the new BAITC degree, and make contact with university administration.

Analysis of test data resulted in four major findings:

1. There is very poor visual and organizational continuity between the HTC Web pages and the SPSU Web site.
2. Users not already familiar with the field of technical communication and the administrative jargon of a university will find the terminology used within the HTC Web pages and the SPSU Web site to be very confusing.
3. Users cannot establish contact with HTC departmental contact persons with reasonable ease, nor can they request information from SPSU (catalogs, applications, and so on) with reasonable ease. The Web site does not easily facilitate "exit points" from which further communication with SPSU faculty, staff, or administration can be initiated.
4. Users cannot find information on tuition with reasonable ease.

Figure 8.3 Executive summary—Team Inertia *(continued)*

(Used with permission of Team Inertia: Anita Carpenter, Henri Dongieux, Cynthia Ravenna, Diane Rhone, Diana Samuels, and Lynn Smith.)

Team Inertia therefore makes the following three short-term recommendations:

1. Minimize abbreviations, acronyms, and administrative jargon within the HTC Web pages and SPSU Web site, and provide the user with parenthetical definitions or glossaries when it is necessary to use unfamiliar or system terms. Rather than excluding many prospective students with the use of too many unfamiliar and even intimidating terms, the HTC Web pages should educate and pique interest in the prospective student, so that he or she will be motivated to explore the educational opportunities in technical communication that the HTC department has to offer.

2. Create a separate Web page that clearly indicates the appropriate HTC departmental contact person or persons for a range of user needs. Make this Web page accessible from a prominent link location, such as the left navigational bar within the HTC Web pages. If users cannot find the information they need within the Web pages, or for whatever reason they want to initiate a dialogue with the department or university administration, an obvious and easy way to make contact should be part of the essential function of the Web product.

3. Present information on tuition by means of a cleanly designed Web page that does not require scrolling in order to view. Make links to tuition information throughout both the HTC Web pages and the SPSU Web site clear and obvious. Since finances play such a big role in decisions regarding education, it is imperative that users be able to quickly find and correctly interpret information on university tuition.

Team Inertia would also like to offer the following two long-term recommendations:

1. Redesign all or part of the HTC Web pages and the SPSU Web site, in order that a noticeable continuity between the departmental and University Web pages can be discerned and appreciated by users. The glaring discontinuity now visible looks unprofessional and simply "makes the university look bad." The present generation of Web-savvy teenagers is unlikely to be impressed by a university Web site that looks patchy and unpolished. For better or worse, in the present case, perceptions of the quality of the university will be largely inferred from the quality of the university's Web site.

2. Implement a section within the HTC Web pages that specifically addresses high-school students, teaching them about the field of technical communication (especially career prospects) in terms they can understand. This section should have a seamless connection with the rest of the HTC site, so that a user having learned the basic information from the site can then move on to the "real" HTC site. Such a section of the HTC site would attract the attention of the bright prospective students in which SPSU is interested; and moreover, it would also attract the attention of high-school guidance counselors and parents who might steer prospective students toward SPSU and the HTC department. High-school students often know very little about college majors and careers; this could be one way to both educate them and attract them to SPSU.

Figure 8.3

the type of study conducted. If the report is lengthy, this section includes a description of the report structure to guide readers in locating information of interest. Figure 8.4 shows the introduction for the Blade Group's usability test report.

Methodology

This section provides the information of greatest interest to those knowledgeable about usability testing. The information for this section can be imported from the

(continued on page 280)

Usability Test Report

*Graduate Student Usability Testing on the
Humanities and Technical Communication
(HTC) Web Site*

Introduction

Report Overview

This report contains the following information:

- *Introduction*—explains the purpose of the usability test, provides an overview of the Web site, includes changes made by the BLADE GROUP (why and when) including screen captures

- *Test Plan*—describes the test plan and procedures, identifies the project goals, user profile information, scenarios used for testing and includes the test schedule

- *Results*—includes results of the time on task and user ratings by scenario

- *Findings*—explains the global, local and favorable findings

- *Recommendations*—lists recommendations based on the testing as well as suggestions for future testing

- *Appendices A–F*—contains complete appendix for each user who participated in the usability testing, including a user overview, their consent form, pre-test questionnaire, pre-task questionnaire, post-task questionnaire, their scenario responses, post-test questionnaire and the logger transcript

- *Appendix G*—contains the original Test Plan

- *Appendix H*—includes the BLADE GROUP Heuristic Evaluation

- *Appendix I*—includes the Rollout Checklist followed for this project

Purpose

This usability test was designed to evaluate the graduate portion of the newest Humanities and Technical Communication (HTC) Web site from Southern Polytechnic State University in Marietta, Georgia. The test sought to:

- establish whether or not the site easily and quickly provides prospective graduate students with specific and thorough information about the HTC program

- determine the overall perception of the program before and after reviewing the site

- determine the overall perception of the site

Overview of the Web Site

The following are facts about the Humanities and Technical Communication (HTC) Web site:

- it is an academic department which is linked from the main Southern Polytechnic State University (SPSU) Web site

---

Figure 8.4   Introduction—Blade Group *(continued)*

- there are no guidelines established by the University regarding standards to be used in Web page design and navigation, so consistency between SPSU and HTC pages was not tested

As part of this project, the BLADE Group made preliminary requested changes to the HTC Web site at the beginning of the usability test. The following change was made on February 26, 2000 prior to the initial walkthrough.

Because the Writing Program is designed for undergraduate students preparing for the Regents' Exam, the BLADE Group changed the link to the Writing Program to show "under construction."

When a user clicked on the Writing Program, an "under construction" message and icon displayed.

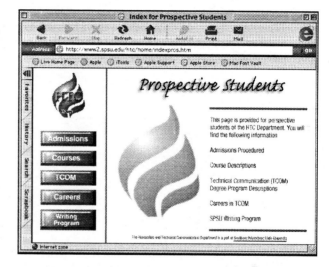

A second set of changes was made based on our initial walkthrough comments. The three changes were:

Change 1—In an effort to facilitate navigation, extended descriptions were made into hyperlinks.

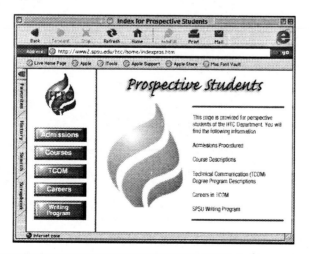

The original screen without the links on the extended descriptions

Figure 8.4   *(continued)*

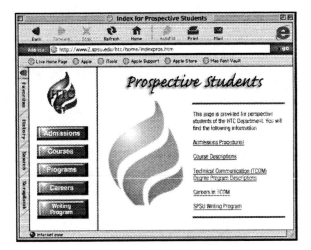

The revised screen with the links on the extended descriptions

Change 2—To clarify the purpose and target market of the Writing Program, an introductory page was added.

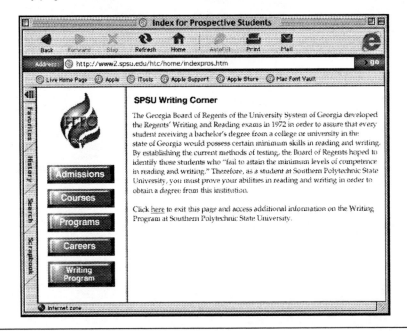

Figure 8.4   Introduction—Blade Group *(continued)*

test plan, if one was created, with the appropriate changes made to match the reality of the actual testing situation. It typically includes the test goals, user profile, number of users, tasks, measurement instruments, testing situation, and so forth. Figure 8.5 provides an example of this section from the Blade Group's report. Figure 8.6 on pages 286–289 is an example of this section, which also incorporates some background information, from Team Inertia's report.

Change 3—To better explain the link from the TCOM button, the button title was changed to read "Program."

The original screen with
the TCOM button

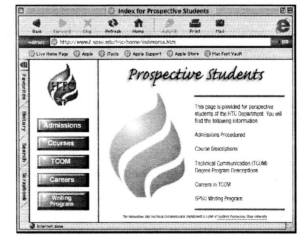

The revised screen with
the Programs button

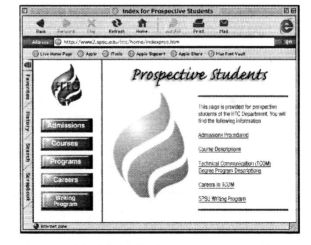

Figure 8.4

Results
This section, which describes the findings from the test, will be the largest part of the report. It is frequently divided into two areas: quantitative results and qualitative results. The discussion of both types of results should include findings from direct observation as well as from questionnaires and unsolicited comments from participants. Results can be further differentiated in the following ways:

- Positive findings
- Negative findings
  - Global vs. local findings
  - Severity rating for each finding

(continued on page 285)

Description of Test Plan and Procedures

Overview

This section of the report provides:

- an overview of the actual test plan conducted
- user profile and screening information
- test schedule
- quantitative results compiled from the time-on-task activities
- quantitative results from survey responses

Goals

The original goals in testing the graduate students on the Humanities and Technical (HTC) Web site were to determine the ease or difficulty of locating the following graduate information:

- admission requirements
- graduation requirements
- programs of study
- class hours
- class content
- job placement
- faculty experience (optional activity if needed)

User Profile

The User Profile was designed to focus on a user who:

- received a Bachelor's degree in a communications-related field
- does not have a Master's degree in technical communication
- is not currently studying technical communication in school
- has an interest in a career that emphasizes communications, such as writing and Web design
- is interested in continuing education
- has at least one year of work experience in professional writing, e.g., producing newsletters, developing multimedia, writing proposals, developing marketing brochures, etc.
- uses a PC in a Win '95 environment
- performs online searches of multiple sites for at least two hours of each week, e.g., business, news, sports, academic, etc.
- has at least 6 months' experience accessing the Internet
- is familiar with basic Web navigation such as how to move backward/forward, click on links, and enter a URL

Figure 8.5   Methodology section—Blade Group *(continued)*

(Used with permission of the Blade Group: Betty Owen, Loretta Joslin, Ardenna Morton, Diana Mason, and Elizabeth Wong Mark.)

- has never applied for admission to a graduate school at Southern Polytechnic State University
- lives in the Atlanta-metro area

Screening Profile

There were five users who participated in this study. In comparing their qualifications against the user profile, the following was found to be true:

- 100% had Bachelor's degrees
- 100% do not have a Master's degree in technical communication
- 100% were interested in continuing their education
- 100% had experience with basic navigation such as moving backward/forward, clicking on links, and entering a URL
- 100% had surfed the Web longer than 6 months
- 100% had experience surfing the Web for business and/or personal information; 75% had experience surfing the Web for news; 50% had experience surfing the Web for travel information
- 100% had at least one year's experience in at least two of the following categories: producing newsletters, writing proposals, training materials, multimedia, brochures, designing graphics, and writing memos
- 100% had experience in a Win '95 environment
- 100% were interested in a career in writing, Web design, etc.
- 100% had not previously applied for a graduate program at Southern Polytechnic State University
- 100% lived within driving distance of Southern Polytechnic State University

In addition to meeting the requirements of the screening questionnaire, the following was also found out about the participants:

- 100% indicated they had *not* surfed the Web for information on academics
- 100% had not made purchases on the Web
- 40% (2 out of 5) were male; 60% (3 out of 5) were female

Scenarios

The following were the scenarios each participant was asked to complete:

Scenario 1—Beginning at the Southern Polytechnic State University Home Web page, explore the Web site and find any graduate program(s) offered in writing, Web design, etc.

Scenario 2—Beginning at the HTC Home Web page, find possible careers available to you after completing the program.

Scenario 3—Beginning at the HTC Home Web page, find the admissions requirements, 3 required courses to complete the program, and the number of hours required to graduate from this program.

Scenario 4—Beginning at the HTC Home Web page, find 3 courses in the program that interest you.

Scenario 5—Continuing from Scenario 4, which graduation option do you think you

Figure 8.5 *(continued)*

would select (if you were currently enrolled in this program)?

Scenario 6 (optional scenario)—Beginning at the HTC Home Web page, review the faculty's experience.

Test Procedures

The testing of the graduate information on the HTC Web site consisted of five scenarios with one optional activity available should time permit. In each of the scenarios the user was requested to find certain information, write down the answer and then call the help desk to signal completion. The logger completed a log of all actions and comments. The time to complete was noted for each task.

Seven questionnaires were completed by each user. Each original completed questionnaire can be found in the Appendix for each user. They were:

Questionnaire Title	Purpose	When Given
Pre-Screening Questionnaire	Select users who fit the profile	Completed **before** user was selected as test candidate
Pre-Test Questionnaire	Determine their knowledge and interest in this graduate program	Completed at the lab **before** the usability test commenced
Post-Task Questionnaire	Obtain feedback after completing scenarios	Completed at the lab **after** scenarios 1, 2, 3, and 5
Post-Test Questionnaire	Obtain overall impressions after using the pages and finding the information	Completed at the lab **after** completing scenario 5

Test Schedule

Listed below are the dates and begin/end times for each user. The tolerant user, selected as the first person to run through the test, agreed to tolerate interruptions and, possibly, not a perfect testing environment. The pilot test user is the first person to "officially" test the Web site.

Date	Begin	End	Subject
3/6/00	5:30 P.M.	6:30 P.M.	Tolerant User
3/13/00	5:30 P.M.	6:30 P.M.	Pilot Test
3/27/00	8:45 P.M.	9:45 P.M.	User #1
4/3/00	5:30 P.M.	6:30 P.M.	User #2
4/8/00	1:00 P.M.	2:00 P.M.	User #3

Figure 8.5   Methodology section

Comments from participants can support the discussion of findings, along with illustrations of problems using screen captures and the like. Figure 8.7 on pages 290–293 shows a portion of the detailed findings from Team Inertia's usability test. When the findings are detailed, a summary, as shown in Figure 8.8 on pages 294–295 from Team Inertia's report, can be helpful for those seeking an overview. Figure 8.9 on pages 296–298 provides a portion of the detailed findings from the Blade Group's report, organized by positive findings, global findings, and local findings.

Recommendations/Actions
As the name suggests, this section describes the recommendations suggested or actions taken on the basis of the findings. This section can follow the findings, or the recommendations and actions can be integrated into the discussion of the findings, as shown in Figure 8.10 on pages 299–301, from Team Inertia's report. In this example, the section ends with a summary of recommendations. Figure 8.11 on page 302 shows the recommendations from the Blade Group's report, with suggestions for future testing. As this example shows, the recommendations section can be used to set priorities for improvements to be done now and those that can wait until later.

Appendices
Optional information, such as completed screening questionnaires, pre-test, post-task, and post-test questionnaires; data logs or observer sheets; milestone charts for planning and conducting the test; and any other information of potential use to some of the report's readers, belongs in an appendix or in multiple appendices. Figure 8.12 on pages 303–304 shows one of the appendices of Team Inertia's report, which is a weekly agenda used by the team, with the accompanying milestone chart. The heuristic evaluation of the Web site conducted by the Blade Group before usability testing is one of the appendices in its report (Figure 8.13 on pages 305–307).

The final report for the Hotmail usability test is included at the end of this chapter in Appendix 8.1.

Getting Feedback

Chauncey Wilson, a usability specialist, recommends getting feedback on your reports to evaluate them for usability. He suggests creating a template of the report format to verify that it will be useful to readers, and then asking them for feedback on the following aspects of the report (3):

- Is the report too long or too short?
- Is there enough detail for managers or developers to understand the problem?
- Do you want me to set priorities or is that the development team's responsibility?
- Do you want me to recommend solutions?
- How much detail do you want on the methods that I used?
- Does the inclusion of screen shots make it easier for the developers to understand the problem?
- Is the language clear and tactful?

(continued on page 307)

Problems and concerns of the test

For the present test, we assumed that the HTC Web environment and the BAITC information within it should do the following things in order to effectively serve the stated business objectives:

- Integrate seamlessly with the SPSU Web site as a whole, so that navigation between the site and the HTC web environment within it is as intuitive and trouble-free as possible.

- Educate the user about the field of technical communication, and specifically the field of international technical communication. This is an integral part of the process because these two fields are not as familiar to the prospective student as, for example, engineering or computer science would be. Should a student become interested in technical communication and international technical communication by using SPSU's Web site, we assume they would have a preference for SPSU's program among others since SPSU's Web site provided the "gatekeeper" information for them.

- Provide specific information about Southern Polytechnic State University itself, the Humanities and Technical Communication department there, and the BAITC degree offered therein. This is important, since the user who has been familiarized with the field of international technical communication would next seek information to help him or her decide whether the particular BAITC offered by SPSU is an appropriate choice.

- Provide specific administrative and/or procedural information. This is important, since the student who has decided to pursue studies within the HTC department of SPSU will next require information on applications, curriculum requirements, tuition, deadlines, and so on.

- In doing the above, serve as a complete and satisfactory alternative to printed material on the BAITC program and the HTC department. This is important for the university as a means of controlling the costs associated with mailing, postage, etc. Though not an explicitly stated business objective, we see any opportunity for reducing costs to be worth exploring.

Given the above, the principal problems or questions that we were concerned with evaluating by means of this test became the following:

1. Can users locate the HTC web environment, and the BAITC pages within it, in a reasonable amount of time, given the starting point of the SPSU homepage?

2. Can users find general information on the fields of technical communication and international technical communication (such as career prospects and typical skills) in a reasonable amount of time?

3. Can users retrieve information about SPSU's HTC department and BAITC degree program that would play an important role in their decision to apply (such as information on tuition, financial aid, housing, and admission deadlines) in a reasonable amount of time?

4. Can users retrieve and make use of critical information on the site, such as course requirements, the payment of tuition, and online applications? This includes the ability to bookmark and print information for later reference.

5. Do users find the information presented within the Web environment to be useful, intuitively presented, and aesthetically pleasing?

6. Is the BAITC and HTC Web environment an effective substitute for a paper-based catalog and application process?

Figure 8.6 Methodology section combined with background—Team Inertia *(continued)*
(Used with permission of Team Inertia: Anita Carpenter, Henri Dongieux, Cynthia Ravenna, Diane Rhone, Diana Samuels, and Lynn Smith.)

Summary data on test participants

As part of the usability test plan, we developed a narrow user profile that we assumed would represent the actual users of the HTC Web environment and the BAITC information within it. This was done with the knowledge that selecting an appropriate—and appropriately narrow—user profile is crucial to the success of a usability test. Five participants were chosen for the test, based on the knowledge that approximately 80% of all usability problems can be found using four to five test participants.

The "ideal user" for this test was a high-school student, comfortable with computers and the Internet, who was interested in writing and preferably studying a foreign language. A number of high-school students were given a screening questionnaire (see Appendix C: Questionnaires) in order to see if they matched the user profile; potential participants were required to match very closely in order to be selected for the test. (For a detailed breakdown of the user profile used in selecting test participants, see Appendix A: Usability test plan.)

The following table summarizes the data collected through a pre-evaluation questionnaire, which was given before the test to those participants who "passed" the screening questionnaire. This table includes data on the five participants whose data are analyzed in this report; information from the "walkthrough" participant were excluded from analysis.

	Participant 1 Rachel	Participant 2 Alia	Participant 3 Adrienne	Participant 4 Anthony	Participant 5 Steven
Date tested	3/21/00	4/3/00	4/4/00	4/15/00	4/18/00
Age	15	15	15	17	16
National origin	American	American	American	American	American
Web experience	Can use search and design her own sites	Quite comfortable using the Web	Quite comfortable using the Web	Very comfortable	Very comfortable
Typical Web content sought	School, entertainment, sites about books	Email, topics of interest	Pictures, games, school info, MP3s	Email, entertainment	Email, pictures, school info
Preferred Web browser	IE 5.0	IE 5.0	IE 5.0 and Netscape 4.7	Netscape 4.7	IE 5.0
Number of times per week "bookmark" feature used	5–10	7+	4–5	1	3
Number of times per week pages printed from the Web	2–3	1–2	5–6	0	6–10
Number of times per week search engine used	6–7	3	2–3	0	10+
Foreign language?	Spanish, 2 years	Spanish, 3 years	French, 2 years	None	Spanish, 2 years
Plans after high school	College, major unsure	College, major in science field	College, major in science or English	Unsure	College, major in science or graphic design

Table 1:   Summary of participants, data taken from pre-evaluation questionnaires

Figure 8.6   *(continued)*

Tasks and methods of the test

Having conformed sufficiently to the user profile, users were then asked to perform a range of tasks within the HTC Web environment, some of which were specific to the BAITC degree program. Data were recorded as participants worked within the Web environment, to be compiled and analyzed later. Analysis proceeded along methodological lines similar to a qualitative case study.

User tasks

The tasks that we asked test participants to perform included the following:

- Find the HTC homepage from the SPSU homepage

- Find some of the career options in International Technical Communication

- Find the contact person or persons for the HTC department and BAITC program

- Find the application deadline to SPSU for the summer semester of 2000

- Begin the online application process

- Find tuition and financial aid information

- Request an undergraduate catalog

Tasks were thematically organized into three scenarios, each of which addressed an increasing level of interest in the BAITC program. Scenario 1 was exploratory in nature, Scenario 2 involved finding departmental and BAITC-specific information, and Scenario 3 involved information and tasks necessary to apply to and pay for courses at SPSU.

Performance measures and subjective measures

In developing the usability test plan, we defined two kinds of measures—*performance measures* and *subjective measures*—by means of which to analyze the data gathered from the usability test. These kinds of measures allowed us to record both the actual performance of users within the HTC Web environment (purely quantitative data) as well as to capture their subjective opinions, perceptions, and frustrations (which could be either quantitative or qualitative, depending on the method by which the data were gathered).

Team Inertia counted the following (quantitative) performance measures by means of the records kept by the logger (see Appendix E: Log data):

- Number of participants able to complete each task within the allotted time

- Time taken to complete each task

- Number of general errors (cannot print, link, bookmark, and so on) for each task

Team Inertia also recorded the following qualitative subjective measures by means of the questionnaires administered by the briefer/debriefer (see Appendix F: Questionnaire data):

- What information was difficult to locate?

- What information was easy to locate?

- Was there enough information about the BAITC?

- Was anything confusing?

- How does the HTC Web environment compare to other sites?

- Other general comments from each section

Figure 8.6   Methodology section combined with background—Team Inertia *(continued)*

Team Inertia also recorded a quantitative subjective measure for each task that participants were asked to perform (see Appendix D: Scenarios). Participants were asked by the briefer/debriefer to rate the ease of each task with a number from 1 through 5, with 1 being "Very easy" and 5 being "Very difficult" (see Appendix F: Questionnaire Data).

Additional data and triangulation

As a supplement to the above measures, Team Inertia also recorded three additional kinds of data during testing:

- Participant comments, both verbal and nonverbal (such as groans and sighs).

- General observations made by members of the test team.

- An *issue list* compiled by the team from the log data. The issue list identifies each usability issue or problem encountered and the number of times it was encountered or "hit." (For the issue list, see Appendix E: Log data.)

Taking into consideration all of the types of observations—performance measures and subjective measures in conjunction with comments, observations, and the issue list—we were able to get a broad and multifaceted view of the usability issues and problems associated with the HTC Web environment and the BATIC information within it. The analysis and synthesis of such multiple types of data is known in the usability-testing field as *triangulation*. It is a way of "pulling it all together" to discover what the real usability issues and problems are.

Analyzing the scope and severity of usability problems

For each usability problem encountered, Team Inertia assigned a *scope* and a *severity*, based on the standard practices within the usability-testing field. Scope refers to the scale or distribution of the problem within the system, while severity refers to how serious the problem is.

The scope of a problem is either *local* or *global*. A local problem is one that affects only a particular user task or a specific area of the user interface (in this case, one or two related Web pages). A problem linking to the online application, for example, is a local problem. A global problem, in contrast, is one that affects multiple parts of the system. The lack of visual continuity between the HTC Web environment and the SPSU Web site is a global problem, because it manifests itself on every page of the HTC Web environment.

The severity of a problem is rated in four levels:

1. Level 1: The participants cannot complete the task

2. Level 2: The participants are delayed significantly in completing the task and are frustrated by the delay

3. Level 3: The participants complete the task with minor delay and frustration

4. Level 4: There is no significant impact on task performance, but participants indicate that they would like to see a change in the future

The categorization of problems by scope and severity helps the usability test team in its recommendations as to which usability problems are of the highest priority. It is often easier to fix local problems than global ones, but the prioritization of fixes is usually more dependent on severity than it is on scope. In terms of severity, Level 1 problems should be attended to first, while attention to Level 4 problems can be delayed until the next substantial revision of the HTC Web environment.

Figure 8.6

Findings, Explanations, and Recommendations

This section, being the crux of this report, describes in detail the findings of Team Inertia in the usability test of the HTC Web environment and BAITC program information. It includes both detailed and summarized recommendations, based on the findings, of changes to be implemented for the improvement of both usability and information quality.

This section is broken down into the following subsections:

- The concept of triangulation in usability analysis
- Charting performance measures
- Charting subjective measures
- Identifying usability problems
- Explaining usability problems, with detailed recommendations
- Summarizing the recommendations

The concept of triangulation in usability analysis

Triangulation is the preferred method of analysis in the usability testing field, as it allows the test team to focus narrowly on usability problems by taking advantage of the three different types of data collected: performance measures (numbers taken and "crunched" from the logs), subjective measures (numbers and comments taken from questionnaires and interviews), and the issue list (a chart of participant encounters with various usability problems). Performance and subjective measures are addressed in this section; for the issue list, see Appendix E: Log data.

Triangulation can be graphically represented in the following way:

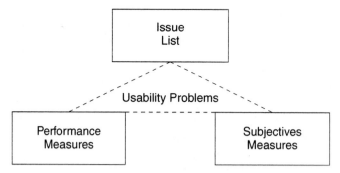

Figure 1. Triangulating usability problems.

Charting performance measures

Figure 2 shows the percentage of participants who successfully found information in the areas indicated.

Figure 8.7 Detailed findings from Team Inertia report *(continued)*

(Used with permission of Team Inertia: Anita Carpenter, Henri Dongieux, Cynthia Ravenna, Diane Rhone, Diana Samuels, and Lynn Smith.)

In the estimation of Team Inertia, those tasks with a 60% or lower success rate show that there is room for usability improvements in their respective areas. Of particular concern, given the data, is the low (40%) success rate for participants in finding what we consider to be critical pages within the HTC Web environment: the HTC homepage and the page at which a catalog may be requested. The success rate for finding information on foreign language requirements is also unacceptable, especially given the international emphasis of the BAITC degree.

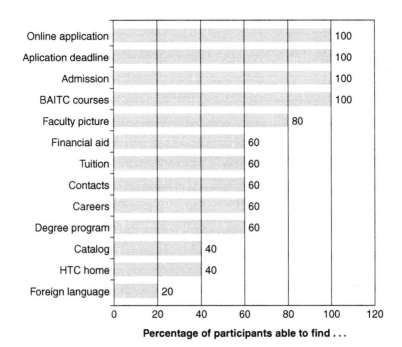

Figure 2. **Performance Measures:** The percentage of test participants able to find various information and pages within the HTC Web environment.

Charting subjective measures

Figure 3 shows the subjective impressions of test participants regarding the level of difficulty of the tasks indicated. By means of post-task questionnaires and interviews, we asked participants to rate the difficulty of each task on a scale from 1 to 5, with 1 being the easiest and 5 being the most difficult. The mean response for each question is charted.

Of particular concern, given the data, is the difficulty that participants perceived in requesting a catalog and finding information on tuition. Also of significant concern to Team Inertia is the level of difficulty participants perceived in finding information on foreign language requirements, the HTC's degree programs, the specific BAITC courses, and contacts. And lastly, the level of difficulty that participants attributed to finding the HTC homepage, from the starting point of the SPSU homepage, is something we consider serious and unacceptable.

Figure 8.7   *(continued)*

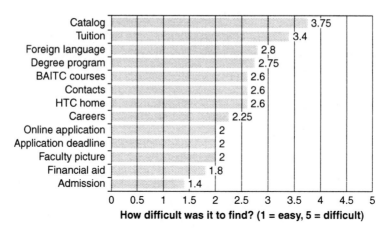

Figure 3. **Subjective measurements:** The level of difficulty attributed by participants to various tasks within the HTC Web environment.

Figure 4 shows the subjective impressions of test participants regarding the general navigability of the HTC Web environment. By means of a post-test questionnaire and interview, we asked participants to rate the level of difficulty of three navigational "checks" as well as to rate, for a second time, the difficulty of locating the HTC homepage from the starting point of the SPSU homepage. Again, the scale ranged from 1 to 5, with 1 being the easiest and 5 being the most difficult. The mean response for each question is charted.

The level of difficulty that participants attributed to the first two navigational checks—tracking and changing one's position within the HTC Web environment—is a matter of concern for Team Inertia. Also interesting is the drop in the perceived difficulty of locating the HTC homepage—in the post-test questionnaire, the average rating dropped from 2.6 (see Figure 3) to 2.0.

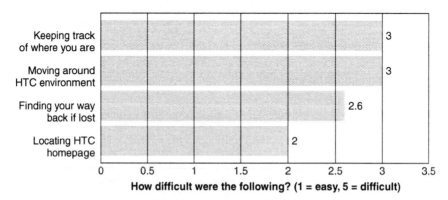

Figure 4. **Subjective measurements:** The level of difficulty attributed by participants to three navigational checks and one task within the HTC Web environment.

Figure 8.7   Detailed findings from Team Inertia report *(continued)*

Identifying usability problems

Having triangulated data from performance measures, subjective measures, and the issue list, we then identified 9 usability problems with the HTC Web environment and the BAITC program information within it. Of the 9 problems we identified, 4 are local and 5 are global.

Again, the severity of a usability problem is rated in 4 levels:

1. Level 1: The participants cannot complete the task

2. Level 2: The participants are delayed significantly in completing the task and are frustrated by the delay

3. Level 3: The participants complete the task with minor delay and frustration

4. Level 4: There is no significant impact on task performance, but participants indicate that they would like to see a change in the future

The following table presents problems 1–9 alongside their scope and severity. Local problems are presented first, followed by global problems. Within these two subsets, problems are listed in order of severity, from most severe (Level 1) to least severe (Level 4).

Problem #	Description of Problem	Scope	Severity
1	Contact and catalog information is difficult to find	Local	1
2	Tuition information is difficult to find	Local	1
3	The course/curriculum distinction is not clear	Local	2
4	There is a lack of BAITC-specific information	Local	4
5	System terminology is confusing to users	Global	1
6	Information should be presented in manageable chunks	Global	2
7	Visual continuity between the HTC Web environment and the SPSU Web site is poor	Global	3
8	The right frame should be more thoroughly hyperlinked	Global	3
9	Mouseovers should be more thoroughly implemented	Global	4

Table 2: Usability problems, scope, and severity.

Figure 8.7

Summary of Findings

This section presents a summary of the findings of Team Inertia's usability test of the HTC Web environment and the BAITC information within it. This summary section approaches the findings by presenting data gleaned from the test as direct answers to the test questions that we outlined in the usability test plan.

Question 1: Can the user locate the HTC web environment and the BAITC information within it in a reasonable amount of time, given the starting point of the SPSU homepage?

Locating the HTC homepage, given the starting point of the SPSU homepage, proved on the whole to be too difficult for participants. Only 40% of participants were able to locate the HTC homepage at all within the allotted time for the entire first scenario (whose three tasks were allotted approximately 10 minutes; see Appendix D for the full text of Scenario 1). For the two participants who managed to find the HTC homepage, average task time was approximately 2 minutes, or within the range that Team Inertia defined as a reasonable amount of time.

Question 2: Can the user find general information on the fields of technical communication and international technical communication (such as degree programs and career prospects) in a reasonable amount of time?

About half of participants found information on the fields of technical communication and international technical communication. There is room for improvement in this area. We observed that 60% of participants were able to find the degree program descriptions and another 60% of participants were able to find the career descriptions. Only 40% of participants, though, managed to find *both* the degree program *and* career descriptions. Of the 4 participants who were able to find at least one of the two Web pages that we had in mind, 3 found the page or pages within the 2 minutes that Team Inertia defined as a reasonable amount of time.

Question 3: Can the user retrieve information about SPSU's HTC department and BAITC degree program that would play an important role in their decision to apply (such as information on admission, tuition, and financial aid) in a reasonable amount of time?

Locating admission information proved to be reasonably easy: fully 100% of participants were able to find information on SPSU's freshman admission requirements and application deadlines, and all task times fell within the range that we defined as reasonable. Tuition information was far more difficult for participants to find, even with the benefit of the substantial improvements to the Web environment implemented by Team Inertia in both phases of the redesign (see Appendix H: Web redesign). Only one participant found tuition information in less than 9 minutes; we defined a reasonable amount of time for this task as 2 minutes. We observed that 60% of participants were able to find financial aid information, and the task times of those who were successful in finding this information all fell well within what we defined as a reasonable amount of time (1:30).

Question 4: Can the user retrieve and make use of critical information within the HTC Web environment and the SPSU Web site, such as course information, con-

Figure 8.8   Summary of findings from Team Inertia *(continued)*

(Used with permission of Team Inertia: Anita Carpenter, Henri Dongieux, Cynthia Ravenna, Diane Rhone, Diana Samuels, and Lynn Smith.)

tacts, and the online application? This includes the ability to bookmark and print information for reference later on.

Information on courses was reasonably easy to find, with 100% of participants finding the appropriate information and 80% of these finding it within what Team Inertia defined as a reasonable amount of time (2:30). Finding contact information for the HTC department and the BAITC program proved to be somewhat more difficult: only 60% of participants provided an acceptable contact name (either Dr. Herb Smith or Donna McPherson). Those who did provide the correct contact information did so within what Team Inertia defined as a reasonable amount of time (1 minute). Finding the online application proved to be reasonably easy, but the process still has room for improvement: though all participants (100%) were able to find and initiate the online application process, only 60% of these did so within the 2:30 that we defined as a reasonable amount of time.

Question 5: Do users find the information presented within the HTC Web environment to be useful, intuitively presented, and aesthetically pleasing?

The HTC Web environment has several design qualities that participants liked, but there is still a need for substantial improvement in aesthetics and the organization of the information presented. Participants liked the information presented in mouseovers and the fact that there were a number of link options (both on the navigational bar and in the text itself) between pages. The same participants, though, complained that there was too much information in the site. Participant 1, Rachel, remarked that the Web environment was easy to navigate but the information wasn't what she was looking for. Several participants became mired in the "Writing Corner" pages and were unable to understand exactly how these pages fit into the overall scheme of the HTC department and Web environment. Lastly, several participants found the HTC flame logo—or as Steven (Participant 5) called it, "that big thing"—to be either confusing, in bad taste, or both.

Question 6: Is the HTC Web environment an effective substitute for a paper-based catalog and application process?

During the course of the test, Team Inertia's position on this question changed. We realized that a Web-based product such as the HTC Web environment and a paper-based product such as the Undergraduate Catalog should be seen as complementary to one another. We came to understand that the Web and print media each have distinct strengths and weaknesses, related to their modes of presentation and interaction, and they therefore cannot be compared in this simple and reductionist manner. A more appropriate question, which presented itself during the usability testing process, is the following:

Can the user make the transition from the HTC Web environment to a paper-based means of communicating with SPSU administration with reasonable ease?

We observed that only 2 participants (40%) were able to find the Web page through which an undergraduate catalog can be requested. One of these took nearly 9 minutes to find the appropriate page. The other participant found it very quickly (9 seconds), but this quick performance is probably attributable to both phases of the Web redesign implemented by Team Inertia, which made the task of requesting a catalog obvious in the extreme (see Appendix H: Web redesign). A number of participants did not recognize that the Web page featuring the first-level heading "Request more information" was, in fact, the page at which to request a catalog.

Figure 8.8

Favorable Findings

#1	Users indicated their level of knowledge regarding the Master's Program in Technical Communication was greatly increased after completing the usability testing.
User Comments	• "By viewing several different pages, the information became easier to find."
	• "Spending time in the site can really assist the user in finding relevant information."'
Test Results	The average user rating increased from 1.4 to 4.2 when users rated their knowledge of the TCOM Master's Program (before the testing versus after completing the testing).
#2	Users commented on the thoroughness of the information contained on the Humanities and Technical Communication Web page.
User Comments	• "Video is pretty hot . . . graphic design . . . Web page authoring . . . a lot of people are getting Web pages so that's good."
	• "This is a good page (list of courses) that tells prospective students what is offered in the program. I'm sure there are plenty more."
	• "The part about studies is good."
Test Results	• The average user rating increased from 1.4 to 4.2 when users rated their knowledge of the TCOM Master's Program.

Global Findings

Navigation	Users found requested information through a trial-and-error approach. Users did not see an obvious path to find specified information within the Humanities and Technical Communication (HTC) site.
Severity	Level 1
Cause(s)	• Overall Web site organization of prospective student, current student and peers and professionals did not provide a clear division for the target audience. The site is organized by the department's hierarchy of information and not by the user's need to find information.
	• There is no search function within the HTC Web pages.
	• There is no site map for user's reference.
	• Link buttons and terms were abbreviated and may not have been clear or understood by all users.
User Comments	• "I'm just clicking, hoping to stumble on some information."
	• "I'll try to find where I was before . . . I experience most of my success by surfing, clicking around trying to find information."
	• "I'm going to look at the front page again to make sure I didn't miss anything (pause) well, I don't seem to see anything."

Figure 8.9   Detailed findings from Blade Group report *(continued)*

(Used with permission of the Blade Group: Betty Owen, Loretta Joslin, Ardenna Morton, Diana Mason, and Elizabeth Wong Mark.)

Global Findings, continued

User Comments
- "Perhaps the graduate program needs to be clearly marked."
- "I just noticed the links (frame navigation buttons) on the left." (User has nearly completed the first two scenarios.)

Test Results
- 6 out of 25 (24%) of all answers to the scenarios rendered incomplete or incorrect information from the users.
- 2 of the 5 scenarios (40%) of the activities took more than 7.2 minutes to locate the information.
- At least one straight path was not obvious in some of the scenarios, and for all the scenarios, the users took a long time to find the information.

Short-Term Remedy
- Add an index or site map.
- Expand the link descriptions, include more relevant links in the middle of and at the bottom of pages.

Long-Term Remedy
- Separate and clearly distinguish graduate and undergraduate information.
- Use parallel hierarchy for both graduate and undergraduate page organization.
- Add a search function.

Local Findings

Navigation
Users had trouble finding the total number of hours required to complete the program on the Master of Science program page and the required courses.

Severity
Level 3

Cause(s)
- Users tended to scan the pages and overlook information in the process.
- Some pages are text-heavy and require users to scroll through several screens, increasing the chance that important information may be overlooked.
- There is no explanation or way to draw users to the link to the Tracks of Study.

User Comments
- "I'm going to try programs . . . (clicks on the MSTPC link) it talks about different plans again. Not immediately apparent what the three courses are."
- "Hours seem to depend on the options (A, B, or C) . . . no, I take that back."
- (User furrows eyebrows) "I'm seeing some information but I don't see the required hours."
- "I just noticed the pop-ups (mouseovers)."

Figure 8.9   *(continued)*

Test Results	• None of the users found the Tracks of Study, identifying the professional, graphics, and technical options.
	• 2 out of 5 (40%) could not determine how many hours were required to complete the program.
Short-Term Remedy	• Arrange text so it is easier to read. Use more headings, bulleted lists, and hypertext links.
	• Make mouseovers permanent to direct users more quickly.
	• Add more prominent links to Tracks of Study.
Long-Term Remedy	• Separate and clearly distinguish graduate and undergraduate information.
	• Use parallel hierarchy for both graduate and undergraduate page organization.
	• Add a search function.
Feedback	Users selected links to the Writing Program, Virtual Tool Museum, and Electronic Gallery, although these pages did not relate to the scenarios. Users expressed uncertainty about what they would find on these pages.
Severity	Level 2
Cause(s)	• Links to the Writing Program, Virtual Tool Museum, and Electronic Gallery contain minimal information about corresponding pages.
User Comments	• ". . . let me try the Electronic Gallery . . . and another screen comes up that doesn't look like where I should be."
	• Clicks on Virtual Tool Museum, hits back button.
Test Results	• 2 out of 5 (40%) selected the Electronic Gallery or Virtual Tool Museum when searching for information requested in a scenario, although these pages did not relate to the scenarios.
Short-Term Remedy	• Add introductory pages for the Writing Program, Electronic Gallery, and Virtual Tool Museum, explaining each section's purpose.
	• Make links to the Writing Program, Electronic Gallery, and Virtual Tool Museum more specific to each section's purpose.
Long-Term Remedy	• Reconsider the location of the links to the Writing Program, Electronic Gallery, and Virtual Tool Museum on the Humanities and Technical Communication page.

Figure 8.9   Detailed findings from Blade Group report

Explaining usability problems, with detailed recommendations

The following subsection enumerates usability problems 1–9, explains their emergence in terms of the three kinds of data collected, and provides 14 detailed recommendations for the improvement of both the HTC Web environment and the SPSU Web site.

Problem 1: Contact and catalog information is difficult to find

The problems of finding contact and catalog information are combined into a single problem because they both reflect the trouble participants had in attempting to establish contact with either SPSU or the HTC department beyond the confines of the Web interface.

Only 60% of participants managed to find the name and email address of either Dr. Herb Smith or Donna McPherson in response to the task which requested the name of a contact person for BAITC information, and only 40% found Dr. Herb Smith, the technically correct contact name. Since the Web environment does not include a great deal of BAITC-specific information (see Problem 4 below), providing the user with a means of getting more information is crucial. If a potential BAITC applicant cannot get more information through establishing contact, there is a risk that their interest in the BAITC program will drop off.

Only 40% of participants succeeded in requesting a catalog. Participant 1, Rachel, required a task time of 8:54 in order to locate the appropriate page. After Team Inertia's Web redesign made the catalog-request page extremely obvious, Participant 4, Anthony, located the page in only 40 seconds (see Appendix H: Web redesign). Participant 5, Steven, actually landed the browser on the appropriate page but never figured out that it was the correct page: the first-level heading on the page reads "Request More Information," and it is only by reading a paragraph of text (which Steven did not read) that the user finds out that this is the catalog-request page. Participant 3, Adrienne, strayed so far off course as to look in SPSU's Library pages for catalog information.

Again, if a potential applicant cannot "feed" their interest with more information on SPSU, this interest may well drop off.

Team Inertia therefore recommends:

1. Contact information should be made more prominent, and the distinction between Dr. Herb Smith (contact for BAITC) and Donna McPherson (contact for MSTPC) should be drawn more sharply. Designers might consider making a green button in the left navigational frame that reads "Contacts," which would lead the user to a dedicated contacts page.

2. The "Request More Information" page should be more specifically oriented. Designers might consider using radio buttons or check-boxes so that the user can request either the undergraduate or graduate catalogs, an application, a financial aid prospectus, or all of the above. Alternatively, a dedicated and unambiguous page entitled "Request A Catalog" could be created and linked to from a number of pages.

Problem 2: Tuition information is difficult to find

Only 60% of participants, or 3 out of 5, managed to find, within the time available, the cost of tuition for a resident full-time undergraduate student at SPSU. Of these 3 participants, 2

Figure 8.10 Findings and recommendations combined in Team Inertia report *(continued)*

(Used with permission of Team Inertia: Anita Carpenter, Henri Dongieux, Cynthia Ravenna, Diane Rhone, Diana Samuels, and Lynn Smith.)

took an excessively long time (9:51 and 13:00) to find the information. After a substantial Web redesign, Participant 4, Anthony, located the information in only 50 seconds (see Appendix H: Web redesign). On a scale of 1–5, participants ranked the difficulty of finding tuition information at an average of 3.4, which was the second-highest ranking given to any task. We observed that those participants who did find the correct page were slowed down in their search for tuition information by having to scroll horizontally (that is, the page is too wide for the frame).

As university students ourselves, we can attest that financial information, such as the cost of tuition, is one of the most influential variables in a decision to attend a particular university.

Team Inertia therefore recommends:

3. Tuition information should be easy to find from a variety of different places within both the HTC Web environment and the SPSU Web site. Having reached the page within which the tuition information is presented, users should not have to scroll horizontally.

Problem 3: The course/curriculum distinction is not clear

All test participants were able to "find the undergraduate courses associated with the BAITC degree," as the task was listed in Scenario 1 (see Appendix D: Scenarios). The high success rate of participants for this task, though, is attributable to the fact that we accepted both the undergraduate course descriptions in TCOM *or* the BAITC curriculum pages as the correct page. Therefore, despite the high success rate of participants and the medium-to-easy difficulty rating that they gave this task (2.25), we observed that there was substantial confusion between courses and curriculum. For example, Participant 3, Adrienne, never found the foreign language requirements because she assumed that this information could be found within the TCOM course descriptions.

Knowing which undergraduate courses are offered in a particular department is quite a different thing from knowing all of the courses one is required to take, throughout the entire university, in order to meet the requirements for a specific degree. According to our observations, participants did not adequately understand that courses in technical communication were only part of the requirements.

Team Inertia therefore recommends:

4. The distinction between course descriptions and the curriculum outline should be made more prominent. The BAITC curriculum page should be made more accessible, with each course number and title being linked to its respective description. It should be made clear to users that the BAITC degree involves courses other than those taught in the HTC department.

Problem 4: There is a lack of BAITC-specific information

The distinctions made within the HTC Web environment between the BAITC, the BS, and the MSTPC degrees are not strong enough. Before the Web redesign we implemented, there was no information on the site about the field of international technical communication—what is unique about the field, what it involves, what the career prospects in the field are, and perhaps most importantly, why it is such an exciting field. Participant 3, Adrienne, never understood the differences between the BAITC and BS, and she was unable to find any BAITC-specific information throughout her evaluation (see issue list in Appendix E: Log data).

Given the newness of the fields of technical communication and (especially) interna-

Figure 8.10   Findings and recommendations combined in Team Inertia report *(continued)*

tional technical communication, Team Inertia contends that it is imperative that the HTC Web environment provide background information about these fields. Given SPSU's small size and its limited offerings in foreign language courses, a point needs to be made *very strongly* regarding why SPSU and the HTC department are qualified to offer such a multidisciplinary and cutting-edge degree as the BAITC.

Team Inertia therefore recommends:

5. More information should be given on the field of international technical communication and the BAITC degree. The strengths and unique qualifications of faculty members, especially their international experience, should be emphasized.

6. More generally, a stronger distinction should be made between all three degrees (BAITC, BS, and MSTPC). A start to this would be to offer, at the top of the "Admissions" page, a choice between descriptions of the undergraduate and graduate programs—rather than defaulting to the graduate program description (see Appendix H: Web redesign).

Summarizing the recommendations

In order to ameliorate the most pressing usability problems with the BAITC program information, the HTC Web environment, and the SPSU Web site, Team Inertia recommends that designers and developers implement the following changes:

1. Make contact information more prominent

2. Make the process of requesting a catalog clearer and easier

3. Present information on tuition clearly and prominently

4. Draw a clear distinction between courses and curriculum

5. Include more BAITC-specific information

6. Draw clearer distinctions between the three degrees offered in the HTC department

7. Moderate the use of system terms and define/explain them when necessary

8. Consider creating a separate Web environment for potential TCOM majors who happen to be high-school students

9. Refine information into smaller and more manageable chunks

10. Offer traditional paper information via PDF downloads

11. Integrate the HTC Web environment and SPSU Web site visually

12. Consider a total redesign of the SPSU Web site as a whole

13. Provide dense links for pages in the main frame, as an alternative to the left navigational bar

14. Increase the use of mouseovers and other dynamic elements that minimize errors

Figure 8.10

Recommendations

The BLADE Group provides a short-term and a long-term remedy for each finding. The following is a compiled list, which groups the findings into a few categories.

Short-Term Recommendations

- Add an index or site map.
- Add an introduction page to the Writing Program, Electronic Gallery, and Virtual Tool Museum.
- Make the mouseover information permanent.
- Emphasize visual design by adding white space, tables, bulleted lists, and boldface for important terms and headings.

Long-Term Recommendations

- Organize the information by undergraduate and graduate information.
- Add links to relevant administrative information.
- Add a search function.

Suggested Future Testing

The BLADE Group recommends that continued usability testing be done on this Web site to assure it is consistent, predictable, and organized in the users' language and by users' tasks.

Figure 8.11   Recommendations from Blade Group report

(Used with permission of the Blade Group: Betty Owen, Loretta Joslin, Ardenna Morton, Diana Mason, and Elizabeth Wong Mark.)

FEBRUARY

Tues, February 8:	Complete team formation, review schedule and responsibilities
	Discuss preliminary findings of heuristic evaluation

	Assignment:	Compile and circulate findings of heuristic evaluation (2/15)

Tues, February 15:	Identify test goals and objectives
	Finalize user profile
	Identify which aspects of the site we want to test
	Decide on 3–4 test scenarios
	Identify measures

	Assignment:	Write/edit test plan for submission (2/21)
		Develop screening questionnaire (2/22)

Tues, February 29:	Review additional information on BAITC
	Discuss changes needed to the Web site
	Final review screening questionnaire
	Review status of participant gathering
	Identify "tolerant" user
	Try out lab equipment

	Assignment:	Confirm "tolerant" user (3/7)
		Find, screen and schedule participants (3/11)
		Make preliminary changes to Web site (3/7)
		Develop scripts for briefer/debriefer (3/7)
		Develop test questionnaires (3/7)

MARCH

Mon, March 7:	Walkthrough with tolerant user
	Assignment: Make any changes necessary (3/13)

Mon, March 13:	Pilot test
	Assignment: Document, as appropriate, findings of pilot test
	Make changes to Web site (4/3)
	Make changes to scenarios, etc. (4/3)

Tues, March 21:	Spring break (or catch-up, if needed)

Tues, March 28:	Final project planning (as needed)
	Assignments: Confirm schedule with participants (3/31)

APRIL

Mon, April 3:	First evaluation
	Assignment: Compile findings (4/4)

Tues, April 4:	Second evaluation
	Assignment: Compile findings (4/10)
	Make changes to Web site (4/10)

Mon, April 10:	Third evaluation
	Assignment: Compile findings (4/11)

Tues, April 11:	Fourth evaluation
	Assignment: Compile findings (4/18)

Tues, April 18:	Finalize findings
	Identify portions of video for highlights
	Assignments: Prepare draft written report (4/25)
	Prepare draft oral report (4/25)
	Edit videotape (5/1)

Tues, April 25:	Review reports
	Assignment: Make changes to reports based on team review (5/1)

Figure 8.12 Appendix of weekly agenda from Team Inertia report *(continued)*

(Used with permission of Team Inertia: Anita Carpenter, Henri Dongieux, Cynthia Ravenna, Diane Rhone, Diana Samuels, and Lynn Smith.)

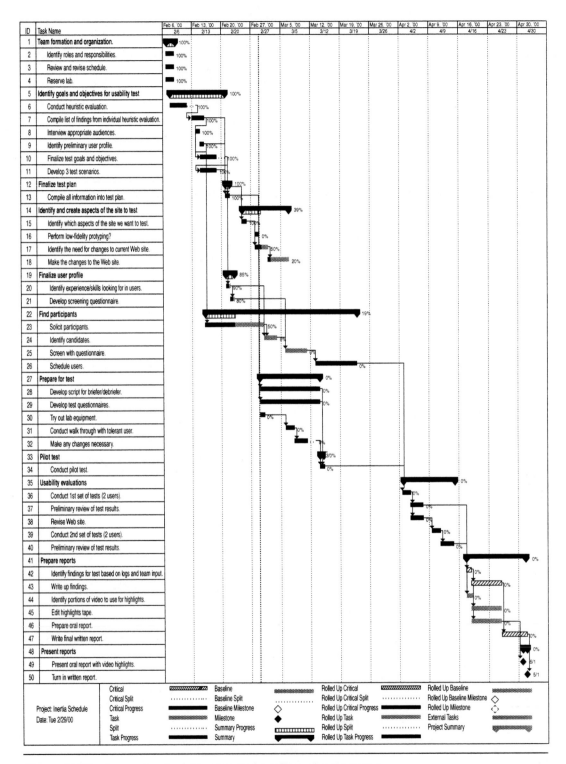

Figure 8.12 Appendix of weekly agenda from Team Inertia report

Heuristic Evaluation of the Humanities and Technical Communication Department's Web Pages

Based on Jakob Nielsen's 10 usability heuristics, each team member conducted a heuristic evaluation of Southern Polytechnic State University's (SPSU) Humanities and Technical Communication (HTC) Web pages.

As an aside, this evaluation is not intended to address other departmental pages. However, the colors and design on these pages vary by department and are not consistent with the top-level SPSU pages. Consistency among the departments would give the university a cohesive, coordinated appearance.

We reviewed our heuristic evaluations and used it as a basis for developing our test plan. A comprehensive summary of issues identified by our heuristic evaluations follows.

Visibility of System Status

- Unanimous agreement regarding the Writing Program link: based on the program's primary audience being undergraduates, this link should be moved to a section that undergraduates, not graduates, would be more likely to view—perhaps as an option within the undergraduate course options. As our target user is the prospective graduate school candidate, the Writing Program will not be included in the following heuristic evaluation.

- Site navigation could be clarified with a site map, more links including "home" to prevent the user from having to rely on the "back" button.

- Add a search function by key word.

- In the first level after the homepage, frame buttons offer navigation but the same button words as listed in the main frame are not links; this appears problematic.

- The user needs visual feedback as to where one is on the site (selected link is a different color).

- Section titles were clear. Titles matched links for the most part, although some links were a little vague, like "Guidelines," "Procedures," and "TCOM." With regard to the TCOM navigation link, all the HTC Web pages are about (humanities and) technical communication. We suggest renaming the navigation link Program Overview, Degrees, or simply Overview to fit.

Match Between System and Real World

- All headers should spell out TCOM and MSTPC. A user may jump into the middle of the Web page rather than start from the beginning and follow the links to TCOM.

- Clarify where the navigation links go. Specify on the homepage, at least, for Prospects, Current, Peers; there should be details, subcategories, or explanations of what's in the frame choices—not just as a mouseover.

- Graduate admissions information does not include costs or the deadline for application. However, the undergraduate section includes deadlines. Graduation requirements should be set off as a separate link. Add related navigation links to HTC home, program description, and graduate course catalog.

Figure 8.13 Appendix of heuristic evaluation from Blade Group report *(continued)*

(Used with permission of the Blade Group: Betty Owen, Loretta Joslin, Ardenna Morton, Diana Mason, and Elizabeth Wong Mark.)

- The terminology "tracks" is not self-explanatory. Suggest changing it to "areas of concentration."
- "SRS"—Savannah River Site—is not defined anywhere. Too many unfamiliar terms in the site have the potential of alienating the user.
- On the schedule page, information like CRN# does not need to be listed first. It is not the most important information and makes for a more muddled table.

User Control and Freedom

- Add site map to HTC homepage.
- To offer the user more control, make navigational links of each word in the unordered list that repeats in the link button frame.
- Add navigational options so the user does not rely on the back button.
- Add more internal links to the course description page to take users back to the top.
- If a user goes to the HTC homepage and bypasses the SPSU links, the user does not know that this department is part of Southern Polytechnic nor can the user go to SPSU's homepage, other departments, or other information such as fees and registration.

Consistency and Standards

- Site identification is really important, as is the repetition of frames (and how the frames look), colors, and fonts. Why aren't frames used on the HTC homepage?
- Make Peers and Professionals consistent with the others. The faculty bios do not have a link back to HTC.

Error Prevention

- No major errors detected. However a link to a page that is under construction may give the user an impression of an error or lack of preparedness.

Recognition Rather Than Recall

- Some of the pages could use more identification in the title or header. The buttons in the frame section should indicate where the user is. The subpages of a topic need to show the topic.
- The alt tags or dialog boxes that display only when the user places the cursor over a certain portion of the screen can be confusing.
- Using frames for navigation may not be intuitive for some users. Printing with frames may also be an issue.

Flexibility and Efficiency of Use

- While the pages tested are not set up with accelerators to speed up interaction for the expert user, given the frames navigation, the HTC pages may likely confuse the early-stage Internet novice.

Figure 8.13 Appendix of heuristic evaluation from Blade Group report *(continued)*

- Add links to the basic information on SPSU pages like fees, calendars, dates, online registration, etc.

Aesthetic and Minimalist Design

- HTC pages are branded with flame logo and "HTC" but the pages lose a connection to SPSU. In relation to other information on the page, the flame is overpowering. SPSU was only mentioned at the bottom of pages as a link back to the SPSU homepage, and the link was SMALL. Add the name and location of the school on every page. If students are looking at a lot of different schools, it might be easy to confuse one with another if pages are not marked. It would also be helpful to list the full department name, phone number, and email somewhere on each page—it doesn't have to be big—it's just nice to have access to that information.

- The color and font changes make the pages appear inconsistent.

- There could be more white space in some sections with extensive information. These portions could be divided up with progressive levels of detail. The more general information could be on the top levels and, as the user drills down, more details could be included.

Help Users Recognize, Diagnose, and Recover From Errors

- Additional navigation links and a TCOM home button in the Writing Program section would be a great service to users who browse in that section.

Help and Documentation

- Adding a search function (at least on the major heading pages) or index would be helpful.

- Including technical communication professional resources and other Web sites, perhaps as a link from the career options, would enhance professionalism and credibility.

Figure 8.13

Previewing the Report

Because this type of formal report can be lengthy, especially when it serves the dual purpose of communicating the results of testing and documenting all aspects of the testing process, some companies send out a quick, short report right away as a preview for the longer report to come. One company calls this quick report the *roadrunner report*, which, to be effective, needs to conform to the following guidelines (Harrison and Melton 15):

- Catch readers' attention with a catchy name and graphics (they use the roadrunner graphic).
- Keep it brief, generally one page.
- Include charts and graphics.
- Speak the readers' language.
- Include user comments.
- Include pats on the back (positive feedback).
- Tie the results to the original usability goals.
- Emphasize the need to read the final report for full results.
- Include a short summary/implications section.

Template for Common Industry Format

Title Page

Names the product and version tested, who led the test, when the test was conducted, the date the report was prepared, who prepared the report, and contact information for additional inquiries.

Executive Summary

Provides information for procurement decision makers; meant to be a stand-alone document. Includes the description of the product; summary of methods of testing, including the number and type of participants and their tasks; results expressed as mean scores or other measures of "central tendency"; the nature of the test; and a tabular summary of performance results.

Introduction

Divided into two parts:

Full product description. Identifies the product name and release or version and the parts evaluated. Identifies the user population and any special needs groups, describes the environment in which the product should be used, and the type of work supported by the product.

Test objectives. Describes the objectives and any special areas of interest. Includes testing performance of tasks and subjective satisfaction.

Method

This is the first key technical section. It must provide enough information to allow an independent tester to replicate the testing procedure. It includes the following information:

Participants. Provides detailed demographic, professional, and computing experience of participants.

Context of product use in test. Describes the tasks, scenarios, and conditions under which testing was performed.

Experimental design. Describes the measures used for gathering data. Includes a description of the procedure, participant general instructions, and task instructions.

• *Procedure*: provides all aspects of conducting the test, from greeting participants to the use of non-disclosure agreements, warm-ups, pre-task training and debriefing. Describes the steps the team used to

---

The Common Industry Format

A standardized format for reporting the results of usability testing, called the *Common Industry Format* (CIF), is being tested for use by companies interested in evaluating the usability of software products being considered for purchase. It is not intended for use in formative evaluation, but rather for summative evaluations of products to reflect data on performance measures of the product. The intended audience for the report is purchasing agents to assist them in buying decisions, as well as usability professionals within the purchasers' organization to allow them to replicate the results of product testing to see how the product works for their own employees.

conduct the test sessions and record data; specifies how many people interacted with the participants; describes team roles and location of team members during the test; states whether participants were paid.

- *Participant general instructions:* all materials used with participants, included here or in an appendix; describes how participants were to interact with other people present and how to ask for assistance.

- *Participant task instructions:* summarizes the task instructions; places scenarios in appendix.

Usability metrics. Explains what measures were used for each category of usability metrics: effectiveness, efficiency, and satisfaction.

- *Effectiveness:* common measures include percent task completion, frequency of errors, frequency of assists and of access to help or documentation.

- *Efficiency:* the most common measure is related to time on task and completion rate.

- *Satisfaction:* measures user's satisfaction with the product, using a Likert or similar scale.

Results

This is the second major technical section of the report. Includes a description of how the data were scored, reduced, and analyzed. Provides the major findings in quantitative formats.

Data analysis. Should be presented in the following ways:

- *Data scoring:* the method of data scoring, including the exclusion of outliers, categorization of error data, and criteria for scoring assisted or unassisted completion.

- *Data reduction:* the method by which data were reduced, including how data were collapsed across tasks or task categories.

- *Statistical analysis:* the method by which data were analyzed, including statistical procedures. Scores reported as means must include standard deviation and standard error of the mean.

Presentation of results. Reports the Effectiveness, Efficiency, and Satisfaction results. Both tabular and graphical presentations should be included.

Appendices

Include questionnaires, participant instructions, scenarios, plus any updated information about the product release since the product was tested.

Source: Version 1.1, October 28, 1999. Available at National Institute of Standards and Technology Web site. Version 2.02, June 15, 2001, is now also released. Both versions are available at <http://www.nist.gov/iusr/documents/CIF.html>.

The effort to produce the CIF is being financed and facilitated by the National Institute of Standards and Technology at the urging of large companies like State Farm, Boeing, Fidelity Investments, and Eastman Kodak (Orenstein).

See the sidebar above for an overview of the CIF template.

Although the written report of the findings from a usability test is certainly an essential method for communicating the results and maintaining a history of the events for future reference, other methods can also be used to communicate results and advocate future usability testing. One common method is to present the results orally, either informally or formally. We take up this subject in the next section.

Preparing an Oral Report

It is standard practice in many organizations to prepare an oral report, in addition to preparing a written report of the results of your work. Frequently, the audience for an oral report is larger than that for the written report. Even for those who may be on the distribution list for the written report, the oral report may be your only real opportunity to communicate the results of your testing, as some may not read the written report. As well, the oral report gives you the opportunity to advocate more usability testing as part of user-centered design. The oral report can be formal or informal. It can be scheduled as part of a meeting, or even the main event. Or it can be a special presentation to an invited group of managers and other interested attendees. Regardless of the degree of formality or informality, the presentation should be planned, prepared, and rehearsed to assure that the opportunity is not wasted and that the team appears knowledgeable and professional. Of course, if you have not had experience in giving an oral report before, you should consult one of the many books on strategies for planning, preparing, and delivering an effective oral presentation. A good place to start would be Gurak's *Oral Presentations for Technical Communication* (2000).

What we offer here is an overview of how to organize the information you will want to present in your oral report, including the option of showing a video-highlights tape. If you have been working as a team, the entire team may want to participate in the presentation of the results, or you may decide that you want a subgroup to do the oral presentation, while another subgroup does the written report or the video-highlights tape. If you're using all three reporting mechanisms, then you will most likely have planned these activities as part of your overall planning for the test. Each one takes time and a special set of talents. Naturally, the best writers and editors on the team should take the lead on the written report, while the best speakers should take the lead on the oral report. For the oral report, you will want to plan the organization, the delivery (and timing), and the visual aids you will use, as well as the way in which you will incorporate a video-highlights tape, if your team is preparing one. Later in the chapter we discuss the preparation of such a highlights tape.

Organizing Your Presentation

Every presentation needs a beginning, a middle, and an end. Effective presenters make clear to the audience the structure of the organization and the plan for presenting the information in the beginning. They remind the audience of where they are as they move through the presentation, using transitions, forecasting statements (to project the organization of information to come), and internal summaries (to brief the audience on where they have been). They conclude the presentation with a sense of finality, while also restating the objective and summarizing the points covered. Then they ask for questions, unless they have let the audience know that they want to entertain questions during the presentation. The sidebar entitled "Guidelines for Oral Reports" provides a checklist you can use when planning and giving your presentation.

Guidelines for Oral Reports

Introduction	Effectively captures the interest and attention of the audience Gives the necessary background to understand the subject Clearly states the purpose of the talk Clearly states the order of the points of discussion
Organization	Recognizable through the use of: • sufficient introductory information • transitions from one point to the next and between points • appropriate use of summary statements Distinguishes main ideas from one another Leads naturally to the conclusion
Content	Presents adequate data to support generalizations Relates well to the subject and purpose of the report
Conclusion	Gives a sense of finality to the report through one of the following: • Conclusion reached • Problem solved • Results obtained • Value of the findings for the audience • Recommendations offered • Summary of the main points covered and their importance
Visual Aids	Present information in a clear, simple style that can be seen by all Support key points and facts and figures Enhance the presentation
Question Period	Speaker(s) effectively handle questions by: • Showing respect for the question • Giving evidence of intelligent listening • Giving brief, but complete, answers
Delivery	Good body language Good eye contact Enthusiasm and confidence Adequate voice projection Evidence of practice with notes Avoidance of distracting mannerisms Avoidance of distracting expressions like: • You know • OK • All right

If you are doing a team presentation, you will want to begin by introducing all the members of your team, not just the ones making the presentation. Also, if there are members of your audience who are not familiar with usability testing, you will want to provide an overview of the process and the approach you used. Certainly, you will want to explain the goals and objectives for the test and the areas you tested. As well, information about your users and the tasks they were asked to perform will be useful. With this essential information, the audience will have the right context to understand your findings, which will make up the bulk of your presentation.

You will also want to support your findings with visual aids, which we discuss next.

Preparing Visual Support

Visual support for your presentation can be of several types:

- Slides, overhead transparencies, or a PowerPoint presentation using projection equipment
- Handouts—summary of findings or handout of PowerPoint slides
- Video-highlights tape

The choice of slides, overhead transparencies, or a PowerPoint presentation will be dependent on several factors:

- Formality or informality of the speaking situation
- Availability of the equipment
- Conditions of the room in which the presentation will take place

For instance, if you are making the presentation at a meeting in a conference room to a small number of people, you might want to use a handout created from PowerPoint slides, rather than setting up an LCD projector and laptop computer. However, if the setting is more formal and the group larger, you will want to use the highest level of quality possible. PowerPoint presentations via computer and LCD projector are becoming increasingly common, almost the norm, in many organizations, as the projection equipment becomes smaller and more portable and laptop computers are ubiquitous. Within a PowerPoint presentation, you can insert clips or stills of participants from the videotapes to add multimedia technology to the presentation. If your team has these capabilities, you should use whatever tool will create the strongest impact on your audience. We will say more about multimedia reports later in the chapter. Lower-level technology using overhead transparencies can still be used effectively in presentations, and these can be created via PowerPoint or other presentation software to give them a consistent and professional appearance.

If your team has created a video-highlights tape, you will want to incorporate this into your presentation. There are two ways to create a highlights tape to incorporate into your presentation:

- Prepare a tape with representative clips that are spliced together with some blank tape in between each one. The presenter sets up each clip by telling the audience what they will see and the usability issue being presented. As each clip ends, the presenter puts the tape player on pause and explains what the audience will see on the next clip. Or the presenter stops the tape and returns to it later in the presentation to set up and show another example.

- Prepare a tape with an audio track that explains the clips and their implications. The presenter explains what the audience will hear and see on the videotape and then the tape can run without interaction from the presenter.

In the next section, we talk about how to prepare a video-highlights tape.

Preparing a Video-Highlights Tape

As we've said before, when it comes to usability testing, "Seeing is believing." For those who could not observe the test, the video-highlights tape does for the audience what a football-highlights tape does for sports fans who missed the game. It creates a sense of being there by focusing on the key events. In the football-highlights tape, the announcer tells what happened in each play. Likewise, the best usability highlights tape is one that includes the "announcer's" descriptions to set up each play (finding) of significance. This requires some video production expertise on the part of at least one member of the team or the willingness of a team member to learn how to use a tape-editing tool to create the highlights tape. Although equipment varies and it is beyond the scope of this book to provide a detailed explanation of the video-editing process, the basics are fairly simple and similar across different analog-editing systems. They are these:

1. You will need a source tape and destination tape (and two tape decks).
2. From the source tape, you select the place where you want to start a clip. This information could come from your log, which is easy to find if your logging software has a time stamp function. If not, the team may have indicated start and stop times for tasks or scenarios to help you locate the place on the tape where you want to copy a segment.
3. The place to start a clip (mark in) and the place to stop a clip (mark out) need to be determined.
4. Once you have located the exact start and stop points (using the "jog" dial on the tape editor), you will record this segment, pressing the "assemble editing" button.
5. This clip is now "assembled" onto the destination tape.
6. You can set up an audio track in front of each assembled clip by laying down the audio track first or allowing sufficient space for it, followed by the clip, then the next audio track, and clip, etc. More complex editing allows you to use voice-overs while the clip is playing.

Digital editing, which is becoming more popular as the prices for the required software fall, uses a somewhat different process. Tutorials for common analog and digital editing processes can be found at the companion Web site for *Usability Testing and Research* <www.ablongman.com/barnum>.

A highlights tape of 10 minutes (no more than 15 minutes) generally works effectively to maintain the interest of your audience. As we have suggested earlier, it is important to include the positive findings, as well as the usability problems, in reporting the results of testing. A great place to start the video-highlights tape is with positive findings, as this communicates the good news to those members of your audience who may be sensitive about what's to come. If the tape can be used independently of the presenter, the "announcer" can explain what will be shown on the tape. The detail that can't be shown on the tape can be included in the report. Because you cannot show everything you've learned, you will need to select representative users and make it clear that the problems you present are typical of other users, not just the ones you're showing. Another technique is to show several users experiencing the same problem, providing a very short clip of each person's experience. This approach conveys how widespread the problem is. Also, if you can capture a particularly salient comment from one or more users, even funny comments, these go over well with an audience. The entertainment value derived from using video is not to be underestimated. Users may make us laugh, but they also show us what needs to be changed to improve the product.

Planning for the creation of the video-highlights tape will make the production aspect a whole lot smoother. Be prepared for this process to take a long time, depending on your level of experience when you start. Although you are not aiming for Academy award-winning production quality in doing a video-highlights tape, a good rule of thumb is that it takes one hour to create a minute of video (Dumas and Redish 364). If you're familiar with the equipment or software and the process, you may need less time. However, you should be prepared to invest even more time if you are learning how do this for the first time. A planning document, circulated to the team, will allow everyone to agree on the approach being used. See Appendix 8.2 at the end of the chapter for an example of a planning document and the accompanying "announcer" script for a usability highlights tape of a desktop software product.

Using Multimedia

Other, more sophisticated tools are now available to help you communicate the results of testing. These include multimedia and Internet media. One company describes how the report and highlights tape are combined into one archive by digitizing the video from the VCR or camcorder and placing it onto a PC that can send the report out via the company's Intranet (Harrison and Melton). The multimedia report in HTML provides text, audio, and video at the audience's individual workstations through a URL. Multimedia reports can also be produced on CD-ROM, using an authoring tool such as Director or Authorware. This approach allows for search capabilities and portability on a CD. The report can contain text, audio, video, stills, graphics, and even prototypes of the product or of recommended improvements to the product.

A software tool called NetSearchable Video uses advanced image and audio analysis to read an analog or digital video signal and generate a storyboard of browsable images, while also extracting any text in the video image. An index allows you to search for the exact video clip you want, create the video, and post it on the company's Intranet with searching capabilities. Users can access the video from their Web browser, enter search terms, and receive the matching video clips. Sorting capabilities allow the user to create a video clip to watch or email to others.

These kinds of state-of-the-art tools clearly make it easier to communicate results and distribute them widely. Although they are currently expensive and in most cases not yet widely available, they suggest the direction the industry may go in improving the ability to document and share the results of testing. In the meantime, the tried and true tools work well and can be used effectively in communicating results.

Summary

In this chapter, we have presented the methods commonly used to analyze the data gathered from usability testing and then report your results. We described approaches to interpret the data and determine the extent of the problem. Labeling the problem as *local* or *global* identifies the *scope* of the problem. Identifying the *severity* of the problem helps determine which recommendations need to be made now and which can be made later.

When this analysis is complete, you are ready to report your results. We discussed several avenues commonly used to report results:

- Written report
- Oral presentation
- Video-highlights tape

We also looked briefly at some of the multimedia options available for reporting results. If you have followed the usability process sequentially, as we have presented it in this book, you now have all the information you need to understand how usability testing fits into the process of user-centered design and you know how to prepare for testing, conduct a usability test, analyze the results, and report your findings.

Coming Up

Although we have referred to usability testing of Web sites throughout this book and have used examples of Web testing in our discussions, we have set aside the last chapter, coming up, to focus on the specific nature of Web usability testing, as this is the hottest topic in usability testing today. If you have a particular interest in Web testing issues, you will want to press on and read this chapter.

Questions/Topics for Discussion

1. Define *triangulation* and explain its relevance to analyzing the results of usability testing. List some of the types of data that can be used for triangulation.
2. Define the meaning of "scope" as it relates to usability findings, differentiating between *local* problems and *global* problems. Give examples of each type of finding.
3. Describe how you would use a *severity scale* to rate the findings from a usability test. What scale would you use?
4. Discuss the different types of reporting options available to report the results of testing. Identify the most appropriate audience for each type of report.
5. Identify the essential parts of a written report. Explain what should go into each part.
6. Discuss some of the newer multimedia options available for reporting usability testing results. What advantages do these options provide?

Exercises

For Your Project

1. Using the flip chart sheets containing the findings from all participants in your usability test, convene a team meeting to analyze the findings and make recommendations. For each finding, you will need to decide on:

   - Scope (global or local finding)
   - Severity (using an agreed-upon scale)
   - Number of participants experiencing the problem

   You will also want to collate the quantitative data from the questionnaires and compare these to your goals and benchmarks for the test. In addition, you will want to collate any positive findings.

2. Plan the reports you will prepare. For the written report, you will want to map out the sections it will contain and outline the information that should appear in each section. The team should decide how to draft the report: all together, in parts for editing by the whole, or written by one person and edited by one or more members of the team. Your decision on how many team members should be involved in drafting and reviewing the written report may depend, in part, on whether you will also present an oral report and video-highlights tape.

3. For an oral presentation, decide on the method the team will use: all participate, some participate, or one person speaks, while other members of the team prepare the visual support and the video-highlights tape.

4. Schedule an editing workshop to review the written report. Schedule a practice session to present your results orally, using visual support and a video-highlights tape.

References

"Common Industry Format," Version 1.1. 28 Oct. 1999. National Institute of Standards and Technology <http://www.nist.gov/iusr/documents/CIF.html>.

Dumas, Joseph S., and Janice C. Redish. *A Practical Guide to Usability Testing.* Norwood, NJ: Ablex, 1993.

Gurak, Laura J. *Oral Presentations for Technical Communication.* Boston: Allyn and Bacon, 2000.

Harrison, Charles, and Shane Melton. "Are Your Product Teams Reading Your Usability Reports?" *Common Ground* 9.1 (Jan. 1994): 14–15, 18.

Orenstein, David. "Getting Tough on Ease of Use: Software is Too Hard to Use!" *Computerworld,* 23 Aug. 1999 <http://www.computerworld.com/home/print.nsf/all990823bc62>.

Rubin, Jeffrey. *Handbook of Usability Testing.* New York: Wiley, 1994.

Wilson, Chauncey. "Usability Techniques and Tips." *Usability Interface* Oct. 1977: 2–3.

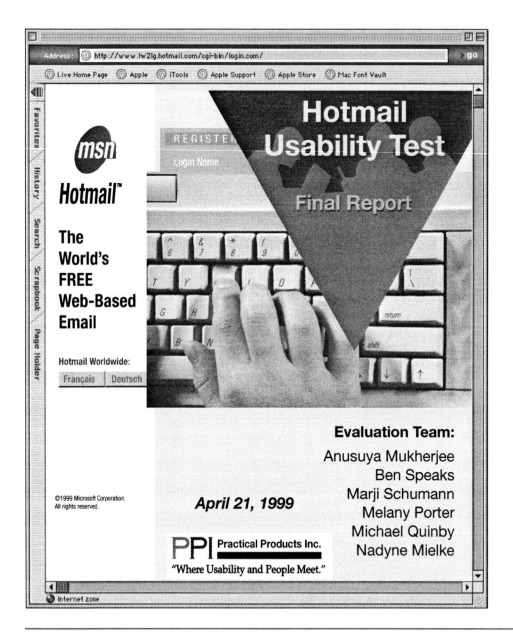

Front cover of report

Hotmail Usability Test
Final Report

Evaluation of Hotmail Internet Email Application

April 21, 1999

Report for Microsoft's Hotmail Development Team

Practical Products, Inc.

5234 East Technology Place
Anywhere, USA

Table of Contents

Abstract

This report contains the following sections:

The **executive summary** briefly describes our test, summarizes the results, and lists our main recommendations for improvements to Hotmail.

The **description of the usability study** outlines the processes we followed to design the test, select test participants, and develop criteria to gauge test results.

The **test results** describe the amount of time test participants spent completing scenarios, the types of data collected, and the categories used to group usability problems.

The **findings and recommendations** provide detailed information about the test results and Practical Product's recommendations for resolving problems.

The **conclusion** summarizes the results and discusses reasons to address the usability problems identified in the test.

The **appendices** contain copies of actual documents used during testing.

Executive summary

In response to Microsoft's request for usability testing of Hotmail, its Web-based email product, Practical Products, Inc. performed a formal usability test with several representative users of the product. We tested six people ranging from rank novices with no previous email experience to advanced users who were highly experienced with email products.

Our tests, conducted in a usability lab, involved observing users while they completed a broad range of real-world messaging tasks. The test results and post-test interviews revealed several strengths and weaknesses in Hotmail, as detailed in the body of this report. The following table briefly reviews the most significant usability problems and our recommendations for addressing them.

Problems	Recommendations
The Hotmail Search feature failed.	Enable the Hotmail user Search feature or remove it if this is not possible. The Search feature to locate other Hotmail users did not work.
It is difficult to attach files.	Reduce the number of steps required to attach files and change the default file type to "all files."
User feedback is lacking.	Provide better and more visible feedback to users. Our users needed more and better confirmation that they had successfully performed certain tasks, including moving messages into folders, attaching files, and logging off.
Internal and network errors are common.	Research the causes for internal errors and network errors and determine ways to improve the robustness of the product.
The Enter key does not always work.	Allow users to use the Enter key and Submit button interchangeably.
Users weren't sure how to reply to mail.	Make more obvious the functions of radio buttons versus links. Many users mistakenly clicked on radio buttons when attempting to reply to messages.
Icons, buttons, options are sometimes hard to find.	Consistently position buttons, icons, options, etc. so that users become "trained" concerning where to expect to find these items. In addition, Hotmail should avoid duplicating options on a single window (e.g., "Inbox" on the Folders window) to prevent confusion.
The password clue was confusing.	Use a more familiar password reminder, such as "mother's maiden name."
Some language was confusing.	Find a synonym for the word "compose" to label the option that users select to write a message. Also, one of our international test participants commented that "first name" and "last name" are terms international users might fail to recognize.

Description of the usability study

This section describes the purpose, content, and design of the Hotmail usability test that Practical Products, Inc., performed for Microsoft. In addition to this report, our lab produced an annotated 10-minute "highlights" video that captures key responses of the test participants as they complete the usability test.

Test goals

Practical Products, Inc.'s goal for this test was to provide Microsoft developers with a list of findings and recommendations they can implement to improve the usability of Hotmail, Microsoft's no-cost, Web-based email product.

We addressed as many of the issues Microsoft developers raised as practically possible, given time, budget, and technical constraints, as explained following.

Background

Microsoft contracted with Practical Products, Inc., to research the strengths and weaknesses of Hotmail, Microsoft's no-cost Web-based email application. According to our Hotmail liaison, Hotmail's audience is quite broad, consisting of anyone with Internet access who is interested in having anonymous email capabilities.

Microsoft presented Practical Products with a set of features to test. We addressed most of the requested issues, as discussed below, with a few noted exceptions.

"Specific" test requests. We were asked to assess Hotmail's ease of use in the following *specific* areas:

* Registering for Hotmail
* Logging in and logging out of Hotmail
* Composing an email
* Sending and retrieving email (to include sending attachments)
* Using the Hotmail member directory to look up member email addresses
* Sorting messages in the Hotmail InBox
* Creating an address book that contains frequently used addresses
* Setting up folders to store messages by category

"General" test requests. The developers also asked us to address concerns of a more *general* nature. They asked us to collect information about Hotmail user habits and perceptions, including:

* How users currently use email
* The level of effort required to use Hotmail
* Satisfaction with Hotmail (determining whether users continue using it, recommend it to others, etc.)
* Perceived reliability of Hotmail
* Perceived speed of Hotmail

2

Test requests we excluded. The test team decided to exclude from formal testing four test issues that Hotmail developers requested. We based this decision on our opinion that it would be better to address these issues in a focus group or through questionnaires and interviews:

1. **What users think of Hotmail's performance.** Because of the wide variety of computers used, modem speeds, variations in Internet traffic volume, and other factors, we determined it would not be helpful to address this issue as part of the formal usability test. We decided to assess the test participants' impressions about system performance using a post-test questionnaire.
2. **The password retrieval process.** We omitted a study of the password retrieval process because it requires setting up password "prompts" that would require time to elapse for users to forget their passwords or password clues. However, we did collect information about the password entry process, because it revealed some problems for users.
3. **Reminders.** We excluded a study of "reminders" because we believed they would be used by only a small subset of advanced users.
4. **Accessing other email through a POP account.** We chose not to test POP account access because of the difficulty in setting up the test (e.g., queuing messages up from another account while the usability test was in progress) and because of potential proprietary conflicts with other email accounts.

Hotmail test description

The discount usability testing approach. Practical Products conducted the Hotmail usability test following our customary "discount usability testing" approach. This widely embraced approach to usability testing involves testing a relatively small, representative group of users in order to yield reliable results, reduce testing costs, and reduce the amount of time spent conducting and analyzing test results. Industry studies confirm that carefully designed tests with a small number of test participants (4–6, typically) discover at least 80% of the usability problems revealed in formal tests with much larger numbers of test participants.

In addition, we have found that discount usability testing significantly reduces test turn-around time, allowing our lab to provide prompt feedback to clients. This is especially important to clients who may be working under very limited time constraints—such as development staff who must implement recommended changes within a small window of time before a product is released.

Test format. The complete test for each test participant involved the following activities:

Pre-test activities consisted of phone calls to qualify the users and completion of a pre-test questionnaire designed to confirm that the user met our user profile requirements.

Formal testing in a usability lab involved testing individual users in a lab environment set up much like a home office. Users completed real-life scenarios using Hotmail while we recorded their activities on video and observed them through a one-way mirror.

3

The usability evaluation room (where test participants worked) was furnished with three video cameras set up to tape participants from various angles. Test participants worked at a desk with a Pentium computer running Windows 95 with Netscape Communicator and Internet Explorer software. They were connected to the Web through an Ethernet T–1 Internet connection.

The observation room contained an AV console, audio channel mixer, VHS recorders, a special effects generator, and a speaker with a pickup to the usability evaluation room. While the participants worked, the evaluation team logged and categorized observations using a computer running U-Loggit usability testing software.

Walkthrough tested our scenarios and the general "do-ability" of the test. We invited a sample test participant to complete the test scenarios in the lab while we logged the results. We used the results from our walkthrough user to confirm that the test scenarios were readily understandable and to review our timing assumptions. The walkthrough experience gave us a chance to revisit some awkward wording and revise our test time limits.

Pilot test confirmed that our revisions had corrected all critical problems with the test. After refining the test scenarios and questionnaires, we conducted a pilot test under authentic test conditions.

Post-task and post-test activities consisted of short questionnaires administered between scenarios and a longer questionnaire and interview administered after the final scenario. The test team used the final interview as an opportunity to ask participants about specific issues that arose during their individual tests.

Summary sessions conducted after each test allowed the evaluation team to quickly examine test results and categorize usability issues discovered in the test.

Test times. We tested Hotmail both on weekday evenings and on Saturday mornings. We tested two users per 3-hour session.

Test participant selections
Based on Microsoft's assertion that Hotmail is geared for all levels of users, Practical Products' evaluation team decided to test two groups of users: novice users and advanced users. We reasoned that by selecting users on both ends of the experience scale, we could collect a broad range of feedback that would be generally applicable to users falling in the middle of the continuum. By testing novices, we were more likely to collect information about the intuitiveness of the application. By targeting advanced users, we could be confident of assembling a group of people capable of performing the more difficult tasks we were asked to test.

Novice profile. We selected novice users who met our requirements of having basic computer experience, including keyboarding skills, Windows experience, and the ability to access and navigate a Web browser. We purposely selected people for this group

4

who have NO email experience as a way to ensure that prior experience with other email packages would not skew the test participants' reactions.

Advanced profile. We selected advanced users who met the minimal requirements of the novice users, but who in addition had previous experience using other email programs (except for Hotmail). We limited this study to users who had extensive Web experience (6 months +), and who had used email for at least 6 months.

In addition to selecting test participants who met the experience profile, we also worked to ensure that the users were sampled across a broad demographic range. Our users were a mixed gender group ranging from age 15 to 45+ years.

Test problems
User selection problems. We originally recruited and qualified three novice users and three advanced users, each group containing a mixture of ages and genders. However, during one evening testing session, Hotmail was unexpectedly taken down for maintenance. We had to excuse our sole male novice user and recruit another on short notice. The replacement was a 45+ year-old female with advanced user skills.

Because of this substitution, our final test sample was composed of four advanced users and only two novice users.

Wide variations in Hotmail response. We noticed a considerable difference in system responsiveness depending on the time of day that the tests took place. Hotmail was very slow on weekday evenings, but quite responsive on weekend mornings. This is important to note because it may help explain why there is such a wide divergence of opinion among the test participants concerning the "speediness" of Hotmail.

Scenario and questionnaire design
We created a set of scenarios designed to test the issues discussed previously. Each scenario was designed to require between 15–25 minutes to complete. We constructed the scenarios to be as real-world as possible, containing multiple related tasks (e.g., reading an email message and then responding to it).

The questionnaires administered after each scenario and after the complete tests were designed to collect some of the qualitative data omitted from the formal testing. The questionnaires asked test participants for their perceptions about Hotmail and how well they understood and liked the product.

Scenario design. We revised our test scenarios slightly because of some problems that occurred during testing. The final scenarios and tasks were as follows:

Scenario 1: Registering for Hotmail and Logging On

(time limit: 10 minutes)

Scenario 2: Reading, Composing, and Sending Messages

(time limit: 15 minutes)

Task A: Check for email messages received from Hotmail.
Task B: Write an email message and send it.
Task C: Check for a new message and respond to it.

ADVANCED USER SCENARIO
Scenario 3: Sending Attachments, Creating a Message Folder, and Creating an Address Book

(time limit: 15 minutes)

Task A (Discontinued because application wouldn't support a search for existing Hotmail users)
Task B: Send a message with an attachment.
Task C: Create a folder and store a message there.
Task D: Create an address book and store an email address there.

Scenario 4: Deleting Messages and Leaving Hotmail

(time limit: 10 minutes)

Task A: Erase all messages in the Inbox.
Task B: Sign off from Hotmail.

TIME LIMITS. We allotted 50 minutes for the test participants to complete all four scenarios.
When we originally designed the scenarios, we believed that because of their limited abilities and experience, novice users might not have enough time to attempt Scenario 3, which tests the advanced Hotmail tasks (attachments, folders, address books). However, because our novice users were able to complete scenarios 1, 2, and 4 reasonably quickly (setting aside system-imposed delays), we decided to allow them to attempt the more advanced tasks. As a result, the test scenarios and time allotments are the same for the two groups of users.

Test questionnaires and interview design. We designed a series of questionnaires to qualify potential test participants and to collect subjective feedback from them during and after testing. The Appendix contains the completed questionnaires.

PRE-TEST QUESTIONNAIRE: To qualify test participants, we asked a series of questions designed to collect demographic information and to assess their level of computer and Internet experience. We accepted for testing those who met our minimum requirements for novice or advanced users.

POST-TASK QUESTIONNAIRES: After the test participants completed each scenario, we administered a post-task questionnaire. The questionnaire was designed to capture feedback about Hotmail tasks while the test participant's memory was fresh. The questionnaires asked test participants to rate the ease or difficulty of the tasks, describe whether Hotmail's terminology relative to the task was clear, and provide free-form comments concerning the tasks.

POST-TEST QUESTIONNAIRE: After the test participants completed the final scenario, we administered a questionnaire designed to capture their general opinions about Hotmail. The questionnaire asked them to rate their interest in having anonymous email capabilities, their impressions about Hotmail's speed and responsiveness, and their overall satisfaction with the product.

POST-TEST INTERVIEW: After each of the test participants completed the post-test questionnaire, the test briefer (the evaluation team's liaison with the test participant) scanned the questionnaire and asked the test participant to explain some of the responses. As the need arose, the briefer occasionally presented the test participant with additional questions that the evaluation team compiled while observing the test.

Test results

Timing results
The test participants completed the test scenarios as outlined in the following table.

	Scenario 1 (10 min)	Scenario 2 (15 min)	Scenario 3 (15 min)	Scenario 4 (10 min)	Total Time (50 min)
Participant 1 (Novice)	9:29	4:34	14:25	3:36	**32:04**
Participant 2 (Advanced)	1:04	5:52	17:33	1:24	**25:53**
Participant 3 (Advanced)	13:43	6:13	9:42	1:12	**30:50**
Participant 4 (Advanced)	5:40	5:57	6:50	0:49	**19:16**
Participant 5 (Novice)	17:03	6:56	10:12	1:02	**35:13**
Participant 6 (Advanced)	6:35	5:43	8:11	1:03	**21:22**

Explanation for exceeded time limits. The time limits presented few difficulties for the test participants, with the following exceptions:

Scenario 1: Participant 3 exceeded the time limit on Scenario 1 because she thoroughly read the terms of service agreement and the mail group descriptions. Participant 5, a novice, exceeded the time limit primarily because system response time was very slow at the time of testing.

Scenario 3: Participant 2 exceeded the time limit primarily because he tried several times without success to use the Hotmail search feature.

Types of data collected

Quantitative data: Quantitative data consists of "hard," measurable results that we analyzed to determine how the participants performed compared to established benchmarks. Some of the quantitative information we collected included time spent on task, the percentage of participants succeeding or failing at tasks, and so on.

Qualitative data: Qualitative data consists of records of subjective impressions and opinions. Some of the qualitative information we collected included individual opinions about Hotmail's quality, perceptions about Hotmail's speed and ease of use, and so on. We captured some of the qualitative commentary during testing, but also received good qualitative feedback in the questionnaires and post-test interviews.

Quantitative data collected during testing

We collected the following information during formal testing:

- Time to complete each task
- Number of test participants completing tasks within allocated time
- Number of test participants completing tasks with extra time
- Number of problems encountered
- Number of errors (unsuccessful tries)
- Number of local problems
- Number of global problems
- Number of times each test participant used the online help
- Number of times each test participant accessed advertising sites
- Length of time each test participant spent browsing advertisements

Qualitative data collected during testing

During and after the test we also collected qualitative data, consisting mostly of commentary recorded during the tests. This commentary provides additional insight into some of Hotmail's usability difficulties.

We collected information including:

- Facial expressions
- Verbal comments when test participants "thought out loud"
- Spontaneous verbal expressions (comments)
- Miscellaneous activities (stretching, requesting breaks, etc.)

We also collected qualitative data during:

- Interviews after the test scenarios
- Interviews after the test was completed

Usability criteria

To categorize the test observations, we applied a usability test analysis model that categorizes product usability problems according to whether they fail to meet any of the following 10 criteria:

1. **Concept:** Does the product use effective metaphors? Is it intuitive?

8

2. **Consistency:** Does the product look and perform similarly through all parts of the application?
3. **Content:** Is the content accurate, appropriately complex, and provided in the right amount?
4. **Feedback:** Does the product provide appropriate feedback to the user?
5. **Interaction Model:** Are user responses and other system interactions handled according to established models?
6. **Navigation:** Is it easy to get where you want to go in the product?
7. **Terminology:** Is the interface's language easy to understand for the audience(s)?
8. **User Assistance:** Does the product supply an appropriate amount of user help (e.g., online help, how to get customer service, other instructions)?
9. **User Preference:** Does use of the product cause difficulty for individual users in other ways not covered in these categories (e.g., does it favor "mouseusers" over "keystroke users"; is it perceived to be too slow)?
10. **Quality Assurance:** Is the product robust? Does it fail in ways that prevent users from performing tasks?

Our test results produced findings in most of these areas, which we rated using the rating scales discussed in the following section.

Scope and severity ratings

After identifying usability problems, we rated their scope and severity. **Scope** refers to how widespread the problem was throughout the product, and **severity** codes rate the seriousness of the problem.

Scope. **Local problems** consisted of problems that occurred only in a particular part of the application, while **global problems** indicated far-reaching design flaws. In general, global problems tend to be critical to correct, because they affect usability of the entire application. However, some local problems are critical enough to hamper severely the users' ability to perform key tasks.

Severity. We used the following severity codes to classify the seriousness of the problems we discovered:

1. **Prevents completion** of a task
2. **Causes significant delays** in completing a task
3. **Causes minor usability problems,** but users can complete the task
4. **Minor annoyance**—does not significantly impact usability, but should be corrected if time allows

Findings and recommendations

Using the evaluation criteria discussed previously, we analyzed the test results to develop a set of findings. This section discusses:

- Usability problems noted during the test (findings)

9

- Recommendations for improving Hotmail
- Feedback we collected from test participants using questionnaires and post-test interviews

Findings

The following table summarizes usability problems noted in the usability test, ordered by severity level. The narrative following the table provides recommendations related to the findings.

Usability problems	Number of participants affected	Severity level	Scope
1. Test participants were unable to find users in Hotmail's directory.[1]	2	1	local
2. The process for sending attachments confused participants. (Four participants thought they had successfully attached a document when they had not.)	4	2	local
3. Test participants were unsure if items had been moved into the selected folder.	2	2	local
4. Test participants received internal and network errors.	2	2	local
5. Test participants expected to be able to press the Enter key to submit information, but this worked only in isolated instances.	3	3	global
6. Test participants were unsure whether to click on the radio button or the link to reply to email.	4	3	local
7. Test participants had problems finding the "create folder" icon.	3	3	local
8. Test participants were unsure if they had signed off from Hotmail successfully.	2	3	local
9. Test participants were unsure which button allowed them to compose an email.	1	3	local
10. Test participants had trouble navigating between Inbox screen and Folder screen.	2	3	local
11. Test participants were confused about the password hint question.	4	3	local
12. International test participants were unsure of the terminology "first name" and "last name."[2]	W	3	local
13. Test participants complained about excessive amount of reading material in the Terms of Service.	4	4	local

10

Usability problems	Number of participants affected	Severity level	Scope
14. Test participants were unable to find messages they had sent.	1	4	local
15. Test participants disliked the Compose window.	1	4	local

[1]We removed this task from our scenarios after the first two test participants were unable to complete the task and the evaluation team confirmed that the task could not be completed.

[2]This finding was collected from our walkthrough participant, whose other testing results are not recorded in this report. We included this finding because it may be of special interest to developers interested in internationalization and localization issues.

Recommendations
We recommend the following improvements to Hotmail based on the test findings.

1. Enable the Hotmail User Search feature
The search feature on Hotmail ("Searching for Another Hotmail User") did not work over the course of our testing. After it failed for our walkthrough test participant and first advanced user, we removed it from the scenarios. Later attempts to use it by the test team were similarly unsuccessful. We recommend that Hotmail enable this feature (or entirely remove it). In the future, if it (or any portion) of Hotmail is not available, we recommend that Hotmail not allow users to attempt to use the facility.

2. Simplify the Attachments feature
The attachment feature caused problems for each of our test participants. Each test participant found the process to be difficult. Of our six test participants, only two were able to successfully attach it, although all *thought* they had done so. We recommend the following:

- **Change the default file type on the "browse" option from HTML files to "all files."** Because the test participants were not sending HTML files, they experienced trouble finding the correct file type.
- **Remove the second step from the attachment procedure.** Once the user has chosen the file to attach, the second step confuses the user. The "attach to message" process should occur automatically.
- **Add highlighting or an icon to the email Compose screen to notify users that they have successfully attached a message.** None of the test participants noticed the "attachments" portion of the email Compose screen.

3. Notify users when folders are created successfully
Some test participants had trouble using the Folders feature. It is easy to move items between folders, but there is no confirmation that an item has been moved to a folder. We recommend that Hotmail add a notification after the user has moved the item.

11

4. Improve "robustness" of the application

During our tests, Hotmail experienced issues such as internal and network errors. (For example, some users encountered an internal server error after submitting their registration and after creating a new folder.) While these are not usability issues per se, they do affect the general usability of Hotmail and user acceptance of the product. We recommend that Hotmail research these issues and take steps, such as increasing server capacity, to avoid them in the future.

5. Allow users to submit using the Enter key

Test participants expected to be able to hit the Enter key when submitting information. Many other Web sites do this. In some places, Hotmail does not accept it; in others, it does. We recommend that Hotmail allow users to press Enter to submit information on every portion of the Web site, not just selected portions.

6. Make obvious the function of radio boxes and links

All Folder screens feature a radio box next to the message, and a hyperlink on the message itself. Test participants were unsure of the function of each. We recommend that Hotmail make more obvious the function of radio boxes and hyperlinks.

7. Make it easier to find the Folder "Create" option

Test participants experienced difficulty finding the "Create" option on the Folders screen. Users searched on the screen to find it, taking up to five minutes to find it. We recommend that Hotmail add highlighting to draw attention to the "create" link.

8. Notify users that they have signed off

Many test participants were unsure whether they had actually signed off from Hotmail. We recommend that Hotmail add a screen notifying users that they have successfully signed off before taking them to the MSN homepage.

9. Provide different term to replace Compose

Test participants had issue with the "compose" button. They did not understand the terminology. One of our test participants stated during the test that "it would be better if it said 'send a message.'"

10. Remove duplication of menu items

Some test participants had trouble navigating between the Inbox and Folders screen. They were unsure if the menu would take them where they wanted. One test participant also expressed confusion over the Inbox being listed both on the menu and in the Folders screen.

11. Use a more familiar password retrieval metaphor

Most test participants were confused about the password hint question. If a user forgets his or her password, they can contact Hotmail and get their password if they answer this question properly. Test participants thought that they were supposed to supply their password to answer this question. This compromises the security of the users and of Hotmail, since the answer to the question appears on the screen (thus giving away the user's password). We recommend that Hotmail use the verification method widely used in business, where the user gives mother's maiden name to verify his or her identity.

12. Change "last name" to "family name"
Our walkthrough test participant was international. He found the terminology "first name" and "last name" to be confusing. We recommend that Hotmail change this terminology to embrace the needs of international users.

13. Reduce quantity of information in the TOS
All participants complained about the amount of information in the Terms of Service. Only one test participant tried to read the entire TOS, and she started skimming after approximately five minutes. We recommend that Hotmail decrease the amount of information given at the beginning for users to read, and make it more clear where the TOS can be referenced later.

14. Make the "save message" option more visible
Test participants expected to be able to find the messages they had sent. They did not notice the option on the email Compose screen that they can set to keep a copy of the message. We recommend that Hotmail make this option more visible, add an option to allow users to choose an on/off setting to specify that they want to keep all sent messages, or (as many other mail programs do) automatically keep copies of sent messages.

15. Add color/other design elements strategically
Test participants commented that the email Compose window was "boring." We recommend that Hotmail add more color, highlighting, or other graphical elements to the screen.

Other feedback (questionnaires and interviews)
We collected detailed feedback from test participants concerning what they liked and disliked about Hotmail. Following are summarized results collected from the post-test questionnaires.

On the following scale, rate your need for/interest in having anonymous email capabilities.

Test participant	No interest/ need	Low interest/ need	Don't feel strongly either way	Moderate interest/ need	High interest/ need
#1				X	
#2					X
#3	X				
#4				X	
#5			X		
#6				X	

13

On the following scale, rate your impression of Hotmail's speed and responsiveness.

Test participant	Very slow	Moderately slow	Neither fast nor slow	Moderately fast	Very fast
#1					X
#2				X	
#3		X			
#4				X	
#5		X			
#6			X		

Will you use Hotmail in the future?

Test participant	Never	Rarely	Sometimes	Fairly frequently	Very frequently
#1				X	
#2		X			
#3	X				
#4		X			
#5					X
#6			X		

On the following scale, rate how highly you would recommend Hotmail to your friends and associates.

Test participant	Would not recommend	Would recommend with reservations	Don't feel strongly either way	Would probably recommend	Would strongly recommend
#1					X
#2	X				
#3	X				
#4			X		
#5		X			
#6				X	

If you plan to use Hotmail at all in the future, please indicate how you might use it:

Test participant	While traveling for pleasure	While traveling for business	At work for business use	At work for personal use	At home	Not applicable will not use
#1	X				X	
#2					X	
#3						X
#4						X
#5		X				
#6				X		

Following are free-form comments from the test participants.

What did you like MOST about Hotmail?
1. Test Participant #1: It's fast and pretty easy to use.
2. Test Participant #2: Easy to send email to another Hotmail member, easy to delete messages.
3. Test Participant #3: Log off.
4. Test Participant #4: It's very fast. Also, the screens aren't cluttered.
5. Test Participant #5: The in-box (once you are familiar with it) was fairly straightforward—nice to know how many messages you had (new and unopened).
6. Test Participant #6: Fairly easy to follow without printed instruction sheet or manual.

What did you like LEAST about Hotmail?
1. Test Participant #1: There's not confirmation for signing off and sending messages sometimes.
2. Test Participant #2: File attachment difficult and not clear.
3. Test Participant #3: Attaching files, moving email to folders.
4. Test Participant #4: I don't think people who've never used email will find it easy to use—at least initially.
5. Test Participant #5: It seemed to take a long time to get from one section to another.
6. Test Participant #6: Didn't see a button to allow review of "sent" messages.

What would you change about Hotmail?
1. Test Participant #1: Get good pictures on the homepage.
2. Test Participant #2: Clarify and simplify file attachment process.
3. Test Participant #3: Lose the horizontal toolbar with Reply, Reply All, etc. Add drop down menus. Allow right-click shortcut menus.
4. Test Participant #4: The OK button after sending email. The lack of instructions for moving and deleting mail.
5. Test Participant #5: Maybe the layout and design.
6. Test Participant #6: Need an obvious out-box.

15

Optional comments
Please add any other comments about Hotmail that might be useful in helping Hotmail improve this email product.

1. Test participant #2: Reduce amount of options—high percentage of PC users very seldom use more than sending/receiving messages in home environment—perhaps if you target businesses, they will have more use for various options.
2. Test participant #3: Make it look like Outlook Express.
3. Test participant #5: The flow (or ease of going from one section to another) could use some improvement. Not all sections seemed as easy to maneuver as others did. The address book was a nice feature because it stored quite a bit of useful information that may not always be easily accessible.
4. Test participant #6: File attachment seems to take longer than either Lotus Notes or Eudora.

Positive feedback summary. Test participants offered several positive comments about Hotmail. They liked:

- The ability to log into Hotmail from any location—noted as a plus when traveling on business.
- The ease of sending and deleting messages.
- Hotmail's overall simplicity of use: "I didn't need an instruction manual to use it."
- The uncluttered, simple layout of the site.
- The thoroughness of the Address Book feature—it lets you add considerable biographical information about people.
- The quick responsiveness of Hotmail (this from users using Hotmail at low-traffic times).

Critical feedback summary. Some of the test participants commented on issues they would like to see improved in Hotmail. They criticized:

- The wordiness of the terms of service text.
- The limited amount of graphics. Some users commented that the site should be made more visually attractive.
- The slow response time (this from users using Hotmail during high-traffic times).
- The excessive number of "clicks" required to attach a file.
- The inconsistent location of options. Sometimes options are placed in the left frame of the window, sometimes in the middle of the window, and sometimes at the bottom of the screen.
- The "wordiness" of the online help text.
- The fact that Hotmail asks new users for demographic information about themselves although it touts itself as an anonymous email product.
- The spell check feature. It does not provide you with feedback to confirm it is checking words.

Conclusion

The fact that users who were unfamiliar with Hotmail learned to use it fairly easily suggests that Hotmail is a basically sound product. Even novice email users were able to complete the majority of Hotmail tasks successfully, and most test participants offered up positive comments about Hotmail along with their criticisms.

Even so, Microsoft could do much to improve the product. It has been Practical Products' experience that clients who implement usability recommendations report a significant improvement in user acceptance and fewer calls to technical support. In the case of this Web-based product, Microsoft might reasonably expect greater numbers of new registrations and greater amounts of time spent at the site—both of which would increase exposure for Hotmail's advertisers.

Many of the problems with the product could have been discovered through earlier testing of the product and through iterative testing at different stages in the application's development. We recommend that Microsoft perform iterative usability testing on the revised parts of Hotmail whenever major changes are made to the application.

Appendices

The attached appendices consist of the following items used in testing or as a basis for test analysis:

- Appendix A: Pre-test Questionnaire
- Appendix B: Test Scenarios
- Appendix C: Post-task Questionnaires
- Appendix D: Post-test Questionnaire
- Appendix E: Evaluation Team Checklists

Appendix A: Pre-test questionnaire

Practical Products administered the following questionnaire to qualify our test participants.

Thank you for considering being a volunteer for our usability test. We will work to make sure the test environment is pleasant and fun for you, with a casual dinner being served. The results from our usability test will be used to help improve a computer software product's ease of use.

Please answer the following questions. We will use your answers to determine if you will be a participant in our usability test.

The testing will take place on March 22 and March 29 from 6–8 P.M. The usability test will require 1½ hours of your time.

Please place a check next to the dates on which you are available, if any.

March 22 _____ March 29 _____ Either Date _____ Neither Date _____

Please disregard the rest of the questionnaire if you are not able to attend one of the dates. Thank you again for your consideration.

Name: _____

Home Phone: _____

Work Phone: _____

Age:

☐ 15–20   ☐ 21–30   ☐ 31–40   ☐ 41–50   ☐ 51 or above

Sex: ☐ Male   ☐ Female

☐ Right-handed   ☐ Left-handed

Please answer the following questions about your computer experience:

1. Do you use an IBM or compatible personal computer?

   ☐ Yes

   ☐ No

   If you answered "no," please disregard the remaining parts of the questionnaire.

2. What kind(s) of programs have you worked with? Check all that apply.

   ☐ Word processing

   ☐ Spreadsheets

   ☐ Graphics

   ☐ Other(s) specify _____

3. How long have you been using personal computers?

   ☐ 0–3 months

   ☐ 4–6 months

   ☐ 7–9 months

   ☐ 10–12 months

   ☐ More than 12 months

4. Have you ever used a Web browser?

   ☐ Yes

   ☐ No

   If you answered "no," please proceed to question 7.

5. Which Web browser have you used? Check all that apply.

   ☐ Microsoft Internet Explorer

   ☐ Netscape Navigator

   ☐ Other(s) specify _____

6. How long have you been browsing the Web?

   ☐ 0–3 months

   ☐ 4–6 months

   ☐ 7–9 months

18

☐ 10–12 months

☐ More than 12 months

7. Which Internet Service Provider(s) do you use? Check all that apply.

☐ AOL

☐ Prodigy

☐ CompuServe

☐ Mindspring

☐ Other (specify) _____

☐ I do not use/have an Internet Service Provider

8. Does your Internet Service Provider (ISP) OR your work/school location provide an email program?

ISP   ☐ Yes   ☐ No   ☐ Not applicable—I have no ISP

Work/School   ☐ Yes   ☐ No   ☐ Not applicable—I don't use email from work/school

If you answered "no" or "not applicable" to BOTH of the categories in this question, please proceed to question 11.

9. Which email program does your Internet Service Provider OR your work/school location provide?

	ISP	Work, School
Microsoft Outlook Express	☐	☐
Express	☐	☐
Eudora	☐	☐
Other (specify) _____	☐	☐
I do not know.	☐	☐

10. How long have you been using your Internet Service Provider's OR your work/school location's email program? (If you use multiple programs, indicate the time period corresponding to the program for which you have the MOST experience.)

☐ 0–3 months

☐ 4–6 months

☐ 7–9 months

☐ 10–12 months

☐ More than 12 months

11. Do you use the World Wide Web for email?

☐ Yes

☐ No

If you answered "no," please proceed to question 14.

12. Which World Wide Web email program(s) do you use? Check all that apply.

☐ Yahoo!

☐ Hotmail

☐ Netscape

☐ Other (specify) _____

13. How long have you been using your World Wide Web email program(s)?

☐ 0–3 months

☐ 4–6 months

☐ 7–9 months

☐ 10–12 months

☐ More than 12 months

14. Where do you use email? Check all that apply.

☐ From a personal home account

☐ From an account at work

☐ From a public access terminal (library, Internet cafe, other)

☐ From school

☐ Other (specify) _____

15. What do you use email for? Check all that apply.

☐ Work

☐ Personal

☐ Other (specify) _____

16. Do you know how to send attachments to someone via email?

☐ Yes

☐ No

17. Do you know how to make files for the email you receive so similar emails can be grouped?

☐ Yes

☐ No

18. Do you know how to create and send a simple email message?

☐ Yes

☐ No

Thank you for completing our questionnaire. We greatly appreciate your consideration and time. We will contact you if you are selected to participate in our usability test. Thank you!

Appendix B: Test scenarios
Practical Products tested participants using the following scenarios.

Scenario 1—Remember: THINK OUT LOUD! You have recently decided to sign up for email using a service called Hotmail. Using your Web browser, go to the following address:

www.Hotmail.com

Once you are at the Hotmail Web site, go ahead and sign up for a free email account. If you need any assistance, feel free to use the online help provided by Hotmail.

When you finish signing up for Hotmail, take some time to look around the site and explore its features—but for now, don't try to look at or send any email.

Scenario 2—Remember: THINK OUT LOUD!

Task A Check for any email messages that you may have received in Hotmail. Open a message you received from Hotmail, and close it when you finish reading it.

Task B Send a message to the following email address:

Bill.smith@i-solutions.com

Be sure to tell the recipient that you are sending out this message to test your new Hotmail account.

Task C Check to see if you have received any new email messages while you've been working in Hotmail. Look for a message with the subject line "Usability," and respond to it with a message telling the sender that you got the email.

Scenario 3—Remember: THINK OUT LOUD!

Task A **(Discontinued—go to Task B.)**

Task B You decide that you want to send your friend Marji a message to tell her about your new Hotmail account. Along with your message, you also decide to send her a file she's been asking for. Go ahead and write Marji an email telling her you have a Hotmail account, and attach the file to it. The file you are sending is located on the A drive and is titled "Test.doc." (Marji's Hotmail address is **marji_miller@hotmail.com**)

Task C Place one of the emails you have received in a holding area called "My Stuff." If this holding area isn't there, create it.

Task D You just realized that you would like to keep Marji's email address accessible for future correspondence. Create a place in Hotmail to store her address for other mailings.

Scenario 4—Remember: THINK OUT LOUD!

Task A Erase all of the messages in your mailbox.

Task B Sign off from Hotmail.

Appendix C: Post-task questionnaires
Attached are the questionnaires that Practical Products administered after the test participants completed each of the scenarios.

We reviewed the results and asked follow-up questions concerning these questionnaires in the post-test interviews with test participants.

Scenario 1 Questionnaire: *Signing Up for Hotmail and "Looking Around"*

1. Rate how easy or difficult it was to sign up for Hotmail.

Very difficult	Moderately difficult	Neither easy nor difficult	Moderately easy	Very easy
☐	☐	☐	☐	☐

2. Was Hotmail's wording clear (easy to understand)?

Very unclear	Moderately unclear	Some clear/ some unclear	Moderately easy	Very clear
☐	☐	☐	☐	☐

3. What was MOST DIFFICULT to do or understand? (If you need more room, write on the back of this page.)

_____

_____

_____

_____

4. What was EASIEST to do or understand? (If you need more room, write on the back of this page.)

_____

_____

_____

_____

5. When you were exploring the Hotmail site, what items, features, or ads did you look at? What were your observations about what you saw? (If you need more room, write on the back of this page.)

_____

_____

_____

_____

6. Optional: Please add any additional comments. (If you need more room, write on the back of this page.)

_____

_____

_____

Scenario 2 Questionnaire: *Checking for New Messages, Writing a Message, Replying to a Message*

1. How many new messages did you have when you first signed into Hotmail?

_____

2. Rate how easy or difficult it was to determine whether you had new messages when you first signed into Hotmail.

Very difficult	Moderately difficult	Neither easy nor difficult	Moderately easy	Very easy
☐	☐	☐	☐	☐

3. Rate how easy or difficult it was to write and send messages in Hotmail.

Very difficult	Moderately difficult	Neither easy nor difficult	Moderately easy	Very easy
☐	☐	☐	☐	☐

4. Rate how easy or difficult it was to notice you had received a *new* message *during* your Hotmail session.

Very difficult	Moderately difficult	Neither easy nor difficult	Moderately easy	Very easy
☐	☐	☐	☐	☐

5. Rate how easy or difficult it was to respond to a message in Hotmail.

Very difficult	Moderately difficult	Neither easy nor difficult	Moderately easy	Very easy
☐	☐	☐	☐	☐

6. Was Hotmail's wording clear (easy to understand)?

Very unclear	Moderately unclear	Some clear/ some unclear	Moderately clear	Very clear
☐	☐	☐	☐	☐

7. What was MOST DIFFICULT to do or understand? (If you need more room, write on the back of this page.)

_____

8. What was EASIEST to do or understand? (If you need more room, write on the back of this page.)

_____

9. Optional: Please add any additional comments. (If you need more room, write on the back of this page.)

_____

Scenario 3 Questionnaire: *Attaching Files, Storing Messages, Storing Addresses*

1. Rate how easy or difficult it was to attach a file to an email message.

Very difficult	Moderately difficult	Neither easy nor difficult	Moderately easy	Very easy
☐	☐	☐	☐	☐

2. Rate how easy or difficult it was to create folders to store messages in Hotmail.

Very difficult	Moderately difficult	Neither easy nor difficult	Moderately easy	Very easy
☐	☐	☐	☐	☐

3. Rate how easy or difficult it was to create a place to store an email address (create an "address book").

Very difficult	Moderately difficult	Neither easy nor difficult	Moderately easy	Very easy
☐	☐	☐	☐	☐

4. Rate how easy or difficult it was to add a new address to the address book.

Very difficult	Moderately difficult	Neither easy nor difficult	Moderately easy	Very easy
☐	☐	☐	☐	☐

5. Was Hotmail's wording clear (easy to understand)?

Very unclear	Moderately unclear	Some clear/ some unclear	Moderately easy	Very clear
☐	☐	☐	☐	☐

6. What was MOST DIFFICULT to do or understand? (If you need more room, write on the back of this page.)

_____

_____

_____

7. What was EASIEST to do or understand? (If you need more room, write on the back of this page.)

_____

_____

_____

8. Optional: Please add any additional comments.

_____

_____

_____

Scenario 4 Questionnaire: *Deleting Messages, Signing Off from Hotmail*

1. Rate how easy or difficult it was to erase messages in Hotmail.

Very difficult	Moderately difficult	Neither easy nor difficult	Moderately easy	Very easy
☐	☐	☐	☐	☐

2. Rate how easy or difficult it was to sign off from Hotmail.

Very difficult	Moderately difficult	Neither easy nor difficult	Moderately easy	Very easy
☐	☐	☐	☐	☐

3. Was Hotmail's wording clear (easy to understand)?

Very unclear	Moderately unclear	Some clear/ some unclear	Moderately easy	Very clear
☐	☐	☐	☐	☐

4. What was MOST DIFFICULT to do or understand? (If you need more room, write on the back of this page.)

_____

_____

_____

5. What was EASIEST to do or understand? (If you need more room, write on the back of this page.)

_____

_____

_____

6. Optional: Please add any additional comments. (If you need more room, write on the back of this page.)

_____

_____

_____

Appendix D: Post-test questionnaire

Practical Products administered this questionnaire after the test participants completed the final scenario.

We reviewed the results with the test participants in post-test interviews.

Thanks for completing the usability test. Please answer the following questions about your experience with Hotmail. We will use your answers to provide important feedback to Hotmail's marketing and development staff.

Hotmail allows you to send and receive mail independent of any email programs you maintain through your ISP or through work/school. Hotmail is accessed through the World Wide Web, and your mail is therefore not tracked through your ISP or work-provided email.

1. On the following scale, rate your need for/interest in having anonymous email capabilities:

No interest/ need	Low interest/ need	Don't feel strongly either way	Moderate interest/ need	High interest
☐	☐	☐	☐	☐

2. On the following scale, rate your impression of Hotmail's speed and responsiveness:

Very slow	Moderately slow	Neither fast nor slow	Moderately fast	Very fast
☐	☐	☐	☐	☐

3. Will you use Hotmail in the future?

Never	Rarely	Sometimes	Fairly frequently	Very frequently
☐	☐	☐	☐	☐

4. On the following scale, rate how you would recommend Hotmail to your friends and associates:

Would not recommend	Would recommend with reservations	Don't feel strongly either way	Would probably recommend	Would strongly recommend
☐	☐	☐	☐	☐

5. If you plan to use Hotmail at all in the future, please indicate how you might use it (check all that apply):

☐ While traveling for pleasure

☐ While traveling for business

☐ At work for business use

☐ At work for personal use

☐ At home

☐ Not applicable—will not use

26

6. What did you like MOST about Hotmail?

_____

_____

_____

7. What did you like LEAST about Hotmail?

_____

_____

_____

8. What would you change about Hotmail?

_____

_____

_____

9. Optional: Please add any other comments about Hotmail that might be useful in helping Hotmail staff improve this email product.

_____

_____

_____

Appendix E: Evaluation team checklists

Following are the checklists that each of our evaluation team members used to organize their activities during testing. A checklist was used for each key testing role:

- Narrator
- Logger
- Test administrator
- Camera operator
- Briefer
- Test assistant

CHECKLIST FOR THE NARRATOR

Before each participant comes:

_____ Know the product/system well.
_____ Know the objectives of each task.
_____ Know the steps related to each task scenario.
_____ Know the team's objectives as related to video and data captures.
_____ Coordinate efforts with the data recorder to ensure results are captured.

During each task session:

_____ Provide information to the data recorder.
_____ Work with the data recorder to verify the accuracy of actions and comments.

Checklist for Scenario #1
Scenario 1
You have recently decided to sign up for email using a service called Hotmail. Using your Web browser, go to the following address:

www.Hotmail.com

Once you are at the Hotmail Web site, go ahead and sign up for a free email account. If you need any assistance, feel free to use the online help provided by Hotmail.

When you finish signing up for Hotmail, take some time to look around the site and explore its features—but for now, don't try to look at or send any email.

_____ How does the user enter the URL for hotmail.com?
_____ Pay attention to how the user navigates the page (mouse versus tab).
_____ How does the user navigate information forms (mouse versus tab)?
_____ Does the user access the online help?
_____ Does the user click on any banner ads?
_____ Note any facial expressions to the logger.
_____ Note any verbal comments to the logger.
_____ Note any body gestures to the logger.

Checklist for Scenario 2
Scenario 2
    Task A
Check for any email messages that you may have received in Hotmail. Open one of them, and close it when you finish reading it.
    Task B
Send a message to the following email address:

Bill.smith@i-solutions.com

Be sure to tell the recipient that you are sending out this message to test your new Hotmail account.
    Task C
    Check to see if you have received any new email messages while you've been working in Hotmail. Look for a message with the subject line "Usability," and respond to it with a message telling the sender that you got the email.

_____ Note to the logger how the user navigates the Inbox Screen.
_____ Can the user understand the radio box concept?
_____ Pay attention to how the user navigates the page (mouse versus tab).
_____ How does the user navigate information forms (mouse versus tab)?
_____ Does the user access the online help?
_____ Does the user click on any banner ads?
_____ Note any facial expressions to the logger.
_____ Note any verbal comments to the logger.
_____ Note any body gestures to the logger.

28

Checklist for Scenario 3
Scenario 3
    Task A
(discontinued)
    Task B
You decide that you want to send your friend Marji a message to tell her about your new Hotmail account. Along with your message, you also decide to send her a file she's been asking for. Go ahead and write Marji an email telling her you have a Hotmail account, and attach the file to it. The file you are sending is located on the A drive and is titled "Test.doc."
    Marji's Hotmail address is
    marji_miller@hotmail.com
    Task C
Place one of the emails you have received in a holding area called "My Stuff." If this holding area isn't there, create it.
    Task D
You just realized that you would like to keep Marji's email address accessible for future correspondence. Create a place in Hotmail to store her address for other mailings.

_____ Note to the logger how the user navigates the Attachment page.
_____ Note to the logger how the user navigates the Folders page.
_____ Note to the logger how the user navigates the Address Book page.
_____ Pay attention to how the user navigates the page (mouse versus tab).
_____ How does the user navigate information forms (mouse versus tab)?
_____ Does the user access the online help?
_____ Does the user click on any banner ads?
_____ Note any facial expressions to the logger.
_____ Note any verbal comments to the logger.
_____ Note any body gestures to the logger.

Checklist for Scenario 4
Scenario 4
    Task A
    Erase all of the messages in your mailbox.
    Task B
    Sign off from Hotmail.
_____ Note how the user interacts with the radio box/pull down deletion menu.
_____ Note the user's facial expressions when logging off from Hotmail.
_____ Pay attention to how the user navigates the page (mouse versus tab).
_____ Does the user access the online help?
_____ Does the user click on any banner ads?
_____ Note any facial expressions to the logger.
_____ Note any verbal comments to the logger.
_____ Note any body gestures to the logger.

CHECKLIST FOR THE LOGGER
Before the test:
_____ Turn on logging computer.
_____ Check error codes in logging software.
_____ Enter new test information into logging software.
_____ Check headphones and microphones for logger and narrator.
_____ Test logging software.
_____ Check video feeds.
_____ Check logger's monitor.
_____ Change monitor views as necessary.
_____ Check cable from logging computer to printer.
_____ Check paper and ink in printer.
_____ Do a test print from logging software.
_____ Check paper and toner in copy machine.
_____ Do a test copy.

After each test participant:
_____ Print report.
_____ Copy report.
_____ Distribute copies to evaluation team members.
_____ Place original in test participant's folder.
_____ Set up logging software for next test participant (if any).

At end of day:
_____ Print final report.
_____ Make sure all members of team have copies.
_____ Have logging software ready for next team.
_____ Turn off computer.
_____ Refill printer (if necessary).
_____ Turn off printer.
_____ Refill copier (if necessary).
_____ Turn off copy machine.
_____ Order paper (if necessary).
_____ Back up logging software data files.

CHECKLIST FOR THE TEST ADMINISTRATOR
Before each test participant comes:
_____ Make sure each evaluation team member has a copy of the scenarios, questionnaires, etc.
_____ Monitor the evaluation team members to confirm they are using their checklists.
_____ Greet the test observers.

During each test session:
_____ Manage any problems that arise.
_____ Observe and take notes, noting real problems and "big picture" issues.
_____ Collect follow-up questions to review with the test participants.

After each test session:
_____ Collect test paperwork (questionnaires, notes, etc.).
_____ Make sure the computer is set up for the next test participant and clear the room of any materials left behind by the test participant or briefer.
_____ Bring test participants into the observation room and describe the testing process from the evaluation team's point of view.
_____ Lead the team in a brief session to catalog results and identify any usability issues discovered during the test.

After each day of testing:
_____ Conduct a brief review with the other members of the evaluation team to summarize the test day's findings.

CHECKLIST FOR THE CAMERA OPERATOR

Before each test participant comes:
_____ Turn on the equipment.
_____ Adjust the cameras to the proper setting for taping.
_____ Check the sound both in and out of the monitoring booth.
_____ Label the tapes for the session.
_____ Load the tape into the VCR.

During each test session:
_____ Synchronize starting times with the data recorder.
_____ Run the equipment.
_____ Select the picture to record and handle the recording.
_____ Adjust the sound as needed.
_____ Change the videotapes when necessary.

After the test participant leaves:
_____ Rewind the tapes used during the session.
_____ Check to make certain the tapes are labeled properly.
_____ Turn off the equipment.

CHECKLIST FOR THE BRIEFER

Before each test participant comes:
_____ Make sure the evaluation room is properly set up. Turn on the computer equipment. Get the product ready.
_____ Make sure the documentation is in place, if appropriate.
_____ Have a pad and pens or pencils for taking notes.
_____ Have an ink pen ready for the test participant to use in signing the Consent form.
_____ Check the folder for that test participant. Make sure all of the forms are in the folder.

At the beginning of each test session:
_____ Greet the test participant.
_____ Check the test participant's name to be sure that this is the person whom you expect.

_____ Make the test participant comfortable. Offer food and beverage.
_____ Bring the test participant into the evaluation room.
_____ Let the test participant see the cameras and other equipment.
_____ Show the test participant where to sit.
_____ Give the test participant a brief introduction to the test session.
_____ Ask if the test participant has any questions.
_____ Remind the test participant to think out loud.
_____ Remind the test participant to tell you when he or she has completed each task.
_____ Put the "Testing in Progress" sign on the door.

At the end of each test session:
_____ Ask the test participant to fill out the post-test questionnaire.
_____ Go in to the evaluation room and thank the test participant for his or her help.
_____ Debrief the test participant. Go over the test participant's responses to the post-test questionnaire.
_____ Give the test participant the payment or other incentive.
_____ Offer to show the test participant the observation room. Show the equipment and introduce the team.
_____ Thank the test participant and show him or her out.

After the test participant leaves:
_____ Put all the forms in the test participant's folder.
_____ Turn off the equipment in the evaluation room.

CHECKLIST FOR THE TEST ASSISTANT
Before each test participant comes:

_____ Make sure that there is sufficient paper and that all of the evaluation team members have writing instruments to take notes.
_____ Label each page of the notes with the project name, test participant's number/name, date, and time.

During each test session:
_____ Take notes on problems and other observations.

After each test participant leaves:
_____ Review and edit notes so that they are legible and clear.
_____ Put notes in that test participant's folder.

(Used with permission of the SPSU Hotmail team: Marji Schumann, Anusuya Mukherjee, Nadyne Mielke, Melany Porter, Benjamin Speaks, and Michael Quinby.)

APPENDIX 8.2

Spinn Team Video Presentation Documentation

Videotape presentation scope statement

Scope
To illustrate the 4 most important recommendations the Spinn Team identified during testing.

- Concept
- Interaction Model
- Terminology
- Consistency

Objective
Primarily, to convince managers of various departments as well as upper management that these changes need to be made. As a secondary objective, to convince these same managers that usability testing is a worthwhile pursuit.

Audience
Upper and middle managers of various departments.

What they will do with the information
Change the documentation per the Spinn Team's recommendations for a product that is about to be shipped.

Constraints
Do all this in under 10 minutes.

1

Video presentation script

```
McClain                    Mon Jun 3 08:15

  LOG                 WRITER    DAY    DATE   TIME   REV. BY    ON           STATUS TIME
VIDEO PRESENTATION    mcclain   Wed  may 29  08:48  mcclain    Jun 3 08:15  LOCKED 3:31
===============================================================================
```

VIDEO   AUDIO

<MUSIC UP>

SCREEN SHOTS:

[FADE SCREEN UP FROM BLACK]
THE SPINNAKER SOFTWARE
SPINN TEAM PRESENTS:
[FADE SCREEN TO BLACK]

[FADE SCREEN UP FROM BLACK]
USABILITY TESTING OF
BETTERWORKING DESKTOP
[FADE SCREEN TO BLACK]

[FADE SCREEN UP FROM BLACK]   ANNC:
USABILITY...[TYPE OUT]
[FADE SCREEN TO BLACK]   "THE SPINN TEAM IS THE USABILITY TESTING
                                     UNIT OF SPINNAKER SOFTWARE. YOU MAY
<MUSIC UNDER, OUT>   ASK, WELL, WHAT -IS- USABILITY TESTING?
[FADE SHOT UP FROM BLACK]   WE'LL ANSWER THAT QUESTION AND ALSO
MS ANNC STANDUP   SHOW YOU HOW USABILITY TESTING CAN HELP
                                     MAKE A PRODUCT LIKE BETTERWORKING
[FADE SHOT TO BLACK]   DESKTOP EASIER TO USE.

<MUSIC UP, UNDER, OUT>
SCREEN SHOTS:

[FADE SHOT UP FROM BLACK]
                                     ANNC VO:
                                     USABILITY IS A PART OF EVERY PRODUCT,
                                     BUT IT DOESN'T REFER TO -HOW- THE
                                     PRODUCT WORKS,
                                     IT REFERS TO HOW PEOPLE "GET ALONG"
                                     WITH THE PRODUCT . . .

MS SHOT OF COMPUTER/USER
USABILITY ISN'T HOW WELL THE PRODUCT
WORKS . . .

                                     USABILITY IS USER-ORIENTED.
USABILITY IS HOW PEOPLE WORK WITH THE   USERS USE PRODUCTS TO IMPROVE THEIR
PRODUCT . . .   PRODUCTIVITY.
                                     USERS ARE BUSY PEOPLE TRYING TO
USABILITY: ACCOMPLISH SPECIFIC TASKS.
-FOCUS ON USERS   AND IT'S THE USER WHO WILL DECIDE IF A
-USERS USE PRODUCTS   PRODUCT IS EASY TO USE.

-USERS ARE BUSY PEOPLE   THE GOAL OF USABILITY TESTING IS TO
                                     IMPROVE THE EASE OF USE OF A PRODUCT.

Mcclain   Mon Jun 3 08:15

-USERS DECIDE EASE OF USE.
[FADE SCREEN TO BLACK]

TRUCK SHOT VICTIM AT DESK WORKING
CU VICTIM OVER SHOULDER W/COMPUTER
PAN/ZOOM VICTIM TO MIRROR CONTROL ROOM
        FROM VICTIM SIDE
PAN/ZOOM REVERSE FROM CONTROL ROOM SIDE

<MUSIC UP>

SCREEN SHOTS:
<MUSIC UNDER, OUT>

[FADE SCREEN UP FROM BLACK]
THE PRODUCT...[TYPE OUT]
[FADE SCREEN TO BLACK]

[FADE SCREEN UP FROM BLACK]
WELCOME TO BWD (OR WHATEVER)
BWD MAIN MENU, HIGHLIGHT WITH CURSOR
EACH ITEM WHEN MENTIONED...

<MUSIC UP, UNDER, OUT>
SCREEN SHOTS:

[FADE SCREEN UP FROM BLACK]
THE LABORATORY...[TYPE OUT]
[FADE SCREEN TO BLACK]
EXT MS SCT SIGN
EXT LS OUTSIDE BUILDINGS
INT MS LAB ENTRANCE
TRUCK SHOT REVERSE VICTIM AT DESK
WORKING
CU CAMERAS
CU CAMERA MONITORS IN CONTROL ROOM
CU LOGGING IN CONTROL ROOM

<MUSIC UP, UNDER, OUT>
SCREEN SHOTS:

[FADE SCREEN UP FROM BLACK]
THE PARTICIPANTS...[TYPE OUT]
[FADE SCREEN TO BLACK]

[FADE SCREEN UP FROM BLACK]
USER PROFILE
-HOME OFFICE/SMALL BUSINESS
-FAMILY MANAGER
-ADMINISTRATIVE ASSISTANT

-COMPUTER EXPERIENCE
-DOS EXPERIENCE
-JOB EXPERIENCE

TEST PARTICIPANTS REPRESENT REAL USERS
WHO DO REAL TASKS WITH THE PRODUCT
WHILE TEST TEAM MEMBERS, IN THIS CASE
THE SPINN TEAM, OBSERVE AND RECORD WHAT
THE PARTICIPANTS SAY AND DO.
AFTER THE TEST THE TEST TEAM MEMBERS
ANALYZE THE DATA COLLECTED, DIAGNOSE
PROBLEMS AND MAKE RECOMMENDATIONS TO
IMPROVE THE PRODUCT.

BETTERWORKING DESKTOP IS A SUITE OF
PRODUCTIVITY PROGRAMS CONSISTING OF
A MEMO PAD, AN ADDRESS BOOK, A WORLD
CLOCK, A CALENDAR, A TO-DO LIST, A
LABEL MAKER, A TYPEWRITER, AND A SUITE OF
DOS UTILITIES.

FOR THE USABILITY TESTING OF
BETTERWORKING DESKTOP, WE CHOSE AN
OFFSITE USABILITY TESTING LABORATORY AT
SOUTHERN COLLEGE OF TECHNOLOGY, IN
MARIETTA. HERE, TEST PARTICIPANTS CAN
EVALUATE THE PRODUCT WHILE THEIR
COMMENTS ARE RECORDED ON VIDEOTAPE AND
LOGGED ON A COMPUTER FOR EXAMINATION BY
THE TEST TEAM.

OUR TEST PARTICIPANTS WERE SCREENED
ACCORDING TO OUR USER PROFILE, WHICH
WAS BASED ON WHO WOULD USE
BETTER WORKING DESKTOP.

USERS WORK OR HAVE A SATELLITE OFFICE
FROM THE HOME, MANAGE A FAMILY,
OR ARE SECRETARIES OR ADMINISTRATIVE
ASSISTANTS.

USERS ALSO HAVE AT LEAST 6 MONTHS
COMPUTER EXPERIENCE, INCLUDING DOS
APPLICATIONS, AND AT LEAST ONE YEAR OF
CURRENT WORK.

3

Mcclain   Mon Jun 3 08:15

[FADE SCREEN UP FROM BLACK]   THE SPINN TEAM TESTED PARTICIPANTS WITH
CALENDAR W/FACE   REAL-WORLD EXAMPLES OF THE CALENDAR,
LABEL MAKER W/FACE   THE LABEL MAKER, AND THE ADDRESS BOOK
ADDRESS BOOK W/FACE   PORTIONS OF BETTERWORKING DESKTOP.
[FADE SCREEN TO BLACK]

<MUSIC UP, UNDER, OUT>
SCREEN SHOTS:

[FADE SCREEN UP FROM BLACK]
THE FINDINGS...[TYPE OUT]
[FADE SCREEN TO BLACK]

[GOOD FINDINGS COLD]

TEST	PAGE	MARK
T1T1	3	(G1)
T1T2	2	(G2)
T2T3	2	(G3)
T1T1	4	(G4)
T2T3	3	(G5)
T2T4	2	(G6)
T1T2	1	(G7)

                                           ANNC VO:
BWD SHOTS WHILE SOT   PROBLEM AREAS WE FOUND DURING TESTING
                                           CAME UNDER 4 BASIC AREAS: CONCEPT,
                                           INTERACTION MODEL, TERMINOLOGY, AND
                                           CONSISTENCY.
                                           CONCEPT IS THE USER'S MENTAL MODEL OF
                                           THE PRODUCT, OR, WHAT THEY BRING WITH
                                           THEM AS EXPECTATIONS -TO- THE PRODUCT.
                                           HERE, A TEST EVALUATOR LOOKS OVER THE
T1T2 2   (1)   TUTORIAL...
"...IF I WERE THE NEW ADDRESS INFO,
WHERE WOULD I BE?"

T1T2 2   (1)   HERE, CONFUSING TUTORIAL HIERARCHY
"...OH, I ALREADY DID THIS...IF I HAD   CONFUSES AN EVALUATOR...
READ PROPERLY..."

T2T3 3   (3A)   AFTER USING THE CALENDAR APPOINTMENT
VO ZIP CODE MISPLACED   SCREEN, AN EVALUATOR MISPLACES THE ZIP
                                           CODE ON THE ADDRESS BOOK...

T1T1 5A   (5A)   THIS EVALUATOR EXPECTED A MORE
"...TOO EASY..."   SOPHISTICATED USER INTERFACE...

T2T4 2   (6A)   THE INTERACTION MODELS ARE USERS'
"...IF I DIDN'T ALREADY KNOW...HOW TO   ASSUMPTIONS ABOUT HOW THE PRODUCT
MOVE FROM AREA TO AREA..."   OPERATES BASED ON PRIOR EXPERIENCE.

T2T4 5   (6C)   THESE EVALUATORS EXPECTED A BLAND
"...ACTUALLY A LABEL WE HAD PREVIOUS..."   SCREEN WHEN THEY OPENED A NEW ITEM...

T1T1 3   (6B)
"...I'M ASSUMING IT'S OK TO OVERWRITE
THIS INFO..."

4

Mcclain   Mon Jun 3 08:15

T2T3 1A   (9)   EVALUATORS WERE NOT CLEAR ABOUT THE
"...ISN'T CLEAR TO ME IF YOU TYPE ENTER   <ENTER> COMMAND CONVENTION...
OR HIT ENTER..."

T2T4 1   (10)
"...DON'T KNOW IF I'M SUPPOSED TO HIT
ENTER..."

T1T2 1   (11)
"...DID I HIT <ENTER>?"

T2T4 2   (12)   TERMINOLOGY IS THE LANGUAGE THE PRODUCT
"...SAY DIALOGUE BOX, BUT I DON'T KNOW   USES TO CONVEY CONTEXT.
WHAT THAT MEANS..."

T1T2 1   (13)
"...INSTALLING ON DRIVE C...I THOUGHT
IT WAS DRIVE A...PRESS ANY KEY..."

T2T4 2   (19)
"...SAYS RECORD UPDATED, I'LL ASSUME
THAT MEANS SAVED..."

T1T2 2   (16)
"...BUT, WHAT ARE NOTES?"

T1T1 1   (23)   CONSISTENCY IS HOW THE PRODUCT IS
"...THE MESSAGE ISN'T EXACTLY THE   ORGANIZED SO USERS CAN FEEL CONFIDENT
SAME..."   GOING FROM SECTION TO SECTION.

T1T1 2   (21)   HERE, AN EVALUATOR IS CONFUSED ABOUT A
"...DON'T HAVE TO PRESS <ENTER>..."   DATE ENTRY WINDOW THAT ISN'T EXPLAINED
                                   PROPERLY IN THE DOCUMENTATION...

T1T2 1   (22)   OTHER EVALUATORS HAVE CONSISTENCY
"...DOESN'T SAY YOU'RE -ABOUT- TO..."   ISSUES...

T2T4 2A   (24A)
"...LOOKS LIKE I SKIPPED OVER THE
CALENDAR..."

T2T4 3A   (24, 25)
"...SAYS IF I PRESS <ESC>...SAYS I
SHOULD HAVE THE CALENDAR...BUT..."

SCREEN SHOTS:
<MUSIC UNDER, OUT>

[FADE SCREEN UP FROM BLACK]
SPINN TEAM RECOMMENDATIONS [TYPE OUT]
[FADE SCREEN TO BLACK]

[FADE SCREEN UP FROM BLACK]   ANNC VO:
                                   THE SPINN TEAM'S RECOMMENDATIONS FROM
VARIOUS SHOTS PARTICIPANTS   THIS TEST ARE TO RE-WRITE PROBLEM AREAS
                                   IN THE DOCUMENTATION AND FOCUS SOFTWARE
                                   DEVELOPMENT TOWARDS A WINDOWS '95
                                   VERSION OF BETTERWORKING DESKTOP.

T2T4 3A   (24, 25)
"...HEAL, HOLY MY SCREEN..."

5

Mcclain   Mon Jun 3 08:15

<MUSIC UP, UNDER, FADE WITH FADE>
[FADE SCREEN UP FROM BLACK]
IN CONCLUSION [TYPE OUT]
[FADE SCREEN TO BLACK]

[FADE SCREEN UP FROM BLACK]

VARIOUS SHOTS PARTICIPANTS

AS USEFUL AS USABILITY TESTING IS, IT
CANNOT STAND ALONE. USABILITY TESTING
WILL SHOW THE PRODUCT, IN THIS CASE
BETTERWORKING DESKTOP, IN ITS INTENDED
ENVIRONMENT: IN THE HANDS OF THE USER.
USABILITY TESTING WILL EXPOSE SOME
POTENTIAL PROBLEMS USERS MAY HAVE WITH
THE PRODUCT. IF THESE PROBLEMS AREN'T
ADDRESSED, IT CAN IMPACT NOT ONLY THE
CURRENT PRODUCT, BUT FUTURE PRODUCTS AS
WELL.

ANNC STANDUP:
WORKING WITH USERS TO UNDERSTAND WHAT
THEY'RE THINKING AS THEY USE OUR
PRODUCT IS A VALUABLE DESIGN TOOL. IT'S
UP TO YOU AND ME TO SEE THAT IT'S PART
OF SPINNAKER'S OVERALL DESIGN STRATEGY."

<MUSIC UP, UNDER, FADE WITH FADE>
[FADE SCREEN UP FROM BLACK]
EXITING TO DOS
EXITING DESKTOP
[FADE SCREEN TO BLACK]
<MUSIC FADE>

Video presentation B-roll log

Note: Counter reset at 00:00:00 from head video of music beds

Music Beds

Music beds start at 11:20
Music beds end at 17:35

B-roll

Sitting at computer over the shoulder	18:00
Truck shots computer head-on	18:20
Over shoulder computer (Fade Up, Fade Out)	18:40
Zoom into control room glass	19:00
Zoom out of glass (FO)	19:26
Truck shots computer reverse	19:50
Control room monitor shots	20:20 (20:50!)
CU keyboard typing	21:00

Graphics

The Spinnaker Spinn Team presents (FUFO)	21:28
Usability Testing of BWD (FUFO)	21:44

6

Usability . . . [typed out] (FUFO)	22:00
Usability *isn't* how product . . .	22:40
Usability *is* how people . . .	22:54
Usability	23:08
Focus on users	23:46
Users use products	24:00
Users are busy people	24:23
Users decide ease of use	24:46
The Product . . . [typed out] (FUFO)	25:15
The Laboratory . . . [typed out] (FUFO)	26:25
The Participants . . . [typed out] (FUFO)	27:34
User Profile (FUFO)	28:50
Have office (FU)	30:56
Family manager	31:21
Admin asst	31:46
(next set)	
Computer exp	32:11
DOS exp	32:29
Job exp	32:49
(next set)	
18 years old	33:19
HS education (note: **misspelled do not use!**)	33:55
The findings . . . [typed out] (FUFO)	37:20
Spinn Team recommendations . . . [typed out] (FUFO)	38:30
In conclusion . . . [typed out] (FUFO)	39:40
Procedural step format	40:34
Confusing directions	41:05
Overview task confusion	41:40
Unnecessary steps in doc	42:30
Obscure wording	42:54
Unclear wording	43:08
Screen doesn't match doc	43:33
Doc difficult to read	43:58
Info overload	44:14

Program

BWD hello screen	45:24
Menu steps	45:38
(in order: Memo pad, address book, world clock, calendar, to do list, label maker, typewriter, set of DOS utilities)	
Exit to DOS?	47:40
Exit BWD?	47:46
c:\BETTER	48:00

(Used with permission of William McClain.)

7

## CHAPTER 9

Web Usability

 If you've been reading this book in a chronological sequence, you may be wondering what can be said about Web usability that hasn't already been said in previous chapters. As you know, we have covered many usability issues that are equally as applicable to the Web as they are to any software or hardware product. And we've included examples from Web testing in our illustrations throughout the text. On the other hand, if you've come directly to this chapter without stopping to read anything that has come before, you may be here because you want a quick summary of the special issues affecting Web usability. After all, it is THE hot topic in usability testing. One study placed the number of Web users at 332 million in 2000 ("Numbers"), and Jakob Nielsen, a Web usability specialist, estimates that this number will grow to 500 million by 2005 (*Designing* 348). With numbers like these, interest in the subject will surely grow along with the increasing user population. For as Nielsen says:

> Usability rules the Web. Simply stated, if the customer can't find a product, then he or she will not buy it.
>
> The Web is the ultimate customer-empowering environment. He or she who clicks the mouse gets to decide *everything*. It is so easy to go elsewhere; all the competitors in the world are but a mouseclick away. (*Designing* 9)

So, whether you've come to this chapter as the last in a logical sequence of chapters or as the first chapter you're reading in this book, there are some things to say about the Web that demonstrate how this medium is different from other media and how this difference translates into unique usability issues. This chapter covers the following topics:

- Problems with the Web today
- The needs of Web users
- Design principles for Web architecture
- Web heuristics

- Tools for Web analysis
- Lab or field testing of Web usability

We begin with the problems, which are many and well-documented.

Problems with the Web: Does It Have to Be This Hard?

Jakob Nielsen said it best in the title of one of his monthly online columns: "The Web Usage Paradox: Why Do People Use Something This Bad?" In this column, he estimated that 90% of all commercial Web sites are too difficult to use because of problems that many others cite as well:

- Lengthy download time
- Lack of clear navigation
- Obscure site structure, oriented toward the products rather than the needs of the site visitor
- Wordy writing style more suitable for print than for the Web

As a result, most people fail in their attempts to use the Web, leaving the site without accomplishing their goal. And once they leave, they generally don't return.

Much recent and relevant research supports how frequently users fail to achieve their goals and how the statistics on Web usability haven't improved much since the Web emerged in the early 1990s. In 1999, the fifth annual survey from NetSmart showed that 83% of Web surfers left sites because of bad performance, citing poor navigation and slow downloads as the main reasons (Thompson).

Poor usability of many Web sites results when companies stress speed to get a presence on the Web over all other considerations, on the premise that they can "throw it at the wall and see if it sticks" (Nielsen, "The Mud-Throwing Theory"). If the user's experience is bad, he or she will probably not try again and may tell others not to try the site either. As an added problem, if the designers make changes to the site based on feedback about problems from the first launch, those customers who have made it through the problems to learn the site may be unhappy with changes resulting from a redesign, even if it improves the site. According to Forrester Research, Fortune 1000 companies spend $1.5 million to $2.1 million per year on site redesigns, "without knowing whether the redesign actually made the site easier to use" (Kalin). In just one example of a redesign of the *New York Times* Web site, a daily reader of news about Asia complained on an Asian studies listserv that the changes made it much more difficult for this reader to see the entire newspaper, which had previously been available. In the previous version, the user could select text version and then scan the newspaper quickly for articles of interest about Asia, which could be found in many different sections of the paper. With the redesign, the text version button disappeared from the homepage, although it could be located several subpages below the main page, using the following path:

- On the *Times* homepage, look for a box entitled "Services."
- Click on the site index.
- Scroll down to the bottom of the page.
- Under the "Services" banner, click on "Text version."

Whereas the user had previously been able to get to this place with one click on the homepage, the designers, believing that readers would want to select a subpage of Asia-Pacific hard news stories instead, deleted the option preferred by this user, which allowed him to scan the paper for news in sports, books, film, theater, and other sections of the paper.

As further evidence of the problems with Web usability, the Boston Consulting Group determined the following about Web users from its research, reported in March 2000 ("Winning the Online Consumer"):

- In 1999, 28% of all attempted online purchases failed.
- Four out of 5 people who have purchased online failed at least once in 1999.
- Only 2% of Internet users say they originally went online to shop; 80% went online to communicate.

Here's more bad news (Gordon):

- 75% of shoppers abandoned their shopping carts without making a purchase (as reported by Bizrate.com).
- 27% of all Web transactions are abandoned at the payment screen (as reported by Forrester).
- $6 billion in sales may have been lost during the 1999 holiday season (as reported by Creative Good).

Although all these statistics are about customers using e-commerce sites, the situation is equally bleak for business-to-business (B2B) sites, as indicated by Forrester Research, reported in the *E-Commerce Times* (Dembeck). Using 30 B2B sites and 25 business-to-consumer sites, Forrester found that all 30 B2B sites failed basic tests of ease of use and reliability because the sites were designed from a company perspective, rather than a customer perspective.

Internet start-ups are no better, even those with large budgets. Nielsen reports that these start-ups typically spend "300 times as much money on advertising as they spend on usability" ("Usability as Barrier"). While advertising will get people to the site, without site usability, they won't stay and they won't return. In other words, they won't "convert" to customers. Statistics bear out this problem with small conversion rates, as reported by Creative Good in June 2000 (*The Dotcom Survival Guide* 6–7):

- The average, industry-wide conversion rate is 1.8%.
- Companies that make the effort to improve the customer experience increase their conversion rates by 40–140%.
- An improved customer experience raises the average order size by 10%.
- A 10% increase in industry-wide order sizes will increase revenues by $5.18 billion.

What do all these startling statistics tell us? That the customer experience is everything. How to understand the customer and the experience (good or bad) that the customer has on the Web? Usability testing. How to plan for effective usability testing of Web sites? Get back to the basics of user-centered design. In the next section, we talk about the first critical step in getting back to the basics: understanding the user's goals, which means putting the user first.

Putting the User First

It seems so simple to state that usability means putting the user first. And that means understanding the user's goals. The problem is summarized succinctly by Mark Hurst of Creative Good (*Dotcom Survival Guide* 10):

> Clearly, there's a difference between what the Web gives its customers and what they actually want. Customers want simplicity, but the Web offers complexity. Customers want service, but the Web offers technology. Customers want to accomplish their goal, but the Web offers "compelling features." In each case, the Web doesn't offer the experience the customer wants. This is the "customer experience gap": the difference between what customers want and what they get.

There seem to be many reasons (excuses) as to why the customer doesn't get what the customer wants. Rod Amis, in his online article "The Truth About Web Design," has one explanation. A Web designer himself, Amis says that "the vast majority of sites on the Web today are designed by individuals and teams who choose (or are forced by backend database architects, bosses, and/or clients) to use design elements, code, utilities and plug-ins" that will crash the user's system or force the user to leave because of specific browser requirements or versions to use the site, or because of too-slow downloads from too much animated advertising or complex graphics. He further states that the Web press and many businesses "require that Web designers ignore the needs of the end users. We Web workers are producing pages which meet the needs of bosses, clients, and our peers primarily."

Nielsen comes to much the same conclusion, describing pages that may look good superficially but do not work once users attempt to use them, because they don't help users *solve problems*, which is why they have come to the Web in the first place. Either the sites don't have the information users want or they don't allow users to make the transactions users want to make. The problem, according to Nielsen, is that "usability does not happen automatically: Web designs *always* turn out bad unless project management takes explicit care to apply usability engineering throughout the design process" ("Users First: Web Usability").

The problem is generally not one of cost, since Web sites can be highly cost-effective. A report entitled *Usability Is Good Business* states that the cost-benefit ratio is typically $1:$10–$100. That is, for every dollar spent on usability, the organization will realize a benefit of between $10 and $100. Usability should not be viewed as an additional expense, but rather as an investment with the following returns (Donahue, Weinschenk, and Nowicki):

- Increased sales and customer satisfaction
- Better notices in the media

- Reduced development and maintenance costs
- Improved productivity and operational efficiency

If usable Web sites can be so cost-effective, it behooves companies to put the focus back on the user, which means understanding real users' needs, the subject of the next section of this chapter.

Understanding Real Users' Needs

If we agree that the first step in planning a usable Web site is to consider the needs of the users, as is the case in planning any usable product, then the first questions to ask are: What do users want to do? What motivates users to come to your Web site, and, more important, what motivates them to return? Far too often, a Web site is designed to answer questions about what the company wants the site to do and not what the user wants to do on the site. Without addressing the needs of the user first, which means understanding the user, the needs or goals of the company cannot be met successfully.

Users want to use the Web for three reasons:

- Information (content)
- Sales (commerce)
- Interaction (communication with other people)

Some sites serve all three of these user needs. Other sites are primarily for information or primarily for communication. It should never be assumed, however, that some sites are primarily for commerce (even if that is the site's underlying objective). As the research about users shows, they rarely make a purchase the first time they visit a commerce site. The first time and perhaps for several return visits, they may visit for information, which, if easily accessible and useful, may bring them back later for a purchase. If the site is arranged from the organization's perspective or uses terminology that requires knowledge of the organization or its products (domain knowledge), it will not be useful to the uninitiated user.

Take the case of a person we'll call Mel. Mel is interested in purchasing a video camera, so he decides to visit the Sony Web site, because he believes that Sony makes good products and he wants to learn about its video cameras. When Mel goes to the Sony Web site, he finds the following alphabetical listing, which contains some Sony brand product names, some common names for products, and some technical terms for product categories:

accessories	digital satellite systems
boombox	Glasstron®
cd Walkman®	Handycam® camcorders
cassette Walkman®	home audio
clock radio	home audio es
digital imaging accessories	home entertainment
digital video	home video
dvd	md disc camcorder

md Walkman®	telecom products
network Walkman®	television
portable radios	video walkman
radio Walkman®	Webtv™ internet terminal
tape recorder	world band radio/scanners

If Mel scans the list quickly, looking under "v" for video camera, he sees "video Walkman" but not "video camera." In Mel's second attempt to achieve his goal, he might try "c" for camcorder, but he finds nothing there to help him. If Mel persists in trying to figure out how Sony lists its entry for video cameras, he might return to the top of the list and read every item until he finds one that might match his search. The first one he comes to is "Handycam® camcorders," but if he reads the whole list, he also finds "md disk camcorder." As Mel may not understand the distinction between these two choices, he'll probably click on the more familiar-sounding one: Handycam® camcorders. Here the page that appears offers little help, as the list of specifications of the video recorder seems to require domain knowledge, which Mel doesn't have. It doesn't help him to know that the video camera has ¼ in. CCD with 270k Pixels, 20X optical/200X digital zoom, and 6 Mode Program Auto Exposure, which are the first three items on the list of features. Mel can click to get "more specifications," but he's hesitant to dig deeper because he's afraid that the information will become even more technical, taking him farther from his goal. What Mel really wants to know, but can't seem to find, is information about whether this camcorder will fulfill his need for an upcoming vacation he has planned. And, if he wants to compare the features of this camcorder to others that Sony makes, Mel has to return to the homepage and click on the other entry and then write down information about both products to make his own comparisons. It seems it would be easier to get in the car and drive to an electronics store where Mel could compare many products and brands, as well as talk to someone who can answer his questions. In fact, Sony may not want customers like Mel to use its site, because it provides a way to "scroll for store locations" rather than providing the information potential customers might want to know before going to a store. So, if the site is not meant to serve potential customers who are likely to go there in search of *information*, then who is the intended user of the site?

To make the Web site speak the user's language and to provide a good experience for first-time visitors, the designers have to ask the usual questions about the audience that any technical communicator or Web content developer knows to ask:

- What do users *want* to know or do when they visit?
- What do users *need* to know?
- What's *most important* to them?
- What's the *problem* they're trying to solve?

This last question is probably the most important. In thinking of visitors as problem-solvers, Web content developers can focus the Web site on providing solutions to their problems.

The best way to determine what users want is to understand users' goals and then match the users' goals with the Web site's goals. Because users are goal-directed (as discussed in Chapter 3), the design of the Web site should focus on helping users achieve their goal. When users achieve their goal easily and completely, they're much more likely to come back to the site again. When they return, they will have a different goal. When their goal for information is satisfied, if the site is an e-commerce site, they're likely to move to the next step, which is to attempt to make a purchase. This user represents the *conversion* factor—from visitor to customer—that we spoke of earlier. Now that this user has converted to a customer, the organization's main goal shifts to help this customer successfully complete the transaction without leaving the site prematurely. At this point, the goal of the organization and the goal of the user are one and the same: a successful purchase.

Even when a site is primarily for information purposes, it may still have a "selling" function. Academic Web sites fit this category. Users come to an academic Web site for information about a college or university. If they like what they see and find the site easy to navigate, they may request a catalog or even apply online: the completed application is the "sale." In planning a usability test of a Web site for a private women's college, the team knew from research about Web visitors' usage that most visitors were on the site for several minutes (longer than is typical), but that their time on the Web site did not translate into downloading the application or requesting that one be sent. Usability testing revealed that the methods for obtaining the application or for requesting additional information were confusing to users. Later in this chapter, we say more about academic Web sites as a special-use category. In the next section, we focus on the specific characteristics of Web users.

Most Users Are Novices

Part of understanding user needs is understanding who Web users are. Because the Web has been around since the early 1990s, it is a commonly held belief that most Web users are now experienced with the Web. Instead, the research shows that Web users continue to be novice users. This assertion is based not only on the fact that the number of new users grows every day around the world, but also on the fact that most users don't move beyond the novice stage, even when they return to a site. Nielsen states emphatically that "all Web users are novices all the time, since you very rarely use any individual website long enough to become an expert user." A user will spend only a few seconds acclimating to a new site; if the site design isn't obvious, the user leaves ("End of Web Design").

Most Users Are Conservative

Users are conservative, meaning they resist change. They are reluctant to accept innovations in Web design. They want consistency in the look and feel of Web sites, as they move from one site to the next. To users, the Web is an environment in which their "expectations for narrative flow and user options" should be consistently met (Nielsen, "Increasing Conservatism"). One study shows that users place their mouse in the target location on the screen where they *expect* to be able to click on a menu option, even before the menu options appear (Byrne et al., "Eye Tracking"). In this way, users make their selections even before the page loads.

Users Are Goal-Driven

Because users are goal-driven, speed is of the essence. They are very impatient with long download times, with 10 seconds being the limit of their tolerance (Nielsen, *Designing* 48). In a 1999 report, Zona Research cites an even shorter requirement of eight seconds, and the eight-second rule must be applied to the still large audience with 14.4-kb modems. Although the number of users who have higher-speed modems is increasing, with 52.7% of users reporting a recent upgrade (according to the latest WWW user survey conducted in late 1998 by the Graphics, Visualization, and Usability Center or GVU), one-quarter of the respondents had not upgraded and had no plans to upgrade. This group was represented primarily by those who had less than one year's experience on the Web, which, as we said earlier, continues to be the predominant group of Web users. The GVU survey found that the average age for someone with less than one year on the Web is 41.5 years old, an increase of 4.5 years over the previous survey. Even with increased numbers of higher-speed modem use for Web access, the GVU survey found that the percentage of users with 56.6-kb/sec modems is still largely in the United States (34.4%) with a smaller number in Europe (13.3%). Zona Research reports that shoppers with 14.4-kb modems who are unable to load Web pages within eight seconds represent a potential loss of $73 million a month in e-commerce sales, $3 million a month in the securities trading industry, and over $2.8 million a month in the travel and tourism industry.

Once users have successfully downloaded a Web site, they are goal-driven to perform some task (get information, make a purchase, make a connection). Research by User Interface Engineering (Spool et al.) shows that users ignore banner ads while focusing on their task. Only when users have successfully completed their goal will they notice other elements of a Web site, such as banner advertising. Other studies show that users resist the requirement to register at a site, especially if they are barred from entering the site without first registering. Because users are goal-oriented and come to a site seeking information, the studies show that they should be able to get into the site and get access to some of the information they seek. Then, and only then, should they be asked to register: at the point where they would like to do more on the site. One study by Intuit of its online mortgage site, QuickenMortgage.com, shows that usage doubled after the registration requirement was postponed until a later stage in the process (reported in Nielsen, "Web Research"). Other studies by Creative Good demonstrate how a confusing sign-in or registration process on Web sites deters customers from making purchases (Rehman).

Users Skim and Scan Text

Users don't "read" on the Web. Here are four reasons why (Nielsen, *Designing* 106):

1. Reading on the screen is hard on the eyes and 25% slower than reading on paper.
2. Readers use the Web to get information, and they're in a hurry to act. Because it is a user-driven medium, readers want to "click" on things and move around.

3. Each Web page competes with "hundreds of millions" of others for the user's attention. Users move fast if they don't find what they want right away.

4. Modern life is hectic and people don't have time to work too hard for information.

Thus, Web users are scanners and skimmers of text, not readers, searching for keywords that match their goal for information. In particular, they are looking for hyperlinks, highlighted words or phrases that will take them into deeper levels of information they're seeking. So, the most important hyperlinks (from their perspective) should be placed first, and above the fold, or the part of the screen that is visible to them without scrolling. Because users prefer to navigate a site via the text links (vs. graphic images), the more descriptive the link, the better (Spool et al.).

Also, because the computer screen is not the same medium as the printed page, Nielsen recommends making text 50% shorter to make the experience a pleasant one for users ("Be Succinct!"). However, shorter text blocks do not necessarily lead to the conclusion that generous use of white space is a positive finding for Web sites. Spool et al. found that white space actually makes information seekers' task more difficult, whereas the opposite is true for readers of paper-based text. On the Web, white space means more scrolling, and users prefer not to scroll, especially on navigation pages like the homepage. Although Nielsen contends that people are more willing to scroll nowadays than they were when he was first doing Web testing in 1994 and 1995, their willingness to scroll may be attributed more to their knowledge that Web pages are poorly designed and require scrolling. Still, they prefer to make their selections for hypertext links from the information they see "above the fold" (*Designing* 112–115). If information is grouped and descriptive hyperlinks are provided, dense text can be easy to use, so long as paragraphs have clear topic sentences to support skimming.

Another study, which tested the white-space finding from Spool et al., asked users to locate information on three identical Web sites, where the only difference was in the amount of white space (Bernard, Chaparro, and Thomasson). Although the researchers found no significant differences in the amount of time participants took to find information, there were significant differences in the participants' satisfaction levels with the amount of white space. Highest preference and greatest satisfaction were given to the site with "medium" white space. Too little white space made the site difficult to read; too much white space gave the site an "empty" look and required more scrolling.

As for the amount of time users spend searching for information, another research study found that users spent 12% of their time searching for items on a page, another 13% requesting information (filling out forms), and 5% responding to requests (e.g., providing a file name for downloading). However, most of their remaining time was spent waiting or scrolling. When combined with waiting for pages to download, users spend about 1 hour and 27 minutes of 5 hours either waiting or scrolling (Byrne et al., "The Tangled Web").

More Men than Women Use the Web

Although more men than women use the Web, the gap is narrowing. The February 2000 Nielsen/Net Ratings showed that 53 percent of Web users are men and 47 percent are women. The ratings also show that there may be differences in the ways in which men and women use the Web, with men spending one hour and 35 minutes more online per month than women in February 1999 and two hours and 12 minutes more than women in December 1999 (O'Connor). Forrester Research analyst Ekaterina Walsh believes that the differences may be attributed to the ways in which men and women differ in their view of technology, with men preferring to play with technology and women preferring to use it as a tool to get something done. Also, according to Melissa Moss of the Women's Consumer Network, women are more loyal than men in their usage patterns on the Web, meaning that men prefer to browse or surf and women prefer to return to a site they like. Since women account for 70 percent of household purchases, companies selling products traditionally purchased by women should understand these differences and build sites that are task-oriented with lots of product information (reported in O'Connor). Another study of gender differences found that gender is "one of the most important variables in learning" on the Web. The differences have to do with spatial orientation: men relate more easily to visual displays of information (spatial orientation) than women, based on evidence from magnetic resonance imaging (MRI) experiments that studied brain activity patterns and the differences between men's and women's responses to verbal and spatial displays (Hall and Hickman). Still another study of gender differences, this time among teenage boys and girls, found that boys are more interested in learning about technology, playing games, and building Web pages than girls, who are more goal-oriented, using the Web for homework and to communicate with others (Bowman).

These findings should not lead designers to conclude that they need to design a Web site, or even a part of a Web site, specifically for women, according to an online article in *Web Informant* (Strom). Rather than design a special part of a Web site specifically for women, as one car-buying Web site does, the author recommends providing better service and better tools for anyone visiting the site, thus improving the experience for all.

Older vs. Younger Users

Two studies look at the differences between older and younger users on the Web. One study found that older users spend more time on the Web than younger users, with increasing age leading to an increasing amount of time spent on the Web. Although teens are typically early adopters of new technology, the study found that teens between the ages of twelve and seventeen were online eight days per month with 303 minutes of connection time. This was compared to people between the ages of eighteen and thirty-four, who went online thirteen days and spent an average of 656 minutes per month, and people between the ages of thirty-five and forty-nine, who went online fifteen days and averaged 804 minutes. The main difference between older and younger Web users is that younger users view the Web as an entertainment tool, whereas adults view it as a productivity tool (Bowman). In another study that looked at age and gender differences with regard to speed and task completion issues on the Web, the experience levels of users seemed to be the determining factor, not age or gender (Palmiter et al.).

International Users

Because the World Wide Web is designed for a worldwide audience, it is highly likely that your Web site will have international visitors. Therefore, to be effective, it should take their needs into consideration. The number of Internet users in non-English speaking countries is growing at a considerable pace, and U.S. leadership is decreasing, as a result of a significant number of new Web users in Europe and the Asia-Pacific region. According to an eMarketer eGlobal report, the number of Internet users around the world will top 362 million by 2003, with just under 37% of these users being in the United States ("Internet Users").

If a user and task analysis shows that a segment of your audience reads English as a second language, you should consider a design that allows for translation and localization. Translation requires space for English to expand when translated into other languages (or vice versa, to contract when going from other languages to English). The rule of thumb is to allow for 30% expansion room when going from English to other languages. That means that you need to allow 30% more space for text in languages other than English. The simpler the layout of the page, the easier it will be to translate the information into other languages. If you have text inside graphics, for instance, you will have problems when the text is translated.

Unlike translation, which addresses language only, localization means making the content meaningful to audiences in different countries and cultures. The best way to localize Web sites is to avoid country- or culture-specific examples or references in text, as well as in graphics and icons. Localization issues must also be considered when writing in English for use in other English-speaking countries; for there are differences in language, usage, spelling, and degrees of formality or informality when going from American English to British English, as well as using English in Canada, Australia, New Zealand, and elsewhere. Effective localization may also mean reorganizing the information on the site to give prominent placement to the most relevant or meaningful information to people in different countries or cultures.

Treatment of dates is just one area that needs to be addressed in localizing Web sites. If your site requests information about dates, you should specify how it needs to be entered: mm/dd/yyyy is one way, but there are several others, including the more common European model of dd/mm/yyyy. Time, as well, differs in different countries, with the United States more frequently using a 12-hour clock and Europe more frequently using a 24-hour clock. First name, last name requests can also be confusing, as some cultures reverse the order of the names, beginning with their "last" name, followed by their first name. Better to use words like "surname" and "given" name to avoid confusion. Likewise, when requesting address information, people in different countries may not use zip codes; better to call this item a postal code. Another issue to consider is print format. If you want to make forms available for print, you need to provide both the U.S. letter size and the A4 format used by much of the rest of the world. In using dimensions or distances, as well, you will want to specify both metric and U.S.-based measurement systems.

The meaning of color can also be culture-specific. White, for instance, may mean "death" in some Asian countries, whereas it may mean "pure" in some Western countries. Red may mean happiness in China, danger in the United States, and death in Egypt. Hand gestures, animals, symbols, numbers, and images can also carry different meanings in different countries and cultures. Some images convey no meaning beyond their own culture, such as national monuments or sports references. Other images, such as icons, need careful consideration; however, common usage has given meaning to some icons where a cultural meaning does not exist. The champagne glass, for instance, is meaningless in many countries in Africa, but the icon for "fragile" is still typically presented as a champagne glass. My own experience points up another example that may be less well known. On a recent trip to China, I was struck by the fact that the highway signs display the icons of a knife and fork to indicate restaurant locations. In a country where I have yet to see a knife and fork, I found it odd to see such icons. When I asked a group of Chinese faculty participating in a technical writing institute in Nanjing, China, to create an icon for a restaurant stop on a highway, some drew rice bowls, while others drew the knife and fork. Those drawing the knife and fork demonstrated that they had internalized the meaning of the icon, even though it didn't fit their culture and custom. In cases such as this one, consistency in icon usage may be more helpful than localizing with culture-specific examples.

Although there is much more that can be said about designing Web pages for international audiences, the subject is only one among many that bear consideration when thinking about audience. As with everything we've covered in this section, it comes down to the simple point of knowing what real users need. But this is only the first issue to consider. Once you know who your users are and what they need from your Web site, you must apply what you know to designing a Web site that works for them. This topic, called information architecture or Web architecture, is the subject of the next section.

Design Principles for Web Architecture

No amount of guessing or even thinking about what users want will replace learning about users' needs by observing them actually using your site or a competitor's site. Sending the team or a representative to users' homes or offices to watch them work and learn from them will teach the team how to build a site (or rebuild an ineffective one) that will match the user's goals. Applying the information learned about users from such field studies is but one step in a multistep process of user-centered design, as we have described throughout this book. Information gathered from site visits can help the design team not only identify who the users are, but can also help the team formulate the users' goals, the users' preferences for tasks, and the users' mental model for where and how to find the information. In this section, we discuss the design principles that apply to Web architecture.

One way to approach Web design is to copy what everyone else does. In fact, that's exactly what Nielsen advocates, using the following yardstick ("When Bad Design"):

- If 90% or more of the big sites do something in a single way, this is the standard you must comply with.
- If 60–90% of the big sites do something in a single way, there is a strong convention to do the same.
- If less than 60% of the big sites do something in a single way, there is no established standard yet, and this gives you some flexibility; however, it's best to look for a model used by at least 20% of the big sites.

As we've said earlier, the reason for such design compliance is that users arrive at your site with expectations from experience at other sites. They expect to be able to use the site without training and to use what they've learned at previous sites to make the effort fast and easy. Although Nielsen's design yardstick seems to take away most of the designer's choices, it, in fact, leaves open quite a few decisions regarding information architecture because the *content* of the site, or its information, must be built to suit the unique needs of the site. It is this important emphasis on content that causes many technical communicators to now call themselves information developers or information architects.

The importance of content itself and the arrangement of the content on a Web site is borne out by a study that evaluated 32 features on the Web sites of 28 cyberstores with a large product selection. The study revealed that variations in the following design features had no impact on sales (Lohse and Spiller):

- Choice of background color or pattern
- Availability of help screens
- Consistency of selecting new pages from the top, side, or bottom
- Homogeneity of product listings
- Number of buttons on the homepage
- Use of icon-only, icon-plus-text, or text-only buttons
- Number of clicks required to reach an item

Rather, the research revealed that it was the following item, alone among 13 items identified as affecting sales success, that accounted for the greatest difference: how the products were listed. The best lists were those with text descriptions, graphics, and navigation buttons that provided additional information. Any improvement in the basic list box increased sales. The authors concluded that a user interface that allows potential customers to effectively browse a product list and easily get the information they seek is more important in generating sales than any other factor.

This is compelling data, and it points once again to the importance of content, shaped to serve the needs of users. How do you determine what that content should be? One sure way is to conduct an early prototype test, as the site is being planned, to learn how users use the content. One such prototype technique uses a card-sorting strategy to determine where users would expect to find information. By using a set of note cards or sticky notes with each topic of information listed on a separate card, users can sort through the cards to arrange the information under the categories that make the most sense to them. Once a consistent pattern emerges among users, the developers can feel confident that the Web architecture will match the user's mental model. In addition, any terminology issues can also be sorted out, so that the names or descriptions of the items match the users' vocabulary. If you recall the Sony example used earlier, a simple card-sorting exercise of the products on the Sony Web site would quickly reveal the problems with the current architecture.

Sometimes, an alphabetical list makes sense, but other times, it's better to sort items in a list or elements on a homepage by those most likely to be of interest to users. How to determine this? Nielsen suggests a number of ways ("Prioritize"):

- Use best-sellers, placed at the top of your list
- Highlight items that will be of most interest, even while placing them in an alphabetical list
- Mark recent entries as "new" in a list with an appropriate icon
- Track server traffic to learn where users go most often and make this information prominent and easy to locate (requiring fewer clicks)

At the same time, it makes sense to comply with the design standards that have become commonplace. One of the most widely accepted standards is the use of blue, underlined text to indicate a hyperlink. Even though Nielsen and others have commented that blue is not the best color choice, as it is a cool color that recedes rather than comes forward to stand out on the screen, it has nonetheless become the design standard. That means users expect it. So, don't change it. Likewise, when they have clicked on a hyperlink, the color of the link should change to pink or rose, as this is a standard users recognize.

Other standards are not as universally adopted, but still a few choices are commonly understood by users. For instance, an institutional logo and banner generally occupy the very top of the screen. Menu bars for local navigation are most often located either at the top of the screen or down the left side. In the early days of Web development, menu bars might be anywhere on the screen, including at the bottom, below the "fold," or viewing area. Users frequently missed them, not knowing where to look, until the choices for location were standardized. Another example is the shopping cart, which e-commerce users recognize as the place to make selections for purchase. In answer to the question, "Do Interface Standards Stifle Design Creativity?" Nielsen says, "no": "A **standard ensures that your users can understand the individual interface elements** in your design and that they know **where to look for what features**" (bold in original).

Top-10 Web Design Mistakes

Even when designed according to standards, interfaces frequently are riddled with problems. Nielsen's top-10 list of these problems is shown in Table 9.1 ("Who Commits"). His survey was first conducted in 1996, then repeated in 1999, with many of the same mistakes appearing on both lists.

As you can see, the number-one problem is slow download time, made so by too many graphics, especially those that don't add anything substantive to the site. While Nielsen's data refer to popular Web sites, he also cites data for the 10 largest corporations' Web sites, with an average violation rate of 20%, higher than that of the most popular Web sites. Nielsen concludes that it is no accident the most popular Web sites have such a low rate of violation, as these Web sites are popular because they are so easy to use. The reason for the higher violation factor for major corporate Web sites is download time: the corporate homepages took 19 seconds on average to download, whereas the popular Web sites averaged 8 seconds to download. These measurements were taken on the weekend, using a high-speed ISDN line, not the more typical analog modem that is in common use.

Because download speed continues to be the biggest problem in Web usability, Web Pages That Suck.com presents two ways to determine if a homepage takes too long to download (Flanders):

1. As you click the URL, hold your breath and if the page is still loading when you gasp for air, it's too big.
2. As you parachute out of an airplane holding a wireless laptop, click on the URL and don't open your chute until the page finishes loading. If you crash before it loads, the page is too big.

Of course, you don't really want to try these techniques yourself, but the humor evinced in these methods highlights the significance of the problem.

TABLE 9.1	Top-10 Mistakes of Web Design
Design Mistake	**Violation Score (%)**
Slow download times	84
Non-standard link colors	17
Long scrolling navigation pages	15
Scrolling text or looping animation	12
Frames	11
Orphan pages	10
Bleeding-edge technology	7
Complex URLs	6
Lack of navigation support	4
Outdated information	1
Average	**16**

Source: Jakob Nielsen, "Who Commits the 'Top 10 Mistakes' of Web Design?" Alertbox, 16 May 1999 <http://www.useit.com/alertbox/990516.html>.

In addition to design issues associated with download speed and navigation, a key element of effective design is page layout, which we discuss in the next section.

Elements of Page Layout

As shown in Table 9.2, four elements of page layout affect the overall feel and use of a Web site (User Interface Engineering).

Although these considerations apply to any and all Web pages, certain applications, such as Intranets and academic Web sites, involve special considerations. We discuss these applications next.

Intranet Design Components

An Intranet is a company's own internal Internet, containing information to support the work of the employees. While few companies apply as much effort to Intranets, either in their development or in their usability, poorly designed Intranet sites can account for a lot of lost productivity. Many have no main portal, or homepage, that serves as a starting place for all employees, and many are an ununified conglomeration of different information compiled by various departments, making the site difficult to navigate and search. Nielsen recommends that Intranets should all have a portal homepage with the following three components:

- *Directory hierarchy:* provides a structure for all the site content
- *Search field:* connects to a search engine that indexes all the pages and makes distinctions between more important and less important pages
- *Current news:* provides information about the company and employee interests; can replace an employee newsletter, email announcements, and memos

When a company focuses on improving its Intranet, it can reap substantial savings. When Bay Networks invested $3 million in Intranet usability, it reaped an estimated savings of $10 million per year for its 7,000 users (Nielsen, "Intranet Portals"). When Sandia National Laboratories redesigned its Intranet, the design-

TABLE 9.2	Elements of Page Layout for the Web
Page element	**Description**
Page length	The number of screens the page occupies. If longer than one screen, users must scroll to see below the fold.
Page density	The amount of information on the page. Pages can be lightweight, using a lot of white space and meaningless graphics, or dense, packed with useful text and graphics.
Levels of information	Pages might contain a single level of information or a hierarchy of multiple levels.
Grids, panels, and frames	Well-designed pages use a consistent grid of columns, plus navigation aids in left, top, or bottom panels (or in more than one location).

Source: Adapted from "Four Elements of Page Layout." User Interface Engineering. 15 April 2001.
<http://www.uie.com>.

ers set as an objective that users would be able to locate information 80% of the time. The first revision of the site produced a 73% search success rate with an average completion time of 113 seconds. A further revision to the site, based on the usability data learned from the first testing, improved the success rate to 84% with an average completion time of 57 seconds (Baca and Cassidy).

Academic Web Sites

Academic Web sites have both an Intranet (internal) and an Internet (external) audience. The internal audience needs both current and archived information. The external audience may represent prospective or current students (each group with different needs), plus alumni and potential employees. The most common problem of academic Web design is that the design reflects the hierarchy or structure of the college or university, making the information most relevant to the various audiences difficult to locate. As Steve Johnson, an instructional technologist and Provost of St. Petersburg Junior College, put it ("Expert Reveals" 6):

> A common mistake is to let the culture and politics of the institution drive the Web design to the point that people are not being served information that matters to them. Students want grades and transcripts online—they do not want to click through a welcome message from the registrar before they can get their grades. Potential employees want job listings—they do not want them buried beneath piles of links and pages related to board minutes. Staff want a quick and accurate telephone directory, not a fancy animated splash screen between them and the number they are looking for.

If you stop and take a look at your college or university Web site (or that of your alma mater), ask yourself how well it works for you. In the case of my university's Web site, when it was first designed, it was organized according to the major divisions of the university, with Development and College Relations being the first one listed! After a redesign, improvements were made; however, students seeking information about registering for classes had to click on an item in the main menu labeled Admissions (because registration was located within Admissions in the university's organizational chart). More recent redesigns have improved the site for real users. In another situation, officials at the University of Kentucky found that the university's Web site, which was designed by computer technicians, was too technical, resulting in very low traffic. After a major redesign, the hits increased tenfold ("The Sun Shines" 7).

A major survey of 10,000 college-bound high-school students shows that they rated college Web sites as their main source of information ("What 10,000 Students Want"). The quality of the Web site experience closely correlated to the students' impressions of the college. Students start searching for college information on the Web in the tenth grade, and the Web is a major influence in the early stages of their decision making.

The survey results point to the follow requirements for effective Web sites for college-bound students:

1. Present complete and clear tuition costs and financial aid information.
2. Make sure that a link to the admissions page is prominently listed on the homepage.

3. Place a link back to the homepage on all pages, as students hate to have to hit the back button.
4. Provide a profile of incoming freshmen—SAT scores, GPA, ethnic diversity, etc.—and pictures of current students.
5. Include an overview of the college location and description of the surrounding community.
6. Make the site design distinctive—make sure positioning messages are clear and the homepage isn't generic (students equate generic design with a boring institution).

Whether your Web site is for internal or external use, for e-commerce, or for a university, you should still design it to support the goals of the user. But how do you go about following all of this good advice for creating effective Web sites and avoiding all the pitfalls of bad Web design? By adopting a user-centered design process, of course. Now that we've examined the first steps in this process—understanding users and their goals and creating prototypes to test the concept for the site—we can move to the next step in this process, which is to conduct a heuristic evaluation of the Web site, either in its present form or in the development stage. In Chapter 2, we presented several sets of heuristics, or rules, for evaluating any product. In the next section, we present specific heuristics for the Web.

Usability Heuristics for the Web

Most people who conduct heuristic evaluations are familiar with Jakob Nielsen's 10 usability heuristics (see Chapter 2). Recently, Nielsen and others have clarified these rules to show how they apply to Web usability evaluations. As Table 9.3 on pages 380–381 shows, Nielsen's original list ("Heuristic Evaluation" 30) can be applied to Web reviews, with the help of a few specific comments from two usability experts, Denise Pieratti and Keith Instone.

Pieratti adds other categories to these 10 heuristics that have specific application to the Web (23):

- *Respect for users and their skills.* Does the Web site support, extend, supplement, or enhance a user's skills, background knowledge, and expertise?
- *Pleasurable and respectful interaction.* Do users' interactions with the site enhance the quality of their work life? Does the design reflect the users' role as they navigate through the site? Is the design both visually and functionally pleasing?
- *Quality of work.* Does the user's interaction with the Web site produce usable output?
- *Privacy.* Does the Web site help protect personal and private information and interactions?
- *Readability and legibility.* Is the text readable?
- *Information structure.* Is the information ordered into a hierarchy based on precedence, significance, and frequency of use? Does the underlying structure support intended functions, which are based on user tasks, goals, and needs?

Nielsen weighs in with some comments of his own regarding the original list of 10 heuristics, especially concerning *reset, cancel,* and *undo* options in Web applications ("*Reset* and *Cancel* Buttons"). He contends that the reset and cancel buttons, if removed, would improve usability. Although cancel makes sense in a GUI-based application, because it allows the user to close a dialog box without accepting any changes the user may have made, it does not match what the user does in a Web environment. The same with undo, which works well in editing systems, because it allows the user to revert to a previous state. However, Nielsen contends that the user prefers the back button to escape from any unwanted situation on the Web, making reset and cancel options confusing or redundant. Worse, when the reset button is placed beside the accept button, users can click on the wrong choice and thus lose all the data they may have entered on a form. Cancel can be used sparingly in situations where the user is completing a multipart form, progressing through several pages. In this case, the back button would not undo the information; thus, cancel is useful. An additional button needed in sales transactions is a remove button to delete items placed in a shopping cart. This lets users know they can take things out of their cart without cancelling the order or going back to a previous page.

A special issue of *Technical Communication*, devoted to articles on heuristics for Web communication, focuses on information sites. The researchers whose articles appear in the special issue created five new sets of heuristics for Web development and evaluation, based on the following aspects (van der Geest and Spyridakis 304):

- The rhetorical situation as it is created by authors for and with their readers
- Navigation as a means to signal the information structure of a site and to guide visitors to and through the information
- The presentation of verbal information so that users can comprehend it
- The visual display and presentation of information
- The involvement of users, either directly or indirectly, in the design and evaluation of Web sites

Each of the articles in this special issue covers one aspect of these Web heuristics. Well-researched and tested by both students and Web professionals, the heuristics are complex and detailed. However, each article ends with a checklist, which can be accessed, along with the complete articles, at the journal's Web site, <www.techcomm-online.org>.

As we have discussed in this section, heuristic evaluation provides an excellent way to assess a Web site against a list of rules, or guiding principles. It is one tool in the usability toolkit. In the next section of this chapter, we discuss other tools that provide different kinds of information.

Other Tools for Web Analysis

Other tools for Web analysis fall into one of two categories: (1) computer-based tools that generate data without human intervention and (2) computer-based tools that use humans to provide feedback.

(*continued on page 382*)

TABLE 9.3	Nielsen's 10 Heuristics Adapted for the Web*
Nielsen's heuristics	*Web adaptation*
1. *Visibility of system status.* The system should always keep users informed about what is going on, through appropriate feedback within reasonable time.	Are the URL line and the status line used to provide effective feedback? (P) Most important to users is to know "Where am I?" and "Where can I go next?" That requires branding each page and indicating what section it belongs to. Links to other pages should be clearly marked. (I)
2. *Match between system and the real world.* The system should speak the user's language, with words, phrases, and concepts familiar to the user, rather than system-oriented terms. Follow real-world conventions, making information appear in a natural and logical order.	Does the Web site reflect users' language, tasks, and intentions? (P) Because users come from different backgrounds on the Web, this issue is a challenge. (I)
3. *User control and freedom.* Users often choose system functions by mistake and will need a clearly marked "emergency exit" to leave the unwanted state without having to go through an extended dialogue. Support undo and redo.	Can users select and sequence tasks? Can they easily return to where they were if they choose an inappropriate path? (P) Even though many emergency exits are provided by the browser, a "home" button on every page is a simple way to let users feel in control of the Web site. Be careful when forcing certain font choices, colors, screen widths, or browser versions, including the use of "advanced technologies" that users may not have. (I)
4. *Consistency and standards.* Users should not have to wonder whether different words, situations, or actions mean the same thing. Follow platform conventions.	Do the Web pages work with different browsers? Can people resize windows or adjust browser options without compromising information or the task? (P) One of the most common cases of inconsistent wording is with links, page titles, and headers. Inconsistent wording can confuse users when the destination page has a different title from the link that took them there. Standards on the Web mean following HTML and other specifications. Deviations will create opportunities for unusable features to creep into your site. (I)
5. *Error prevention.* Even better than good error messages is a careful design, which prevents a problem from occurring in the first place.	Does the Web site give enough directions and information so that users can find desired pathways and complete desired operations? If an error does occur, can users recover easily? (P) Because of the limitations of HTML forms, inputting information is a common source of user errors. GUI-style widgets, coming into more common use, cut down on the errors, but you still have to doublecheck these after submission.

TABLE 9.3 (Continued)	
Nielsen's heuristics	*Web adaptation*
6. *Recognition rather than recall.* Make objects, actions, and options visible. The user should not have to remember information from one part of the dialogue to another. Instructions for use of the system should be visible or easily retrievable whenever appropriate.	For the Web, this heuristic is closely related to system status (#1). If users can tell where they are by looking at the current page, they are less likely to get lost. Good labels and descriptive links are crucial for recognition. (I)
7. *Flexibility and efficiency of use.* Accelerators—unseen by the novice user—may often speed up interaction for the expert users to such an extent that the system can cater to both experienced and inexperienced users. Allow users to tailor frequent actions.	Do links take users where they expect to go? Are images and data loaded as effectively as possible? (P) Some of the best accelerators, like bookmarks, are provided by the browser, so pages should be easy to bookmark. Do not use frames in a way that prevents bookmarking. (I)
8. *Aesthetic and minimalist design.* Dialogues should not contain information which is irrelevant or rarely needed. Every extra unit of information in a dialogue competes with the relevant units of information and diminishes their relative visibility.	Are the best media and screen images used to convey a message? (P) Extraneous information on a page is a distraction and a slow-down. Make rarely needed information accessible via a link. Use links for progressive levels of detail. If users jump into the middle of a progression, make sure there's a way to go "up" to get the bigger picture. (I)
9. *Help users recognize, diagnose, and recover from errors.* Error messages should be expressed in plain language (no codes), precisely indicate the problem, and constructively suggest a solution.	Every error message should offer a solution or a link to a solution. For example, if a search yields no hits, don't just tell the user to broaden the search: provide a link that will broaden the search. (I)
10. *Help and documentation.* Even though it is better if the system can be used without documentation, it may be necessary to provide help and documentation. Any such information should be easy to search, focused on the user's task, list concrete steps to be carried out, and not be too large.	Is the site self-documenting? (P) For the Web, the key is to integrate the documentation into your site, either through links to specific help or into each page. (I)

*Pieratti's comments indicated by P; Instone's indicated by I.
Source: Heuristics from Jakob Nielsen, "Heuristic Evaluation." *Usability Inspection Methods.* Eds. Jakob Nielsen and Robert L. Mack. New York: Wiley, 1994, p. 30. © 1994 John Wiley & Sons, Inc. (Reprinted by permission of John Wiley & Sons, Inc.) Web adaptations from Keith Instone, "Usability Heuristics for the Web." Webreview.com 28 June 1999 <http://webreview.com> and Denise D. Pieratti, "Usability and the Web." *Intercom* June 1998, pp. 20–23.

Tools Without Human Intervention

Tools that provide data without human intervention are popular at some companies, because they can work behind the scenes at all times without interrupting product use. These tools track a user's time and location on a Web site. The most basic tool of this type extracts information from server log files, such as the number of visitors to a site in a given time period, the types of requests made for information, including the date and time of the request, and any errors that occurred. The advantage of using such tools is that they can provide insight into real users performing actual tasks in natural working conditions vs. the artificial setting of a lab. As well, they can represent the activities of many users over a long period of time vs. the small sample of users in a short time span, as is typically the case in lab testing. In addition to basic log file data tracking, more specific types of tools in this category, such as WebCriteria and Evity, track page-loading time, the time it takes a user to complete a purchase, changes per week to a site, and so forth. WebCriteria provides an added feature through its Max model (a model for Maxwell or Maxine), which creates a "typical" user based on data collected in a number of categories reflecting human behavior. Max is then instructed to crawl through a site and report on the average user's experience regarding page-load times, page visits, and so forth. Or Max can compare searches for the same types of data on competing Web sites and report the comparisons to the client. However, tallying where a user goes to get information does not shed any light on whether the user's *goals* are being met. For that, you need human testing.

Tools Used by Humans

Vividence adds people to the testing process by inviting visitors to its Web site to participate in a usability test. Its database supports a team of 95,000 live users. From the Vividence database, 50 or more participants who match the demographics for a study can be quickly recruited for a Web evaluation. While selected users are doing a usability test, boxes pop up to ask them why they have chosen a particular action; as well, users can supply their own comments whenever they wish.

Another way to get feedback from users is to provide a questionnaire on a company's Web site or to send an email to all registered customers, requesting that they complete a survey. Although the user population will be restricted to current visitors or customers, as well as to those visitors or customers who fill out surveys, a large response can provide useful and relevant data, especially when the response suggests problems or issues shared by many. In addition, the cost of such feedback is very low and the volume of responses can be quite high.

Although each of these tools can provide useful data, none should be the only method used to determine the usability of a Web site. All can provide data that may improve a site, but only when real users participate in controlled tests can these results be confirmed. In the next section, we look at the specific tools used and the unique characteristics of usability testing for Web sites conducted in the lab as well as in the field.

Lab or Field Testing of Web Usability

Usability testing of Web sites can be conducted in the lab or in the field. Increasingly, the "field" for a Web site can be anywhere in the world, so remote testing is becoming a more frequently used option. Regardless of whether you're testing in the lab or in the field, one chief difference in the testing procedure is the number of participants used. We discuss this important topic first and then look at tools to support both lab and field testing.

Number of Participants Needed in Web Testing

Jakob Nielsen's "Rule of 5," as it is sometimes called, may not be applicable to Web testing. (For information on the number of participants needed in a discount usability model, see Chapter 1.) The determining factors affecting Web testing appear to be a diverse user population accessing a Web site for a wide variety of reasons and using numerous problem-solving strategies in pursuit of their goal. When users are homogeneous and share a common goal, such as high-school students searching college Web sites for information, the rule of 5 applies. In other instances, it does not, as some recent research suggests. At the Usability Professionals' Association Conference in August 2000, Jared Spool, a usability specialist, reported that it took 18 users to find 40%, or a whopping 247 problems, on a Web site related to CDs, because no two users approached the site in the same way. Based on this finding, he estimated statistically that it would take 90 users to identify an estimated 600 problems (Spool).

Part of what causes the problem, according to Spool, is the choice of verbs used in task scenarios to describe the tasks users are asked to perform. Spool contends that tasks are much harder to define for Web sites; thus, it is hard to determine what verb to use. In typical software or documentation tests, for example, "find" tasks produce good results; however, in Web testing, Spool and his colleagues at User Interface Engineering discovered that slight variations in the wording of tasks—"Find layoffs at GTE" vs. "Find job cuts at GTE"—produced very different results (Spool).

Thus, in Web testing it may be necessary to create tasks based on user interviews to learn what users want to do on the Web. With this information, the team can observe how well the users accomplish their stated goals. Another approach Spool recommends is to create "compelled shopping tasks," in which participants are told that they should prepare a shopping list in advance to go shopping on the Web with a certain amount of money to spend. When they arrive for the test, they already have a goal. Still, it takes a much larger number of users to uncover the many findings different users will expose in a Web usability test, even while sharing the same goal (Spool).

Others who have arrived at similar conclusions about the number of participants needed in Web testing include Rolf Molich, the developer and coordinator of the CUE–2 (Comparative Usability Evaluation 2) test of Hotmail, in which nine independent tests of the Web site were conducted, using a common list of issues that the sponsor provided, with the result being very little correlation of findings.

Of the 300 combined findings from the nine tests, none were found by all nine teams. The common findings were as follows:

- 1 found by seven teams
- 1 found by six teams
- 4 found by five teams
- 4 found by four teams
- 16 found by three teams
- 48 found by two teams
- 226 found by one team

For more information about the test and the results, see the CUE–2 report at <http://www.dialogdesign.dk/cue2.htm>.

When Vividence conducts Web-based remote usability testing, which we discuss in the next section, it advocates a participant base of at least 50 users and as many as 200 to evaluate the overall customer experience. If different user populations are involved, subsamples of at least 50 are required, because significant problems may not be discovered if a single testing group doesn't access the part of the site where the problem exists ("Sample Selection for Web Evaluations").

Eye-Tracking Devices Used in Web Testing

In addition to the variable in the number of participants needed in a Web test, another possible variable is in the use of an eye-tracking device. Although eye-tracking devices have been used to test traditional software products, they have gained in popularity in Web testing. With an eye-tracking device, the team gets a record of where a user looks on a screen and how the user's eye moves around the screen. One eye-tracking study found that users ignore graphics when they are seeking information, once they determine that the graphics contain little information of value (Ellis). Another study tracked where users looked on a prototype Web page when searching for information. The study found that users typically look first in the center area, then in the left panel, then in the right panel. Users were more likely to move outside the center area when they spent time searching for the correct link or when they returned to the page. New and experienced Web users scanned in the same way, suggesting that experienced users expect to find the most useful information by following this pattern and that new users quickly learn this pattern for effective scanning. While users notice bright colors and animation, their eyes don't rest there long. The borders of ads stop users' gaze (User Interface Engineering, "Testing Web Sites with Eye-Tracking").

Remote Web Testing

When testing users in far-flung locations, remote Web testing is becoming a cost-effective option. Test instructions can be sent via the Web or through the mail in advance of the scheduled test. Then the test administrator phones the user at a pre-arranged time, and the user follows a think-aloud protocol, using the phone. As users describe what they're doing, the test administrator in the home location can "observe" the process by staying on the same page as the user. Meeting software can provide more information by making the administrator's computer show the activities occurring on the user's screen. Of course, as Nielsen points out, remote usability testing has its drawbacks (*Designing* 338):

- International phone calls can be quite expensive.
- The test administrator may have to work at odd hours of the night to accommodate the normal work hours in the host country or in a far-flung time zone.
- The test administrator is dependent on the verbal explanations of the user to be able to follow along (unless remote meeting software is used).

Even with these drawbacks, remote usability testing can provide vital information for Web site use when users represent an international audience. Some of the benefits of remote Web testing include the following (Vividence):

- The testing experience more accurately reflects the user's normal Web conditions, as the user works at his or her computer with its own Internet connection.
- Because the user works from his or her own computer of choice, the user can choose to perform the test from work, home, or elsewhere.
- Potential bias introduced by a test administrator is minimized; if the test is done without a connection to the administrator, this bias is eliminated.
- If the participant completes evaluation forms anonymously, this anonymity can encourage participants to be more candid.

Thus far in this chapter, we've looked at different approaches and processes to use in identifying usability issues related to the Web. In the next section, we look at a way to put these together into a coherent process.

Putting All the Methods Together

As we've often said in this book, a user-centered design process is not dependent on any single method or tool to build usability into a product. Web site usability is no exception to this principle. So, how do you incorporate the methods and tools described in this chapter to bring a user-centered design process to Web site development? Tech-Ed, a usability consulting firm, proposes the following 12-step design process (*Assessing Web Site Usability* 12–13):

1. Design site
2. Develop prototype
3. Perform heuristic evaluation
4. Incorporate feedback into alpha site
5. Perform usability test of alpha site
6. Incorporate feedback into beta site
7. Perform log analysis of beta user activity
8. Use log analysis data to identify areas for further testing
9. Perform usability test of beta site

10. Incorporate feedback into first release
11. Perform ongoing log analysis of site
12. At intervals, use log analysis data to identify areas for further testing and improvement

Summary

In this chapter, we have covered the issues unique to Web usability testing. These include:

- Research that documents the extent of problems with Web sites today
- The need to focus on users, which includes understanding who Web users are, how they use the Web, and what they want from Web sites in both domestic and international markets
- The application of Web-site design principles to provide consistency and to avoid the major mistakes of many Web sites today
- Usability heuristics for the Web, including the ways in which the rules are the same and the ways in which they are different for Web sites
- Special tools, such as tracking software, used to generate data for Web analysis
- Special considerations for Web testing, such as the number of participants and the types of tasks users perform
- Special tools for Web testing, such as eye-tracking devices
- Special processes in Web testing, such as remote testing, used to gather specific information about Web users in the field
- A process for putting these options into a plan for user-centered design of Web products

In Closing

By the time you read this book, much of what is said in this chapter may be changing or may have already changed. Some make it their business to predict where the Web is going. I am not one of these. But I do acknowledge the pace at which change takes place in the environment of the Web, as well as with products we use at home, at work, at school, and at play. For all these products, usability will be an increasingly critical component of their success.

Until recently, usability was a word that was little understood and infrequently applied to product design and development. If I can make one prediction about which I feel confident, it is that usability is moving center stage. By the time you read this book, it may be a word requiring no explanation. It may represent an expectation, perhaps even a demand, on the part of customers who will no longer tolerate inefficient, "quirky" interfaces that require users to learn how to work according to their plan, rather than supporting users in the ways in which they want to work. I agree with Jakob Nielsen when he says that usability has become a "core competency that is necessary for business survival" (*Designing* 389).

Although he makes the statement about Web sites, I believe that usability will become a core competency for all products, if the companies that develop them are to survive. Companies that ignore usability do so at their own peril.

You can contribute to the increasing prevalence of usability as the watchword of user-centered design by becoming a usability advocate. You have already become one, I suspect, from reading this book (if you weren't already a convert before you started). You can now make sure that the message goes out to the companies you work for now or will work for in the future. If they're not yet doing usability testing and incorporating a user-centered design process in product development, you have the knowledge to show them how to get started. All it takes is a first step. Just pick a place in the process, justify the method for doing it by showing how little time, budget, and human effort it takes, and spread the results far and wide. Once you begin, you will likely win converts to your cause.

The most exciting part of usability testing is watching users struggle, because you know that what others may see as problems are actually opportunities for product improvements and company sales improvements. As well, if you have an interest in usability, you will find many opportunities to develop along with the field, as it grows and expands into product areas and improvements that haven't even been thought of yet.

Questions/Topics for Discussion

1. Describe some of the problems that make Web sites difficult to use.
2. Name the three things that users want to do on the Web. If you are a Web user, describe your top three favorite sites and explain what you like about them. If you are not currently a Web user, pick an area of interest—like music, movies, or books—and visit one Web site that deals with this interest in one of the three ways that users generally visit the Web. Describe your reaction to your first visit to this site, including what you liked and what you didn't like.
3. Study the Web site for your college or university or for your company. Describe what you think the strengths and weaknesses of the site are for a first-time visitor to the site. Does the site make it plain to new visitors what its purpose is? Can these new users achieve their objective easily on the site?
4. Describe some of the differences between Web readers and readers of paper-based text. How do these differences affect the usability of Web sites?
5. What special considerations must be taken into account when designing Web sites for international audiences? For women audiences? For novice users? For seasoned users?
6. Describe some of the "standards" in Web design that users expect to find in every Web site. Explain the effect of applying these standards to Web design. What are the advantages and disadvantages of using these standards. What role does creativity play if Web sites follow a standard for design?

7. Describe the ways in which tracking tools generate useful data about Web sites. Explain the strengths and weaknesses of using such tools. Where do tracking tools fit into user-centered design?

Exercises

1. Identify a Web site that causes problems for you when you try to perform a few basic tasks. If your classroom or training room has Internet access, call up the site and present the problems with the site to your classmates. If you do not have Internet access to show the site, use screen captures of the homepage and several other pages and present these as handouts or on transparencies.
2. Identify a different Web site of the same type as used in exercise 1. Compare and contrast the usability of the site in performing the same basic tasks. Use the same technique as described in exercise 1 for presenting your findings to the class.
3. Evaluate a Web site using the usability heuristics presented in Table 9.3. If everyone evaluates the same Web site, the class can collate the findings and see how much overlap results. If everyone evaluates a different Web site, the class can determine how many similar kinds of findings result when examining different sites. In either case, once the results are collated, the class can assign severity codes to the findings.
4. Visit one of the Web sites that provide information about Web site usability. Present information from one of the articles on the site. Some places to start looking include <www.uie.com>, <www.websitesthatsuck.com>, or <www.useit.com>.

References

Amis, Rod. "The Truth About Web Design." The Andover News Network 19 Nov. 1999 <http://www.andovernews.com/cgi-bin/news_column.pl?442>.

Assessing Web Site Usability from Server Log Files. Tech-Ed White Paper, Dec. 1999.

Baca, B., and A. Cassidy. "Intranet Development and Design That Works." *Proceedings of the Human Factors and Ergonomics Society 43rd Annual Meeting,* 27 Sept.–1 Oct. Houston, 1999: 777–90.

Bernard, Michael, Barbarba Chaparro, and R. Thomasson. "Finding Information on the Web: Does the Amount of Whitespace Really Matter?" *Usability News* Winter 2000 <http:wsupsy.psy.twsu.edu/surl/usability%20news/volume2_winter/whitespace.htm>.

Bowman, Lisa M. "Adults Surf Web Way More Than Kids." ZDNet 12 Sept. 2000 <http://www.zdnet.com/zdnn>.

Byrne, Michael D., et al. "Eye Tracking the Visual Search of Click-down Menus." *CHI 99 Conference Proceedings,* 15–20 May 1999. Pittsburgh. 402–409.

Byrne, Michael D., et al. "The Tangled Web We Wove: A Taskonomy of WWW Use." *CHI 99 Conference Proceedings*, 15–20 May 1999. Pittsburgh. 544–51.

"CUE-2." 8 Nov. 1999 <http://www.dialogdesign.dk/cue2.htm>

Dembeck, Chet. "Report: B2B Web Sites Fail Usage Test." *E-Commerce Times*, 11 Jan. 2000 <http://www.ecommercetimes.com/news/articles2000/000111-6.shtml>.

Donahue, Goerge M., Susan Weinschenk, and Julie Nowicki. *Usability Is Good Business*. Compuware Corp. and the Weinschenk Consulting Group. 27 July 1999 <http://www.compuware.com/intelligence/articles/usability.htm>.

The Dotcom Survival Guide: How to Tap the $19 Billion Customer Experience. Creative Good 12 June 2000 <http://www.creativegood.com/survival/>.

Ellis, Steve. "What Eye Movements Tell Us About Software Usability: A Follow-up Study and Workshop." *Common Ground* 9.1 (Jan. 1999): 11–13.

"Expert Reveals How Institutions Can Redesign Their Web Sites." *Enrollment Management Report* 4.1 (2000): 6.

Flanders, Vincent. "How Big Can I Make My Page?" Web Pages That Suck 28 Feb. 2000 <http://www.webpagesthatsuck.com/478.html>.

Gordon, Seth. "Shoppers of the Web Unite: User Experience and Ecommerce." ZDNet 3 Mar. 2000 <http://www.zdnet.com/devhead/stories/articles/0,4413,2448211,00.html>.

"GVU's WWW User Surveys™: Results of GVU's Tenth World Wide Web User Survey." 14 May 1999 <http://www.gvu.gatech.edu/user_surveys/survey-1998-10/tenthreport.html>.

Hall, Richard H. and Lewis L. Hickman. "The Effect of Contiguity and Complexity of Web Page Displays on Subjective Ratings: The Role of Gender." American Educational Research Association, Mar. 1997 Chicago. <http://www.umr.edu/~rhall/research/aera/aera97.html>.

Instone, Keith. "Usability Heuristics for the Web." Webreview 28 June 1999 <http://webreview .com/wr/pub/97/10/10/usability/sidebar.html>.

"Internet Users: 362 Million by 2003." International Business Advisor 31 Mar. 2000 <http://Advisor.com/Articles.nsf/aid/FRASS296>.

Kalin, Sari. "Usability: Mazed and Confused." *Web Business Magazine* 1 April 1999 <http://www2.cio.com/archive/printer.cfm>.

Lohse, Gerald L. and Peter Spiller. "Quantifying the Effect of User Interface Design Features on Cyberstore Traffic and Sales." *CHI 98 Conference Proceedings*, 18–23 Apr. 1998. Los Angeles. 211–18.

Nielsen, Jakob. "Be Succinct! (Writing for the Web)." *Alertbox*. 15 Mar. 1997 <http://www.useit.com/alertbox/9703b.html>.

———. *Designing Web Usability: The Practice of Simplicity*. Indianapolis: New Riders, 2000.

———. "Do Interface Standards Stifle Design Creativity?" *Alertbox*. 22 Aug. 1999 <http://www.useit.com/alertbox/990822.html>.

———. "End of Web Design." *Alertbox*. 23 July 2000 <http://www.useit.com/alertbox/20000723.html>.

———. "Heuristic Evaluation." *Usability Inspection Methods*. Eds. Jakob Nielsen and Robert L. Mack. New York: Wiley, 1994. 25–62.

———. "The Increasing Conservatism of Web Users." *Alertbox.* 22 Mar. 1998 <http://www.useit.com/alertbox/980322.html>.

———. "Intranet Portals: The Corporate Information Infrastructure." *Alertbox.* 4 April 1999 <http://www.useit.com/alertbox/990404.html>.

———. "The Mud-Throwing Theory of Usability." *Alertbox.* 2 Apr. 2000 <http://www.useit.com/alertbox/20000402.html>.

———. "Prioritize: Good Content Bubbles to the Top." *Alertbox.* 17 Oct. 1999 <http://www.useit.com/alertbox/991017.html>.

———. "*Reset* and *Cancel* Buttons." *Alertbox.* 16 Apr. 2000 <http://www.useit.com/alertbox/20000416.html>.

———. "Usability as Barrier to Entry." *Alertbox.* 28 Nov. 1999 <http://www.useit.com/alertbox/991128.html>.

———. "Users First: Web Usability: Why and How." ZDNet Developer. 15 Sept. 1998 <http://www.zdnet.com/devhead/stories/articles/0,4413,2137433,00.html>.

———. "Web Research: Believe the Data." *Alertbox.* 11 July 1999 <http://www.useit.com/alertbox/990711.html>.

———. "The Web Usage Paradox: Why Do People Use Something This Bad?" *Alertbox.* 9 Aug. 1998 <http://www.useit.com/alertbox/980809.html>.

———. "When Bad Design Elements Become the Standard." *Alertbox.* 14 Nov. 1999 <http://www.useit.com/alertbox/991114.html>.

———. "Who Commits the 'Top Ten Mistakes' of Web Design?" *Alertbox.* 16 May 1999 <http://www.useit.com/alertbox/990516.html>.

"Numbers." *Time* 31 July 2000: 17.

O'Connor, Eileen. "Gauging the Gender Gap Online." CNN.com. 11 July 2000 <http://www.cnn.com/SPECIALS/views/effect/oconnor.genders.jul11/index.html>.

Palmiter, Susan, et al. *Validating Max™ for Task-Based Browsing Bahavior: White Paper* Web Criteria Nov. 2000 <www.webcriteria.com/white_papers>.

Pieratti, Denise D. "Usability and the Web." *Intercom.* June 1998: 20–23.

Rehman, Aamir. *Holiday 2000 E-Commerce: Avoiding $14 Billion in "Silent Losses."* Creative Good Oct. 2000 <www.creativegood.com>.

Spool, Jared. "The Latest Findings from Usability Research." Usability Professionals' Association Conference, Asheville, NC, 14–16 August 2000.

Spool, Jared M., et al. *Web Site Usability: A Designer's Guide.* San Francisco: Morgan Kaufman, 1999.

Strom, David. "eCommerce for Her, Another Dumb Idea." *Web Informant* #205. 6 July 2000 <http://www.strom.com/awards/205.html>.

"The Sun Shines Bright on That New Kentucky Home." *Enrollment Management Report* 4.1 (2000): 7.

Thompson, Maryann Jones. "How to Frustrate Web Surfers." *The Standard* 9 Aug. 1999 <http://www.thestandard.com/research/metrics/display/0,2799,9826,00.html>.

User Interface Engineering. "Four Elements of Page Layout." 15 April 2001 <http://www.uie.com>.

————. "Testing Web Sites with Eye-Tracking." 24 June 1999 <http://www.uie.com>.

van der Geest, Thea, and Jan H. Spyridakis. "Developing Heuristics for Web Communication: An Introduction to This Special Issue." *Technical Communication* 47.3 (Aug. 2000): 301–10.

Vividence Research. *Sample Selection for Web Evaluations.* Methodology Best Practices Series. July 2000 <www.vividence.com/public/Research/methodology.htm>.

"What 10,000 Students Want in a College Web Site." Lipman Hearne 9 Mar. 2000 <http://www.lipmanhearne.com/wses/>.

"Winning the Online Consumer: Insights Into Online Consumer Behavior." The Boston Consulting Group Mar. 2000 <http://www.bcg.com/new_ideas/new_ideas_subpage4.asp>.

Zona Research. "Estimated $4.35 Billion in ECommerce Sales at Risk Each Year." 30 June 1999 <http://www.zonaresearch.com>.

Making It Work as a Team

Because user-centered design is a process that involves everyone who is a stakeholder in the product, the development of products using user-centered design is a team effort. Not only is it important to include the goals of the user in developing user-centered products, but it's also important to include the goals of all those who touch the product: developers (both system developers and information developers), marketing and sales representatives, trainers, and technical support staff. Some organizations advocate including the user as a team member in a development approach called *participatory design*. Putting together a multi-disciplinary or cross-functional team with representatives from all the appropriate groups is an important part of creating user-centered products, beginning with the conceptual design of the product and continuing through the phases of product development and usability testing.

But this is no easy task. It is frequently made more difficult because team members may be united by a common goal, but are often left without the tools to know how to communicate well with each other to reach that goal. Being in an organization that recognizes the importance of the team approach, although a good start for developing user-centered products, does not assure success. Team effort, as anyone knows who has worked in teams, is fraught with problems and pitfalls that can sabotage the efforts of individuals, the team, and the product. In *Contextual Design*, Holtzblatt speaks for many when she describes teamwork: "It is a struggle of personalities as we try to work in cross-functional teams to produce a shared direction. It is hard to remember that one smart guy working alone probably doesn't have the whole answer. We simply have to realize that design is about people working together, and that's what makes it hard" (xviii).

To complicate matters, organizations are typically not set up to foster teamwork, even considering the most basic question of where the team should meet. The typical cubicle arrangement doesn't provide enough space for team meetings, and conference rooms are normally at a premium and have to be booked by the hour. Material needed for meetings has to be set up and dismantled every time. "Is it any wonder," say Beyer and Holtzblatt, "that designers and engineers consider meetings a waste of time? The very physical structure of a typical large corporation announces plainly that real engineering happens alone in cubicles and that when people gather in a meeting room, they are not doing real work" (14). Beyer and Holtzblatt contend that "working together effectively means having workplaces where real work, done by multiple people working face-to-face, can happen. It also means giving these people the interpersonal skills and process to make their sessions effective" (14).

Knowing some of the keys to successful team development and understanding the roles that people play and the tasks that teams perform will increase the likelihood of a successful team collaboration. This appendix addresses these issues. If you are a student or practicing professional who has not had previous training in the principles presented here, you should find useful information to make the process work better for you. If you have already received some training or instruction in methods of successful team interaction, this appendix can be a refresher for you, as these principles need to be constantly reinforced to help each of us understand what we do and why we react to the behavior of others in teams.

Why Work in Teams?

The old adage "two heads are better than one" has stood the test of time because when two or more people put their heads together to solve a problem, the results are generally better, more creative, and more reasoned than when one tries to come up with solutions alone. As well, today's products are generally too complex to be developed by one person alone. To increase the quality of products and get them to market faster, organizations support teamwork, particularly cross-functional teams. And to support the success of cross-functional teams, companies and training organizations offer seminars and workshops on skill-building for team effectiveness. Indicative of the interest in the technical communication community, a special joint issue of two professional organizations' journals—IEEEs *Transactions on Professional Communication* and STCs *Technical Communication*—selected cross-functional teams as the focus of the combined issue (Smart and Barnum).

Donald Norman stresses the importance of putting together a multi-disciplinary team to develop products that are "human-centered." Human-centered products require an understanding of the user's experience, which means that team members must have at least six skills, representing a broad spectrum of disciplines:

- *Field studies* to observe potential users in their normal settings
- *Behavioral designers* to create a conceptual model that will form the basis of design
- *Model builders and prototypers* to build prototypes and mock-ups that can be tested quickly
- *User testers* to do feasibility and usability studies quickly

- *Graphical and industrial engineers* to merge the conceptual and behavioral aspects of the product with the requirements of the technology
- *Technical writers* to understand the audience and the user's activities and to translate "the often idiosyncratic and unplanned design into something that appears to make sense (191)"

Despite the fact that the technical writers are sometimes left off the design team, Norman stresses that "the technical writers should be the key to the entire operation" (191).

In addition to the benefits to be derived from establishing a team to focus on the user, other benefits of multi-disciplinary or cross-functional teams include (Parker, "Cross-Functional" 49–50):

- *Speed.* Teams work especially well in product development because they employ "parallel" development, rather than "serial" development, meaning that team members develop different aspects of the project at the same time, rather than in sequence.
- *Complexity.* Teams improve the organization's ability to solve problems because they bring differing perspectives to the process. In other words, the product design is not the domain of one group but interrelates with all groups represented by the team members.
- *Customer focus.* Teams help focus on the organization's goal of satisfying customers' needs.
- *Creativity.* People from different disciplines come together to focus on the problem, thereby increasing creativity.
- *Organizational learning.* Teams teach each other about the work that they do, and teamwork can increase cross-functional training, as well as provide the opportunity to work with people from different backgrounds.
- *Single point of contact.* Working together, teams serve as a single point of contact for information and decision making, rather than duplicating effort or working at cross-purposes.

Not only are cross-functional teams used to improve product development, but they have also proven to be more effective in usability testing, as suggested by research reported at the 1998 Human Factors and Ergonomics Society Annual Meeting (Jacobsen, Hertzum, and John). The research focused on what is called the *evaluator effect*, meaning the influence of the evaluator in determining the number and severity of usability issues catalogued during a test. The study involved four usability experts who separately evaluated the same videotapes of four users in a usability test. Of the 93 problems detected by the combined observations of all four evaluators, the researchers discovered the following:

- Only 20% of the problems were detected by all four evaluators.
- Almost half (46%) of the problems were detected by a single evaluator.
- From the top-10 most severe problems noted by each evaluator, none of the evaluators shared the same list of 10; in other words, no single top-10 finding appeared on all four evaluators' lists.

The implications of this research are two-fold: (1) a high degree of personal analysis and interpretation occurs on the part of each evaluator, and (2) working as a team, each evaluator can contribute his or her own observations and views to a discussion of the issues and the severity of those issues resulting from a usability test, thereby strengthening the analysis and conclusions.

In the next section, we look at some of the challenges that teams face in trying to work together, even when they share a common goal. These challenges are based on group dynamics and the important part they play in group communication.

Dimensions of Group Dynamics

If the case has been made that cross-functional teams have many advantages over work done by individuals or work done within one department and then handed off to another, then it might seem that everyone would want to work in teams. So, why is that when you are told you will be working in a team, your reaction may be less than enthusiastic? Is it because you have had a bad experience working in a team before and you fear it could happen again? Or is it because you know you will work very hard, but you're afraid to trust that your other team members will work as hard as you do? In fact, do you fear that they may get in your way and make it harder for you to work? Or is it that you know that there will be conflict, and you don't know how to handle this when it arises? These are just a few of the many issues people have (or fear having) when they work in teams. Largely, these problems result from not knowing how to set the stage for effective teamwork and how to establish the rules that will shape the team into a well-functioning unit.

To prepare for your participation in a team, you'll need some background to help you understand the stages of group formation, the roles and functions in groups, the meaning attributed to nonverbal communication, the issues associated with conflict (both positive and negative) and leadership, and the meeting management skills needed to keep the team goal-oriented, productive, and *satisfied* with both the product and the process. If you find yourself wanting to know more, you can expand your understanding by consulting some of the sources listed at the end of this appendix.

Stages of Group Formation

When a group forms, the members of the team may know each other, may know of each other, or may not know each other. Some members may have worked together before, or perhaps none have. Whatever the situation, the group will need to go through a several-stage process that, if successful, will allow it to function properly and be productive. These stages have been characterized in different ways by various researchers, but a popular designation is to divide the process into four stages (Tuckman, reported in Harris and Sherblom 53–59):

1. Forming
2. Storming
3. Norming
4. Performing

Forming

In the *forming* stage, group members come together as individuals holding differing attitudes about the task and process before them. Some members may feel excited, others wary, still others suspicious, or even hostile. The group may have a designated leader, but the leader's style and skill are still unknown. Perhaps the purpose of the group is also unknown or undefined. A team-building activity, such as a paper-prototyping exercise, can get the team working together quickly to jump-start the forming process. The exercise does not have to be related to the product the team will be designing and testing. A popular paper-prototyping exercise, described in Chapter 4, requires the team to build the interface for a fast-food kiosk in a food court, so that a family of four can make individual food choices. The usefulness of this team-building activity or any other is that it gets the team working together quickly with a shared goal as they are getting to know each other. The advantage of participating in such an exercise for a product-development team is that the entire team has equal say in the design decisions, as the expertise of the programmers or engineers is no more valid than that of any other person who can wield a pair of scissors or a pad of sticky notes.

Storming

In the second stage of group development, called *storming,* the necessary struggle for leadership ensues, along with the sorting out of roles people will assume in the group. Politeness and tentativeness from the forming stage give way to open conflict in this stage. Members may argue about the nature of the task, the approach to the solution, the responsibilities of members, the frequency and location of meetings, and so forth. Leadership and power struggles also emerge during this stage. However, this stage is essential in the development of the group, as the rules of the group are established, along with the roles of the members. Once this stage is complete, members are ready for the next stage, in which the rules are understood and used.

Norming

In the *norming* stage, members demonstrate acceptance of the rules of the group and its leader. They act according to their understanding of these rules, which brings cohesion to group effort and allows the group to begin seriously focusing on the task. Previous competition turns into cooperation, as rules, roles, and responsibilities are understood. Norms can include an understanding and acceptance of such issues as:

- *Dress:* formal or informal
- *Seating position:* designated seats or undesignated seats at meetings
- *Method of address and recognition of members:* first name or more formal address; raised hands to be recognized or free flow of conversation

- *Attendance and absence:* advance notification of absence expected; regular attendance for all members expected, or not
- *Cell phones and pagers:* turned on or off; acceptable or unacceptable to leave meeting if paged or called
- *Decision-making process:* by majority vote, consensus, or decision of leader

Performing

As the name suggests, the *performing* stage is the final stage in the process when the work of the group gets done. The group now has the ability to constructively criticize each other and to work through conflict productively. The group feels connected and united in its efforts, fully functioning as a team. Although this process has been described as linear and often is, it is also quite frequently cyclical, particularly when membership or conditions change. If a new member is introduced to a team or a member leaves, groups in the performing stage may have to back up and go through some or all of the previous stages again. Or if the definition of the task changes, it can cause the group to retrace earlier steps in the process. Some groups will move very quickly through the early stages to arrive at the performing stage. Others may have to struggle through storming and norming for weeks or even months before performing. And, of course, some groups may never reach the performing stage. The reasons for this may have something to do with the roles of the members of the group, as we explore in the next section.

Roles in Groups

Whether we like it or even admit it, we all play roles in groups. These roles are determined partly by personality and partly by the needs of the group. According to the work of Benne and Sheats (reported in G. Wilson; Harris and Sherblom), roles can be divided into the following three categories (see Table A.1, Harris and Sherblom 42–43):

- *Task roles* are product-oriented and help a group achieve its goals.
- *Maintenance roles* are process-oriented and intended to keep harmony and goodwill in the group. They develop to ease the tensions and disagreements that naturally arise in the team process and to build and sustain group cohesiveness.
- *Self-centered (self-oriented) roles* arise when an individual's needs become more important than those of the group. These roles are counterproductive to the process and the task.

Most teams understand the nature of task roles, especially when the objective or task function of the group is identified in the forming stage. However, many teams, especially those without training, do not give due consideration to the importance of the maintenance roles in effective group process. Frequently, when the maintenance roles are downplayed or not given time to develop, group cohesiveness suffers. Leaders who focus on tasks only, because they fail to appreciate the importance of interpersonal support and interrelationship development within the group, may find that the group doesn't come together or

(continued on page 400)

TABLE A.1	Group Role Behavior

Group Task Roles	Group Maintenance Roles	Self-Oriented (Selfish) Behaviors; Not Positive Group Roles
Initiating: Proposing new ideas, proposing goals, plans of action, or activities; orienting; prodding the group to greater activity; defining the position of group in relation to an external structure or goal; offering suggestions and approaches.	**Encouraging:** Praising, expressing warmth, support, and appreciation; recognizing the value of others' contributions; indicating positive feeling toward group members; reinforcing group unity and cohesiveness.	**Blocking:** Preventing progress toward group goals by constantly raising objections, repeatedly bringing up the same topic or issue after the group has considered and rejected it (although it is not blocking to raise an idea or topic the group has not really considered); preventing the group from reaching consensus; refusing to go along, accept, or support a group decision.
Elaborating: Clarifying ideas, suggestions; expanding on ideas or suggestions; developing a previously expressed idea; providing examples, illustrations, and explanations.	**Supporting:** Agreeing or expressing support for another's belief or proposal; following the lead of another member; accepting another's suggestions and contributions.	**Being Aggressive:** Criticizing, threatening other group members, being a "noble fighter" preventing collaboration.
Coordinating: Integrating; putting together parts of various ideas; organizing the group's work; promoting teamwork and cooperation.	**Harmonizing:** Helping to relieve tension; mediating differences; reducing secondary tension by reconciling disagreement; suggesting a compromise or a new acceptable alternative; working to reconcile angry members.	**Withdrawing:** Remaining indifferent, refusing to contribute; avoiding important differences; refusing to cope with conflicts; refusing to take a stand; covering up feelings; giving no response to comments.
Summarizing: Pulling work and ideas together; orienting the group; reviewing previous statements; reminding the group of items previously mentioned or discussed.	**Gatekeeping:** Keeping communication channels open; helping "quiet" members get the floor and be heard; suggesting turn taking or a speaking order; asking someone to offer a different opinion.	**Dominating:** Interrupting, refusing to accept others' conclusions as being as valid as one's own, forcing a leadership role.
Recording: Keeping track of the group's work; keeping group records, preparing reports and minutes; serving as group secretary or historian.	**Process Observing:** Making comments on how the group is working, how the members are coordinating and working together.	
Evaluating: Critiquing ideas or suggestions; expressing judgments on the merits of information or ideas; proposing or applying criteria for evaluating information.		

(continued)

Group Task Roles	Group Maintenance Roles	Self-Oriented (Selfish) Behaviors; Not Positive Group Roles
Giving or Seeking Information: Presenting data; offering facts and information, evidence, or personal experience relevant to the group's task; asking others for facts and information, evidence, or relevant personal experience; asking questions about information provided by others; requesting evaluations; asking if the group is reaching consensus. **Opinion Giving:** Stating beliefs, values, interpretations, judgments; drawing conclusions from facts and information. **Clarifying:** Interpreting issues; making ambiguous statements more clear; asking for examples or further clarification. **Consensus Testing:** Asking if an apparent group decision is acceptable to all; suggesting that an agreement may have been reached and asking for verification of that. **Proposing Procedure:** Suggesting an agenda of issues, or a decision-making method; proposing a procedure to follow.	**Setting Standards:** Helping to set goals and standards for the group; assisting in setting norms or making norms explicit; suggesting rules of behavior for members; challenging unproductive ways of behaving; giving a negative response when another violates a rule or norm. **Tension Relieving:** Using humor, joking, or otherwise relieving tension; helping new members feel at ease; reducing status differences; encouraging informality; stressing common interests and experiences within the group; developing group narratives, themes, and fantasies to build a common spirit and bond or to test a tentative value or norm.	**Status or Recognition Seeking:** Stage hogging, boasting, and calling attention to one's expertise or experience when not necessary to credibility or relevant to group's task; game playing to elicit sympathy; switching subject to area of personal expertise. **Special-Interest Pleader:** Demanding group time and resources for special-interest pleading; constantly advocating for one's subgroup or special interest; not allowing group influence over one's perceived self-interests.

Source: Harris, Thomas E., and John C. Sherblom, *Small Group and Team Communication*, pp. 42–43. © 1999 by Allyn and Bacon. (Reprinted by permission.)

gel and that people seem to be at cross-purposes or have varying degrees of commitment to the project. Effective leaders value and support both types of roles (task and maintenance) for maximum group effectiveness. In the performing stage, groups will perform best when they feel secure in both the tasks they are each performing and their value as members of the team. They will also accept that a certain group member will tell a joke at the right moment (tension-reliever), that another group member will draw out a quiet member (gatekeeper), or that still another group member will express praise for the contributions of a member or members (supporter-encourager).

In addition to understanding how groups form, it is important to understand how to interpret the nonverbal communication aspects of group interaction, the subject of the next section.

Nonverbal Communication

Nonverbal communication is the language of the unspoken. It includes facial expression, tone of voice, body language, use of time, distance, and so much more beyond the actual words used to communicate. Researchers in this field claim that at least 85% and as much as 93% of what we understand or interpret as meaning derives from nonverbal communication codes or cues (Mehrabian and others, reported in Beebe and Masterson 138–39). In the next sections, we discuss the following types of codes or cues (Schultz 71–81):

- Artifacts
- Physical environment
- Proxemics
- Kinesics
- Paralanguage

Artifacts

Artifacts include such cues as dress, hair style, physical features, and overall appearance. The choice and style of clothing, jewelry, the way people wear their hair, their body shape and size all make impressions on people, who then make judgments about other people's intelligence, confidence, seriousness, persuasiveness, and so forth. These cues are most important in establishing new groups. Once people get to know each other, different cues take precedence.

Physical Environment

The physical attractiveness of the environment also has an impact on communication. Factors include room size, temperature, and general appearance. In a classic experiment (reported in G. Wilson 130–31; Schultz 72), subjects were asked to rate a group of photographs in three settings: a janitor's closet (ugly room), a professor's office (average room), and an attractive living room (beautiful room). The subjects gave the most positive ratings in the beautiful room, enjoyed the task, and stayed with it longer. Subjects in the janitor's closet complained that they felt irritated and didn't want to finish the task. The implications of this study are that physical environment can have a direct correlation with job satisfaction and productivity and can account in some measure for a group's sense of harmony or discord.

Proxemics

Even more important than the physical characteristics of the room is the arrangement of the people in the group, particularly regarding their distance from one another and choice of seating. These cues are called *proxemics*. Member participation and leadership can be directly influenced by the choices in spacing and positioning. The need to be close for socializing and distant for privacy will be influenced by the familiarity with group members, plus other factors such as personality type, people's feelings about other team members' sex, race, and age. Studies show that cohesive groups occupy less space than noncohesive groups. People of the same age, sex, and race sit closer together than mixed groups. Women sit closer to one another than do men, who not only require more space but also show discomfort when placed in a small room. In contrast, closeness can increase interaction among women. Introverts need more space than extroverts. Higher-status individuals tend to claim more space for themselves (called *territoriality*) than do lower-status individuals in a group.

Seating arrangement also sends nonverbal cues. People who choose the head of the table, for instance, are generally the designated leaders or desire to be. Other arrangement factors influence the flow of communication. The emergence of a group leader is largely determined by the person who is in the best position to maintain eye contact with the largest number of members. One study (Howells and Becker, reported in G. Wilson 131–32; Schultz 75) studied the impact of seating arrangements of five-member groups at a rectangular table. In groups with two on one side and three on the other side of a table, 14 out of 20 leaders were selected from the two-member side. This is attributed to the fact that the two-member side had more eye contact with the three members on the opposite side and that it is more difficult to maintain eye contact with a person sitting next to you than with a person sitting opposite you.

Another experiment (Leavitt, reported in Schultz 74–75) describes the variables on communication flow when comparing various communication networks: the wheel (with a center point), the chain (a straight line), the Y, and the circle. The arrangement of the networks influences the communication flow, the number of messages that can be sent, and the length of time it takes to complete a task. The study showed that "although the wheel is more efficient than the Y, the Y more efficient than the chain, and the circle the least efficient, people are less satisfied when they participate in the wheel, Y, or chain patterns" (74). Thus, the circle, which allows for optimum group participation, is the least efficient but most satisfying arrangement for group members. It naturally follows that group work almost always takes more time than individual effort, but the results can be better and more satisfying if the communication network and corresponding seating arrangement are carefully selected.

Kinesics

Kinesics is a term encompassing gesture, posture, movement, and the way people express themselves through the body and orient themselves toward or away from others. Research shows that leaders give more positive head nods and gestures than do others in a group. Emerging leaders do so as well. Members turn or lean toward those they like and away from those they do not. Members who sit at an angle from the rest of the group may feel excluded or may not want to be included. When members are communicating well, they imitate each other in what is called "postural echoes, body synchrony, or body congruence" (Brilhart and Galanes 147). People tend to follow the leader, as the old game is played. By studying who is imitating whom, you can determine who is perceived as the leader.

Control of the floor, or the right to talk, is also largely regulated by body movement and eye contact. A speaker concluding a point often changes head and eye position or shifts body position. A listener can gain the floor by leaning forward and trying to make eye contact with the leader. Eye contact can also measure a person's status. High-status people receive more eye contact than do low-status people. When eye contact accompanies a message, the message is better received. And, of course, facial features, although often difficult to interpret accurately, can communicate interest or boredom, understanding or the lack of it, interpretation and acceptance or rejection, or, in some people, nothing! What's more, we've all had the experience of not being able to "read" someone's reaction.

Paralanguage

Paralanguage refers to vocal cues, those characteristics of our voice that include inflection, pitch, rate of speech, pauses, and other variables. We often make decisions about a person's education level, ethnic background, and personality on the basis of these vocal cues. In North America, people who talk softly are generally thought to lack persuasiveness because they seem to lack conviction. Others whose vocal qualities change "too often" may be seen as irrational, causing a lack of trust in listeners. Common nonverbal cues—ums, uhs, uh huhs, mmms—tend to show others that we're listening (Brilhart and Galanes 148).

Given all the cues being transmitted via nonverbal communication channels, you may become anxious about future small group encounters. Rather than becoming anxious, you can focus on ways to improve the message you send or to increase your chances of being understood, accepted, and valued. However, effective interpretation of nonverbal communication behaviors may not prepare you for conflict and the role that it plays in small group communication. In the next section, we look at the positive and negative aspects of conflict in groups.

Conflict in Groups

Conflict occurs when an individual's goals are at odds with those of one or more other members of the group. Using this definition, we see that conflict is not the same as disagreement. If you disagree with someone, you do not necessarily have a conflict that interferes with the achievement of your goals or the group's goals.

Contrary to popular belief, conflict is not all bad. In fact, a lack of conflict could be very bad, leading to a phenomenon called *groupthink,* in which everyone agrees, no one points out potential problems, and the group sees itself as an invincible force. The theory was devised as a result of the Bay of Pigs decision, an ill-conceived attempt by the Kennedy administration to overthrow Fidel Castro, as well as decisions regarding Pearl Harbor (Janis, reported in Harris and Sherblom 46–48).

Many groups operate under the mistaken notion expressed in the following three myths about conflict (Beebe and Masterson 270):

Myth #1   In group discussions, conflict should be avoided at all costs.

Myth #2   All conflict occurs because people do not understand one another.

Myth #3   All conflict can be resolved.

Contrary to myths #1 and #2, conflict can be productive, creative, and positive, leading the group to the best solution by providing ideas and information that challenge group members to think of many options and to analyze advantages and disadvantages of each. Groupthink can be avoided by understanding this healthy aspect of conflict. Conflict can be counterproductive, however, when it leads people away from the task, causes them to lose faith in one another, or, in extreme cases, causes the group to break apart and disband. Thus, contrary to myth #3, some conflicts cannot be resolved.

Because conflict can be productive or counter-productive, it is important to recognize which type is occurring so that you can adopt a strategy to manage it. Burnett ("Conflict"; "Substantive Conflict") describes three types of conflict:

- *Affective:* deals with interpersonal disagreement and emotional reactions
- *Procedural:* deals with disagreements about how a group should be run (the norms)
- *Substantive:* deals with disagreement about content, context, and concepts

Substantive conflict is healthy for groups and should be encouraged. This type of conflict produces a better analysis of the problem and a stronger solution, helps groups avoid groupthink, and makes groups stronger, as it builds cohesiveness among group members and results in a greater commitment to the solution. Harmony at any price is likely to guarantee mediocrity. If you expect conflict and view it as natural, inevitable, and healthy when it is substantive, you can make conflict work for the group's success.

Although substantive conflict is desirable and productive, the other two types of conflict—affective and procedural—need to be managed and minimized. Left unmanaged to fester and grow, these types of conflict can cause bad feelings among group members, lower group cohesiveness, and even split the group apart. One management technique for dealing with these types of conflict is reliance on the roles of members in the group. *Gatekeepers, harmonizers, supporters,* and *tension relievers,* to name a few of the essential roles, can all contribute to the resolution of conflicts that can otherwise be destructive to group goals. Leaders can remind members of the norms for group process to help manage conflict. If these group processes do not defuse the conflict, the leader may have to meet privately with the member or members causing the conflict and try to resolve it before it affects the work of the group. In extreme cases and where possible, a member may have to be removed and replaced by another person. This should be a last resort, as it will be disruptive to the group to introduce a new member, frequently requiring the group to go back to an earlier stage of group development to absorb the new member.

In conflict management, the group looks to the leader to handle the situation and keep the group on track. We address the subject of leadership in the next section.

Leadership in Groups

Groups need leaders, even when they claim that they do not, as in the case of self-managed teams. When groups form without a designated leader, one will emerge. Researchers at the University of Minnesota studied this phenomenon to understand how leadership emerges in a small group (Minnesota Studies, reported in Beebe and Masterson 325–26). They determined that the process involves two phases:

Phase 1. Leaders emerge through a process of elimination. The first to be eliminated are the quiet ones, viewed as the introverts. Next are the talkative ones, perceived as overly aggressive or dogmatic.

Phase 2. After half the members are eliminated, the other half vie for the leadership spot. The group rejects people one by one in a sometimes painful process until one or two remain whose style is perceived by others as appropriate for the group. Task- or product-oriented groups reject process-oriented leaders, with the reverse being true for process-oriented groups.

Becoming the leader and being effective as the leader are not necessarily the same thing. In the next section, we look at ways to be an effective leader.

Being an Effective Leader

Whether a leader emerges from a leadership struggle or a group has a designated leader, that individual may not have the skills to lead effectively. Although it was once thought that "leaders are born, not made," this view of leadership, called *trait theory,* has largely given way to other views of leadership. Some people may feel more comfortable in leadership roles than others, but everyone can profit from learning to be a more effective leader in a group, particularly as different situations require different types of leadership. For instance, when a task must be performed under tight deadlines, a more autocratic style of leadership or decision making may be appropriate. However, if the group's objective is problem solving and consensus building, a more participatory leadership role will be effective.

A leader must recognize which role is appropriate to motivate the group and accomplish the task. Leaders have to choose the most appropriate decision-making mechanism from the following three approaches (Smart and Thompson):

- *Command:* decisions made by the leader or imposed by another manager onto the group
- *Consult:* decisions made when the leader confers with those members who are most knowledgeable
- *Consent:* decisions made with involvement of all members equally

These decision-making mechanisms may depend on the time, the circumstances, and the makeup of the group, as well as the personality of its leader.

Regardless of the variations in leadership, effective leaders:

- Understand the goals and tasks of the group
- Are good listeners
- Are active participants
- Have good communication skills
- Can clarify issues
- Are open-minded
- Are sensitive and supportive
- Are flexible
- Share rewards and credit with the group
- Can handle problem participants
- Can effectively resolve conflicts

In cross-functional teams, the leader plays a crucial role because of the diverse nature of the group. Leaders must have the technical background to understand the subject matter and to recognize the contributions made by diverse members of the team. Leaders must also have the people-management skills to foster good communication and full effort from all members. These people skills are even more important when the members have had little experience working together or have had bad experiences in the past. Chief among the skills required of an effective leader is the ability to manage effective meetings, the topic of the next section.

Managing Effective Meetings

So much has been written about meetings, most likely because so many of us have spent so much time in meetings that are badly run or should never have been held, or that included the wrong people or didn't allow participants to adequately prepare. The following statement presents a common view about meetings:

> A meeting is an event at which
> the minutes are kept
> and the hours are lost.

A survey conducted by the Annenberg School of Communications at the University of Southern California reveals that the typical meeting takes place in a conference room, lasts 1 hour and 55 minutes, occurs after 2 hours' notice, has no written agenda distributed in advance (although an agenda is usually available at the meeting), and generally does not cover the agenda completely because 11% of the time is spent on irrelevant issues ("Survey Reveals" 1). Perhaps this survey confirms what so many of us have experienced: meetings are frequently a waste of time because of poor planning and preparation and poor leadership. In his book *Information Anxiety,* Richard Saul Wurman sums up what many of us feel about meetings:

> Meetings are a peculiar form of communication that seem to continually inhibit the very things they seek to accomplish and bring out people's worst personality traits. I've seen more good ideas squashed, egos ruffled, danders raised, and time killed in meetings. Yet we spend such a sizable chunk of our lives in them that we ought to learn how to make them more productive. (323)

As user-centered design is most effective when it uses cross-functional teams, you can improve the effectiveness of the process by making your meetings more productive, whether you are the leader or a participant. See the sidebar entitled "Guidelines for Leading Effective Meetings" for suggestions about the leader's role in making meetings effective. A critical element in meeting effectiveness is planning, which we cover next.

Meeting Planning

If a meeting is worth having, it's worth planning. Meeting planning means determining the purpose and amount of time needed, preparing the agenda, and informing the participants of the objective and their anticipated roles or responsibilities in the meeting. A discussion of these topics follows, beginning with the agenda, which is typically the most often overlooked aspect of effective meeting planning.

Agenda

In an article about meetings published in *Harvard Business Review,* Antony Jay states unequivocally: "The agenda is by far the most important piece of paper. Properly drawn up, it has a power of speeding and clarifying a meeting that very few people understand or harness" (49). However, in an evaluation of 100 meetings conducted by McDonnell Douglas (reported in *Meeting Management News)* the lack of an agenda was cited as the biggest problem contributing to poor meetings. Figure A.1 ("Conference Room Plaque" 2) shows the top eight problems identified with meetings, with the lack of an agenda contributing to most of the other deficiencies noted.

The agenda should contain the date and place of the meeting, starting and ending time, purpose of the meeting, and itemized list of topics to be covered. Many people like to include the amount of time allocated for each topic and the person with the main responsibility for that topic. This is particularly effective

Guidelines for Leading Effective Meetings

Managers usually call a meeting to achieve an objective. Since meetings are rarely stand-alone events, before embarking on a series of meetings, a manager should ask the following questions:

10 Questions Every Manager Should Ask

1. **Should I call a meeting?** Before calling a meeting or beginning a series of meetings, consider alternatives to holding the meeting. Alternatives could include phone calls, memos, electronic mail, one-on-one get togethers, or coordination through other meetings (e.g., staff meetings). If a meeting is the most appropriate way to accomplish an objective, then ask the following questions about each meeting in the series.

2. **Who should I ask to participate?** Be clear about who needs to be invited to the meeting to accomplish the objective.

3. **How does my objective fit into the larger organizational picture?** Before calling a meeting, decide whether accomplishing the objective of the meeting is more important than the current use of participants' time.

4. **Have I clearly communicated the objectives to the participants?** The objective of the meeting should be clear to the person who called it and shared with those asked to attend, preferably in advance through memo, phone conversation or an agenda.

5. **Have I communicated to each participant his or her role in the meeting?** If each participant knows what is expected, he or she will be better able to prepare for the meeting.

6. **Can I accomplish the meeting's objective in the time allotted?** Meetings should start and end on time. Match the objective to the time allotted to the meeting.

7. **How am I conducting the meeting?** Successful meeting management requires clear presentation and open but focused discussions.

8. **Have I set clear tasks for follow-up?** At the end of each meeting the leader should make certain that each participant is clear about follow-up steps and his or her own responsibilities for the next meeting.

9. **When should I call the next meeting?** The scheduling of later meetings should be driven by the tasks that need to be accomplished and the support that individuals performing those tasks might need rather than assuming that a regularly scheduled meeting will be most effective.

10. **Do I need to change the structure of future meetings in the series?** Each additional meeting in a series should re-examine the issues raised above. For example, some later meetings in a series may require only some of the original participants, or the meeting leader may need to add different participants at different stages.

Source: Meeting Management News 3.1 (Jan. 1991), p. 6.

Courtesy of the Wharton Center for Applied Research. Reprinted with permission from 3M Meeting Network <http://www.3M.com/meetingnetwork>.

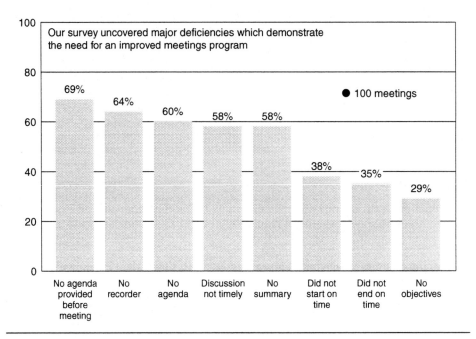

Figure A.1 Major deficiencies in meetings

Source: "Conference Room Plaque Reminds Leaders and Participants of 'Keys to Good Meeting.'" *Meeting Management News* 1.4, p. 2. (Reprinted with permission from 3M Meeting Network <http://www.3M.com/meetingnetwork>.)

with cross-functional teams, as different members will likely have different areas of responsibility and will need to know when they are expected to report on these at team meetings. As time is usually in short supply, time allocations keep everyone informed about the depth of discussion anticipated. To help members prepare for a meeting, the agenda should be distributed in advance. If new material or previous reports are needed for the meeting, these should be attached to the agenda or referenced for retrieval in advance of the meeting. See Figure A.2 for a sample agenda.

Meeting Time

The meeting should start on time, even if everyone hasn't arrived. If those who arrive on time see that nothing happens, they will soon begin arriving late, making the intended start time of meetings meaningless. One suggestion for getting meetings to start on time is to place an odd start time, such as 1:17 P.M., on the agenda to focus attention on it. Another suggestion is to announce that the fourth person to arrive at the meeting will be asked to take the minutes. This encourages all to be on time (or even early), as few people enjoy taking the minutes.

Meeting Purpose

When the meeting begins, the leader should state the purpose of the meeting and get agreement from the participants on the goal of the meeting and its intended purpose. As the group moves through agenda items, if a particular item takes longer than scheduled on the agenda, the leader can ask the group whether they want to delete something else from the agenda so as to continue the discussion of

Meeting between Southern Polytechnic and Women's College
Concerning Usability Testing of Web site

February 23, 2001, Atrium Building (J 389)
11 A.M.–noon

Purpose

Discuss Web site project, testing approach, and deliverables. Tour lab.

• Introductions	5 minutes
• Discussion of the project to be tested: Women's College	10 minutes
• Discussion of the usability testing process: Barnum	10 minutes
• Discussion of heuristic evaluation: Thomas	10 minutes
• Schedule for follow-up meeting: all	5 minutes
• Tour of lab: led by Barnum and Thomas	20 minutes

Figure A.2   Sample meeting agenda

this item, or whether they want to move on to the next item and continue the discussion of the current item at another meeting. Another possible option is to ask whether the group wants to extend the meeting to allow for this discussion, while still covering all the items on the agenda. Such questions and decisions should be based on the meeting's purpose. The agenda should be used as a tool to guide discussion and decisions, not a rigid document that stifles productive discussion. Group consensus on these decisions, whenever possible, is most productive. At the conclusion of the meeting, the leader should return to the purpose statement and ask the group whether the meeting objective has been met. Some groups like to discuss ways to improve future meetings as a final item before adjourning. This can be a productive activity in the early stages of a group's lifecycle.

If the group is meeting for the first time, the meeting frequently has two purposes:

- *Team building:* getting to know each other; working out norms for meetings, decision making, and so forth
- *Task orientation:* defining the task; understanding the process, the resources, the schedule; developing a plan

In this case, time should be allowed for an icebreaker activity, small talk, or introductions so that team members can get to know each other.

Minutes

Minutes are an accurate record of the meeting issues and actions. If the technique of assigning that task to the fourth person who arrives at the meeting is not in keeping with the norms of the group, then it is customary to have one person regularly take the minutes. Sometimes this person is the group leader, but some group leaders prefer to have someone else take notes during the meeting, as the leader is preoccupied with managing other aspects of the meeting. The minutes can vary in length from a narrative that summarizes all discussion (long) to a list of action items (short). When actions are determined, the person responsible for the action with the due date should be noted in the minutes. Figure A.3 shows the minutes of a meeting with action items.

Even the best planned meetings can run into problems when members talk too much or, the opposite, too little. In the next section, we look at ways to handle each of these situations.

Minutes of Meeting to Plan Women's College Usability Test
Held at Southern Polytechnic State University

March 15, 2001
9 A.M.–noon

Present:

From Women's College
Tom Houston
Candy North

From Southern Polytechnic
Dawn Ramsey
Carol Barnum
Bonnie Brown
Laura Johnson
Barbara Thomas

Purpose:
To plan the Women's College usability Web test and assign team responsibilities.

Actions/due dates:
User profile—Candy (due 3/24)
Post-task questionnaires—Tom (due following review of scenarios)
Scenarios—Laura and Bonnie (due 3/24)
Pre-test and post-test questionnaires—Carol (due 3/24)
Screening questionnaire—Dawn (due 3/24)
Information on guidance counselors—Tom and Candy (due 3/24)
Test goals and objectives—Laura and Bonnie (due 3/24)

An email list has been established for the team, and drafts of all planning documents will be distributed for comment by the list members. First due date for most parts of the test is March 24.

Testing dates:
The following test dates were established:

Walkthrough—Tuesday, April 18, 2:30–5:00 P.M. (participant 3:30–5:00 P.M.)

Pilot—Tuesday, April 25, 2:30–5:00 P.M. (participant 3:30–5:00 P.M.)

Full test days
Tuesday, June 6, 8 A.M.–5 P.M.
Thursday, June 8, 8 A.M.–3 P.M.

Figure A.3   Typical meeting minutes

Handling Problem Participants

During meetings, some members may cause problems for the group, not because the members are combative or hostile, but rather because they exhibit some behavior that is not helpful to the group. Although such behaviors could fall under a host of categories, the most common are of two types:

- *Members who talk too much,* thus dominating the conversation and preventing others from participating
- *Members who talk too little or not at all,* thus denying the group the benefit of their views on the subject

The following strategies can provide some solutions when these problems arise.

Members Who Talk Too Much

Members may talk too much for a variety of reasons. Some like to show off their knowledge and history of the problem. Others can't resist the opportunity to add comments whenever there is a break in the conversation. Still others are just chatty, launching into stories and anecdotes in the belief that the group will be interested in hearing them. When any of these reasons cause members to talk too much, the momentum of the meeting can be lost, members may feel that the group leader has lost control of the meeting, and other members may see the meetings as a waste of time. Thus, a leader must recognize when a member talks too much and apply some of the following strategies (Andrews and Baird 292–95):

- Interrupt the person and summarize what he or she has said, while moving on to someone else.
- Act as a "gatekeeper," indicating that you have already heard from this member and now need to provide time to hear from some others.
- Refer to the agenda and the need to move on to the next person or item.
- Get the team to agree to balanced participation in discussions (a norm for the group).
- Put the member in charge of a subcommittee to present its findings to the group for discussion.
- Ask whether the member is making a new point or merely adding support for a point already made. Establish the norm of discussion to focus on new points only.

Another approach is to assign a group member the task of "rat hole watcher." This person has the responsibility for keeping the meeting on track so that discussion doesn't fall into "an innocent-looking hole in the ground that, if you dive down it, branches and turns until you are totally lost in the dark" (Beyer and Holtzblatt 133). The person assigned this task can keep an eye on the discussion to make sure that members who talk too much don't lead the group down such a rat hole. In this way, the team gives tacit approval to this person to point out when the conversation is going off in the wrong direction.

Members Who Talk Too Little or Not at All

With these members, the leader has the opposite problem of drawing them out. Understanding why these members talk too little or not at all helps a leader select the right strategy to include them in the discussion. Some members are reluctant participants because they feel uncomfortable for reasons that could include new participation in an existing group, a sense of powerlessness in a group, or a lack of expertise in the subject under discussion. Other members talk little because they prefer to listen and observe the discussion, and absorb the comments of the more vocal members. One highly valued role in groups is that of the *silent observer*, who is actively listening but withholding comment until the end. An effective leader wants to learn the views of all participants, so the leader should use some of the following strategies to draw out the more quiet members of a group (Andrews and Baird 295–97):

- In the gatekeeping role, ask if anyone else has a comment to add to the discussion.
- Specifically inquire of a quiet member if he or she would like to add something to the discussion.
- Assign a quiet member to lead a subcommittee and report to the group on its findings.
- Arrange the seating so that the quiet members are more centrally placed in the group, rather than at the corners of tables or in the back of the room.
- Observe the body language of the silent member and respond to nonverbal communication cues like head nodding, smiling, quizzical looks, and so forth.

Certainly, effective meeting management is vital to fostering a good climate for productive participation from all members. But what if your team can't "meet" in the traditional sense, but still needs interaction to do its work? In the next section, we look at the unique issues associated with remote meetings.

Remote Meetings

Increasingly, groups from remote locations that can span the globe form teams to address product development and testing. If your team is not centrally located, you may still have to meet, as certain kinds of decisions and discussions are best handled in meetings. Technology supports such global teamwork, allowing teams to meet remotely through teleconferences or through remote-control software tools such as PC Anywhere, NetMeeting, Reachout, and others. In between meetings, team members share ideas and files, using one of two technological solutions (Ray and Ray):

- *Integrated solutions*, which are typically implemented throughout a large company
- *Non-integrated solutions*, which teams can set up to support specific functions.

Integrated solutions, called groupware, include Lotus Notes, Microsoft Exchange, Novel GroupWise, and other packages used for information management and collaborative communication. Groupware uses established networks to allow team members to access and share information already in the database, as well as new information the team produces. Company forms can be used for meeting minutes and other standard notices. Groupware provides instant messaging and discussion forums to enhance team communication. However, because groupware is expensive, it is typically used only by large organizations that can provide technical support and training.

Non-integrated solutions work well for individual team projects, as they are less complex and are not network-dependent. Microsoft and other companies use Web-based technology that provides a way for teams to collaborate on any computer from anywhere. For example, Microsoft Office 2000 offers Web subscriptions that notify team members when documents have been changed. Using NetMeeting, teams can start a meeting from any Office program, while holding discussions in a chat window and transferring files to other members at the same time. Videoconferencing and whiteboard capabilities allow everyone to see what's happening while participating in a remote meeting.

Chauncey Wilson, a usability specialist who has conducted many remote meetings, offers the following practical suggestions on a professional, private Internet discussion group (used with permission of author):

1. If at all possible, have a face-to-face meeting before meeting remotely. If the team is spread out and large, this may not be practical, but it may be practical to have one or two people from each site attend a face-to-face meeting. Plan a month ahead to get the cheapest airfares. This first face-to-face meeting results in more productive later sessions and also makes the participants who have met each other a little more tolerant of "distance mistakes" resulting from using the tool.

2. Practice with the tool before first using it and write up clear instructions. Test-drive the tool with several people at different sites to minimize problems.

3. If members will be interacting with each other, as they would in a design meeting, it is important that some rules for turn-taking be established. For instance, in a meeting run from Boston with a large group in Boston and Atlanta, the moderator allowed the Atlanta contingent to speak first so that they felt "included" in the discussion right away.

4. Use the best sound system you can. It is worth the money to invest in the best microphones you can afford. A single speakerphone might work for a small group, but for larger gatherings, you might need boom mikes from the ceiling or a really good omni-directional mike that is turned up for sound sensitivity.

5. Send or let people know where all the materials for the meeting are a few days ahead of time. Also send a reminder to people about the meeting.

6. After the first meeting, ask for feedback on how the meeting went. At the beginning of the meeting, tell people that this is an experiment and you

want to improve the process each time, so their feedback is important. Ask people to jot down a few comments on how the system or meeting might be improved.

7. Keep in mind that attention spans can wander at remote meetings. You'll have to balance the length vs. frequency of meetings.

8. If your meeting is used to make decisions, assign someone to record the action items with the whiteboard or word processor and then review the action items at the end of the meeting so everyone is clear about what they must do next. This public presentation of action items before the meeting is over allows people to correct mistakes, add needed people who might have been overlooked, and adjust key dates. Make sure that each action item has a due date and responsible person. It might be useful to send this action-item list along with an agenda a few days before the next meeting as a gentle reminder. A recap of action status at the beginning of the next meeting is also useful. [As Wilson notes, these last two suggestions are aspects of basic meeting structure; however, remote meetings need this type of structure even more so to bind the virtual team together.]

9. If you are using a videoconferencing system, it might be useful to discuss how people are perceived on video, especially if they haven't previously met. Small "tics" like constantly adjusting one's glasses or twisting an earlobe may be distracting. Slumped heads and bodies are viewed by everyone and may be taken as signs of disinterest.

While these suggestions are likely to pave the way for a successful remote meeting when members are fairly homogeneous in culture, additional issues need to be addressed when the team is truly global, representing people from different countries, as well as different cultures. In such cases, the team should have some training on cross-cultural communication issues to learn how to interpret differences in manner, gesture, eye contact, forms of address, styles of dress, deference, control, and numerous other issues that can affect group effectiveness.

Dynamics of Successful Teams

Successful teams define the tasks and resolve problems before they grow out of proportion. They recognize the value of group cohesion and social interaction; thus, they foster the maintenance aspects and value the maintenance roles of members. They realize that teams take time and that teams have a life span involving phases of development. In successful teams:

- Roles are clear.
- Individuals are committed.
- Procedures and structure are understood.

- An effective leader is present.
- Interpersonal problems are solved.
- Team members promote team building and teamwork.

In unsuccessful teams:

- Members behave with caution and resort to guarded communication.
- There is a lack of disagreement.
- Members do not freely share information.
- Criticism is used as a punishment.
- Leadership is weak, absent, or (worse) authoritative.
- There is no evaluation of progress.
- There is no assessment of team process.

See the sidebar on page 416 entitled "Characteristics of an Effective Team" for more insight.

Summary

Because so much depends on the effectiveness of teams working together to plan and develop usability tests and to create user-centered design products, we have presented strategies for making teamwork productive. Applying these strategies is critical for the success of the product as well as the participants' satisfaction with the process. The steps in developing a successful team effort include:

- Recognizing the stages of group formation, including forming, storming, norming, and performing
- Understanding the valued roles in groups, both for tasks and maintenance, as well as recognizing counter-productive roles
- Becoming an effective interpreter of nonverbal communication
- Appreciating the importance of productive (substantive) conflict in groups and identifying the types of conflict that are counter-productive (affective and procedural)
- Becoming an effective leader by understanding the goals of the group and the crucial role that a leader plays in fostering both task and maintenance functions in a group
- Practicing effective meeting management through proper planning, effective goal setting, and leadership of meeting discussion, and appropriate follow-up after meetings
- Learning strategies for handling problem participants, which includes members who talk too much, as well as members who talk too little
- Applying the special skills of planning and running effective remote meetings when members are at different locations

Characteristics of an Effective Team *Glenn M. Parker*

1. Clear Purpose	The vision, mission, goal, or task of the team has been defined and is now accepted by everyone. There is an action plan.
2. Informality	The climate tends to be informal, comfortable, and relaxed. There are no obvious tensions or signs of boredom.
3. Participation	There is much discussion and everyone is encouraged to participate.
4. Listening	The members use effective listening techniques such as questioning, paraphrasing, and summarizing to get out ideas.
5. Civilized disagreement	There is disagreement, but the team is comfortable with this and shows no signs of avoiding, smoothing over, or suppressing conflict.
6. Consensus decisions	For important decisions, the goal is substantial but not necessarily unanimous agreement through open discussion of everyone's ideas, avoidance of formal voting, or easy compromises.
7. Open communication	Team members feel free to express their feelings on the tasks as well as on the group's operation. There are few hidden agendas. Communication takes place outside of meetings.
8. Clear roles and work assignments	There are clear expectations about the roles played by each team member. When action is taken, clear assignments are made, accepted, and carried out. Work is fairly distributed among team members.
9. Shared leadership	While the team has a formal leader, leadership functions shift from time to time depending upon the circumstances, the needs of the group, and the skills of the members. The formal leader models the appropriate behavior and helps establish positive norms.
10. External relations	The team spends time developing key outside relationships, mobilizing resources, and building credibility with important players in other parts of the organization.
11. Style diversity	The team has a broad spectrum of team-player types including members who emphasize attention to task, goal setting, focus on process, and questions about how the team is functioning.
12. Self-assessment	Periodically, the team stops to examine how well it is functioning and what may be interfering with its effectiveness.

Source: Glenn M. Parker. *Team Players and Teamwork.* © 1990 by Jossey-Bass. Reprinted by permission of Jossey-Bass, Inc., a subsidiary of John Wiley & Sons, Inc.

References

Andrews, Patricia Hayes, and John E. Baird, Jr. *Communication for Business and the Professions.* 4th ed. Dubuque: Brown, 1989.

Beebe, Steven A., and John T. Masterson. *Communicating in Small Groups: Principles and Practices.* 6th ed. New York: Longman, 2000.

Beyer, Hugh, and Karen Holtzblatt. *Contextual Design: Defining Customer-Centered Systems.* San Francisco: Morgan Kaufmann, 1998.

Brilhart, John K., and Gloria J. Galanes. *Effective Group Discussion.* 6th ed. Dubuque, IA: Brown, 1989.

Burnett, Rebecca E. "Conflict in Collaborative Decision-Making." *Professional Communication: The Social Perspective.* Eds. Nancy Roundy Blyer and Charlotte Thralls. Newbury Park: Sage, 1993. 144–62.

———. "Substantive Conflict in a Cooperative Context: A Way to Improve the Collaborative Planning of Workplace Documents." *Technical Communication,* 38.4 (1991): 532–39.

"Conference Room Plaque Reminds Meeting Leaders and Participants of 'Keys to Good Meeting.'" *Meeting Management News* 1:4: 2–4.

"Guidelines for Leading Effective Meetings." *Meeting Management News,* 3.1 (Jan. 1991): 6.

Harris, Thomas E., and John C. Sherblom. *Small Group and Team Communication.* Boston: Allyn and Bacon, 1999.

Holtzblatt, Karen. Preface. *Contextual Design: Defining Customer-Centered Systems.* By Hugh Beyer and Karen Holtzblatt. San Francisco: Morgan Kaufmann, 1998.

Jacobsen, Niels Ebbe, Morten Hertzum, and Bonnie E. John. "The Evaluator Effect in Usability Studies: Problem Detection and Severity Judgments." *Proceedings of the Human Factors and Ergonomics Society 42nd Annual Meeting,* 5–9 Oct. 1998, Chicago. 1336–40.

Jay, Antony. "How to Run a Meeting." *Harvard Business Review* Mar.–Apr. 1976: 43–57.

Norman, Donald A. *The Invisible Computer: Why Good Products Can Fail, The Personal Computer Is So Complex, and Information Appliances Are the Solution.* Cambridge: MIT Press, 1998.

Parker, Glenn M. "Cross-Functional Collaboration." *Training & Development* (Oct. 1994): 49–53.

———. *Team Players and Teamwork.* San Francisco: Jossey-Bass, 1990.

Ray, Deborah S., and Eric J. Ray. "Matching Collaboration Technologies to Team Needs: Accommodating Document Management and Communication Goals." Special Joint Issue. *Technical Communication* 47.1 (Feb. 2000) and *IEEE Transactions on Professional Communication* 43.1 (Mar. 2000): 122–26.

Schultz, Beatrice G. *Communicating in the Small Group: Theory and Practice.* 2nd ed. New York: HarperCollins, 1996.

Smart, Karl L. and Carol Barnum, guest eds. "Communication in Cross-Functional Teams." Special Joint Issue. *Technical Communication* 47.1 (Feb. 2000) and *IEEE Transactions on Professional Communication* 43.1 (Mar. 2000).

Smart, Karl L., and Michael Thompson. "Changing the Way We Work: Fundamentals of Effective Teams." *Proceedings of IPCC 98,* Sept. 1998, Quebec, Canada. 383–90.

"Survey Reveals Profile of the Typical Meeting." *Meeting Management News* 1.5: 1–2.

Wilson, Chauncey. "Electronic Collaboration and Interface Design." 17 Nov. 1999. Posted to a professional private Internet discussion group.

Wilson, Gerald L. *Groups in Context: Leadership and Participation in Small Groups.* 4th ed. New York: McGraw Hill, 1996.

Wurman, Richard Saul. *Information Anxiety.* New York: Doubleday, 1989.

INDEX